D0340369

The Language War

THE LANGUAGE WAR

Robin Tolmach Lakoff

UNIVERSITY OF CALIFORNIA PRESS
BERKELEY LOS ANGELES LONDON

Permission to reprint selections from the following
is gratefully acknowledged: Robin Lakoff, "The
(Rise and Fall)ⁿ of Hillary Rodham Clinton," in
N. Warner, J. Ahlers, L. Bilmes, M. Oliver, S. Wert-
heim, and M. Chen, eds., *Gender and Belief Systems*
(Berkeley: Berkeley Women and Language Group,
Linguistics Department, University of California
at Berkeley, 1996); Robin Lakoff, "Many Stories,
Multiple Meanings: Narrative in the O. J. Simpson
Case," in *Links & Letters* 3 (Departament de Fi-
lologia Anglesa i de Germanistica, Universitat Auto-
nòma de Barcelona, 1996).

University of California Press
Berkeley and Los Angeles, California

University of California Press, Ltd.
London, England

Library of Congress Cataloging-in-Publication Data

Lakoff, Robin Tolmach.
 The language war / Robin Tolmach Lakoff.
  p. cm.
 Includes bibliographical references and index.
 ISBN 0-520-22296-2 (alk. paper)
  1. Sociolinguistics—United States. 2. United
 States—Languages—Political aspects. 3. Mass
 media and language—United States 4. Power
 (Social sciences)—United States. I. Title
 P40.45.U5 L35 2000
 306.44'0973—dc21   99-055386

Manufactured in the United States of America

09 08 07 06 05 04 03 02 01 00
10 9 8 7 6 5 4 3 2 1

The paper used in this publication meets the mini-
mum requirements of ANSI/NISO Z39.48-1992
(R 1997) (*Permanence of Paper*). ♾

For My Father,
Samuel Tolmach

Fair moon, to thee I sing,
Bright regent of the heavens,
Say, why is everything
Either at sixes or at sevens?

Contents

Acknowledgments

This book could probably not have been written, and certainly would have been much harder to write, without the help, support, and love of many people.

I have dedicated *The Language War* to my father, Samuel Tolmach, as a very inadequate acknowledgment of his contribution to it, starting with reading *Alice in Wonderland*, first to me, at a tender age, and later with me. That taught me about the logic of the illogic of the world we inhabit and the language we use to talk about it and (particularly germane here) to play games of power and status with one another.

I am always grateful to my son, Andrew Lakoff. While conceiving and gestating books, and bringing them into the world, has its pleasures, seeing a baby grow up into an intelligent, articulate, creative, and humane adult man eclipses them all. Additionally, I can now thank him as a colleague, whose careful reading of parts of the manuscript was most helpful and whose insight and knowledge over many discussions have contributed to my understanding of these topics immeasurably.

I owe a particular debt to my friend and collaborator, Mandy Aftel. Her presence has enriched both my life and this book immensely. Aside from her wisdom and clarity in so many discussions, her reading of part of the manuscript has improved it greatly.

Many other friends have shaped my thoughts on these topics in many ways. To list just a few: Andrée Abecassis, Roberta Johnson, Pat McGrath, Elizabeth and Herbert Simons, Emily Stoper, and Julia Svihra.

Deborah Tannen has been thoughtful, helpful, and perceptive now as always.

I am also grateful to my students, past and present, for so much. Watching their progress through courses, papers, orals, and finally the Big D toward careers as scholars makes being a professor worthwhile and soul-renewing. Many of them have helped make these topics come to life by their questions and comments. In particular, four of them have provided invaluable research help for this task: Mary Bucholtz, Monica Corston-Oliver, Pamela Morgan, and Suzanne Wertheim. I also want to thank John Fiske and Roger Shuy, who both read the complete manuscript and made many insightful and supportive suggestions.

Last (but not least) I am most grateful for inspiration, support, and comments to my editors at the University of California Press, Laura Driussi, Katherine Bell, Jan Spauschus Johnson, and Ellen F. Smith. The first two have worked with me from the inception of this project to its conclusion. Their suggestions have improved it immeasurably, and their enthusiasm has enabled me to give my thoughts the reality of language.

WHAT I AM DOING HERE,
AND HOW I AM DOING IT

A question may occur both to my fellow linguists and to others as they examine this book: What is an ivory tower denizen, a linguist like me, doing in the notoriously real world of politics? Is this what linguists do? Can do? Should do?

While the Ebonics debate of 1996–97 (see Chapter 7) served to bring the field of linguistics to popular awareness (or at least more awareness than it had enjoyed previously, about −9 on a scale of 1 to 10), its workings are still not familiar to everyone. Moreover, even linguists argue among themselves and within themselves about what the field can and should do, what it is about. A book suggesting rapprochement between language and politics is bound to raise questions among the uninitiated and hackles among initiates.

The popular use of "linguist" is very different from its professional acceptation. If you tell a layperson that you're a "linguist," you are very likely to be asked, "And how many languages do you speak?" A "linguist" is someone able to use several languages, that is, use them practically—speak, read, and write in them. In this sense, the consummate linguist must be Francis E. Sommer, described in the *New York Times* (Honan 1997) as "fluent in 94 languages."

The *Times* article calls Mr. Sommer "the Babe Ruth of the Linguistic Society." But in fact, were Mr. Sommer (who died in 1978) to have attended a meeting of the Linguistic Society of America (LSA), he would have found himself both bewildered by the papers presented and the discussions of them, and ignored or patronized by the professional linguists (in the second sense) who belong to the Society and attend its meetings. The one thing most of us seldom do, in our professional capacities, is *use* a lot of languages. Many of us, to be sure, *know* more than one language. A few know many. But we know them in order to study them, rather than to communicate in them. Therefore we are often less concerned with individual languages than with what the totality of languages can show us about *language*—what it is, what properties all languages necessarily share, in what ways languages may differ, and what those facts may tell us about the makeup of the human mind—pardon me, *brain* (that being the fashionable consideration at present).

Linguists of the LSA type therefore tend to be interested in discovering the abstract properties of languages, the grammatical rules that make them up, and the structures that make them different from one another, yet basically similar. Even this is no easy task. English is, for obvious reasons, the best studied language in the world, and yet we are nowhere near a complete grammar of English, nor in all probability will linguistics produce one in the lifetime of anyone reading these words.

The *Times* article mentioned what I think is a first: eminent members of LSA talking about their interest in people like Mr. Sommer (as objects of study for LSA-linguists rather than as potential colleagues). Linguists are quoted as saying that Sommer-linguists have never been studied scientifically by LSA-linguists. But we are beginning to see them as special cases who, if their abilities could be unraveled and scientifically explained, could shed light on the processes the rest of us use with varying degrees of competence when we attempt to learn languages other than our native one.

But even if LSA-linguists agree on what we aren't, there is less consensus on what we are. Are there natural boundaries to our field? How do we differ (if we do) from rhetoricians, literary critics, psychoanalysts, appellate courts, political spin doctors, and others who, theoretically and practically, determine what language means or accomplishes?

When I entered linguistics some thirty-five years ago, the answer was fairly simple. The field had a well-marked turf that distinguished it from other areas in the humanities and social sciences and thereby justified its independent existence. In recent years that certainty has been under some pressure.

Linguistics in this country began, in the early years of this century, as an offshoot of anthropology, another newish area. Both reflected the growing realization that many of America's indigenous cultures were nearing extinction. While earlier observers tended to see this as a good thing (the cultures were "primitive" and non-Christian, the languages not possibly the equals of Indo-European and therefore not of much interest or worthy of preservation), by the early twentieth century scholars were starting to become more sophisticated. They saw these indigenous cultures and their languages as expressions of the complexity and variety of the human mind, and therefore not only worthy of study, but essential to study if we were to understand ourselves as a species. To this end it was necessary to develop objective and scientific methods of investigation, so as to avoid the subjective perspectives that caused earlier scholars to understand other societies and their ways from the vantage point of their own (and thus necessarily as unintelligible or inadequate). The new science of linguistics also had to devise empirical methods of discovery and analysis, in order not to force the data uncovered in the field into the Cinderella's slipper of preexisting theories, themselves often based (knowingly or not) on the Indo-European habits of thought innate to the scholars, all speakers of European languages and members of Western cultures.

So American linguistics was created as empirical and antimentalistic, fitting in nicely (as intended) with the new notion of "social *science*." "Science," then as now, was ipso facto a good word. A field that could claim scientific status had the right to legitimacy. So linguistics identified itself as belonging to the social sciences rather than the humanities, using the empirical methods of the former rather than the interpretive ("mentalistic") techniques of the latter. Ideally, linguistic analysis was concerned with form, not function; structure, not meaning; the concrete artifacts of language, not the abstract deeper structures that gave it sense and purpose. During the first half of the century, therefore, linguists concentrated on word-lists (lexicons) and inventories of sounds (phonology) and affixes (grammatical endings, prefixes, and such—that is, morphology). Syntax involved relationships between constructions (e.g., active and passive voice), and therefore required assessing whether two sentences had similar meanings (that is, were paraphrases), and so could be done only in a very rudimentary and unsatisfactory way in an antimentalistic field. Therefore, in the field's antimentalistic period, it received little attention. Within linguistics proper (excluding philosophy of language and general semantics), semantics (the study of the relationship between language forms and their referents, that is, meaning) and pragmatics (the study of the relation between language forms and language function, to use one definition) played a role that was minimal to nonexistent.

This began to change with the advent of Noam Chomsky in the late 1950's. Chomsky's theory, transformational generative grammar (TGG), permitted—indeed, required—a limited amount of mentalistic analysis. Syntactic relationships were evaluated in part on the basis of paraphrase relations, which required the analyst to make judgments about meaning, albeit on a superficial level. The changes wrought by Chomsky and TGG were spectacular, both on linguistics itself and on many related fields. Not least was the change in the importance of linguistics in the university.

Before the mid-1960's American linguistics was tiny and obscure. Very few universities had full-fledged linguistics departments; some had programs, while many had a linguist or two on their faculties, situated, often uneasily, in anthropology, language, or English departments. But transformational grammar, with its promise that language could be a window into the mind, a glimpse into the universality of language capacities, and hence a way of achieving a fundamental understanding of what it means to be human, seized the intellectual imagination. (Chomsky's emergence in the late 1960's as a radical critic of the Vietnam War also helped to popularize his still-infant field.) At the same time, during these economically flush years many universities were starting from scratch, and others upgrading themselves from small colleges into major institutions. To get recognition, it was essential to acquire intellectual respectability, as quickly as possible. That was most efficiently accomplished by creating a few prestigious departments filled with "name" scholars who could attract the best graduate students and large research grants.

But large and traditional departments are difficult to change. Tenure made it hard to replace older (often undistinguished) faculty members with resplendent new stars. Even for a new university, staffing a first-rank large department was a dauntingly expensive task. But a first-rate small department would put a university on the intellectual map at once, particularly if the department was in a hot field and had ties to other departments and a bit of extra-university glamour. What fitted those definitions better than linguistics? The field prospered exceedingly, so that today virtually every serious research university has its linguistics department, typically with a faculty of ten to twenty tenured or tenure-track professors.

But as linguistics grew exponentially, we tended to ignore the fact that it was now made up of at least three very different kinds of people, who had entered linguistics with at least three very different assumptions—and therefore had diametrically opposite notions of what we ought to be doing, or even what this "scientific study of language" we claimed to be doing *was*, what "language" consisted of, and what "science" included. There were still many who had been trained as social scientists, anthropologists interested in learning about languages other than the familiar Indo-European ones as a way of understanding cultures very different from their own. They found the exoticism of the surface forms of those languages compelling, the idea that languages could differ from one another in seemingly innumerable and unpredictable ways. Others (like me) had been trained as humanists, and our interests lay in the hermeneutic potential of TGG. We wanted a way to determine, from their superficial form, what sentences "really" meant at a deeper level, why people made the choices they made, and what those choices signified about ourselves. Still others entered the field from mathematics or formal logic. For them, language was above all a system whose properties could be formalized in equation-like rules. They were less interested in the relationships between language and culture, and language and thought, than in the relations that held between the parts of sentences. This was the centerpiece of the Chomskyan project, as those of us who had entered it under one of the other auspices would ruefully discover. The three kinds of linguists made strange, increasingly uneasy bedfellows, and the field has yet to achieve a rapprochement among them.

In the 1970's, social-science-minded linguists developed other concerns. Just as sociologists like Erving Goffman had been looking inward into their own cultures and finding them pretty exotic, linguists began to collect and study familiar yet unanalyzed language forms like nonstandard dialects or ordinary conversation. In this they broke away from TGG, which certainly concentrated on English, but in a very different way.

To the formal (that is, strictly Chomskyan) TGGian, the linguist's task was discovering the abstract grammar of the language, the grammar of the "ideal speaker-listener in a completely homogenous speech community, who knows its language perfectly and is unaffected by such irrelevant conditions as memory limitations, distractions, shifts of attention and interest, and errors (random or characteristic) in applying his knowledge of the language in actual performance" (Chomsky 1965, 3). While variants were known to exist, they were deemed of little importance; and while the context in which words were uttered might affect both their form and their understanding, TGGians saw that as essentially irrelevant to the abstract grammar they were seeking to intuit. Hence empirical data, painstakingly gathered from real people's actual utterances, was not only not necessary, it was undesirable: it might be corrupt, tainted by trivial external influences, "performance factors." Transformational theory directed its practitioners to produce the data that they then analyzed, and those analyses then formed the basis of their theories. If this sounds like a dangerously corruptible (and circular) system, let me assure you that today I find it scandalous. The acceptance of these theories and methods drove a wedge between the TGG "mentalists" (both formalists and humanists) and their purported colleagues, the empirical social scientists.

None of the parties was then asking a major question about language: how do we use it to construct ourselves, make deals with one another, and weave our social fabric? To the social science end of the field, the fact that language was social was indisputable, but to answer that question was to wallow in the slough of mentalism, surfacing with analyses that were unreliable because not based directly on superficially observable data.

It might seem that that question would occur naturally to the TGGians and their descendants, especially given Chomsky's extradisciplinary concerns with the politics of language and vice versa. But they had a conservative idea of "meaning." For them, not unlike their more empirical colleagues (Chomsky after all had himself been trained as an American structural linguist), evidence had to be linguistically observable at the surface or not far below it. The assumptions speakers had in mind when they spoke, or their intentions in choosing one form rather than an apparent equivalent, were not part of "linguistics," that is, grammatical analysis. These restrictions made for simplicity and elegance, but created in some of us a gnawing desire to see linguistics work as the "window into the mind" Chomsky had promised us it could be.

So both sides—the social scientists and the mathematicians—were to varying degrees antimentalistic and anti-interpretive. A reasonable justification, for both camps, was that to abandon their use of only superficially accessible data was to go back to that dangerous yesteryear in which anything could be related to anything on the analyst's say-so— the awful results of which could be discerned not only in pre-twentieth-century linguistics, but in contemporary psychoanalysis and literary theory. It also moved linguistics further away from "science," where rational people who craved respectability wished to reside.

The only problem (for me at least) was that accepting these constraints entailed accepting the impossibility of saying almost everything that might be interesting, anything normal people might want or need to know about language. For instance:

- Why do men and women, who "speak the same language," regularly misunderstand each other?
- Why do we late-twentieth-century sophisticates, after a century's barrage of advertising, still find ourselves bedazzled by the language of persuasion, economic and political?
- How do we use language to avoid responsibility for ourselves and allocate it to others?
- How can lawyers on either side in a trial describe the same events in such different ways that jurors fail to agree on a verdict? Or reach a verdict that, to an outside observer, makes no sense at all?
- How do the stories we tell and hear, privately and publicly, give us our understandings of ourselves and the society we inhabit?

And much, much more. Answers to any of these questions must start with close analysis of actual linguistic data and show how the specific forms speakers select have the precise effects they do on social, economic, or political reality. Analyzing the superficial linguistic form of a communication alone cannot explain why *these* particular words, in *those* specific combinations, operate *to this exact effect* on the minds of hearers; much less can it teach us how to be discriminating hearers and responsible creators of language. Looking (like political scientists and communication theorists) only at the effects of linguistic choices as demonstrated in polls and focus groups leaves open the question of what exactly happened to create *this* effect. So if linguistics is going to raise interesting questions and answer them in useful ways, and exist as more than an ivory tower curiosity, linguists must find ways to bring these different forms of analysis together, to look at language closely, but not to stop with language; to consider the complexity of cause and effect in everything we do that involves linguistic expression (which is pretty nearly everything we do). Analysts of language must use their minds, like transformational grammarians, as a filter or conduit: we must ask ourselves how we are affected by particular uses of language. But as social scientists we must use real, spontaneously created language as the basis of our analyses; and we must be sure that our individual mentalities, producing our own interpretations, are not idiosyncratic: the effect that I describe language having on me should elicit an "aha!" from you a good part of the time. Even when you disagree, you should see that my version might work for someone who brings to the interpretation a context different from yours (for discussion of this issue see Tannen 1984).

Modern "core" linguists still shun such endeavors as unscientific, tending to confine their analyses to the safe havens of relatively small and concrete linguistic artifacts: the sound, the word, the sentence. Even many sociolinguists have been loath to engage in analyses that involve intuition or introspection. Occasional linguists (as opposed to, say, discourse analysts) have alluded to the existence of "structure above the sentence level," but mostly in the same tones as pre-Columbian Europeans speaking of what lay beyond the Ocean Sea. There be dragons—don't go there.

Yet we don't make meanings or express intentions at those smaller levels. Meanings become visible in *discourse:* connected language used for a purpose, whether in the form of a conversational turn, a haiku, a how-to manual, a courtroom cross-examination, a novel, or any of the innumerable other linguistic actions in which all of us engage regularly. To do so, we have to have internalized a set of rules or principles dictating what is a possible utterance within the relevant genre and what is not. These rules are part of our linguistic knowledge as much as the rules about what constitutes a permissible cluster of sounds in a language or what makes a string of words intelligible as a sentence. Traditionally linguistics has been unwilling to consider the processes by which we understand larger and more abstract units of language (text or discourse) as a part of a speaker's knowledge of language that linguistic theory must account for. But it seems to me that there is no natural reason to cut off "linguistics" before meaning enters the picture, except as a reflex of the old antimentalism and the desire to keep a tightly formalistic hold on the meaning of "grammar." True, adhering to the old ways will avoid the dangers of solipsism and incoherence (unless you believe, as I do, that formal statements can be just as incoherent as informal ones). But in simplifying your life this way, you make linguistics an artificial field, condemned to turn away just as things get interesting, unable to make a true rapprochement with literary analysis, or psychology, or anthropology, or political science. I know some of my colleagues want it that way, and I wish them success; but they should not force us all into that Procrustean bed.

For this reason, I see all the topics I deal with in this book as "linguistics," ways of understanding "language." Most linguists would go along with me through Chapter 3, which looks at "political correctness" and therefore hovers around the safely linguistic level of the word or phrase. Even Chapter 4, on "sexual harassment," as defined by Anita Hill, still relatively small-scale and concrete, may pass muster. Chapter 7, on Ebonics, will seem unexceptionable as an examination of dialect differences and attitudes toward them—a respectable topic for sociolinguistics. But many esteemed colleagues will part company with me there.

The other chapters all cluster at a more abstract linguistic level. They are about the social and political construction of narratives. Who makes our stories, and how do they develop over time and through an assortment of media venues? What happens, more particularly, when groups or individual members of those groups (the O. J. Simpson jury, Hillary Rodham Clinton) who previously were accorded no right to self-definition through language, take for themselves that right, in very public ways? I see the appropriation of narrative-construction rights as parallel to, and a natural development of, the earlier appropriation of definitional rights at the word level. The narrative-controlling strategy of Hillary Rodham Clinton discussed in Chapter 5 is, in this view, the direct lineal descendant of the reappropriation of "Black" by the civil rights movement in the late 1960's. I'm not saying that the linkage is conscious, just that the recent one could not have occurred at the abstract level of narrative had not the earlier one, more readily graspable at the lexical level, familiarized our society with the idea that language could be reclaimed.

Some linguists will be troubled less by the objects of my analysis than with my analytic procedures. How do I justify my interpretations? Language is the transference of meaning from mind to mind (among many other things). A satisfying theory of how we use language to make and change public and private meaning (which is what this book attempts) can only be tested by what it illuminates and communicates to those who encounter it. There is, alas, no extrinsic, objective, "scientific" test of the claims I will be making. Some might argue that, therefore, what I am doing is not "scientific" and should therefore be read out of both linguistics and decent society. But the scientific method is not the only way we can arrive at understanding. As we enter a new century and a new millennium, it behooves us to keep our eyes open and raise again some old questions: What exactly makes an endeavor "scientific"? And must every way of knowing be "scientific" according to the traditional definitions? Is it, finally, possible to have a linguistics that does what the study of language must: weld the interests and methods of "pure" science, "social" science, and the humanities into one, taking from each what it needs?

Other questions follow from the foregoing. Where do I get my data, and what do I do with it? These too are problematic.

Over the history of linguistics, linguists have been of two minds about the collection and use of data. For transformational syntacticians and their descendants, it is important to determine the limits on the applications of grammatical rules, and therefore it is essential for the investigator to construct sentences that would never occur naturally, as well as sentences that might occur but that might not show up in a normal-sized corpus of naturally occurring data. Hence the syntactician must construct sentences and test their grammaticality as a prelude to proposing rules and grammars.

Empirically minded linguists avoid this mentalism and its hazards, at least overtly. But often they find that, in order to say anything of significance, they must work interpretation (i.e., mentalism) into their analyses in covert form. That can create even greater opportunities for corruption than outright mentalism.

Being forced to choose between these possibilities (often framed by their proponents as Manichean opposites) means that, inevitably, valuable opportunities for understanding will be lost. Eschewing mentalism forces the analyst to forfeit the use of the tool humans naturally use to understand language—the mind. So motives, ambiguities, and subtleties are off limits, and linguistics becomes (to my mind anyway) a sterile enterprise.

On the other hand, if we admit deep interpretation into our armamentarium, whose do we choose, since each of us enters every discourse with our own context and perspective, which necessarily color (some might say distort) our interpretations? How do we justify our results? Can they be verified, or falsified? And if not, can they be "scientific"? And if they are not scientific, can they be useful? Are interpreters of human communication (whether linguists, literary critics, or psychoanalysts) engaged in scientific or humanistic enterprise? I want to answer, whether flippantly, greedily, or properly, both. But how can the methods and perspectives of those very different discovery systems be welded together into a harmonious whole that yields reliable results?

Who, if anyone, is in charge here? Who certifies the interpretation of discourse? At one time many of us thought the responsibility for meaning (in Western culture at least) lay with the producer: the speaker/writer produced *the* meaning; the hearer/reader might or might not perceive the speaker's meaning correctly.[1] But increasingly I think that the speaker does not necessarily encode a single meaning, and that the business of making sense with language is a collaborative and indeterminate business. For most circumstances, though not some of the most interesting ones, if speaker and hearer get close enough to some sort of agreement, that will be fine.[2] But that still leaves open the question of who decides what things "ought" to mean, or "must" have meant. Both speaker and hearer are suspect: they have their own interests. So should we trust an "objective," uninvolved interpreter? She is, to be sure, outside the immediate fray. But she also has an interest, albeit a theoretical one, in the conclusion. And worse, the interpreter is an outsider, and thus inevitably never privy to the totality of shared context between the participants themselves. Without some form of participant observation, meaning is necessarily lost. It is paradoxical but true that the greater the objectivity, the greater the unreliability.

Some scholars, for instance Deborah Tannen (1984) and John J. Gumperz (1982), have tried to circumvent this impasse by making interpretation a several-stage process. Some time after the initial speech event that they have recorded, they go back with the transcription or tape to the original participants. The latter are asked to assess what was going on: Why did you laugh here? What about that long pause there? How did you feel at that moment? How did you take the interlocutor's remark? What did you mean by your response? Then the analyst interprets the participants' interpretations, whether agreeing, offering alternatives, or disagreeing, and explains what's going on at all three levels: the original discourse and the two levels of interpretation. But it's not clear that the original participants are any more reliable interpreters of their own intentions than is the professional linguist, especially some time after the fact. Freud showed that we are unreliable interpreters of our own behavior. And of course the analyst is not above suspicion on several grounds. She might argue that her special knowledge compensates for her distance from the original utterance. But does it, or might it just introduce additional uncertainty?

These questions at present, and perhaps forever, are unanswerable. Arguably this problem destroys any hope of using language as a true window into the mind. Yet much work has been done that seems to the majority of readers, professional and lay, to be rich in insight and even helpful in daily life. Perhaps we are overly pessimistic; perhaps, just as the psychoanalyst Donald Winnicott talked about "good enough" mothering, we can talk about "good enough" linguistic analysis. And if we are aware of the dangers, we can take steps to minimize them if not ever completely avoid them. The awareness of solipsism may enable us to avoid it. I have learned to question my first take on anything, to be alert to the possibility of alternate understandings. Then, almost invariably, any idea that makes it into print has been subjected to a fair amount of discussion with friends and colleagues; offered to students in classes, presented to groups of various kinds as lectures, and explored in the media in interviews and talk shows. Very often my interlocutors offer new insights that I can incorporate. I have learned, finally, that it is almost never true that an utterance has only one possible interpretation. Rather, I am offering here (as elsewhere) understandings of public language that I hope will be plausible. Then too, it is important to realize that I am not trying to state unequivocally what any speaker "meant": that is impossible. Rather I am trying to explain my understanding of that utterance, and thus the understandings of other hearers or readers, but by no means necessarily everyone. I hope thus to be making plausible interpretations, those likely to have been made by people sharing a fair amount of psychological and/or social context.

This conundrum, originating within linguistics as a purely methodological dispute, has connections to an argument raging in the rarefied air of literary theory: who is responsible for the making of meaning (if that is even a rational question)?

On one side are the deconstructionists, for instance Jacques Derrida and his followers. In its strongest form, deconstructionism asserts the undecidability of meaning in any text. Neither the original author nor any subsequent reader holds the key to "the" meaning of anything. Anyone who claims that power can do so only through the illegitimate exercise of political superiority or brute force. This is a highly subversive position, denying as it does the legitimacy of both political and cultural authority, and thus has been the target of much conservative critique of the "liberal" or "radical" university (see Chapters 2 and 3). These critics feel betrayed, having been brought up with the comforting certainty that all was knowable, you just had to know someone who knew. If you were the right kind of person, that could be you! In any case meaning is stable and determinate. Life is serene.

But neither deconstructionist chaos nor authoritarian certitude represents the commonsense world that readers and hearers know. When competent speakers engage in any kind of discourse, they form ideas in their minds about what it means and respond accordingly. Sometimes, to be sure, later evidence reveals that an interpretation is at odds with an intention, with resultant embarrassment. But more often there is sufficient consensus for the discourse to proceed to a satisfactory conclusion: "good enough" understanding.

That commonsense consensus matches Stanley Fish's (1980) idea of the "interpretive community." As in literature, so in communication more generally: we understand what we encounter based on shared contexts and experiences. In its most obvious form, a linguistic interpretive community is a "speech community," defined as consisting of everyone who, in some sense, "speaks the same language." [3] But communicative interpretive communities may also be based on more abstract similarities: gender, political sympathies, aesthetic preferences, occupations. Over the last thirty years feminists have demonstrated the existence of a (formerly private) women's interpretive community whose presence became public and explicit as a result of the Clarence Thomas confirmation hearings in 1991 (see Chapter 4). Hence the rallying cry of those times, "You just don't get it!" signifying the emergence of a community ready and able to make and insist on its own interpretive rules. Conservatives predictably decry such developments as "special interests," "tribalism," or "balkanization," but as I will argue in Chapter 3, they demonstrate something much deeper and more positive, if initially uncomfortable. Special speech communities have always been a part of human existence, but only recently have they emerged into widespread public recognition.

The interpretive community is the best model for the way we as speakers participate in discourse, as well as for the way we as scholars interpret that discourse and in turn create our own. We must see ourselves, in all our language-using roles, as participants in several always shifting communities of meaning-making. As long as our interpretations work, as long as most of the time, most people respond in a way that mostly seems appropriate, we are doing well enough. Meaning is made by consensus: the original speaker contributes form, the original audience response, the analyst an explanation linking the two.

There is seldom a need for, or a possibility of, complete overlap of intention and understanding. A general sense of cohesion among participants suffices for most human purposes. The scholar attempts to identify all latent as well as patent understandings, eventually discarding those that are unlikely in the context and/or disputed by the original participants. But we should never flatter ourselves that we have created the complete or ideal interpretation of anything. Our work is partial and provisional. But it's good enough.

Another controversy arises out of the data I have chosen as the basis of my analyses: largely written, generally mass-media, most often planned discourse. Since the early twentieth century American linguists have seen spontaneous small-group oral communication as "real" language, the only worthwhile object of study. That assessment represents an overreaction to an earlier assumption that only literate communication was worthy of study. Now it's time for the pendulum to return to the center. In a literate society like ours, meaning is negotiated through a wide array of communicative channels: written language and oral; public and private; formal and informal; spontaneous and constructed; direct and mediated. All of these together create our identities as individuals and members of a society. Each contributes to the totality that is *us*. If we are interested in the way language creates and constructs us all, we must consider all the forms our language takes. Any claim that some forms of language are "realer" or more legitimate objects of analysis than others is misguided. The question to ask is, how do all the forms language takes in our time work together to produce the results we see around us?

One more caveat: this book is written with what some will allude to (with a sneer) as a "liberal slant." I realize that true scholars are supposed to display "objectivity," seeing things from both sides, or all sides, or none. Along with many postmodern cultural commentators, I wonder whether there is such a thing as true objectivity, or at least whether, if objectivity exists, it is ever true. Often beneath the objective surface a writer's real beliefs exist in distorted and covert forms, presupposed rather than asserted and therefore difficult to identify and critique. Even in the best case, objectivity creates disengagement, and disengagement is deadly in every sense. So get it: I'm a liberal.

As I write the foregoing, I wonder about it. In doing the research for this book, I read my way through a lot of conservative discourse: George Will, Peggy Noonan, William Bennett . . . I could go on. (What I have suffered for you, dear reader!) However elegantly written, however smartly argued, there is one thing lacking in every example I have encountered: any kind of apologia for its political stance, or even, generally, any explicit acknowledgment that the work is written from any political stance at all.

That is puzzling. Why do I feel a need to explain, if not apologize for, my politics, but George Will doesn't? Despite the wails of conservatives (see Chapters 2 and 3 especially on this point), there is no case to be made for liberal control of public discourse via a conspiracy of the "liberal media." If that were so, "liberal" would be what linguists call the unmarked value, requiring no justification, and conservatives would feel a need to confess. I speak about this issue at some length in Chapter 2.

The foregoing are my assumptions and ground rules. If you can accept them, reader, read on.

LANGUAGE

The Power We Love to Hate

THE STORIES THAT MAKE THE NEWS

Some of the stories in the news over the last few years:

The fight over Political Correctness
The Anita Hill / Clarence Thomas hearings
The David Mamet play *Oleanna*
The role of Hillary Rodham Clinton
The Bobbitt contretemps
The Nancy Kerrigan–Tonya Harding faceoff
The O. J. Simpson saga
Adultery in high places
Sexual misconduct in the military
The Ebonics controversy
The fight to make English the "official" language of the United States
The death of Princess Diana
The "Cambridge Nanny" case
Sex (or whatever) in the Oval Office

Each of these stories is different, but they share at least one striking similarity: we hate to let them go. Each story, each issue, each case spurs passionate discussion, spilling out of the media and into our personal conversations, our private thoughts, our secret dreams.

There are moralists and pundits who are incensed at the amount of attention paid to what they feel ought to be ephemera, especially since it's impossible to get anyone to care about what ought to matter: campaign spending corruption, genocide in Yugoslavia, the collapse of the Asian economy, the standoff in Iraq. Why doesn't anyone want to argue about *those?*

Theories abound. It's "the culture of narcissism." The media's ratings frenzy. The short attention span created by MTV. Bad education. But the stories keep us enthralled despite the pundits' diatribes. The common thread in the explanatory narratives spun by the moralists and experts is a belief in the intellectual deficits of a populace inveigled into an addiction to trivia. The *real* stories, it is said or implied, the ones a serious and intelligent public would be paying attention to, are complex. We decadent Americans are drawn to these narratives by their very simplicity — all we postmodern consumers can understand.

In truth, these tales are as deep and convoluted as they are gossipy and salacious. They grab us by our emotions, or even less dignified parts of ourselves, so that we are often embarrassed at our fascination. But they do so not because (well, not entirely because) our sensibilities have grown tawdry. Rather, these stories stay around much longer than they logically ought to because they involve the complexities of being American, and indeed being human, in the years just before the millennium. Each of these stories, whatever it *appears* to be about, is really about how hard, yet how interesting, it is to be *us,* here and now.

Stories like these are our new mythology, our current just-so stories. As we tell them and hear them, they have a core of real-life truth. We've read about them in the papers, seen them on television. But we embroider them with other meanings, deeper and more troubling, as people have done with their stories since the making of the classic myths. O.J. is our Achilles, Hillary Rodham Clinton our Helen of Troy, and their stories help make sense of our reality.

These fables are diverse in content and even ultimate staying power, but all pass what I call the Undue Attention Test. The UAT selects stories and issues that seem by "serious" standards to be ephemeral and trivial, to merit no more than passing media attention, if even that. But a story that passes the UAT does not fade away quickly. It acquires "legs." It shows up night after night on TV—in purportedly hard-news venues; on infotainment shows; on TV talk shows; on late-night shows; on the magazine shows. It turns up on radio talk shows as hearers call in with empurpled opinions; it occupies the front pages of newspapers and newsmagazines. We talk about it spontaneously. Serious people may deride our fascination, but we are not ashamed. We know that our Attention is not Undue, that something we need to understand is playing out before our eyes.

Some of these stories stay around only briefly (though longer than they should according to serious standards); some lived with us for several years before receding; and some seem destined never to depart. But all have received Undue Attention. Most of these cases involve problems currently causing unrest and dissension at all levels of national discourse: gender and race. A great many focus on the respective roles of women and men: who can do and say what, and what it means. Others ask the same questions about white and black persons; and some of the most persistent refer to both race and gender.

We use these stories to explore the hardest questions we have to face, as ways to circle around our feelings and test possible resolutions, ways to mask our confusion with titillation. We wallow in Schadenfreude concerning the rich and famous and try not to acknowledge that some of the sources of their embarrassment play a part in our own lives.

Several of these stories share a further similarity. They are about language: who has the ability and the right to make meaning for everyone. Language-based controversies like these are really about which group is to enter the new millennium with social and political control. Whose take on things will be *the* take? Who gets to make meaning for us all— to create and define our culture? Culture, after all, is the construction of shared meaning. These cases are about nothing less than our definitions of ourselves and who can make them. Therein resides power, directly or not.

Does this argument seem strange? One reason it might is that we often consider language no more than mere effusions of breath, a representation of reality, not reality itself,[1] and therefore incompetent to be the motive force behind social change. And the power to make language and through it meaning has been vested in one powerful group (typically middle- and upper-class white males) for so long and so totally that that perception became a transparent lens through which we viewed "reality": the view of that group seemed to all of us the plain, undistorted, *normal* and natural view, often the only view imaginable (if you weren't totally crazy). (I will discuss this point at length in Chapter 2.) For those still immured in this perspective, the suggestion that there might be more than one way to construct meaning is meaningless, threatening, or bizarre. The common conception of language as abstract and impotent seems to support this argument. But our passionate opposition to any new understanding of meaning-making gives the lie to that comforting old belief. Often the pundits (typically supporters of the old order) call these news stories superficial and those who pay attention to them mindless because they don't see that both are harbingers of a truly terrifying social change: the democratization of meaning-making.

We are currently engaged in a great and not very civil war, testing whether the people who always got to make meaning for all of us still have that unilateral right and that capacity. The answer that seems to be winning is NO, but those who want to check the YES box are unaccustomed to not having their choices win by default and are fighting back with the zeal common to lost causes.

LANGUAGE MAKES REALITY

Language is, and has always been, the means by which we construct and analyze what we call "reality." The pundits opine that the economy wins and loses elections, but who has actually encountered, touched, or smelled an Economy? What we know of it we know through carefully selected words, images that tell us what we ought to think and believe we know. It is no accident that, at the very moment at which meaning-making rights are being contested, politicians and others in the public eye have developed armies of specialists whose job it is to construct public meanings via the skillful manipulation of language: old-time speechwriters, image consultants, media advisers, press secretaries, spin doctors, spokespersons, PR experts, pollsters, and many more. "Just language" has become big business. If in Calvin ("Silent Cal") Coolidge's time, the business of America was business, in ours the business of America is language.

But how can language have this kind of power—explanatory and cohesive, on the one hand; divisive and threatening on the other? How can something that is physically just puffs of air, a mere stand-in for reality, have the power to change us and our world?

In some of my classes, to illustrate the role language plays in the making of what we call "reality," I write a sentence on the blackboard:

Christopher Columbus discovered America in 1492.

I then point out that, on the one hand, this is a sentence that early on each of us was encouraged to think of as simple, immutable, physically verifiable historical truth. On the other hand, every word in it (particularly including "in") represents an ambiguity or potential point of rational disagreement.[2] Conservative critics rail at the notion that history may not be literally and absolutely "true."[3] And of course, neither I nor any responsible person argues that the literal event the above sentence immortalizes did not actually occur. What is in dispute is the interpretation of that event. In the possibility of multiple interpretations lies the slippage, but without those interpretations the bare "fact" is meaningless. So you can choose between several competing meanings and no meaning at all.[4]

I am suggesting, then, that language not only has the ability to allocate political power for all of us as a society, but also is the means and the medium by which we construct and understand ourselves as individuals, as coherent creatures, and also as members of a culture, a cohesive unit.

There is a paradox latent here. Language is just air after all—it is not a gun, it has no power on its own. Yet it changes reality. How is air transmuted into concrete reality—how does language become action?

The British philosopher of language J. L. Austin (1962) proposed a way. As a first gambit, he suggested that most utterances were "constative," that is, merely descriptive of reality: *The sky is blue; It will snow tomorrow; I like artichokes; Columbus discovered America.* Such utterances could be judged as either true or false, based on comparison with reality.

But there are other kinds of utterances as well. Leaving aside nondeclarative sentence types (*Close the door! Who is this?*), there are sentences or utterances[5] that are declarative in form, but do not describe an externally determinable reality. Rather, by their very utterance they *bring into being,* or perform, the situation they represent. Austin called such expressions "performative."

Performative utterances have specific requirements. They must all contain a first-person, present-tense verb of linguistic activity: *I order you to leave; I excommunicate you; I promise to pay you within a week.* They are not subject to verification procedures. It doesn't make sense to retort to them, "That's false!" since by my utterance of the words themselves I have made the situation they describe true—providing, of course, I have the right and the means to make that utterance *appropriately* or, in Austin's term, *felicitously.* Thus if I give an order but haven't the power to enforce it; or if the order I give cannot be carried out by a human being ("I order you to fly around the room"), the performative will not work. But if a performative utterance is felicitous, it transmutes the air of language into concrete reality. You must leave; you are no longer a member of my church; you expect money from me at a specified future time. Of course, performative utterances can change only those real-world situations that are changeable via language alone.

Thus far Austin appears to distinguish between constative and performative sentence types, with only the latter (a much less common category) having world-changing properties. But toward the end of his book he slips in a subtle but powerful revision. In fact, *all* utterances are performative, even those that *look* merely constative.

His argument is ingenious. Consider the pair of utterances:

I will give you $100 on Monday.
I promise to give you $100 on Monday.

The first utterance could be understood as either a prediction or a promise; the second, clearly a promise, may be constative or performative. If we interpret the first utterance as a promise, and the second as performative, the two are essentially identical in meaning. Yet by Austin's original analysis, based on its form (the verb is not one of linguistic communication) the first could be only constative. That doesn't make too much sense, inasmuch as it *can* (though it need not) be used with performative, that is, reality-creating, force.[6] The same can be said about *any* utterance: *cats eat bats* is an assertion—that is, it performs the speech act of asserting a proposition—and as such it is equivalent to the explicit performative *I say that cats eat bats*. And since function, not form, determines category, it moves from constative to performative. In the same way, Austin suggests that *all* utterances are performative, and all language world-changing. In some cases ("explicit performatives" like "I promise to give you $100"), the performative expression is itself physically present as part of the utterance; in others ("primary performatives" like "I will give you $100"), it is formally absent, but functionally present as much as if it were literally there.

There are categories of performativity. Some kinds of performative utterances have more palpable effects than others, some are more constrained as to who can perform them felicitously, under what conditions (*excommunicate* is highly constrained, *order* less so, and *promise* the freest, although there are conditions for a felicitous promise). Battles over language not infrequently are fought over performatives: who can use which ones to whom, under what conditions. One case that has received a lot of attention of late is the apology.

APOLOGIES AS LANGUAGE POLITICS

An apology is certainly performative: it changes the world for participants in terms of their relative status and their future relationship. In making an apology, the maker (1) acknowledges wrongdoing; (2) acknowledges that the addressee is the wronged party; (3) admits needing something (forgiveness) from the addressee to make things right again.[7] Apologies put their makers at a disadvantage in two ways: as transgressors, and as people in need of something from those against whom they have transgressed. Hence a true apology is always painful, and real apologies tend to occur either between equals, or from lower to higher. Higher ups "never explain, never apologize," first because they don't *have* to, and second because it might threaten their high status.

Yet we persist in making apologies. Why? Because even as we lose status *by* making them, we get credit *for* making them: we are seen as nice, responsible people deserving of forgiveness and even praise. But to commit an error without apologizing to the wronged party is to appear haughty and uncaring, sins as bad as the original malfeasance. Unlike most speech acts it is the *form* of the apology that counts. It is less important whether it is sincere than that it gets made. In fact sometimes a true, obviously heartfelt apology is just what you *don't* want; all you want is a little reminder that you are owed something.

Suppose you're in a movie theater, the movie is in progress, and someone steps on your foot to get to his seat. What would you prefer at this juncture? A long, loud expression of mortification followed by promises of perpetual atonement? Or a grunted "sorry"? (But you *do* want that "sorry.")

Sometimes an apology is little more than a social formula meaning, "I care about you, I hear your distress." Women seem especially prone to this usage, apologizing even when no discernible wrong has been done[8] or the speaker has had no imaginable part in the wrongdoing that has occurred. Sometimes a pro forma apology is used to placate a disappointed interlocutor, even if the speaker had nothing to do with the annoyance. ("Can I speak to Mr. Bigg?" "*I'm sorry*, he's in a meeting.")

Because genuinely apologizing is humiliating, the full, explicit performative form ("I apologize for stepping on your cat") is seldom encountered. Instead, we have a host of indirect and ambiguous ways to accomplish the nasty business.

> I'm sorry I stepped on your cat.
> I'm sorry the cat got stepped on.
> The cat looks upset.
> Why was the cat under my foot?
> Can't the damn animal watch where it's going?
> You shouldn't have let the cat in the room.

You will note the progression from an ambiguous expression that could be either a true apology or a mere expression of regret to an apparent statement of a simple factual observation to an accusation blaming someone else—the cat, or the addressee.

These choices are language politics in action: the way we determine who bears the responsibility for a mishap, who owes what to whom, reflects current power differences among participants and creates their future relationships. The options chosen by a speaker make meaning by creating or acknowledging the existence of a *frame* (see Chapter 2), clues that tell everyone how to understand what has occurred. If I acknowledge fault in the incident, then I am forever after in the eyes of those present either clumsy or a hater of cats, and I must undo the damage or make it up somehow. My identity shifts, however slightly, against my will and beyond my control. If I do not make an unambiguous apology, I may not have to undergo this debasement. Yet I may still get some credit for acknowledging . . . well . . . *something*.

The public apology shares much of its form and some of its function with the private apology, though its consequences may be different. After an "incident," a nation's government must decide whether to apologize, or whether to accept the offending state's apology. If either decision is negative, the only recourse may be war. Sometimes national leaders intentionally perform actions that normally would require apology, and then refuse to apologize—forcing the offended nation into a declaration of war, the only way to save face—as a way to become involved in a war without appearing to be the aggressor. This was certainly the case in the prelude to the Gulf War in the summer and fall of 1991.

Iraqi President Saddam Hussein was known to be a man of passionate temperament, not used to being thwarted, one who did not brook insults calmly. Yet during the summer of 1991 U.S. President George Bush repeatedly stepped on Saddam's figurative toes. He and members of his administration regularly mispronounced Saddam's name—always a sign of contempt. He referred to Saddam as a "butcher" and a "madman" and worse. He announced that he had "drawn a line in the sand," a statement of unilateral power. Through most of this, Saddam maintained remarkable tolerance, but finally he snapped and hostilities began.

The president could have apologized at any point. Instead, he escalated his insults. The absence of apology was itself an act of hostility, and no doubt was intended to be read as one, albeit a slightly cowardly one, in avoiding explicit expressions of aggression while taunting the target to attack.

The absence of any apology from President Bush seems in this case to have been deliberately provocative. But even when there is no affirmative reason to avoid apologizing, a person in power will often take evasive action anyway. A striking instance occurred during the presidency of Ronald Reagan (a man alert to the potency of symbols if ever there was one). The problem arose in the course of the debate over whether to make the birthday of Dr. Martin Luther King an official holiday. Liberals favored it; conservatives were generally less enthusiastic. As the discussion in Congress proceeded, Senator Jesse Helms argued against the proposal on the grounds that, according to information in possession of the FBI, King had been under Communist influence.

At a press conference in October 1983, the president was asked whether he agreed with Helms's assessment. Reagan replied: "We'll know in about thirty-five years, won't we?" apparently believing that the files would be under seal for that length of time (it was actually forty-four years). Democrats immediately demanded that the president apologize to King's widow, Coretta Scott King. According to the *Los Angeles Times* report, as it appeared in the *San Francisco Chronicle:*

> White House press aide Larry Speakes asserted, "The president said what he meant and meant what he said," and declared there were no plans to call Mrs. King. But later the president did.
>
> Speakes said Reagan told her he "thought his remarks were misinterpreted."

After the conversation, Mrs. King was asked by reporters what had transpired. The article reports her comment and its aftermath.

> "He apologized to me," Coretta Scott King said after the conversation. "He said it was a flippant remark made in response to what he considered a flippant question."

White House aides, however, denied that the president had apologized. "It was an explanation," assistant press secretary Anson Franklin said. "He didn't mean the remarks the way they sounded."[9]

A number of interesting questions arise here. First of all, why should Mr. Reagan's remark, superficially a mere prediction of a future discovery, be considered to require an apology? How was it possible for his reported conversation with Mrs. King to be interpreted by her as an "apology" and by his spokesman as an "explanation"? Finally, why was it so important to the Reagan administration that the statement not go into the public record as an "apology" that they were willing to risk offending a significant segment of the (voting) population?

It is relatively simple to see how Mr. Reagan's remarks, if they were as Mrs. King indicated (that is, if he said something essentially equivalent to, "It was a flippant remark made in response to what I considered a flippant question"), could be interpreted as two different speech acts by the two parties involved. Part of the explanation has been suggested above: since apologies are painful, they are apt to be made indirectly, without the explicit performative "I apologize." That provides fertile soil for ambiguity. Mrs. King, hearing the words quoted or paraphrased above (there appears to be no disagreement about *what* the president said), and having in her mind a context (the president had said something that could be construed as offensive) in which an apology was appropriate, heard "flippant" as self-criticism, a not unreasonable interpretation, especially coming from a public figure whose every word is expected to be dissected by the punditry, and who therefore may be presumed to know enough to shun the primrose path of nonliteral expression. (One of the burdens of power, in a democracy that is at the same time a mediacracy, is the impossibility of linguistic playfulness: everything you say had better be literal.) So to Mrs. King, the president's comment was equivalent to, "I spoke irresponsibly, as I should not have done." Since she was the person most closely related to the one harmed by the misspeaking, and since the president made the statement to her, she was reasonably taking it as a true apology: a statement made acknowledging wrongdoing, to the person hurt by it. Furthermore, Mrs. King's response to the president's comments suggests that she not only construed them as an apology, but acted accordingly—expressed forgiveness: "Mrs. King said she replied to the president, 'I understand. We all make mistakes, and I attribute this one to human error.'"

President Reagan (or his spokesman) construed the utterance differently. For him, the emphasis falls on the second part, " . . . in response to what he considered a flippant question." One might still wonder what is "flippant" about a question suggesting that a national hero was in reality a traitor (this colloquy occurred at a time when the Soviet Union was still the "Evil Empire"—in Mr. Reagan's own phrase). In this interpretation, the president's utterance becomes an "explanation," with a communicative force of "It is normal to answer a question in the spirit in which it was asked. So if someone asks you something in jest (flippantly), it is only fitting and proper to respond in kind. If I had responded seriously, I would show myself to be communicatively incompetent, which (as the Great Communicator) I could not possibly be. Therefore, if you understand anything about how communication works, you will see that I did the only rational thing, and your concern (indicating that you took my remark seriously) merely shows that you don't know as much about how to communicate as I do, which is why I have to *explain* it all to you."

It is always preferable to be in a position of explaining rather than apologizing: as much as the latter puts you one-down, the former places you one-up, with your addressee presumably needing something from you (information) and grateful to you for supplying it. But when the speaker in question is a person of authority, it is all the more crucial that he be seen to be on top from start to finish, lest he lose face as a possible wrongdoer. So it was important for the president's staff to insist on the construction of his remarks as explanatory rather than apologetic.

Other interpretations were, and remain, conceivable. But there is an informal rule that whoever publicly makes the first interpretation, especially if it is a personage of influence, generally gets the meaning-making rights. So Anson Franklin's gloss was the last word (that I know of) on the subject.

But how did the president's superficially innocent prediction about the unsealing of the tapes become open to an interpretation ("The Rev. Dr. King was a Communist") reasonably requiring apology? A powerful person's words tend to be subjected to more thorough exegesis than other people's. So if an ordinary person had made Mr. Reagan's remark, it might very well have been taken at face value: everyone has better things to do than expatiate on my meanings or yours. But the President of the United States' meanings—that's another story! Especially a remark by a conservative white president about an African-American heroic figure, in a racially polarized and racially tense society. This social and psychological context figures into the possible "meanings" that can be made, here as elsewhere.

In order to account for the extended (apology-requiring) interpretation, it is necessary to realize first that when an ambiguity is uttered and it involves the possibility of both positive (or innocent) and negative (or harmful) interpretations, the literal surface reading generally is the one with the positive interpretation, the one requiring exegesis the negative. If I say, "You're a real genius," the literal interpretation is the positive one, you're smart; the ironic, that is, the nonliteral one, is negative, you're an idiot. On the other hand, I can't normally say "You're a real idiot," meaning ironically that you're smart. This follows from our natural instincts as social animals for politeness and self-defense: better to be some distance away (or on to a different topic) when the hearer gets what I *really* meant.

Moreover, when public persons say something, in an informational situation like a press conference, the assumption is that what they say will be "interesting." It will be informative, it will say or suggest things we don't know or haven't thought of. So if an utterance under these conditions is capable of multiple understandings, the one preferred in this case (as opposed to that of normal small-talk) is the one that carries the most informational weight, is the most unexpected, or would have the most significant consequences.

The question prompted by Mr. Reagan's remark is, "Just *what* will we know in thirty-five years?" If we have to wait thirty-five years, and it's to be worth the long wait, it had *better* be the richer possibility. In the normal course of events, once the tapes are unsealed, we would then learn one of two things: King was a Communist, or he wasn't. But the latter is much less shocking, and therefore less interesting, than the former. While that interpretation is certainly theoretically possible, it is significantly less likely in the context in which the remark was made. So there are good reasons to demand an apology, and equally good reasons to avoid making one. Once we understand the way language creates and enhances power relations, this otherwise rather odd colloquy begins to make perfect sense.

In similar fashion, the mayor of New York, Rudolph Giuliani, managed to evade a real apology when many demanded one. On Columbus Day it is traditional for New York mayors and mayoral candidates to attend a Catholic mass. The mayor's opponent in the 1997 mayoral election, Ruth Messinger, is Jewish (Giuliani is Catholic). Messinger did not attend the mass, while Giuliani did. According to a report in the *New York Times,* Giuliani described Messinger's absence as a sign of disrespect to those who attended the mass. The remark was seen by some critics as covertly antisemitic and aroused a storm of demands for an apology. Giuliani, whose thin skin is legendary, made a statement which was construed by the *Times* reporter and other observers as an apology.

> I was not suggesting that anyone who has any reservations about going to a Mass or a religious service should be required to go to it, or any pressure should be put on them to go to it. I think people have a right to make those choices for themselves. It was probably a mistake to put the focus on the Mass.

Technically Giuliani's statement could be put into the "apology" category, but only with some serious reservations that take away much of the sting. As the article notes,

> The Republican Mayor pointedly refused to apologize to his Democratic opponent herself, saying his remarks were directed only at "anybody who feels they need an apology." And he said he would not retract his assertion that Ms. Messinger had shown disrespect to Italian Americans and Roman Catholics who celebrate the holiday. (Nagourney 1997)

One essential part of a true apology is absent here: an acknowledgment that it is the recipient who has been wronged, and who therefore has to be the addressee of the apology. Giuliani's phraseology permits the reader to understand that there might be *nobody* to whom the remarks were addressed—the "anybody" he alludes to might not include anyone. In that case there would of course be no "apology" made at all. And there seems to be no acknowledgment of wrongdoing in Giuliani's direction of his remarks to "anybody who *feels they need* an apology"—very different from acknowledging that an actual person had really been wronged and was therefore truly in need of an apology. And since he would not retract one especially hurtful part of the original assertion, it's hard to know just what his "apology" consisted of. In other words, Giuliani's utterance was a skillful exercise in having it both ways: it took the form of an apology of sorts, so that only a crybaby or malcontent could grouse; but for himself and like-minded others, no retreat had been made, and the loss of face consistent with a felicitous apology had not occurred.

Nice work if you can get it.

THE UN-APOLOGY

I have suggested that public figures avoid making apologies. But there is an exception in the eagerness, over the last several years, of high public officials in this and other countries to make public "apologies," almost always for behavior occurring prior to their term of office, usually before they (or those to whom the apology is made) were born.[10] How do we explain this current fad? For one thing it is easier to "apologize" for what people long dead have done to people long dead. President Clinton appears perfectly happy to make explicit apologies for bad behavior by his predecessors (to African Americans for the Tuskegee syphilis experiments of the early twentieth century; to Hawaiians for the overthrow of Queen Liliuokalani at the end of the nineteenth), but he waffled and talked around a direct "apology" to his wife and the public at large in the *Sixty Minutes* interview of the Clintons in January 1992, in response to reports of his marital infidelities; and public dissatisfaction with his apology for an "inappropriate relationship" with Monica Lewinsky in August 1998 almost led to his ignominious demise (see Chapter 8).

When the occasion for an apology occurred outside of the here and now, it is easier for a public person to do the deed. Hence the long list of public apologies for deeds in the more or less distant past. For instance:

- President George Bush's apology to Japanese Americans for the World War II internment camps;
- Canada's apology to its native population for the damage done by "150 years of paternalistic assistance programs and racist residential schools" (*New York Times*, January 8, 1998);
- Japan's apology to Korea for its use of Korean "comfort women" during World War II;
- Switzerland's apology to the Jews for appropriating the moneys of Holocaust victims;
- The French Catholic clergy's apology for the Church's silence in the face of the antisemitic laws passed by the Vichy government during World War II, and their consequences.[11]
- Great Britain's apology to Ireland for the potato famine (although Queen Elizabeth refused to apologize to the Indians for the 1919 Amritsar massacre);
- Australia's apology to its aboriginal population for its mistreatment of them;
- South Africa's apology for apartheid;

- Pope John Paul II's expression of "regret" for the Church's inaction during the Holocaust.

This is quite a list, all the more extraordinary because such behavior scarcely ever occurred before the 1990's. But by now, the genre has become so familiar that it has become the butt of satire. For example, the comedian Steve Martin (1997) writes in the persona of a candidate for public office "looking out over the East River from my jail cell,"

> Once, I won a supermarket sweepstakes even though my second cousin was a box boy in that very store. . . . When I was twenty-one I smoked marijuana every day for one year. . . . Finally, I would like to apologize for spontaneously yelling the word "Savages!" after losing six thousand dollars on a roulette spin at the Choctaw Nation Casino and Sports Book. When I was growing up, the meaning of this word in our household closely approximated the Hawaiian "Aloha," and my use of it in the casino was meant to express, "Until we meet again."

In a similar vein, a cartoon by David M. Hitch shows a political candidate's television ad: RE-ELECT FLEMBRIK: THE REAL SORRY CANDIDATE, with a bemused viewer commenting, "I think things have gotten out of hand with all these political apologies." [12]

Why has the public infelicitous apology become so popular of late? And why (as the parodies suggest) is resentment developing among those in whose name the apologies are made? I suspect it's because the more perceptive recognize that these apologies, for all their literal meaninglessness, have serious consequences, reallocating as they do the right to determine what events mean, and how they shall be spoken of, and who shall speak of them in public. In the past, groups powerful enough to perpetrate the kinds of bad behavior that normally trigger apologies also had the power to refuse to apologize and used their cultural clout to inculcate a general belief that no apology was called for. The only response by the nonpowerful that was deemed appropriate was humble gratitude, thanks to the former oppressor for ending slavery, for instance. So the fact that representatives of the perpetrators must now perform acts of public ritualized contrition is in itself a significant communication. The apology itself, and the specific details of its wording, matter less than the fact that the once grovel-proof have been made to grovel, an ineluctable sign that the times have changed. Beyond this, the patent insincerity, smarminess, and inappropriateness of such apologies make them irresistible targets for ridicule.

THE IDENTITY CRISIS

Public apologetics are not the only current discourse fad that has created controversy. A second seems at first unrelated, although further analysis suggests connections. Contemporary rhetorical style has devised two novelties that are disturbing because they fit so neatly into our tendency to erode or question the concept of individual identity: the use of the third person for self-reference and the erosion of our trust in personal memory, that creator of the cohesive ego that we confidently refer to as "I." In an increasingly diverse society, as more and more of us expect to be active makers of the public discourse, there necessarily arises a nervousness about who "we" are, whether there even is a "we," and if so, how it is created. Only if we see ourselves as a cohesive entity sharing a collective past, similarities of outlook, a common language (metaphorically and otherwise), and common interests, can we allow others the right to interpret any one of us as an individual. If I can trust your good intentions (because you and I have established grounds for mutual trust), at least to a degree, even if at first your view of me sounds outrageous, I may try to listen and may conclude that you are speaking in my best interests. And if you (the interpreter) have more power than I (the interpretee), I will not be overly concerned: I will assume that you will use your power for my good. Even if I don't feel so confident of your goodwill, there is no one to whom I can turn for redress. I won't even have access to a public language to argue against your construction of me. In such a world, one group's interpretation of another goes unchallenged. Stereotypes proliferate. Even their targets may accept them in silence. For there is a covert promise made: assimilate—become just like us—and we will take you in as one of us. And a covert threat: accept our view, or be ignored (or worse).

Once it becomes clear that the cohesive "we" is a fictive construction, the rules change. I can no longer allow you to speak for me. That new perspective enables the underdogs, as well as their masters (who always had that right) to establish sharp boundaries between "we" and "you" or "they." We can still interpret each other, because we "speak the same language." We can still tell our ethnic jokes among ourselves, kid around about our resemblance to the stereotypes. But they can't do that to us any more. We—all of us who are included—now take over the responsibility for constructing both our individual and group identities. I create myself. The differentiation and definition of "I" have effects at many communicative levels, from the concrete choice of personal pronouns to more abstract and complex decisions about the definition of narrative genres and the right to claim a personal memory. Memory is a major source of identity, and whoever determines whose memories are legitimate controls the identity of others.

At the simplest level is an increasing usage of third-person self-reference. Normally we call ourselves "I," "me," or "myself," as in,

I am trying to explain third-person self-reference.

But

Robin Lakoff is trying to explain third-person self-reference,

is third-person self-reference. The form itself is nothing new. Julius Caesar used it famously throughout his memoir, *Commentaries on the Gallic War,* in the first century B.C.E. His choice was that of a master manipulator of language and people, meant to suggest the absolute trustworthiness and objectivity of his account. If he had used the first person, readers might well have discerned an attempt to illegitimately influence the body politic, and might have begun to perceive distortions of the truths—Caesar was well known to his contemporaries as a tricky character. But his third-person presentation lulled his readers into complacency. It felt like history, and history is "truth." How could someone writing about Caesar's exploits in the third person have an axe to grind?

More elaborate structures have lately been built on Caesar's foundation, most notoriously by Lt. Col. Oliver North in his 1987 congressional testimony. Unlike Caesar, North moved back and forth between first- and third-person self-reference. Indeed, North pushed the form still further. He chose his third-person personae from several different evocative options, depending on which image of himself he wished to project at any given point: "This Marine Lieutenant Colonel," to suggest his obedience to orders and his military practicality and toughness; "this American citizen," to link him to viewers on television and underscore his patriotism and trustworthiness; "Ollie North," in refuting rumors about marital infidelities: just a regular guy like you and me, nothing wrong with *Ollie!* He thus created a stageful of characters, all parts of "Oliver North," yet each distinct; none identical with the person ("I") who was testifying; vivid, unlike Caesar's deliberately gray third person, but at the same time impersonal and thus trustworthy: no propaganda, no razzle-dazzle from him! The ploy worked well for the eminently theatrical and charismatic Marine Lieutenant Colonel.

Successful third-person self-reference seems to be confined to people in positions of power, people who naturally see themselves as the cynosure of all eyes, for whom the external point of view invited by the third-person pronoun makes sense. But used by the charisma-challenged, even among the prominent, the device can backfire. Bob Dole, the 1996 Republican presidential nominee, used it a lot, generally in the form "Bob Dole." Despite his position as Senate majority leader and presidential candidate, his persona seemed insufficient to bear the weight, particularly as he used the form both often and predictably. Commentators began referring ironically to "bobdole," and as he fell inexorably behind in the polls, his persistent third-person self-reference began to feel more like a demand for recognition or a gimmick gone haywire than (as it must to be effective) a reflection of presupposed significance.

The burgeoning of third-person self-reference in the public discourse marks the beginning of a slippage: no one can be absolutely sure any more that there is a difference between *I* and *he*,[13] the internal and external worlds; the *I* who knows what is going on inside, the owner of the inner life, the knower of motives; and the *he* who is outside, objective, seeing with and through the eyes of the hearer/reader. The user of third-person self-reference seems to want to play both roles at once. But this advantageous prospect has a downside: "You" don't know who "you" are any more.

Therefore the concomitant creation of another postmodern puzzle is inevitable, namely the argument over what, if anything, distinguishes "fact" from "fiction," particularly in the genre of autobiography or memoir. In the last several years, the formerly hard line between the two, assumed since the development of mass literacy in fifth-century Athens, has grown fuzzier.

The current confusion goes back to the late 1960's with the publication of Truman Capote's *In Cold Blood* and Norman Mailer's *The Armies of the Night*. In both, the line between reportorial factuality and novelistic imagination was blurred, a blurring made more problematic in the second case by Mailer's interjection of himself, in the third person, as a character in the novel—or rather, a subject of the report. (Mailer continued the game in *The Executioner's Tale,* published about a decade later, in which the reporter/novelist entered into the thoughts of a convicted murderer, with whom he had not actually spoken.) Still, there was no dispute about the veracity of the reports themselves—the external world was still trustworthy, its reporters (whether in the guise of novelists or newspapermen) reliable.

Things got more complicated with the publication in the mid-1990's of several allegedly "true" first-person accounts couched as memoir or autobiography, the veracity of which, when subjected to scrutiny, proved dubious. An author's use of a first-person narrator need not require sophisticated readers to believe in the truthfulness of the narrative or the authenticity of the author's borrowed identity. So for instance both the personages and the accounts of "Lemuel Gulliver" in Jonathan Swift's *Gulliver's Travels* and of "Humbert Humbert" in Vladimir Nabokov's *Lolita* are unproblematically fictional. But the recent controversies arose over stories that were represented explicitly as nonfictional, and whose authors represented themselves not only in the narrative proper, but also in interviews and other public discourse as literally identical to the "I" of the narratives, to whom the events described had actually, historically, happened. They kept their own names—not necessarily a statement about their true identities (occasionally a writer of fiction creates an "I" with the writer's own name who is nonetheless understood to be a fiction), but certainly suggestive of identification. In particular Kathryn Harrison and Lorenzo Carcaterra, authors of *The Kiss* and *Sleepers,* respectively, have come under criticism for obscuring the boundaries between "fact" and "fiction," between real-I and fictive-I. Their use of the trustworthy and empathic first-person arouses feelings of betrayal in readers who learn of the blurred lines—more than would be true if the writers had cast their protagonists as more clearly fictional third persons.[14]

Any argument that writers should keep a clear distinction between fact and fiction has to seem naive, if plausible at all, to sophisticated people in the postmodern period. Modern people often feel that a work that knowingly blurs that line and invites readers to examine their resultant confusion is in fact more honest than the sort of thing that has been around for centuries—purportedly true works of alleged nonfiction that skew reality in ways that cannot be checked or controverted: propaganda of one sort or another.

Perhaps at this impasse one is tempted to duck the confusion by retreating back into one's own, trustworthy "I," the deep recesses of the psyche. But there is no refuge there. As Freud pointed out a century ago, we are not in control of our minds, though we believe ourselves to be. Our "memories" may be fictions (or not—we have no way of knowing);

the motives we attribute to ourselves may well not be genuine; that self we have painfully put together out of our memories, motives, and daily interactions is as fictional a construct as the protagonist of a novel. If we can't trust our memories, there is no identity—no "I"—we can claim with certainty. This concern has been part of the culture for nearly a century, but only now are its disturbing consequences becoming manifest.

On whose authority are one's memories (and with them, one's self) to be declared reliable? Here too politics enters the fray. Early in the development of psychoanalysis Freud wondered why his patients had become neurotic. In many cases their recollections included memories of sexual molestation in childhood. When these repressed memories were made conscious, (sometimes) the patient's symptoms would be mitigated. Freud's first hypothesis was simple: the need to repress all memory of the painful events was the cause of neurotic symptoms, themselves distortions of those very events.

This theory not surprisingly found little sympathy in Freud's professional circle, from whose families many of his first analysands were drawn. And Freud himself was the father of three young daughters. Perhaps, too, for a mind as convoluted as Freud's, that theory was ungratifyingly simple and obvious. The "seduction theory" was short-lived; by 1905 Freud had reversed his original hypothesis. By then he had developed his theory of the Oedipus Complex, the claim that children sexually desire the parent of the opposite sex, and that neuroses result from repressing that wish. In this narrative the patient-to-be desires her father; as a result, she fantasizes his act of seduction. So patients' (or anyone's) tales of childhood sexual molestation were ascribed by generations of psychoanalysts to Oedipal fantasy.

That Freud's switch inspired virtually no argument until the late 1960's is not surprising. Males—particularly of the authoritative medical type—were almost universally seen as the realists, females as misty-eyed romantics with a tenuous hold on truth. So fathers' denials were taken as true, female patients' stories as wish-fulfilling fantasies. Thus was authoritative male power again reasserted over female identities, meanings, and memories. Any woman who fought these interpretations was "resisting"—proof positive of the neurosis that made her memory unreliable.

With the rise of the women's movement in the late 1960's, there was a reexamination of male interpretations of women, in psychoanalysis as elsewhere. Writers like Kate Millett, Shulamith Firestone, and Phyllis Chesler (and, almost a generation later, Jeffrey Moussaieff Masson) reexamined the "seduction theory" and suggested that Freud had gotten his story right the first time. The argument had been largely accepted, even, if grudgingly, within psychoanalysis, by the early 1980's, that women's recovered memories were real. The pendulum had swung 180 degrees.

By the mid-1980's it was not uncommon for women who had "recovered" "memories" of early sexual abuse in therapy, spontaneously or under hypnosis, to confront their alleged abusers, sometimes in the courtroom. During the same period there were several large and well publicized trials of day-care workers on similar charges. Popular myth had it that children never "lied" about such things, and popular (as well as professional) opinion saw only two options: they were lying, or their stories were utterly true. Trust persisted in many quarters even when these stories, both the children's and the adults', included bizarre additions like satanic ritual, cannibalism, and multiple murder. In the day-care cases there were a number of guilty verdicts followed by extremely long sentences for those found guilty.

Eventually psychologists began to understand that, especially for young children and adults under the influence of hypnosis, there was something in between "lying" and "truthfulness." While small children do not spontaneously invent such stories, they are notoriously susceptible to suggestion. And hypnosis is, above all, heightened suggestibility. Work by the cognitive psychologist Elizabeth Loftus (1979) demonstrated the unreliability of even adult short-term memory and observation. Sentences began to be overturned, and there were a few cases of therapists being sued by alleged abusers.

The result has been a significant backlash, with several influential books (e.g., Crews 1995; Ofshe and Watters 1994; Showalter 1997) taking an absolutist position against the existence of repression and recovered memory. Once again "experts" (predominantly male) are telling "victims" (predominantly female) what their symptoms "mean," denying them the right or capacity to make their own interpretations. It would certainly be naive and dangerous to accept all reports of recovered memory of childhood sexual molestation as true; but there is equal danger in discarding all, sight unseen, as false. The culture as a whole seems to have a problem with gray areas, preferring either-or to both-and or some-of-each. But—in the (typical) absence of reliably corroborating eyewitnesses—there is seldom a clear diagnostic for telling true stories from confabulations.

So finally we are left in a state of undecidability. In almost any such case, memory (mine, yours, the culture's collective) *may* represent absolute literal truth; *may* represent a construction of truth plus embellishments or reorganizations; or *may* represent pure imagination. There is no way to be sure, and the debunkers' use of one or two or a few demonstrably false constructions merely warns us to be skeptical in all cases— it does not prove that the entire theory of repressed memory is faulty.

The problems raised, both by our doubts about memory and by the absence of any means by which to resolve those doubts, only exacerbates our other uncertainties about the reality of our selves.[15] If our sense of self—the uniqueness, cohesion, and autonomy that we call "I"—is created and justified by our sense of continuity brought about by reliance on the belief in an unbroken and coherent chain of memories; and if we now have to believe that some if not all of our memories, especially the oldest, are mere ex post facto constructions . . . then who are "we"? Even if we no longer surrender to authoritative others the control of our identities via memory, we ourselves must give up those rights as well.

We are dangerously close to the situation in which Alice found herself after her descent down the rabbit-hole. She is no longer the same size and shape she used to be; indeed, she shifts sizes and shapes uncontrollably and unpredictably. So her physical attributes no longer enable her to establish cohesive identity. At the same time she discovers that the psychic determinants of identity have also turned unreliable: she no longer knows the things she used to know. Her painfully garnered (she is seven years old) school knowledge has vanished. And her practical know-how is continually belied by the special rules of Wonderland.

> "Dear, dear! [said Alice to herself] How queer everything is to-day! And yesterday things went on just as usual. I wonder if I've been changed in the night? Let me think: *was* I the same when I got up this morning? I almost think I can remember feeling a little different. But if I'm not the same, the next question is, 'Who in the world am I?' Ah, *that's* the great puzzle! . . ."

> "I'm sure those are not the right words," said poor Alice, and her eyes filled with tears again as she went on. "I must be Mabel after all, and I shall have to go and live in that poky little house, and have next to no toys to play with, and oh, ever so many lessons to learn!" (*Alice in Wonderland*, chapter 2)

The connection between these two dilemmas—the loss of certainty of selfhood and trust in memory, and our current taste for group apologetics—may be that the first creates a need for the second.[16] Implicit in public apology is the invocation, and acknowledgment, of shared memory: *All of us remember that this event occurred.* Such apologies underscore our reliance on presumably shared memory: if we didn't agree that it happened, if we couldn't all be sure that it happened, then the apology would be infelicitous—it couldn't work in our hearts and minds as an apology! So the fact that we accept it as legitimate (if in fact we do) signifies that there is some shared memory we can trust. And that in turn encourages us to go on believing in the myth of ourselves as members of a cohesive society, a valid "we," composed of members such as ourselves, who have at least this group "memory," even if our individual ones are questionable. What Freud hath put asunder, the President of the United States can bring back together.

But difficulties keep arising out of the diffusion and incoherence of our individual selves and the impossibility of keeping "me" distinct from "them." The latter problem is thrust painfully into our attention by the loosening of common bonds in our multicultural society. In the metaphorical melting pot, *you* and *I* might eventually merge. In the newer metaphorical "mosaic" or "salad," the boundary between *I* and *you* remains distinct. So even if all of us spoke English (and worse luck yet, it appears that all of us don't!), we cannot expect to "understand" one another. It has become an article of faith that men and women "speak different languages." But we always suspected as much. Now we are assailed by the realization that words don't mean the same thing under all conditions for everyone (as the O. J. Simpson verdict and its aftermath made painfully clear; see Chapter 6). Context—where, by whom, in what tone words are uttered—counts. And in disputes over meanings, those who could always count on having the last word can't any more. Arguments about what kinds of language are fit for public consumption (see especially Chapter 7) become more rancorous as more sides demand a hearing.

There is public disagreement over the use of troublesome words: for instance, over who determines what constitutes a "slur," and therefore, who determines how a dictionary (once the unquestionable voice of authority) should define the word "nigger," or even if it should be in the dictionary at all. The very dictionary has become overtly political.

According to an article by Torri Minton in the *San Francisco Chronicle* (October 17, 1997), the *Merriam-Webster's Collegiate® Dictionary* Tenth Edition has aroused the ire of the African-American community because it "does not state immediately that the word is offensive." It does say so, but rather as an afterthought: "1: a black person—usu. taken to be offensive," adding at the end of the complete definition, "It now ranks as perhaps the most offensive and inflammatory racial slur in English."

The Merriam-Webster's definition "inflicts extensive emotional damage on young people who have to identify with that definition—because the definition states who they are," according to Jamal-Harrison Bryant, national youth and college director of the NAACP, quoted in the article.

That is an extraordinary statement. First and most obviously, the idea that *anyone*—let alone members of historically unempowered groups—can take issue with a dictionary, its makers, or its definitions, is shocking. But Mr. Bryant's argument is reactionary rather than revolutionary because it reinforces the old order: the reason it makes sense to create a fuss is precisely that the dictionary *is* our maker of meanings, our semantic arbiter: the definition in the dictionary states who you are, your identity still depends on how authority views you. True revolutionaries would reject the authority of the dictionary to define them altogether.

There is an analogous dispute about the use of the word "Holocaust." [17] Must it refer only to the Nazis' killing of six million Jews? Or can it be applied to other cases of mass murder or mass mistreatment of one group by another? Can African Americans appropriate the term to refer to slavery? Does any group have the right to appropriate a word for themselves or their own experience? Again, the use of the word "Holocaust" is only the surface issue; the deeper one is about who gets to decide who can make the language, choose words, assign meanings, mediate between the real-world referent and the concept via language. In the case of "Holocaust," it is true that its original creation, in Greek, in the course of the translation of the Old Testament into Greek from Hebrew, was for the purpose of translating a Hebrew term. But its current capitalized sense did not arise until well after the events it describes, in 1957.

Like "nigger," "Holocaust" packs a real wallop because both words unlock group memories of horrific events. Because both words have become invested with a special mystique, they have meaning for their users beyond the literal. Victims of both slavery and the Nazis want to hold on to the mystique of their words, want them to retain both their terror and their clout, lest we forget in an age in which memory is vaporous. And by asserting control over words that purport to describe the indescribable, the victims of those histories seek to gain some control over their past through control over the language that describes it. But in the normal course of events, nobody retains a copyright on words. (Even manufacturers who try to do so, with words connected specifically to physical products that they own the rights to—like Xerox, Kleenex®, and Scotch™ Tape—have a hard time keeping them specific and uppercase.) Whatever the morality involved, it is unlikely that the Jewish community can retain sole rights to "Holocaust." Inevitably, over time, it will be used more and more loosely, to cover events that are less and less horrific. The word will lose its mythic and mystical power.[18]

We find ourselves in a curious situation. We see ourselves as awaiting the dawn of a new millennium, a time of unparalleled scientific understanding, a time when we ought to be free of the silly superstitions of the past. Yet at the same time, words retain their ancient magical powers. We want to regulate language in order to magically control the course of real world events.[19]

Language is not "just words." It enables us to establish our selves, and ourselves, as individuals and as members of groups; it tells us how we are connected to one another, who has power and who doesn't. The cases I have looked at in this chapter are mostly small-scale: a word, a phrase, or a sentence. Later chapters will examine the way we construct and dispute larger units—whole narratives, even more potent ways to make meaning. Now more than ever language is construed as something worth fighting for, or at least over.

THE NEUTRALITY OF THE STATUS QUO

MEANING AND MARKING

The evidence in the last chapter suggests that making meaning is a defining activity of *Homo sapiens,* and that it is more than just a cognitive exercise, since those who get to superimpose a meaning on events control the future of their society. And since so much of our cognitive capacity is achieved via language, control of language—the determination of what words mean, who can use what forms of language to what effects in which settings—*is* power. Hence the struggles I am discussing in this book are not tussles over "mere words," or "just semantics"—they are battles over the ability to define, and thus create, a large part of our reality.[1]

In homogeneous populations, or those dominated by homogeneous groups, and in societies in which change is imperceptibly slow, the struggle either doesn't materialize at all or happens so gently that it is not noticed. But in times of diversity and change, we notice that some "facts" we had taken to be self-evident and immutable are suddenly reinterpreted as opinions. Deciding whether the quotation marks around "facts" should stay or go is the privilege of the winner of the battle for hearts and minds. Meanwhile, language starts to shift and fuzz, to iridesce like pinstripes on television, to slither out of our control. We thought we had achieved control of language before we entered school, but suddenly we're asked, or forced, to attach new words to old concepts, or vice versa. It's disorienting, especially to those who have reached adulthood believing that they controlled the uses and meanings of language. Remember the Chinese curse: "May you live in interesting times."

"Meaning" itself requires some reflection. We all know what "meaning" means, right? Just as we know what words mean, don't we? Well, yes and no to both. We all, as human beings and members of cohesive societies, possess implicit folk-theories about meaning; but only relatively recently have philosophers, cognitive psychologists, and linguists developed coherent and satisfying theories that make sense of the word.

We all believe that some ideas, terms, concepts, story-lines, and such, are "normal"—natural, simple, expected. Others seem more complicated, less probable, even bizarre. We are prone to consider cases of the former as neutral—not requiring defense or explanation—but we subject the latter to severe tests and often still refuse to accept them. We cherish intuitions about "plausibility," and base upon them conclusions about human behavior that inform fields from science to literature to law, often with serious consequences.[2] We believe that the distinction between what we accept as "plausible" and what we discard as "unlikely" rests on an objectively determinable reality. But psychology is showing, more and more, that this is not typically the case.

Think about the two simple stories below. One seems plausible. The other will seem bizarre.

The baby cried. The mother picked it up.
The baby cried. The mother ate a salami sandwich.

The first represents a cause-and-effect relationship that we have come to think of as "natural." Indeed, this little tale is so normal and obvious that we would not even bother to tell it: it isn't what we call "interesting." It tells us nothing unexpected. The second is more interesting—so much that, by itself, it doesn't work as an intelligible narrative. When we encounter it, we demand explanation: Is something wrong with the mother? Is there a great physical distance between mother and child? Something special has to be going on.[3] The first is a case of "dog bites man," the second of "man bites dog." We differentiate between them on the basis of our expectations, and these in turn are created both by our own individual prior experience, and by the cultural knowledge that we share as members of our society.

Linguists, philosophers, and cognitive psychologists explain these ideas by theories of "markedness" and "frames."[4] In every language, some linguistic forms are said to be "marked," their correlates "unmarked," a binary opposition that goes back to the late-nineteenth-century French linguist Ferdinand de Saussure. Unmarked forms tend to be both semantically and morphologically simpler than their marked counterparts. In English, semantically marked forms have more complex endings than their unmarked counterparts. Marking implies extra meaning and complexity. For instance, in the verbal tense system of most languages that use tense-markings to express time relationships, the ending of the present tense is generally unmarked; the past and future, marked. So in English the simple present has no special marking, but the past is generally marked by the suffix -ed, and the future by the addition of the auxiliary verb *will*. This extra morphology makes sense to us as speakers of English, because it seems intuitive to us that "now" is simpler than "then." It is, after all, what we are experiencing as we speak, not something we have to strain to remember or imagine. Likewise, singular nouns are unmarked, plurals marked: plurality seems to add information. Therefore we mark (most) plurals with -s, but leave the singular bare. But these "obvious" points are creations of our perceptual systems, rather than direct and unmediated reflections of reality. Creatures whose minds worked very differently from ours, whose brains were differently wired, might organize their lexical and grammatical categories in other ways, or conceivably not use markedness as a linguistic option at all.

THE MARKEDNESS OF THE FEMININE
(AND THE FEMALE)

That claim may seem farfetched since it's almost impossible to imagine a language in which singular nouns are more complex than plural, "one" a more difficult concept than "many." But some categories whose markedness not long ago would have seemed to speakers of English as immutable as the ones above, are currently in flux: as society changes, perception changes; as perception changes, language changes with it. "Gender" is a grammatical category subject to marking, and traditionally "masculine" has been unmarked, "feminine" marked. This distinction shows up in the grammar of English in many places.

There are animal species in which males and females are referred to by different forms of the same noun. In most of these cases, the term for the male of the species is morphologically simpler ("tiger" vs. "tigress," that is, "tiger-ess"). The masculine is also the word we use to speak about the species in general: it is understood as including the feminine, not vice versa: "The tiger (*not* the tigress) is endangered."

There exist some interesting exceptions to the rule, again based on human perceptions of and perspectives on "reality," which are in turn based on human experience. With many domestic animals the case is different: the names for males and females are derived from different sources, rather than (as with *tiger:tigress*) one being derived from the other: *Cow:bull; duck:drake; goose:gander.*[5] In many cases, the usual term for the species as a whole is the same as, or closely related to, the female form, rather than the male: *Cows eat grass; there are ducks on the pond; here comes a gaggle of geese.* Here the masculine forms seem more specific and meaningful than their feminine equivalents. One reason is that, in these species, the females are more numerous than the males, and hence, more "typical." But there is nothing intrinsically simpler or more "natural" about them. In the human sphere too, marking can shift. In my youth, when female physicians were a rarity (marked), it was almost obligatory to identify any such person as a "woman (or lady) doctor," while their male counterparts were never "male (man, or gentleman) doctors."[6] If gender-based markedness were purely a morphological formality, it would not have occasioned the amount of heat it has over the last quarter century. Consider the ancient and modern history of the common English word *man*, including compounds like occupational categories (*policeman, congressman, chairman*), as well as other more general terms (*spokesman, freshman, layman*). As feminists have noted, the coincidence of the two senses of *man* in modern English (both "male" and "human being") encourages speakers to see "males" and "humans" as essentially the same, that is, men as unmarked or normal humans, women as marked or not-fully-human. While it might be argued that this lexical dichotomy merely replicates or represents an extralinguistic perception of women as not-fully-human, the linguistic encoding of this perception encourages speakers to see it as inevitable and correct. But this situation is not universal in languages, even in other Indo-European languages, including close relatives of English. Thus German has one word, *Mann*, for "male," and another, *Mensch*, for "human being." Yet no one is suggesting that German speakers are less sexist than speakers of English.[7]

Since gender (unlike most other categories like number) is politicized, the nonequivalence of *man* and *woman* acquires meaning that other kinds of markedness do not. The markedness inherent in gender-related words in contemporary English becomes a sort of scapegoat for many feminists, bearing the blame for the reality of gender inequity, as if the language had created that reality and change in language per se could change the reality of gender inequality.

Because the brunt of gender inequity falls on women, women are more apt to find problems in language that "normalizes" the male. In its Usage Note under "man," the 1992 edition of the *American Heritage Dictionary* discusses the judgments on the usage of *man* made by a panel composed of both men and women. Often the differences in acceptability based on panelist's gender were quite significant: "On the whole, the Usage Panel accepts the generic use of *man,* the women members significantly less than the men." But the list of members of the Usage Panel shows a strong predominance of men. So the sentence *If early men suffered from a lack of information, modern man is tyrannized by an excess of it* is, according to the dictionary, "acceptable to 81 percent of the Panel (including 58 percent of the women and 92 percent of the men)." Note, by the way, that without the parenthetical information, and the ability to discover the gender makeup of the Usage Panel, the simple statement that the above example was acceptable to "81 percent of the Panel" readily permits the interpretation that "normal people" have no problem with this usage. Here is a clear instance of the way in which linguistic choices in storytelling have political implications (especially since such questions have only been asked of Usage Panels over the last quarter century, and women have achieved representation on such bodies in any number even more recently). But the gender-based discrepancy in judgment would be inexplicable without the increased awareness of the politics of gender in recent years. Otherwise, we would have to conclude that women and men literally inhabit different worlds, rather than that their perceptions, based on differing experiences, make their realities (or "realities") different. So linguistic markedness is sometimes based on literal reality (the larger number and greater visibility of female ducks and geese); sometimes on reality mediated by human perception (the unmarkedness of the present tense vs. past and future); and sometimes (as with gender) based on largely psychological "fact" or social construct. Yet once we accept the assignment of items to marked or unmarked categories, we lump all forms of markedness together as equally indicative of the way the world really is.

FRAMES AS MAKERS OF MEANING

In the early twentieth century, an anthropological linguist, Benjamin Lee Whorf, proposed a controversial hypothesis. The forms of a language, he said, force upon its speakers a particular perception of reality. Languages like English that require all verbs to be assigned a tense—past, present, or future—strongly encourage speakers to see time as crucially important and divided into discrete segments: before-now, now, after-now. But a language that doesn't require formal tense endings on its verbs (like many Native American languages) encourages its speakers to see time as fluid, and time spans as indefinite and not highly salient. The hypothesis, while intriguing, is unprovable, since it is impossible to step outside of language to test it. Yet certainly the choices a language has available to its speakers, the distinctions and markings it imposes on reality, must affect speakers' perceptions of reality. But the relationship goes both ways: our prior understanding of the world enables us to endow linguistic forms with markings in the first place.

In the 1970's cognitive theorists began to develop the concept of *frames* as another way of looking at how language and experience affect each other. While the term has been used in many ways by scholars working in many fields over the years since then, we can define a frame as a "structure of expectation" (Tannen 1979) or, more precisely, as "a body of knowledge that is evoked in order to provide an inferential base for the understanding of an utterance" (Levinson 1983). So we can think, for instance, of "restaurants" or "classrooms" or "political debates" as frames, within which we expect certain kinds of utterances and make sense of the utterances we encounter based on our recognition that we are operating within a predetermined frame. When frames shift abruptly, or participants do not agree on the frame involved in an interaction, misunderstanding will occur, as in a scene from *Through the Looking-Glass* (chapter 5). Alice has found herself in a shop tended by a Sheep. Abruptly the shop turns into a river, on which Alice and the Sheep are rowing; at one point Alice commits a rowing error known as "catching a crab," and the Sheep comments, "That was a nice crab you caught!" [8] Alice responds, "Are there many crabs here?" meaning the river they are navigating. "Crabs and all sorts of things," says the Sheep " . . . only make up your mind. Now, what *do* you want to buy?" Alice echoes "to buy!" in "a tone that was half astonished, half frightened," as she recognizes a sudden shift of frame back to the Sheep's shop. The language signifies the frame-shift in a particularly abrupt way. We don't buy things in rowboats, and as soon as Alice figures that out, she perceives the new frame and adapts to it.

As Alice's shock suggests, the ability to recognize the frames in which we find ourselves is comforting, and to be forced to shift them abruptly, disconcerting. To discover that you do not share a frame with someone is equally distressing. Reframing is traumatic, and we resent being forced to do it. We also don't like changes in the rules governing our behavior within preidentified frames. Many people expect that, in a restaurant, a waiter will, simply, "wait": take your order and not initiate communication beyond what is necessary to accomplish what one goes to a restaurant for. But in some restaurants, waiters are encouraged to engage patrons in conversation, introducing themselves by name and offering up bits of small talk (the assumption is that patrons who "know" waiters will tip more generously). But for more conservative patrons, this behavior violates the "restaurant" frame, leading to irritation (and therefore, maybe, a smaller tip).

Frames, then, are essential parts of our cognitive repertoire. They allow us to make predictions and generalizations: I have been in a store before, I know how to operate, I know what's expected, I'm OK. Without them, the world would truly be the "blooming, buzzing confusion" that William James identified as the world-view of the infant (since infants have not had the experiences that would enable them to construct and recognize frames). But once we identify a frame and decide what is right and appropriate within it, we become wedded to it: it becomes extremely difficult to reframe, to change our expectations. We experience demands or requests to do so as threats to our well-being and indeed even our status as full-fledged competent human beings. Frame-shifting seems counterintuitive. New perceptions don't make sense, since they cannot be placed in a familiar frame. Within the frame, things are unmarked: normal, predictable, neutral, orderly, natural, and simple. They do not require explanation. Once a frame shifts, everything changes. We are, in a way, brought back to infantile incompetence.

THE UNCOMMONNESS OF COMMON SENSE

That the familiar seems normal—*is* normal—may be obvious. It is, we say "just common sense." We think of "common sense" itself as based on reality and our own down-to-earth, theory-free, hardheaded observations of that reality. Common sense is one of Americans' favorite populist virtues, one we see as the difference between those we trust (people like us, who have it and use it) and the untrustworthy types without it, who are to be scorned, pitied, and ignored: egghead professors, fuzzy-haired impractical mathematicians, starry-eyed romantics.

But that idealization of common sense doesn't always make sense. For one thing, the beliefs we so categorize are not universal or inevitable. What seems common sense at one moment, or in one society, is anything but in another. Five hundred years ago, it was common sense that the sun revolved around the earth. That perception was reinforced by experience and direct observation. That the blood was pumped through the body by the heart would have been dismissed as nonsense: if it were true, we would continually feel and hear our hearts beating. That a woman played an active role in determining her child's genetic characteristics would have seemed equally absurd: it was "obvious" that she was only the vessel that contained the homunculus donated by the father, which came complete with all heritable traits. Today the frames have changed, and anyone who espouses views like these would be considered ignorant or crazy—that is, devoid of common sense. Such people do exist, but they are marginal and have to justify their positions when challenged, as holders of what is now the conventional (unmarked) view do not. Today, a relatively small group of specialists, widely viewed as impractical eggheads, believes that time is a dimension of space. Many of us accept these ideas as "true" in a purely theoretical way, but cannot imagine what it would mean to live our daily "commonsense" lives accordingly. That would be the stuff of science fiction. But it might become common sense to some future generation of humans.

So the common sense of an idea is determined by its fit within a frame currently accepted by a majority of influential people. And once an idea becomes common sense, included in a generally accepted frame, it becomes very resistant to change. Other ideas accrete around it, lending it credibility and making its abandonment even more disturbing. We need our frames and conventional assumptions. These form the glue that holds cultures together and allows individuals within those cultures to feel like competent members of a cohesive community. We cling to even discredited beliefs, not only out of ignorance, but equally in fear that we would be left alone, bewildered, and not fully human without them.

As troubling as a shift in our understanding of the physical universe may be, that is nothing compared to our reluctance to change our view of how people work. We live by stereotypes, some explicitly recognized, others implicit and unexamined, about who we and others are. And because these views cannot be countered by hard-nosed "objective" scientific evidence, they are particularly hard to dislodge: it is impossible to "prove" as definitively as Copernicus could prove the earth revolves around the sun that all people are created equal, or that IQ has a significant environmental component. People are too complicated, it is almost impossible to control the variables in order to get unambiguous results, and even the words we use—"equal," "intelligence"—do not have determinate or universally agreed upon meanings. In our time many age-old frames are under siege. Change always entails struggle, often as now taking the form of a "language war," because we defend old frames, and create new ones, through language.

There is plenty of evidence that, from their earliest encounters, white Europeans made negative judgments about members of other racial groups and treated members of those groups unfairly on the basis of those preconceptions. That constellation of attitudes and behaviors is what we call "racism" (or "racialism," to use the British term). Yet when I look up these words in my *Oxford English Dictionary* (first published in 1933—when Nazism was on the rise in Europe!—and "corrected" in 1970) neither appears. "Racialism" appears in a Supplement, with its first cited occurrence in 1907. Are we to suppose that the attitudes and behaviors that we call "rac(ial)ism" *did not exist* among speakers of English before 1907 (and were sufficiently uncommon that the word didn't make the main dictionary as late as 1933)? I don't think so. Rather, it was not until recently that our culture evolved enough to enable us to step outside the frame in which such behavior was normal and so invisible. Racism could only be named when speakers could imagine a world in which it did not exist. (Likewise, while the behaviors and attitudes we now call "sexism" have existed for millennia, the word itself came into being only with the raising of female consciousness in the late 1960's.)

We get upset and angry when the connection between frames and reality is challenged. That may explain the ease with which Lani Guinier's proposal for proportional voting was challenged and disposed of, and the ease with which she was tarred with the epithet "quota queen."[9] To suggest that the rule of the majority may be tyrannical, rather than natural, and something that needed inspection rather than being invisible, is to question the frames on which American democracy is based, and through which our sense of ourselves as Americans is formed.

When an idea has not been fully incorporated into a frame, it stands naked in the world, open to inspection and critique, its assumptions

named and acknowledged. The distinction is starkly illustrated in an interview given by Berkeley philosophy professor John Searle. At one point
the interviewer asks Searle:

> You often say unpopular things, one of the most recent being your complaint
> that the white male is being discriminated against in university hiring. Is
> that true?

Searle replies (ignoring the odd presupposition, given the recent over-
whelming passage of California's anti–affirmative action Proposition 209, that such a statement is "unpopular"):

> Absolutely. It's outrageous. I have a brilliant student who's being considered
> for a job at University X. And I heard yesterday that they do think he's the
> best candidate—but they want a woman. Now, just turn that around a bit.
> Suppose someone said, "Well, it's true he's the best candidate, but he's black,
> and we want a white person." We would regard that as an *outrage*. And it is
> an outrage. It's an outrage to discriminate on grounds of race or sex. (Schoch
> 1995, 26)

This is very persuasive, and fully in keeping with American egalitar-
ian ideals and the Fourteenth Amendment guarantee of "the equal protection of the laws." But the story is not so simple in light of the hiring
history of the University of California, Berkeley Philosophy Department
(not unlike that of most philosophy departments at major research universities). Searle has been a tenured member of that department since the
mid-1960's, a period during which time he was very vocal and visible,
and had access to many public arenas. At that time, and continuing into
the early 1980's, the Berkeley Philosophy Department did not have a
single tenure-track (assistant professor or above) female member. Yet
there must have been then (since I know there are now) highly competent
female graduate students in that and other eminent philosophy departments, who could have been a source of tenure-track appointments. The
department did not question its single-sex faculty (until it became an obvious embarrassment and a basis for threats of legal remedy many years
later), nor did Searle, with all his media access, during all the time from
then to now, offer any critique of the situation comparable to his quoted
remarks above. We cannot fairly fault Searle for not speaking of the
problem back then. Like all of us, he was at that time a prisoner of a cultural frame that rendered women essentially invisible to university hiring
committees. It was a truth universally acknowledged by such committees
that a woman *simply could not* be as good as a man. Even if she were,
it was another universally acknowledged truth that at the first opportu-

nity she would get married and pregnant and abandon her career. So it would be ludicrous to imagine hiring a woman—so ludicrous that it was hardly ever mentioned.

I don't think Searle can be charged with having been sexist at a time when the word itself didn't exist; but I do think he can be faulted for not realizing by 1995 that he and his colleagues were guilty in the past of misbehavior equivalent to the kind he is inveighing against (in which case he might have tempered his outrage). For centuries departments of philosophy (and everything else) *implicitly* said, "we want a man." Arguably the implicitness of the statement renders it even more "outrageous" than the explicit form Searle cites. When bias is made explicit, as in his example, it can be identified and criticized. But when it's implicit, hiding behind a frame that renders it invisible, it is impervious to critique or change. We might even argue that Searle's case is *less* outrageous than the one I have described, since hiring a woman (most philosophy faculties are still very predominantly male) would help overcome the current inequity stemming from the earlier, implicit, bias. Thus it would have positive repercussions, while Searle's choice would produce largely negative effects.[10]

Often, attempts to make frames visible or to change generally accepted ideas are met with derision. Because the derision is supported by conventional beliefs, it "makes sense" and does not require explicit explanation or justification. Hence its support may extend beyond its natural conservative constituency. Such is the case of "politically correct" or "p.c." language (see Chapter 3), one aspect of which is the attempt of many nondominant groups to achieve the right to determine what they are to be called and whether their names can be appropriated by outsiders. A number of college and professional athletic teams have names or nicknames that refer to Native Americans: the Washington Redskins, the Atlanta Braves, the Cleveland Indians. The argument of their proponents is that these names "honor" Indians by stressing their bravery and strength. The point is made, however, that we never so honor other minority groups with names like the Brooklyn Jews or the Baltimore Blacks. The very idea seems absurd because those communities have more clout in the public media than the Indian community does and have made it clear that invoking stereotypes this way would be offensive. But even names like these would make more sense to us than would a team named the Des Moines Caucasians. There isn't an "official" Caucasian stereotype, because Caucasians, the group with clout, have created the stereotypes for the other groups.

Many whites find it easy to see American society as "color blind," because to them color *is* invisible, since theirs is unmarked. So for them, African Americans' insistence that they are different and that their differences should be ratified and celebrated (e.g., by "Afrocentric" instruction or the use of Black English in inner city schools) is racist: it seems to insist on a difference that, to whites, is nonexistent or at least unimportant. But if you have experienced differential treatment based on skin color, the denial of that difference will seem to you an attempt to evade responsibility for it. As Bob Blauner (1992), a sociologist at U.C. Berkeley, put it:

> Whites sense racism when students of color assert their differences and affirm ethnic and racial membership, which minority students have been doing more and more recently. To blacks and other students of color, this reaction seems misinformed, even ignorant. They feel that what is really racist is the white assumption that everyone should be like them, that minorities must assimilate to mainstream values and styles.

Law professor Patricia Williams makes a similar point:

> At a faculty meeting once, I raised several issues: racism among my students, my difficulty in dealing with it myself, and my need for the support of colleagues. I was told by a white professor that "we" should be able to "break the anxiety by just laughing about it." Another nodded in agreement and added that "the key is not to take this sort of thing too seriously." (1991, 166)

In more recent writing, Williams (1998) discusses in depth the problem this anecdote typifies. In her story, her young son is diagnosed by his nursery school teachers as "colorblind." She has his eyesight tested by an ophthalmologist, who finds it normal. She investigates, and finds that the basis of the teachers' diagnosis was that the boy "resisted identifying color at all." So, when asked what color the grass was, he would reply, "It makes no difference." Williams realized that the child was merely echoing his teachers' platitudes about race which he, being black, had already grasped as well-meant falsehoods. Indeed, the kids in class "had been fighting about whether black people could play 'good guys.'"

As these excerpts suggest, if you're a member of the dominant group, your attributes are invisible, as your role in making things the way they are is not noticeable. This process is called "exnomination" by the French deconstructionist critic Roland Barthes. He discusses the bourgeoisie as an exnominated group: "As an ideological fact, [the bourgeoisie] completely disappears: the bourgeoisie has obliterated its name in passing from reality to representation. . . . [I]t makes its status undergo a real *ex-*

nominating operation: the bourgeoisie is defined as *the social class which does not want to be named"* (1972, 138; italics in original). Exnominated groups, says Barthes, become "normalized": they become apolitical and nonideological. They just *are*. Their rules become *the* rules: "[P]racticed on a national scale, bourgeois norms are experienced as the evident laws of a natural order" (140). The same claim can be made of white middle-class males in contemporary America. In fact, whites sometimes feel as if they have been exnominated into obliteration. As a consequence, there are attempts at what might be called re-nomination: the formation of white studies departments at universities, male supremacy groups like the National Organization of Men, and racial supremacist groups like the National Association for the Advancement of White People. There is an irony here which can be summarized as: beware of your wishes, for you may get them.

Communications theorist John Fiske defines the exnomination of whiteness in American culture this way: "Exnomination is the means by which whiteness avoids being named and thus keeps itself out of the field of interrogation and therefore off the agenda for change" (1996, 42). In other words, by assuming an apolitical status, the exnominated (major-ity) group achieves its political ends without needing to justify itself, or them. Similarly, the assumption that the status quo is neutral is an ex-nomination made possible by our cultural frames.

The same phenomenon has been discussed by cultural historian Ed-ward Said as "Orientalism." Orientalism, says Said, is "a western style for dominating, restructuring, and having authority over the Orient" (1978, 3). He notes that, for this "discourse" to succeed, it has to have the appearance of pure knowledge—"be nonpolitical, that is, scholarly, academic, impartial" (10). Orientalism is the West's understanding of the Orient, or East, as the Other—something "we" see as infinitely for-eign and different from ourselves, exotic and thus dangerous, and at the same time, secretly, as representing qualities we might desire to have, or actually have, but cannot acknowledge wanting or possessing. This se-cret makes the Other all the more threatening and dangerous. Said gives an example of this attitude from the writings of Lord Cromer, an early-twentieth-century British Orientalist:

> The European is a close reasoner; his statements of fact are devoid of any am-biguity; he is a natural logician, albeit he may not have studied logic; he is by nature sceptical and requires proof before he can accept the truth of any proposition; his trained intelligence works like a piece of mechanism. The

mind of the Oriental, on the other hand, like his picturesque streets, is eminently wanting in symmetry. His reasoning is of the most slipshod description. . . . They are often incapable of drawing the most obvious conclusions from any simple premises of which they may admit the truth. (38)

Thankfully, we now find such statements more embarrassing to their makers than their subjects: we have learned *something* in the last century. But we are not yet free of the consequences of such frame-dependent reasoning. We are still prone to see groups different from *us* as weird and threatening, needing to account for themselves and their behavior as "normal" people like *us* do not. It is this covert assumption that makes it possible (according to *Newsweek*) for the president of the American Broadcasting Company, Bob Iger, to justify the network's cancellation of the sitcom *Ellen* "not because of the star's [lesbian] sexuality, but because 'the character was gay every single week'" (Howard and Gajilan, 1998). Of course, the great majority of TV sitcoms have characters who are straight every single week, often blatantly so. But heterosexuality is *us,* exnominated and therefore unnoticeable. In the same way, the exnominated and the *we* can appropriate the Other as the butt of satire—because they are abnormal, weird, counterintuitive, and dangerous. Particularly when *they* threaten to erode the frame and change the rules, anger is a typical response, represented in the responsible media via satire and sarcasm.

Thus Maureen Dowd (1996) comments in the *New York Times* on the "feminization" of, as she fears, *everything*. As is frequently the case with commentary on things feminine, it both trivializes and ridicules its subject: "This year, women will get credit for a breathtaking achievement: Taking sports out of the Olympics and politics out of the [political] convention." What Dowd and many of her readers do not notice is that the masculine perspective is exnominated. There is an unexamined assumption that the old (male-oriented) ways of reporting and commentating Olympic events, via statistics and physical comparisons, define "sport," while narratizing about the backgrounds and perceptions of the athletes is not only new and feminine, but non-"sport," that is, uncategorizable—threatening and weird. Similarly, "politics" is defined by the traditional campaign speech or convention address: boastful, divisive, impersonal. Something else might be better or worse, but what's scary to proponents of the status quo is simply that it's different. In the column, Dowd does not need to provide reasoned arguments to support her (implicit) position that the new ways are bad ways. Their badness is presupposed as an aspect of their novelty, and her use of sarcasm is effective because many readers share that unexamined presupposition.

WE ARE THE WORLD

By contrast, when *we* consider ourselves at all, we see our ways as normal, rational, and good—if we even think of them as "ways," which would imply the existence of other imaginable ways. They make sense because we have always done so; and we have always done so because they make sense. Their very routineness comforts us; and the knowledge that "everyone else" is acting and thinking similarly also comforts us. The fact that *we* all are this way separates us from the dangerous Other. We are both cognitively "rational" and socially "normal." A new idea, or its proponents, must be powerful indeed to overcome that double bias.

Hence we are apt to dissect ideas identified explicitly or otherwise as "ours" with less scrutiny than ideas whose provenance is more suspicious. This is one reason why conservative argumentation strikes many critics as somehow "smarter" than the ideas of the opposite side. They are smart precisely because they are conservative, tested by time, and neutral. John Searle, in the interview cited earlier, provides an example of this thinking:

> [U]niversities are about quality. . . . Because that's what universities are for in the humanities: the creation and the maintenance of a superior level of intellectual attainment and the powers of discrimination.
> Q: There's a difference between Bugs Bunny and Shakespeare?
> A: That's right. We think, not only is there a distinction between Bugs Bunny and Shakespeare, we think it's demonstrable. You can show people the difference. We can train our students to spot the difference in quality. (Schoch 1995, 27)

I agree with a lot of what Searle says here, but not everything, and not with some of the attitudes (not to say attitude) underlying it. I feel an emotional sympathy with the claim that universities are "about quality," but when I try to embrace it logically I run into problems. While we all respond positively to statements supportive of "quality," what exactly is "quality," and who decides what has it? Searle uses "quality" as if it were like "redness," a word describing a physically present and uncontroversial attribute whose presence observers could use agreed-upon evidence to determine. But members of a university community might not agree about what constituted evidence or examples of "quality." I would even suggest that a great university is one whose faculty is open to the exploration of the ambiguities of terms like "quality," and able to agree that no single one of us or group of us can make that determination for all of us.[11]

A more subtle problem concerns Searle's use of "we," used three times (four if you count "our") in the excerpt quoted. Who is this authoritative and prescriptive "we" that determines "quality" and conveys that definition to "our" students? Every member of the university faculty? Only members concerned with aesthetic distinctions? Only humanities faculty? Actually, I would agree in principle (as who would not, besides some straw professor created by Searle himself) that Bugs Bunny is no Shakespeare. But if by this tautology Searle means to imply that Shakespeare is worthy of study in a university while Bugs is not, I must opt out of his "we." I think the modern research university is big enough and protean enough to embrace two (and many more) kinds of studies with no diminution of "quality." But then, I don't see the mission of the university as merely "the creation and maintenance of a superior level of intellectual attainment and the powers of discrimination." I think what the university is for is the pursuit of knowledge about who we are as human beings, what the universe that we inhabit is like, and what the relationship is between the first and the second. The studies of both Shakespeare and Bugs Bunny tell us who we are: we are creatures who have created both, who need and understand both, who are enhanced by knowing both—in different ways to be sure, but to deny that either one is relevant to our human experience is to diminish that humanity.[12] So Searle's inclusion of me among his quality-seeking "we," however flattering at first glance, needs to be questioned. His is the exnominating *we,* the *we* that makes *our* discriminations invisible, makes our beliefs the only possible ones and thus invisible as choices.

The implicit inclusiveness of the *we,* and the assumption of *our* rationality, has other consequences. The quotation above about Ellen's, and *Ellen's,* being "gay every single week" is a case in point. These assumptions color much of our public discourse: what words mean, and what whole genres of discourse mean; what forms are "reasonable" for it to take; which people, speaking in what ways, are to be judged "credible"; what it takes to make a persuasive case; what forms of expression are to be given aesthetic preference; more subtly, what metaphors and other figures of speech we are to respond to viscerally; on what grounds these judgments are justified, and whether and how they can be changed. Tacitly, the exnominated group assumes a set of shared interests that are reflected in decisions about what kinds of discourse will be taken seriously. And because those taken seriously embody the "neutral" status quo, automatically the conservative side has an edge in any argument: they don't have to make the case that their side is reasonable, or socially responsible, or normal: that's just a given. But the other side has to argue that change—the move away from the familiar and the comfortable, out of frame and toward the marked, is worth the cognitive and social fragmentation that it necessarily entails, a much more difficult argument to make because it forces participants to venture onto unfamiliar and shifting ground.

Conservative critics often inveigh against the very language of the opposition, accusing them of convoluted syntax and lexical neologism: *hegemony, privilege* as a transitive verb, *interrogate* with an abstract direct object, *interpellate*. Thus the conservative journal *Philosophy and Literature* awarded Judith Butler first prize in its annual Bad Writing contest (see Smith 1999). That Butler's prose is discouraging to the deconstructionally challenged is beyond question. Two questions, however, are worth exploring. First, why do conservatives expend so much passion over "mere rhetoric"? And second, why is their writing often much more accessible to readers than its liberal counterpart?

Conservatives often complain that theirs is the harder persuasive row to hoe: they are seen as unfashionably fuddy-duddy; they are "strict" while their adversaries are "permissive"; they are the voices crying in a wilderness of p.c. and deconstructionism among a demoralized and effete intelligentsia. But rhetorically at least, theirs is the easier task: their arguments are intellectually easier to grasp and emotionally more evocative of sympathy. Theirs is the side of "common sense," conventional wisdom, the tried-and-true, Biblical allusion and ancient proverb. Their world views tend to be simple: good vs. evil, right vs. wrong, where liberal discourse often bogs down in the yes-buts and on-the-other-hands.

Their chosen words are certainly more familiar and pleasant on the tongue than the postmodern neologisms of Butler and her colleagues. But it's not just that they are the better writers. Nor is it simply that conservative thought is direct and clear, its opposite convoluted because it is outlandish. Conservative clarity is deceptive, relying on the shared presuppositions that form the basis of our daily vocabulary. They have been with us so long that we don't need to think very hard when we encounter them; they're like a green light on the road; we hardly notice it. They are commonsensical. Thinkers with new ideas must first free readers from the old. That often requires the making of new words; and a new word on the page often works like a gauntlet in the face, a challenge: "betcha can't figure *this* one out!" It infuriates; it distracts; it perplexes. It slows down like an amber light, or stops us cold like a red one. We *hate* red lights: we're in a hurry.

What makes conservative ideas go down smoothly, while new ones stick in the craw, is their bland familiarity. This is the justification Butler (1999) makes in an Op-Ed piece written in response to Dinitia Smith's "Bad Writing" article. But I am not quite ready to go all the way with the deconstructionists on this one. I notice that Butler's Op-Ed piece is couched in clear and elegant prose. Yet it expresses the same difficult and painful ideas as those that allegedly force her other writings into obscurantism. So clarity *can* be achieved even under duress, and Butler can do it.

If you can write clearly, it seems to me irresponsible not to do so. More than irresponsible—paradoxical. To write (or speak) is to communicate. To communicate is to share meanings, make them "common" to all participants in the discourse. (The etymological root of *communicate* means "common.") To express ideas obscurely is to fail to communicate, except to those who are already adepts in the arcana. So obscure communication is either pointless or redundant, except as a power play ("I'm smarter than you"). For this reason Butler's plea for opacity fails to convince me. At the same time, conservative implications that obscurely expressed ideas should be discounted on that basis alone seem to me smug and self-serving, the status quo resorting to its putative neutrality.

For the invisible *we,* much of the spadework is done in advance. Many of the culture's presuppositions about what kind of talk is persuasive, civil, moderate, or beautiful accord with *our* normal modes of linguistic self-presentation. That matters because effective persuasion is the very heart of democracy. We tend to assume universality: there is a direct link between being truthful, saying what you really believe, and the way your words come out—the same for everyone. But this is not necessarily true.

Some years ago I was working with a couple of criminal defense attorneys, observing the process of juror selection. I was interested in their reasons for selecting some panelists and eliminating others (aside from those who were obviously biased). One prospective juror was a young Japanese-American woman. Some of the attorneys' questions were personal and intrusive. In response she would hide her face in her hands and giggle. The defense dismissed her. Later, I asked them why, since her explicit answers sounded sympathetic to their side. She giggled all the time, they said. She was making fun of us—not taking us seriously. We'd never be able to connect with her. Applied to a mainstream American, that judgment might have been sound. But many women of Japanese descent use giggles to hide embarrassment, as a Caucasian American might drop her eyes or become verbally vague or challenge the questioner directly ("That's none of your business!"). The attorneys mistranslated the prospective juror's "meaning," because they assumed a universal link that in fact does not exist between surface expression and deeper intention.

A current example is also telling. In the parade of women who have accused Bill Clinton of sexual misbehavior, who is credible? Observing the televised performances of three women, Gennifer Flowers, Paula Jones, and Kathleen Willey, I had sharply different initial impressions of the credibility of each.

Gennifer Flowers, trained as a television reporter, is well accustomed to media self-presentation. On *Geraldo Rivera* in 1997 she came across (to me) as rather bland: not enough uniquely personal style to draw any conclusions from. That appearance of distance and "objectivity," so important to a news reporter's credibility, worked against her in this role. As an injured woman, she struck me as untrustworthy because she presented her case in that uninvolved, reportorial fashion.

Paula Corbin Jones was different. At her first press conference, I found her unbelievable, partly on the basis of the story itself (is *any* man intelligent enough to become president stupid enough to expose himself without encouragement?), but also because of the way she told it. There she was before a large mixed-sex group of strangers, telling what should have been an excruciatingly painful and embarrassing tale (since her pain and embarrassment were the basis of her lawsuit). Yet she was perky and chipper, talking loudly and making direct eye contact, speaking without euphemisms of what had happened. Her demeanor supported the state trooper's report that she had come out of the hotel room full of cheer and bragging that she might be the governor's next girlfriend.

Kathleen Willey, a White House volunteer, told her story to Ed Bradley on *60 Minutes*. She spoke in a low voice, sometimes almost inaudibly, eyes downcast. She had to be encouraged by Bradley to go on. From time to time, she seemed barely able to produce the necessary words, often euphemisms. Bradley sometimes had to prompt her: "And was he [pause] aroused?" " . . . Yes [pause] he was [pause] aroused." (I.e., "Did he have an erection?" "Yes.")

I found Willey's story perfectly believable. That may have been in part because it was the third such tale I had heard, and, as the Bellman says in Lewis Carroll's *The Hunting of the Snark,*

"Just the place for a Snark! I have said it thrice:
What I tell you three times is true."

But I think I found it credible at first hearing mostly because of the way in which it was told, which accorded with my presupposition that people (especially women) tell embarrassing stories just as she did.

The argument isn't as simple as it seems. Although middle-class white American women often agree with my perceptions (since I am all of those), that judgment is far from universal. Paula Jones herself is working class, Kathleen Willey middle class; so naturally each represented herself "credibly" according to the mores of her own group. But since middle-class whites are unmarked relative to other groups, their (our) mode of credible self-presentation seems to many people, especially those in the media who are also typically members of this group, the only possible expression of truthfulness. Yet that might not be the case, and *there is no way of knowing,* in individual cases, whether it is or not.

Similarly, Anita Hill seemed to me utterly credible during her testimony: she behaved very much like Kathleen Willey. But to members of other groups (black or working-class white women) she made a very different impression. John Fiske reports: "Nancy Fraser gives an insightful class analysis of the currents and counter-currents swirling around the hearings. She cites a *New York Times* article that also reported that blue-collar women . . . were put off by Anita Hill's soft-spokenness and, in their eyes, failure to deal with Thomas on the spot" (1996, 91).

It may seem that these cases, while interesting, have no consequences for real life: the assessments of couch potatoes have no direct effects on events. But there is at least one situation in which judgments made on these grounds probably matter a lot.

In jury trials, jurors are always given some instruction by judges about evaluating witness testimony. Very often judges tell jurors that the credibility of witnesses' stories is to be determined (at least in part) from their "demeanor." Judges typically say no more than that, but jurors undoubtedly understand from that instruction that they are to use their "commonsense" assessments of credibility: eye contact, tone of voice, absence of hesitations, and the like. Juries are often composed predominantly of middle-class people, and defendants (as well as many character witnesses testifying on their behalf) are frequently lower class. Jurors might draw false conclusions on the basis of "commonsense" rules of credibility assessment, unaware that class differences affect people's rhetorical styles.

WHO'S UNCIVIL?

Just as "our" way is credible, it is also "civil," an attribute of discourse currently considered endangered. The charge of "incivility" has been lodged against several TV talk show hosts and their guests. Jerry Springer has lately become the poster boy for talk-show incivility. On his show, guests are goaded to scream (bleeped) obscenities at one another, demonstrate intemperate rage, even engage in physical altercation. Springer's show has been the subject of repeated critique and ridicule in the "responsible" media, yet (or therefore) is now the highest-rated talk show, having displaced the stolidly respectable Oprah.

When the "problem" of talk-show incivility first arose a couple of years ago, there were suggestions that the complaints might stem from class differences between the critics and the show's guests and audiences. The epithets "trailer trash" and "low rent" might have been minted for those guests. They are everything that middle-class respectability militates against: loud, boisterous, obscene, confrontational, direct, and impolite. They dress in clothes that are too short, too tight, too glitzy—tacky. They are *vulgar*—a word that means, etymologically, "of the common people."

It is possible to say that the behavior of guests on, say, *Charlie Rose,* or *The NewsHour with Jim Lehrer* is just as exotic as that of guests on *Jerry Springer* or *Sally Jessy Raphael,* or that the latter are just as "normal" as the former. Those would be the views of a totally objective observer stationed outside the American class structure—say, a visitor from Mars. (You would have to go that far, since almost every place on earth has come under the influence of American culture and stereotypes.) But such statements would strike most of us as counterintuitive. And since it is the middle class, or those members of other classes who have approximated to its values and mores, who get media access, it is the middle-class self-presentation that is portrayed as normal and right. All other classes are "marked"; their behavior is framed as requiring explanation, while middle-class mores go unremarked. This is why, in George Bernard Shaw's 1914 play *Pygmalion,* the remonstrances of Alfred Doolittle, whom Professor Henry Higgins has indirectly transformed from a member of the underclass to a "gentleman," are so comically absurd:

> Who asked him to make a gentleman of me? I was happy. I was free. I touched pretty nigh everybody for money when I wanted it, same as I touched you, Enry Iggins. Now I am worrited: tied neck and heels: and everybody touches me for money. . . . And the next one to touch me will be you, Enry Iggins. I'll have to learn to speak middle class language from you, instead of speaking proper English. (Act 5)

The very idea that Doolittle's Cockney, rather than Higgins's "middle class language," is "proper English" had to be ludicrous to the play's original middle-to-upper-class audience. But to Doolittle, that's a perfectly reasonable perspective.

In a similar vein, but without Shaw's irony, Peggy Noonan (1991) tries to exnominate the working class as *normal* ("the normal human beings who work in laundromats") and renominate the middle class ("the chattering classes"). The class warfare that provides a subtext to much recent political discourse in our classless society also receives comment from Katha Pollitt (1997a), who observes, speaking of the treatment of Paula Jones, "The good news is that the mainstream media have discovered their own class prejudice. The bad news is that so far they've managed to find only one victim: Paula Jones."

The complaint about "incivility" goes beyond a critique of television entertainment. Pundits on both sides have been grumbling for most of the decade about a perceived increase in rudeness or "coarsening" of public discourse. Some of the criticism is about the emergence into the public daylight of language formerly confined to the darkness of the most private confines of our lives: bedroom and bathroom talk. It is certainly the case that words are used with impunity in the mass media that a couple of generations ago gentlemen hesitated to use in "mixed company," even in private, and ladies at least theoretically didn't even know. But the complaints extend further, into a tendency to revile opponents as miscreants and criminals.[13] It is often suggested that this is a new phenomenon, unheard of before the emergence of the speaker's favorite anathema: feminism, rap music, adultery in high places. It is seen as a sign that moral turpitude is reaching new highs.

The jeremiads are convincing to anyone whose knowledge of history goes back no further than last Wednesday. Political discourse has been marred by "coarseness" of various kinds ever since it was invented in fifth-century-B.C.E. Athens. In the first century B.C.E. the Roman republic was in a state of class and ethnic fragmentation. We think of the rhetoric of the period as measured and sedate, laden with Ciceronian *gravitas*. But if you read what orators like Cicero actually said publicly about their political opponents, it is clear that we are a long way from achieving a comparable standard of incivility. In a campaign manual prepared about a year before Cicero's run for the consulship (Rome's highest electoral office), his brother gives him some advice. He worries at the outset that Cicero, a commoner, is at a disadvantage in a class-conscious society when running against aristocrats like his hated adversary, Catiline. Quintus Cicero provides his brother with a model diatribe against the opposition:[14]

> [T]hey are ideal opponents for an ambitious, hardworking, honest, well-educated man supported by influential people. They were juvenile delinquents, sexually irresponsible, always strapped for money. . . . [One] was expelled from the senate on the excellent judgment of the censors. . . . The other—good Lord, what a piece of work he is! He is a man of equally noble rank [as the first], maybe even higher. But he is not afraid of his own ability. What do I mean by that? While [the first] is afraid of his own shadow, Catiline isn't even afraid of the law: born to a father on welfare, sexually educated by his sister, he came into power during the civil war, starting his murder spree under its cover. How can I even bring myself to say this man is running for the consulship—someone who killed a man of the greatest value to the Roman people, beating him with a centurion's staff, all through the city, driving him literally to his very grave, employing every form of torture; and while the man was still alive, cut off his head, grasping the sword in his right hand, with his left holding the head up by the hair, and keeping hold of it while rivers of blood flowed through his fingers. . . . A man who never came to any holy place without leaving behind the taint of impiety. . . . A man of such gall, wickedness, and sexual perversity that he practically seduces little boys in their parents' laps! (*Commentariolum petitionis*, 8–10)

We have not quite attained this nadir of political expression, although we do occasionally come close.

Nor was nasty political rhetoric unknown before the present in American politics. The Adams and Jefferson administrations are called, with good reason, the "era of bad feeling." Paid propagandists churned out vitriol against the members of the opposition party; the Sedition Act mandated severe criminal penalties for anyone who spoke or wrote against the Adams administration. During the first sixty years of the nineteenth century, the discourse of Congress went from bad to worse, as the dispute over slavery got hotter and hotter and the possibility of a peaceful solution faded. There are records of fistfights and invitations to duels on the floor of Congress. The current "coarsening" has not quite reached this point.

For a brief period during and in the aftermath of the Second World War, partisan rhetoric receded to relative mildness (if we forget, as many critics of the "new incivility" seem to, the McCarthy period, when incivility went beyond mere semantics into pragmatics—lives and livelihoods were lost). One reason is that, throughout that period, we were effectively in a state of war against an external enemy. Once the Cold War ended, we had nowhere to vent our normal partisan spleen except back at one another.

Today there is another reason why "incivility" has become a catchword. It is not just a problem of rude language, but of the polarization of views in public discourse. We are continually mired in debates whose presuppositions permit no ground for compromise, give no quarter. Neither side is willing to acknowledge that there might be a middle ground. That leads inevitably to name-calling and ultimately even to death threats and occasionally more than threats by members of the lunatic fringe of one movement or another.[15]

When there is sharp polarization and an essentially even division of the population between the sides; when the fight is such that there is, or seems to be, no possibility of compromise or commonality of view; the debate can only progress by turning up the heat, since there is little chance of turning up the light. In such discourse, we increasingly see the other side as "them," those with whom we share no affinities, who become, in our demonizations, ever less human, more bestial, more satanic. Because we cannot win them over, they threaten our very existence, and we have to fight back with whatever we've got. Because we cannot imagine any future reconciliation, we have nothing to lose by alienating them forever. And when you're getting nowhere, you feel better by letting off steam with heated language.

If those were the only reasons for intemperance, though, the grumbling about "incivility" would be dispersed on all sides. But most of it comes from the conservative camp, who see it as evidence of the decline of traditional values. They are right in that the heating up of the rhetoric does partly reflect deep social change. Our society and its discourse are becoming increasingly diverse. That is true both literally (immigrants, and their languages, are entering the country at a high rate) and figuratively (different kinds of people—women, people of color, those with unconventional sexual preferences—are gaining access to public forums in positions in which they can speak and be heard). That means not only that there is serious pressure on the neutral status quo, but that the opposition is being posed by people who formerly would not have been able to speak or be taken seriously. Now they must be. More meanings are debatable, there is more competition for control of discourse, than ever before. And groups who have been silent for a long time are likely to express themselves in ways that seem "strident" to those who have for eons had control, and so have learned over time to modulate their rhetoric as "gentlemen." Those "gentlemen" shared "special interests" that tempered their rhetorical thrusts. And since they usually had similar upbringing and education (and often were related by blood or marriage), they were likely to "speak the same language," mitigating any distrust. So the reasonable-sounding critique of "incivility" (and who is *for* incivility?) masks a fear that *they* are taking over, that the neutral status quo will be revealed to be partisan and arbitrary.

THE FIGHT FOR THE CENTER

What is "commonsense" is also "mainstream," and therefore "moderate." All these words describe a position well within a predefined frame, away from the marked periphery. So whoever can gain the rhetorical center is apt to win the most friends and influence the most people. The group that enters the discourse with the power can augment that power invisibly by invoking its presupposed right to create and define terminology and apply it: *their* values become central and "moderate," while others are exiled to the periphery as "extremists."

The jockeying for the moderate center has been endemic to American political rhetoric at least since the 1964 presidential election. That year the Democrats defined the Republican nominee, the acknowledged conservative Barry Goldwater, as an "extremist," and thus took control of the neutral center. The Republicans might have adopted either of two strategies of rejoinder: deny the Democratic claim ("We're closer to the center than you!") or adopt the normally lethal title as a badge of honor. They chose the latter. Goldwater's acceptance speech included the famous line: "Extremism in the defense of liberty is no vice. Moderation in the pursuit of justice is no virtue." Rather than seeking to redefine his position as "central" or "moderate," he tried to interchange the connotations of the words *extremism* and *moderation*. Although it wasn't successful in securing a Republican victory, rhetorically it was a triumph. At Goldwater's death in 1998, the line was quoted tirelessly.

Since 1964 both parties have circled nervously around those terms, each trying to paint the other into the "extremist" corner. For a while the Republicans had the upper hand, winning the moderate "center" for their candidates. More recently the Democrats have had some success depicting the opposition as "extreme" in its social views. Behavior and beliefs don't change, and aren't expected to; rather, the parties fight over who gets to choose the words to characterize themselves and the others.

Both sides hurl ferocious rhetoric and then backtrack into the fuzz of credible deniability when pressed to defend their attacks. House Speaker Newt Gingrich caused some consternation a few years ago with his striking comments about the press:

> In a telephone interview yesterday, Gingrich confirmed that he had said that corporate executives "need to find alternative methods" of getting their message across because of the presence of "socialists" on many editorial boards.

"Socialist" in current mainstream American parlance is a word with no real semantics but only pragmatics: it is not attached in people's minds to any external referent (e.g., a political system with specific beliefs) but is purely a term of abuse, applied to something *we* hate. Gingrich's remark occasioned some concern, and his spokesman, Tony Blankley, was asked what the Speaker meant by the term:

> One Gingrich definition of a "socialist" is someone who believes that raising and lowering taxes have no effect on economic conduct, Blankley said. "Certainly there's nothing un-American about being a socialist," he said. ("Newt Warns Against 'Socialist' Press," *San Francisco Chronicle*, March 8, 1995)

Among the manipulations here one might cite the rather unique definition of a "socialist." While Blankley's response might on the face of it seem conciliatory and reassuring, in fact it is something else. Every American knows perfectly well that "socialist" *is* a term of abuse in contemporary discourse. It is virtually equivalent to "Communist," and while the latter may have lost some of its terrifying luster with the fall of the Evil Empire, it is still hardly a pure descriptor. So Gingrich (through his spokesman) is trying to have it both ways: to undermine the press as un-American, and then to deny that that was his communicative intent, so that he cannot be forced to defend his statement with evidence of press "socialism."

But for most of us "socialist" still has discernible cognitive content: it is understood as referring to a certain kind of political-economic system, opposed to capitalism. So (as Gingrich's backtracking suggests) it can be dangerous to use: such a statement can be falsified with real-world evidence. Increasingly partisans seek to de-exnominate the other side with words that suggest only that their referent is "non-neutral," and therefore unlike and unsympathetic to *us*. At the same time they characterize themselves with descriptions that place them in the comfortable and unmarked middle ground. This Wonderland caucus race has spawned the continual redefining and reframing of a whole set of political terms: *liberal, radical, conservative,* and (in a return to 1964) *extremist.* In the 1988 presidential campaign conservatives painted the Democratic candidate, Michael Dukakis, as "liberal" and "ultraliberal." In this way a word that had formerly had specific political meaning was reassigned to the pure-pragmatic, term-of-abuse section of the lexicon formerly occupied by "radical." Since most of Dukakis's ideas were pretty centrist, this use of "liberal" played two rhetorical roles: it made the positive use of the word "liberal" impossible, denying the Democrats a way to define themselves; and it cut Dukakis and his party off from the centrist mainstream, the *we*. The Democrats retaliated by invoking the term "extremist" for their Republican adversaries in the 1992 election, to good effect. By the 1996 elections, "extremist" had become their epithet of choice, as reported by James Bennet (1996):

> In the epithet wars that were the 1996 Congressional and Presidential campaigns, "extremist" proved to be a more dangerous label than "liberal."
>
> Because of more than a year's worth of consistent Democratic and labor advertising linking Bob Dole to Newt Gingrich and assaulting the Republican Congress as extreme, Bill Clinton was able to control the political agenda. He threw Republicans nationwide on the defensive. . . .
>
> But at the same time, a traditional Republican tactic—attacking a Democrat as liberal—may have lost its edge in 1996. Arthur J. Finkelstein, a pollster and Republican consultant known for his relentless use of this line of attack, lost three Senate races, including one against the "embarrassingly liberal" Paul Wellstone.

On the whole, though, the left has probably gotten the worst in the war of epithets, not surprisingly since theirs is the rhetorically harder position. Their options for self-description have been much narrowed, as is not correspondingly true of the right. In the inter-party scrabble over possession, or rejection, or attribution, of the spectrum of political terminology available to American political parties at the end of the twentieth century, the range covering the territory from radical to liberal to progressive to moderate to conservative to reactionary, the right has had considerable success in rhetorical arm-wrestling, repeatedly forcing the left to abandon its older descriptors in an attempt to regain neutral, or respectable, ground. The right has enjoyed considerable success in shifting the connotations of "liberal" leftward, so that for many Americans, "liberal" now applies to a political stance that until recently would have been covered by "radical" (a word in such total disrepute that no one would dream of applying it to themselves).[16] At the same time, there is no discernible movement in the meaning of "conservative" toward "reactionary": the former is still a perfectly respectable self-description. Hence Democrats tend either to align themselves with the "moderate" center (one recent Democratic candidate for governor of California referred to herself as a "Republocrat"),[17] or, among those who persist in their lefty ways, there is an attempt to refashion themselves as "progressives," which sounds like a euphemism, never a good sign.[18]

VICTIMIZATION AND DEVICTIMIZATION

Another way to distance your opponents from those you are trying to draw into your sphere is to describe *them* in words that make subtly negative presuppositions while asserting what can reasonably be called true descriptions. A favorite tactic is the metaphorical use of words that describe a physically unpleasant manner of articulation to suggest that the content of the utterance is as repugnant as the sound, words like *shrill, strident, whine.* When someone's speech is publicly described that way, hearers or readers feel a subliminal need to put space between themselves and the awful noise. That tactic undergirds Newt Gingrich's characterizations of *them* as people who should understand the motto of New Hampshire (in reality "Live Free or Die") as "Live Free or Whine."

"Whining" is further perceived as something that is done by weaklings, the subordinate, and "victims," another conservative anathema. Nobody wants to be a pitiful, helpless "victim" in a society that has always prized rugged individualism and entrepreneurial initiative. But members of historically disadvantaged groups may accurately see themselves as "victimized" by their histories, during which they were at the mercy of powerful others. If you see yourself as a member of the group responsible for the victimization, you have three choices: deny the charge outright (e.g., Holocaust deniers); excuse the past as "past"—it happened, but it has nothing to do with you in the present; or apologize and do something to redress the wrong, however symbolically. Apologies, we have seen, are painful and damaging to their makers' status, and the effects of acknowledging that one's group in the past was a victimizer are much like those of making a public apology. As with apologies, acknowledging past status as victimizer is de-exnominating. It forces past actions to be reperceived not only as shameful, but as deliberately *chosen*. It was possible to have done otherwise. Like apologizing, acknowledgment of the victimizer role places a person in a one-down position relative to the despised victim. So it isn't surprising that conservatives express contempt for both public apologies and claims of victim status. But the latter are harder to avoid: while you can choose not to make an apology, what do you do when people name you as someone who has victimized them? The only way to deal with it and not lose face by either refusing to deal directly with historical claims or suffering the humiliation of making a public apology, is to induce in *them* an aversion to the status of victim by making it as shameful a badge as "victimizer" would be.

A striking instance of that ploy is a column by dance critic Arlene Croce (1994/1995). In discussing Bill T. Jones's piece, "Still/Here," she begins by saying that she had not seen it and had no plans to review it, and then proceeds to do something that is, if not precisely "reviewing it," certainly discussing the artist's motives and the piece's form in detail —a speech event many might characterize as a "review," and Croce might have as well, except that it is not *comme il faut* to review a work one has not seen.

Croce's problem with Jones's work is mainly its subject—it is about having, and dying of, AIDS. She writes: "The thing that Still/Here makes immediately apparent, whether you see it or not, is that victimhood is a kind of mass delusion that has taken hold of previously responsible sectors of culture" (54–55). Croce objects to the ennobling of suffering and victimhood, although that has been a staple of the highest art since the development of Greek tragedy. The wording is tricky. What does it mean to sweep away all victimhood as "mass delusion"? How is the claim that some people have suffered greatly a sign of irresponsibility? Is Croce suggesting that art, by definition, never examines suffering? If so, we are left with very few works of merit.

AIDS is a convenient opening wedge with which to mount an attack against the "cult of victimization": there is no human victimizer. From that vantage point Croce goes on to attack others who use the arts to express the plight of historical victims, concluding with *Schindler's List*, a big hit at that time. But *Schindler's List* is more problematic than AIDS for Croce's purposes: there were certifiable victimizers (unless you're an all-out Holocaust denier). Croce is too sensible to make explicit claims to the contrary or to attack *Schindler's List* as untruthful. Instead she attacks it as unaesthetic, in a context in which she has previously questioned the credibility of "victimhood" in general. Viewing suffering, she suggests, is not *pleasant* and what is not pleasant is not art:

> . . . these grisly high-minded movies like "Schindler's List" (showered with Oscar nominations while the Serbian genocide goes on), these AIDS epics, these performance-art shockers like Still/Here. . . . The quasi-technical attention to suffering that is the specialty of the TV talk shows may be a sham, but it's not such a sham as pretending to tell us how terminal illnesses are to be borne or what to make of Schindler and his list. (60)

By suggesting that these representations are "shams," she suggests that there is no need to identify with the (purported) suffering they show us and no need for us to worry about our roles in bringing such tragedies into being. (I don't understand her parenthesis about Serbia: would *not* awarding the movie its Oscars have ended the genocide?) Too often humans indulge in a form of magical thinking, in which we distance ourselves from those we see as "victims," to avoid incurring similar punishment. (So in the past the healthy have abandoned the dying during epidemics.) Croce is implicitly relying on this unpleasant human trait to bring her rhetorical point home.[19]

The critique of "victimization," like the similar spread of the use of p.c. (see Chapter 3), continues into the present. "The cult of victimization" has become a catchphrase (drawing on the strongly negative connotations of "cult" as well). In a piece on Muhammad Ali, Gerald Early (1998) remarks offhandedly on "the insipidness of victimology." Conservative commentators have attacked public apologies with similar rhetoric. Thus Walter Shapiro (1997) coined the term "contrition chic," a phrase quickly picked up by both Matthew Cooper (1997) and Jean Bethke Elshtain (1997).

These rhetorical tactics work via the presupposition that, again, *our* ideas are neutral and apolitical, *theirs* dangerous and political. That assumption is continually reinforced by the adoption of a vocabulary suggesting that the program of the other side is divisive and hostile to *us,* and by that means is calculated to make its targets unattractive. While this rhetoric shows up mostly in conservative writing, it is also used by liberals like Todd Gitlin in *The Twilight of Common Dreams.* Among the weapons are negative expressions like *identity politics; special interests; tribalization; Balkanization; radical multiculturalism; class warfare; race war; quota.* Hidden in many of these terms is the assumption that *our* demand for rhetorical control is not a "special interest" or political in any way, but "normal." *Our* politics are not "identity politics," because *we* are not asserting an identity, we just have one. This presupposition invests these terms with their potency. We don't see the conservative side as having an agenda or an axe to grind; it's just espousing business as usual. The other side becomes the one with the bias. As Stanley Fish puts it: "the key terms invoked by neoconservatives in the recent 'culture wars,' terms that come to us wearing the label 'apolitical'— 'common values,' 'fairness,' 'merit,' 'color-blind,' 'free speech,' 'Reason' —are in fact the ideologically charged constructions of a decidedly political agenda" (1994, 19).

It's interesting, too, that the groups who have done such a good job of cornering the market on public discourse rights, absolutely for millennia, and now merely predominantly, "whine" (if I may appropriate a term of art) about their "free speech rights" being threatened, the First Amendment stripped bare, because some groups have challenged their right to control the discourse unilaterally. Suddenly, they lay claim to "victim" status and demand protection. This chutzpah rises to extraordinary heights when the right wing appropriates the term "McCarthyism" for what the left is doing rhetorically, quite forgetting that at its worst, no one has demonstrably suffered significant loss as a result of failing to adapt to p.c., while during the period of true McCarthyism on the right, many people lost a great deal.[20]

USING THE *WE*

Plenty of good examples of the right's reliance on their unmarked status are to be found in a *Newsweek* column by George Will (1998), in which the columnist scourges Richard Rorty, a philosopher who had published a book written from a liberal perspective.

A thorough analysis of the sophistries of Will's argument would take us beyond the millennium. But let me touch on a few highlights. Will begins by making use of most people's desire to be in the majority, included in the unmarked *we*. The column begins: "Analyzing the intellectual disarray on the American right—libertarians warring with cultural conservatives—has become a cottage industry. The American left is too marginal to merit much analysis." Will courts the reader's support with the suggestion that he is not biased—he is as willing to criticize disarray on the right as on the left. He doesn't supply a grammatical subject for "analyzing," so we don't know who is doing the analysis: worried right-wingers or gleeful lefties? His concern might demonstrate only healthy self-searching (of which the left is incapable). But while the right might be in "disarray," at least it's *important*. The left, says Will, is "marginal," and later, "peripheral to the nation's political conversation," and "going to earth" like a hunted fox. Who wants to be moribund? Without benefit of evidence or arguments, Will wins readers to his side by sneers alone.

If you're an American, his side (now your side) is *our* side. It's old-fashioned today to fling the C-word epithet (though Will does remark in passing that Rorty might re-read *The Communist Manifesto,* which makes that point more subtly). But you can hint at un-Americanism (i.e., un-*us*-ism) in other ways: by suggesting, as he does throughout, that "Professor" Rorty is contemptuous of regular folk, good Americans, like *us* (Joe McCarthy's pointy-headed intellectuals *redivivi.*). Rorty has the gall not to quote Walt Whitman, "who called this nation 'essentially the greatest poem.'" (A novel indictment: failure to quote poetry.)

"He seems to despise most Americans," says Will, as though criticizing a government's policies is equivalent to despising the people it governs. (If that were true, surely Will could not criticize President Clinton's sexual escapades, as he often has, without incurring the same charge.) From the fact that Rorty uses the words "sadism" or "sadistic" "at least sixteen times" in the course of his "slender" (another dig) book, "to describe American mores or social policies," Will draws the conclusion that Rorty thinks "America is awash with people taking pleasure from the deliberate infliction of cruelty." As a rhetorical device, hyperbole is as effective as it is deceptive.

Will began the column by apparently conceding trouble on the right. But within three paragraphs he has dismissed it: "The left has responded to the conservative ascendancy . . . " Any disarray is illusory. Rorty's statements are brushed aside without examination as "sophomoric rants" and "clumsy japeries," rather than "grown-up discussion." (In other words, Will's side is the one that is implicitly equipped to make aesthetic judgments such as these. They are the grown-ups, the serious persons.) Without even knowing the specifics of Rorty's argument, a reader is led to dismiss it with extreme prejudice. He hates *us*, he's a commie, he's an outsider, he's a child, he's dead. That's all I need to know.

Will makes a claim that goes against much of my argument: that (unbeknownst to Rorty and his ilk) conservatives are the true revolutionaries of our time. "When was the last time Rorty read a newspaper? The right has pretty much cornered the market on radicalism regarding public policy, from privatization of Social Security, to school choice, to a flat tax." True enough. Certainly these proposals are deviations from the current status quo. But I do not think they constitute genuine counter-examples to the claim that conservatives seek to preserve the status quo. All of these daring proposals, however "radical," would if instituted reinforce the pre-existing power—political, social and economic—of the dominant group. You can be radical in defense of reaction. (But I find fascinating Will's use of "radical" for his own side's agenda. Is the word on the brink of rehabilitation?)

A CASE IN POINT: LINGUISTIC PRESCRIPTIVISM

A particularly persuasive case for adherence to the familiar is based on a fear of the erosion of standards and the implication that novelty equals decline. The emotional comfort of the familiar is intellectually buttressed by the claim that the old ways are truly better, so adherence to tradition is both intellectually and emotionally gratifying. A favorite case, endorsed by political conservatives and liberals alike, is linguistic prescriptivism.

The argument is simple and ancient. It has existed at least since the dawn of literacy. (And maybe before that, although literacy facilitates prescriptivism by providing access to records of past usage. In any case, if preliterate people worried about linguistic decline, we have no way of knowing about it.) The language, it has always been said, is going downhill; getting uglier; losing its expressive capacity; losing or garbling meanings. If things keep on this way, pretty soon we'll be unable to communicate at all (the strong position) or not be able to communicate as well or about as many kinds of things, leading to chaos and/or totalitarianism.[21]

This worry evokes the favorite myth of a past golden age when everything, and everyone, was better. Among its current forms are the beliefs that the family has been in decline since the 1950's, and that "values" are not what they were in grandpa's day. Faith in these myths rests in turn on more dubious assumptions: fuzzy (at best) knowledge of the past and how it really was; and a feeling that the way things were is inevitably better than the way things are now, which of course is in turn ineffably better than the way things will be if we let *them* have anything to say about it. These are strong versions of the set of presuppositions I have already identified as trust in the familiar, the unmarked, the within-the-frame. These cases carry that argument further: the way things are right now, the status quo, is already a system in grave decline. Only in a past so long gone that none of us alive now can even recall it were things the way they should be. We cannot turn the clock back, but we can at least try to stop time in its tracks and keep things from getting worse. As Alice remarks to Humpty Dumpty in *Through the Looking-Glass,*

"One can't help growing older."
"*One* can't, perhaps," said Humpty Dumpty; "but *two* can" (chapter 6)

implying the murderous intent implicit in the desire to make time stand still.

The notion of death as the only way to stop change is especially appropriate to language. Language seems to its users to be fixed and stable, unchanging except in very minor ways (a word here or there added to the vocabulary). Even when we read a century-old novel, we are not terribly struck by its linguistic differences from "high" or formal prose today. It's only when we go back several hundred years, to Shakespeare or, further still, to Chaucer, that change becomes apparent. But because most nonspecialists read older literature fragmentarily—*Gulliver's Travels* (eighteenth century); *Paradise Lost* (seventeenth century); *Hamlet* (sixteenth century); *The Canterbury Tales* (fourteenth century)—rather than as an unbroken sequence, they may feel that change, when it occurs, is abrupt and occasional, the exception rather than the rule.

But in language change is the norm. Like any living thing, language evolves. Historical linguists and sociolinguists have demonstrated persuasively that language is continually in flux, that English is at this very moment changing, mostly beneath our consciousness. The changes we notice—the introduction of slang words, for instance—are apt to be ephemeral. The deeper changes are mostly too subtle for us (even linguists) to catch as they happen. But because change comes in tiny and continuous increments, it virtually never creates chaos or causes the loss of meaning or expressive capacity. And since there is no objective standard of what makes a language "beautiful," it makes no sense to charge that change is making a language "ugly."

All of this linguists have known, and written about, often in accessible styles and places, for some time.[22] But no one listens. Authoritative speakers *want* to feel that their language is in imminent danger of decline and fall. As I suggested in *Talking Power,* we find that an attractive idea because in a world in which reality is changing at a frazzling pace, we (want to) feel that language at least can be brought under control. So worrying about language decline could get results. If we can stop language from changing, and if language both reflects and creates our reality, we could . . . just maybe . . . stop real-world change. If language change functions as a symbolic equivalent of real-world change, by refusing to use "hopefully" as a sentence adverb, one can (to be sure, only symbolically—but our species has gotten where it is by the deft manipulation of symbols) keep everything else as it was, or might have been.

This belief is in itself\ harmless, if useless. But other arguments for keeping language "pure" are more pernicious. Statements bewailing linguistic decline almost always originate with people in positions of authority and power, the people who determine what "good English" (or whatever) is. It is always *they*—members of the underclass, women, nonnative speakers—who are using language "badly" and thereby creating the decline. By pointing out the sad discrepancy between the way things are and the way they ought to be, authorities shore up their own influence and make it harder for outsiders to get a serious hearing (if they don't speak "right," they are not "making sense," so there is no need to listen to them). These authorities know that language control *is* control of meaning-making *is* political and social power.

It's not that linguists don't believe in rules of grammar. It's just that what we mean by "rules," and "grammar," is different from what most people mean. The rules linguists talk about are *descriptions* of the way people actually speak: the forms that are found vs. those that are not. A linguistic rule is a statement about what is actually found, as well as a prediction of what is going to happen in the future, based on what has been observed in the past. We model our rules on observations of fluent speakers of English, who often produce sentences similar to the first example, and never any like the second:

Three men were arrested by the police.
*Three dollars were cost(ed) by my socks.[23]

Even if you have never encountered anything like the second example (and unless you've taken a linguistics class, you probably haven't), you know, if you are a fluent speaker of English, that there is something wrong with it. You know (implicitly) a rule of English: verbs like *cost, weigh,* and *fit* do not have passive equivalents (in one of the meanings of each). But this rule causes no distress; you will not find it in any handbook of English grammar, because no one is apt to get it wrong. Speakers are normally not even aware of the existence of such rules, any more than we are aware of following descriptive rules outside of language: *Ice cream tastes good,* for instance.

On the other hand, there are rules we have to learn through explicit instruction, rules we may incur penalties for breaking. *Cross the street with the green light* is one. The rules for English usage we learned in school are similarly prescriptive, for instance, *Don't use multiple negations*, the rule that prohibits us from saying, when we are on our best behavior,

I didn't do nothing to nobody.

If educated speakers weren't warned against this usage early and often, it would probably be the norm. Even so, it exists in a great many non-standard dialects of English, though it is heavily discouraged in "good English"—the standard dialect, the speech of those with education and status.

Speaking the standard reinforces the feeling of being one of *us,* and *their* not speaking it gives *us* a "good" reason to ignore *them.* But the standard dialect itself is an exnomination. As long as you're speaking it, your choice is invisible, "normal." But lapse into any nonstandard form, from New York ("Brooklynese") to Ebonics (see Chapter 7), and you may be sure it will get noticed—and not favorably.

"Bad language" is a favorite topic for comment, by both pundits and commoners, in the public media. It is often the subject of complaints by writers to advice columnists like Ann Landers, Dear Abby, and Miss Manners:

DEAR ABBY: What has happened to the English language?
    The excessive use and misuse of the word "like" is an abomination! . . . "Hopefully" is used far too often and invariably ungrammatically. (*San Francisco Chronicle,* February 25, 1992)

DEAR ABBY: . . . Although I myself am not easily irked, there are a couple of phrases infesting the language today that I am sure you will agree would irk a saint.
    To wit: "I need you to" in place of "Will you please" ("I need you to sign here"); . . .
    Then there's this obnoxious "Enjoy your (whatever)." (*San Francisco Chronicle,* June 16, 1990)

Abby herself provides her personal irk list (*San Francisco Chronicle,* June 15, 1992), including the loss of the distinction between *lie* and *lay; all are not* for *not all are; between you and I; try and . . .* instead of *try to; irregardless;* the overuse of *basically;* and much more. Clearly nonstandard and neologistic English hits a raw nerve. But the pain extends beyond the populism of advice columnists' correspondents. Just to select a few cases:

The *New York Times* Sunday column "Metropolitan Diary" (compiled by Enid Nemy with Ron Alexander) of June 7, 1998, leads off with the following item:

> Dear Diary:
>
> Visiting an editor at Random House, I stepped into a crowded elevator and found myself pressed close to the control panel.
>
> "Has everybody got their floors?" I asked.
>
> After a moment's silence, a young female voice from the rear said, "His or her."
>
> "I beg your pardon?" I said.
>
> "His or her. It's 'Has everybody got his or her floors?' Your pronouns don't agree."
>
> "And shouldn't it be 'his or her floor,' not 'floors'?" a young man piped up. "Each of us gets off at only one floor."
>
> "And wouldn't it be better to say 'Does everybody have?' rather than 'Has everybody got?'" a third voice chimed in.
>
> I stood corrected—and red faced. But I was glad to know that good grammar is alive and well.
>
> RICHARD CURTIS

I am tempted to suggest that one function of prescriptivism, amply attested here, is that worrying about *how* people talk avoids the necessity of paying attention to *what* they say—which could be a real problem. Crowded elevators naturally encourage trivia talk—you don't want to get personal with someone with whom you're already up close. And a publisher's elevator must be the *locus classicus* for such gamesmanship.[24]

Another case comes from a *New York Times* book review of *The New Fowler's Modern English Usage*, a revision of the hallowed prescriptive authority, by Christopher Lehmann-Haupt (December 26, 1996). The original *Fowler's*, published in 1926, is conservative even by the standards of its day and place (England), and a reconsideration of Fowler's strictures was overdue. But the reviewer is disconcerted and disoriented by some of the changes in the revision. He is peeved at the new editor's redefinition of his mission: "Not to tell readers what is correct, as Fowler did, but allow them to 'make sensible choices.'" But if, as we have seen, language is continually in flux, giving readers a basis on which to make decisions on their own is surely more useful than giving them a hard-

and-fast list of no-no's which may be obsolete before the book hits the stores. Fowler, grumbles the reviewer, quoting an earlier editor, Sir Ernest Gowers,

> "held that the proper purpose of a 'grammarian was to tell the people not what they do and how they came to do it, but what they ought to do in the future.'"
>
> By revising Fowler in the manner he has done, Mr. Burchfield [the present editor] has betrayed him to the enemy camp and transformed him from an upholder of standards into a passive observer of trends.

Gowers's comment is a perfect illustration of exnominated prescriptivism. Note in particular the reference to "the people": a distinct case of *them* from the pen of an upper-class Briton at a time when class really mattered! Note further Lehmann-Haupt's characterization of the revision as a "betrayal" of Fowler to "the enemy camp." Not for nothing do I speak of "the language war."

RE-NOMINATING THE STATUS QUO: RECOGNIZING NON-NEUTRALITY

The continued belief in the old presuppositions and the discourse options they permit is possible so long as exnomination is not recognized, and especially so long as it is not contested. But the language war is being fought over just these issues: who must be named, who can choose whose names and what meanings. The demand that the exnominated "neutrals" acknowledge their active role and political status goes along with the ability of formerly speechless groups to demand that their own language choices be accorded equal status with the conventional ones. The fact that the official namers are themselves no longer invisible, exnominated, or unnamed means that their linguistic activities are no longer normal or unmarked. Those activities can now be commented on and criticized. They no longer define our cultural frames unilaterally and uncontroversially. Competition will arise, the discourse become more heated and less open to "reasonable" compromise (since reasonableness itself is no longer obviously definable).

How are meaning-making rights to be determined? How can we devise, as a community, a language that will speak equally for and to all of us? One solution at first glance seems ideal: suppose we all agree to be "color-blind," "gender-blind," and so on; suppose people in the formerly excluded groups agree to accept exnominated status and thus become just like everyone else. This hope underlies many of the arguments against affirmative action; indeed, some opponents of affirmative action have even argued that that golden age has arrived already; or even further, that in the "good old days" before *they* became uppity and demanding, we all got along and everybody really *was* color-(etc.)-blind. Those arguments can most generously be dismissed as naive, but what if we were all to make a good-faith effort to change our ways *right now?* We might avoid the perils of legal remediation and restore goodwill. Of course, the formerly disempowered are expected to make the first good-faith move. Some spokespersons for those groups, especially those who are prominent and admired, are willing to do so (they are, after all, "honorary whites/males/etc." to begin with). So, according to John Fiske (1996, 48–49) when the basketball superstar Michael Jordan is asked how he wants to be treated, he replies that he wants to be treated as "just a person," not as a black person. Similarly, one thing that made Bill Cosby's sitcom a smash hit for many years was the delighted realization of the predominantly white audience that here were "invisible" black people, people whose skin color could conveniently be overlooked, because their behavior was so unthreateningly white! *We* could enjoy the moral gratification of feeling that *they* were just like *us*, without having to make any embarrassing accommodations. The same sort of dynamic probably underlay O. J. Simpson's great popularity (pre-murder). He acted like a white person, he hung out with white people, he even married a (very) white woman . . . he is not someone to fear, because—while of course he is not quite "just like us"—he *wants* to be, which is even better.

THE POWER OF THE PERSONAL NARRATIVE

When I say that "language" behavior is being reinterpreted and new meanings assigned, I am thinking of "language" in all its senses, from single word to complex narrative. Over the last decade or so, a surge of interest in narrative has swept through the humanities and social sciences. Psychotherapists and psychoanalysts have begun to see narrative as the foundation of personal identity; when a person's life-story is distorted or fragmented, distress arises that can only be mitigated by the client and therapist working in collaboration to reweave the narrative fabric (see Aftel 1996; Schafer 1980; Spence 1982, 1986). In law, interest in narrative has taken several forms (see Farber and Sherry 1993; N. A. Lewis 1997; P. Williams 1991b). Lawyers increasingly recognize that a trial is "about" the construction and control of a narrative. The prosecution in its opening statement offers the jury a model narrative of what happened, then fleshes out the tale and gives it credibility through witnesses and evidence. The defense's job is to poke holes in that narrative and make the jury see that things could have happened another way, or even that they could not have happened *that* way (see Lakoff 1990, chapters 5 and 6).

More controversially, in the newly developed subfields of critical legal studies (CLS) and critical race theory (CRT), narratives have been incorporated into the very heart of the understanding of the law and how it functions. CLS's proponents argue that laws do not get their meanings solely from their authors at the time they are encoded, but rather that the meaning and applicability of any statute evolves with time, to fit the requirements of continually changing culture.[25] What the Eighth Amendment prohibition against "cruel and unusual punishment" meant to the founders who placed it in the Constitution is not necessarily how it will or should always be understood. For the founders, most Constitutional scholars would agree, the death penalty was neither "cruel" nor "unusual." But if society should change its opinion about appropriate remedies for crimes, a majority of Supreme Court justices might come to see the death penalty as both cruel and unusual (whatever, precisely, they understand those words to mean) and outlaw it as unconstitutional. It follows that the law may mean different things to different people in a multicultural society (a point made by scholars working in the area of CRT), since nondominant groups have very different experiences with it from the majority (and therefore have different frames for its understanding). A clear demonstration was the O. J. Simpson verdict, in which a predominantly minority jury essentially told the white majority, through the medium of a nationally televised trial and verdict, that its understanding of how America's laws and justice system worked was not in accord with what we read in high school civics texts, and that therefore they did not understand *our* laws as applying to people like *them* (including O.J., whom the jurors saw as one of *them;* see Chapter 6).

CLS contradicts conventional understandings of the legal system, which hold that the meaning of a law is immutable (the function of appellate courts being merely to determine whether a particular case fits a specific statute, rather than to reinterpret the preexisting statute in terms of current understanding). Its proponents have found new ways of approaching the question of what laws mean and how they apply, abandoning the old one-size-fits-all statistical and normative standardizing model. More conservative legal theorists see the law as "objective" and identically applicable to everyone. But CLS (and especially CRT) call that a sham: there is plenty of evidence that race, class, and gender are brought to bear in generally invidious and covert ways in the application of laws to individual cases. And (a still more radical position) even if the argument were true, perhaps it should not be so: since our race, class, and gender cause each of us to understand reality differently, it makes little sense for laws promulgated to advance the interests of the white male middle-class majority (or rather, to be accurate, minority) to be applied identically to all of us, especially since we have not participated equally in making them, adjudicating them, and enforcing them. But if statistical norms and generalizations are not valid justifications for the making or interpretation of laws, what basis can we use?

One possibility is the personal narrative. CLS/CRT uses narratives both to illustrate the unequal effects of laws on different kinds of people and, more implicitly, to counter the presumption that the law is impersonal and generic. The legal use of personal narratives also suggests that objectivity itself is neither an ideal nor normally even a possibility: narratives are necessarily subjective, expressing one person's viewpoint. And unlike statistical samples or broad generalizations, narratives are collaboratively made: the hearers, as interpreters, make the story as actively as does the teller. A narrative can be ambiguous: it may—like a sophisticated novel—mean different things to different readers or hearers, and as long as each one can make a plausible case for his or her interpretation, based closely on the text itself, every reading is equally valid. There is no ultimate authority, whether derived from original authorship or the current reader's professional status. Thus narratizing styles of legal discourse are inherently democratic and therefore deeply disturbing to the hierarchical organization that is the law. Finally, narrative theory is subversive to an authoritarian legal system precisely because it wrests control of the story—the law—from the authorities who enforce and interpret it. When statistics and norms are the means of understanding, meaning continues to be controlled by those who know and can make sense of them. But anyone can tell a story, and any hearer is entitled to derive his or her own meaning from it. Storytelling is democratic, and so it is dangerous.

More conservative legal scholars have, predictably, attacked CLS/ CRT. A favorite rejoinder is that its theories and methods "defy common sense," a statement attributed to Suzanna Sherry, a law professor at the University of Minnesota: "The problem with denying any objective reality is that there is no way of mediating among the competing perceptions of reality except power. And what they ultimately want is more power for their perceptions" (quoted in N. A. Lewis 1997). Absolutely true, except for the implication that only *they* want that. We do, too, and in fact, it's what *we*'ve always had. But *ours* has been invisible, and *theirs* is not, so *theirs* seems political—that is, power-driven. Additionally, the comment makes an assumption that traditional legal discourse represents "objective reality"—that is, a single reality every rational person would accept. But what is the evidence for that? It's true that in CLS there is no way of determining "the truth" from amid a welter (well, maybe a couple) of competing truths. But many would argue that that represents a truer understanding of the way we all experience the world than the traditional imposition of an "objective reality" by fiat and sometimes brute force. Narratizing the law brings home the message that justice is relative, like most other human creations and experiences. It isn't that the reality has become more chaotic: it's that our perception of it has moved from a false rigor to a more accurate confusion, a better match with the way things really are. Sherry also claims that her opponents deny *any* objective reality. But that is certainly not true (see note 1 to this chapter). When Sherry accuses CLS/CRT of defying common sense, she's again correct. But as we have seen, common sense is neither necessarily common to us all, nor does it automatically make sense.

Interestingly, when critics of CLS/CRT attack it, they often do so through anecdotes—narratives themselves. Even they realize the explanatory and persuasive powers of narrative. But (unlike their opponents) they don't appreciate the possibilities of multiple interpretation, and so tell stories with evident ambiguities as if there were only one meaning to be derived from them. For example, Sherry and her coauthor, Daniel Farber, in their critique of "radical multiculturalism" (i.e., CLS/CRT) *Beyond All Reason* (1997), relate a story that at first reading is genuinely disturbing, especially for a reader who spends a lot of her time in classrooms. They are arguing against a belief in the legitimacy of multiple understandings of historical events, the indeterminacy of "truth."[26] They cite a story from a colleague, a law professor at the University of Wyoming, about a horrific experience after the very first lecture of the first class he ever taught. After class a student came up and told him that something he said deeply disturbed her and he'd better learn not to make such mistakes again.

> Naturally [he continues] I was mortified . . . [and] told her that I'd appreciate knowing what it was I'd said, so that I could be more careful the next time. She told me, and I am essentially quoting, "Slavery was not bad. There were a lot of individual slaveholders who mistreated their slaves, and that gave slavery a bad name. My family were slaveholders, and our slaves loved us. What you have given us was the Union version of the War, but the victors always get to write the history."
>
> I was speechless. I know we live in a relativistic world, but I thought it safe to work from the premise that a couple of things, say slavery and the Holocaust, were evil. But I guess I was wrong. (110)

The teller (and Farber and Sherry) intend this narrative as an indictment of subjective interpretationism. But I see it as an illustration of the perils of inexperienced pedagogy. Students often come into classes with ill-considered ideas. Our job as teachers is to help them learn to discriminate between valid and invalid ideas—that is, to reason. I'm not sure what the narrators of this story would see as a better ending: For students never to dare to make unpopular statements out loud (but of course, they would go on believing them, because there is no opportunity to discuss and correct them)? For the professor to hoot such a student down, telling her unequivocally that authoritative persons such as himself know that her family is a bunch of (probably inbred) morons, and she'd better not believe such trash any more? These approaches represent old modes of authoritarian teacher-student interaction, but hardly ideal teaching. Teachers should be happy that occasional students now feel brave enough to express peculiar points of view, so that we get a chance to correct them (or, on occasion, be persuaded by them). A good thing (in my view) to have said in the above case is something like, "Even if your family were totally benign to all of its slaves; in fact, even if every slave owner were totally benign to all of his slaves, slavery would still be evil. It isn't the treatment per se that makes slavery evil, it's slavery itself that corrupts all parties to it. Nothing can overcome that." You don't contradict the student's narrative (it's probably mythic, but whose family history isn't?). You are allowed, I believe, even in this postmodern relativistic world, to suggest that some values are absolute. The ball is now in her corner: she has to tell you why slavery may be OK, so she's forced to do some thinking and will probably learn something from the encounter. In any case, I don't see this story as an illustration of the evils of postmodern narrativity but as a reminder that teachers have as much to learn as students.

The telling of each story is a skirmish in the language war. Eventually, the side with the better stories will win. The rest of my narrative examines several favorite contemporary stories.

"POLITICAL CORRECTNESS" AND HATE SPEECH

The Word as Sword

MEANING IS COMPLEX

Neutrality is advantageous only if it can be exploited and extended into an effective means of persuasion. Language both creates a message, through devices like framing and presupposition, and uses that message, winning the uncommitted over by assuming the "normality" and "neutrality" of the speaker's position, as transmitted through arguments that (because they rely on neutrality) need not even be overtly stated and therefore need not be exposed to the rigors of examination. This and the remaining chapters of this book explore several recent cases in which language becomes a locus of struggle over self-definition and societal cohesion. The battle is joined at all levels of language from word to sentence to narrative. This chapter focuses on the use and definitions of the small and concrete details of the linguistic message, words and phrases: who gets to make up the words of our contemporary language and invest them with meaning. Later chapters will explore the creation and function of the stories we contemporary Americans construct out of these elements and the question of how our conclusions about who gets to make up our stories and give them meaning are based on, and contribute to, our current continual reevaluations of the roles we play.

Meaning goes beyond semantic reference. True, the meaning of a word connects it to an object or concept it refers to. If I say "desk" to you, as a speaker of English, you will form in your mind an image of a particular sort of piece of furniture. If I say "table," your mind will produce another image, with some similarities to and some differences from "desk." In these cases reference is all we need to worry about: most of us don't attach positive or negative connotations to these words. But there are many words that involve much more complex kinds of understanding. These are the words that win (or lose) wars, the shooting kind and the more subtle kind we fight with one another in the name of politics, religion, and relationships. New words are created, old ones given new meanings. Links between form and meaning are forged and strengthened when people use those words in specific contexts, with specific nuances and connotations. Whoever gets to establish those connections first and best controls the meanings (in the larger sense) of these new words and expressions. And since words are at the forefront of our persuasive efforts, controlling meaning brings victory in the continuing war for hearts and minds by defining our cultural "values" and personal "identities"— themselves words currently in the front lines.

When I was about fifteen, I read Shakespeare's *Julius Caesar*. At the time I was starting to learn Latin and reading Caesar's *Gallic War*. I found him a fascinating figure and set out to read what I could about him. I read the play on my own, with no authority I could turn to for interpretive guidance. Things were pretty clear until I got to the funeral scene, where Brutus offers the citizenry a justification for his assassination of Caesar. "As Caesar loved me, I weep for him; as he was fortunate, I rejoice at it; as he was valiant, I honor him; but, as he was ambitious, I slew him," he says. That is all the people need to hear: they express their hearty support.

I was confused by the argument. Clearly Brutus meant to contrast Caesar's worthy qualities, for which Brutus admired him, with one bad enough to justify his murder. But where was that? The last clause, introduced by "but," rhetorically and semantically ought to be the bearer of the bad news, but I could find none. As an adolescent in 1950's America, I had encountered "ambition" only in a favorable sense: the get-up-and-go that is the quintessential American virtue. I couldn't imagine what Brutus's problem was. *Kill* someone because he was ambitious? You might as well kill someone for eating apple pie or ice cream!

If I had checked a dictionary, I might have solved the mystery. The basic sense of "ambition," desire for fame, wealth, status or power, has remained constant throughout its history in English. But society's view of that desire has changed over time. *Ambitio,* the Latin source of "ambition," meant literally "going around soliciting votes," a respectable enterprise in the Roman Republic.[1] But metaphorically it came to mean going around soliciting favor, an insatiable desire to please, and a willingness to do whatever it took to get whatever one wanted. In this sense the word came into French and thence into Middle English, in the form *ambicioun,* meaning "excessive desire for honor, power, or wealth," a meaning the word kept into the seventeenth century.

By then English society was changing: the government was becoming more democratic, and Calvinism encouraged the accumulation of wealth. So by the eighteenth century, desire for honor, power, or wealth was seen as a good thing, something it was hard to have too much of. As the values of society changed, the connotations of "ambition" shifted with it, so that today if we want to use the word with Shakespeare's negative assumptions, we have to call it "blind" ambition.

In this case, no one made a deliberate attempt to bring about a change (that would have been much harder anyway without modern mass media). Recent conscious efforts to shift meaning have sometimes succeeded. Barry Goldwater's struggle to change the connotations of "extremism" largely failed. But his party's later shift of "liberal" from neutral to bad has had considerable effect on our current political discourse (see Chapter 2).

MAKING WORDS, MAKING SENSE

Definition, then, may not be as neutral an act as it appears to be, but may be used with the explicit motive of giving more power and legitimacy to those who already have enough of it to control the connection between word and definition.[2] Who has that power? Today we think of the dictionary as an impersonal, disinterested arbiter of meaning and usage. But it was not always so.

Early dictionary makers were not as punctilious as their modern counterparts try to be. Dr. Samuel Johnson, the eighteenth-century English lexicographer, is notorious for sneaking political import into some of his definitions. He defined "oats" as a food that in England was used to feed horses, but in Scotland, people—a sneer at Scotland's poverty. But even though current lexicographers are more careful, unconscious bias sneaks in, which (because the dictionary is *the* unquestionable authority) is often difficult to identify and impossible to extirpate. And since biases generally work to the disadvantage of the powerless, it is all the more unthinkable that a definition might be called into question.

We are becoming suspicious of apparent neutrality, and groups formerly without language control are achieving it. Occasionally outright battles erupt over the control of dictionary definitions of especially charged words. In Chapter 1 I discussed an article (Minton 1997) reporting on a dispute between the publisher of the *Merriam-Webster's Collegiate® Dictionary* and the NAACP over the definition of "nigger" —whether the word should be considered "a definition of a person's race," essentially a neutral term, or should be defined primarily as "a slur," or "a derogatory word," according to NAACP President Kweisi Mfume. Should the derogatory sense of the word be treated as its principal denotation or (as *Merriam-Webster's* had done) as a connotation of a word with another principal meaning? The dictionary did indicate the offensive nature of the word, but only after an initial bland definition of nigger as "black person."

With this explicit public recognition that dictionary definition is political, rather than purely scientific and objective, comes a very new understanding of the role of both dictionaries and their users in constructing definitions. The user is increasingly thought of not as a passive vessel into whom meanings are poured by the disembodied authority of the dictionary, but an evaluator making choices, matching definitions to the real world contexts in which the word is being used.

Meaning has been contested outside the dictionary too. Our sociopolitical discourse sometimes covers over, sometimes brings into sharp focus disagreements about the meanings, or connotations, of words like *addiction, drug, baby, fetus,* and *sexual harassment.*

It is no accident that many contested terms are associated with frames representing controversial or problematic attitudes or behaviors. The disagreement over meanings related to "addiction" implies competition in the culture over what habits should be criminally regulated (are cigarettes or alcohol "drugs" like cocaine?) as well as what behaviors should be considered subject to a person's free will and which beyond our control. We readily accept (as earlier generations did not) the "physical illness/ beyond intentional control" model for "controlled substances," but what about "sex addicts" or "shopaholics": are they also to be considered "ill," or merely "weak willed" or "misbehaving"? There are serious consequences attached to the place where we draw the line: we *punish* people we understand to be *intentionally* misbehaving, but *treat* people who "can't help it." The extension of the meaning of "addict," and the proliferation of its semantic equivalent, the suffix "-holic" (from "alco-holic" to "workaholic," "chocoholic," "sexaholic," and "shopaholic") provide the opening wedge for the shift.

Not all neologism is politically loaded. But the introduction of any new word into the popular lexicon is world-changing because it alters our presuppositions: it identifies the new concept as both real and wor-thy of mention, assigns it to a frame, and so enables us to talk and think about it. Dictionary makers struggle to keep up with the new terms, but it's no easy task. The last few years alone have witnessed the births of (among others) "trailer trash"; "GIGO"; "high/low concept"; "high/low maintenance";[3] "megabyte"; and a continuing stream of "-gates," deriving from "Watergate," to describe misbehavior in high places: Koreagate, Iran-Contragate, Travelgate, Chinagate, and (to cite just some of the terms battling for supremacy) Monicagate, Sexgate, Tailgate, Zip-pergate, and Peckergate (see Chapter 8). Yet none of these has achieved the celebrity of "political correctness," or "p.c."

POLITICAL CORRECTNESS: WHO OWNS P.C.?

From an article in a recent issue of the *San Francisco Chronicle:* "The political right seizes on cases like this [Mapplethorpe's homoerotic pho-tographs, Serrano's "Piss Christ"] because they seem patently, overtly outrageous. Supporters of the NEA are thrown into a defensive posture in this era of timid political correctness, muttering about free-speech pro-tection when they ought to be trumpeting the endowment's convictions" (Winn 1998). What is remarkable here is not the trotting out, yet again, of the old p.c. war-horse, but rather the fact that it is used here with al-most a reversal of its usual connotation ("timid" as opposed to "dan-gerous" or "brazen"), if it has any meaning at all. That may be a good sign. Often before a verbal fad is consigned to the dustbin of history it is bled of all discernible meaning, becoming only a way to fill out a para-graph when there's nothing much to say. The usage here is just such an instance of the decline from rapier to penknife, the hand slapping away a gnat: "I hate to sound p.c., but. . . . ," "Oh, that's *so* p.c.!"

It was not always thus. In 1990, p.c. would have been an excellent choice for *Time*'s word of the decade (if *Time* had such a category). For over ten years it served as the weapon of choice to defang what was per-ceived, or represented, by the right as the threatening menace of the left.

Paradoxically, many on the left have participated in p.c.-baiting. "Political correctness" has been the epithet of choice used to discredit a wide array of discursive practices generally thought of as lefty, among them:

- the development of campus codes against hate speech
- the questioning of the established literary canon
- attacks on, and examinations of, sexism and racism
- the adoption of self-descriptions originated by the minorities they described (e.g., "woman" for "girl" or "lady"; "African American" for "Negro"; "gay" for "homosexual"; "Asian" for "Oriental")
- the deconstructionist/postmodern doubting of the knowability or reality of historical truth and the trustworthiness of authority

"Political correctness," "politically correct," and the common abbreviation for both, "p.c.,"[4] cover a broad spectrum of new ways of using and seeing language and its products, all of which share one property: they are forms of language devised by and for, and to represent the worldview and experience of, groups formerly without the power to create language, make interpretations, or control meaning. Therein lies their terror and hatefulness to those who formerly possessed these rights unilaterally, who gave p.c. its current meaning and made it endemic in our conversation.

We may ask why there was a need for such a term, and such a concept, at this time: why language rights seemed, to a broad enough swath of the populace to make the terms household words, worth fighting over just now. One answer is that we are a species as contentious as we are social, never really happy without a *them* to unite against. With the decline of the Evil Empire during the 1980's, and its final demise in 1991, we lost that essential Other. There was no one else worthy of that status (we tried to use Saddam Hussein in that capacity, but he was not up to the task). We had to turn on each other.

During this time, some of the revolutions of the 1960's were bearing linguistic fruit. Late in that decade the Black Panthers had reclaimed "Black" (see Chapter 2), recognizing that the use of terms based on euphemism ("colored," "darky," "Negro") would necessarily imply inferiority. Only by re-appropriating and re-contextualizing the word that characterized the most salient difference between them and the majority community could they undo centuries of damage. That decision was shocking: since when did a disempowered group have the right to *name itself?* That was a contradiction in terms. Yet it stuck: by 1970, "Black" was in common use in the national media.

Women did much the same thing in the 1970's, with less striking results (we had millennia, not mere centuries, to overcome), but results nonetheless. Others followed. By the 1980's those groups were moving beyond words to narratives. Whose story was *the* story, the "history"? Was there a "true" story at all? Whose reading of the language, in literature and elsewhere, was "the right" interpretation—or was that not even a meaningful question? Power and authority had previously been able to answer those questions firmly and unambiguously: *My* word, *my* story, is the right one. But suddenly, power and authority were losing control. At the very moment that a new scourge was needed, one conveniently emerged, and the language war was born.

There are more than a few ironies in the history of political correctness. The New Right virtually copyrighted the term as its own, yet they did not originate it, but borrowed it from the enemy, the Old Left. As Paul Berman notes:

> "Politically correct" was originally an approving phrase on the Leninist left to denote someone who steadfastly toed the party line. Then it evolved into "P.C.," an ironic phrase among wised-up leftists to denote someone whose line-toeing fervor was too much to bear. Only in conjunction with the P.C. debate itself did the phrase get picked up by people who had no fidelity to radicalism at all, but who relished the nasty syllables for their twist of irony. (1992, 5)

Something important had changed in the translation from left to right. In the left's ironic use p.c. was just teasing, "all in the family," and so, "for your own good." But in the mouths of the right it became a term of abuse leveled at outsiders, *us* versus *them,* a humorless and vitriolic sneer.

The terms of the "debate," if such it was (since the other side was only rarely heard from) are ironic too. The terror masked by the anger of p.c. is that *they* are taking over the language, preventing *us* from speaking at all.[5] Yet every aspect of the discourse—its tone, its terms, its targets— was defined by the right, leaving the left the capacity only to react, if even that. That makes the entire p.c. complaint self-contradictory. If the left has unleashed p.c.—as the right claims—as a totalitarian threat to language and mind, it hasn't done it very well at all.

While there have been some attempts to define p.c., a complete and satisfying definition has not been achieved, as a selection of attempts makes clear:

In the name of "sensitivity" to others and under pain of being denounced as a sexist or racist, the postmodern radicals require everyone around them to adhere to their own codes of speech and behavior. (Berman 1992, 2)

Newsweek asserted that "P.C. . . . attempt[s] to redistribute power from the privileged class . . . to the oppressed masses." (Neilson 1995, 77)

[T]here is a large body of belief in academia and elsewhere that a cluster of opinions about race, ecology, feminism, culture and foreign policy defines a kind of "correct" attitude toward the problems of the world, a sort of unofficial ideology of the university. . . .
    Central to p.c.-ness, which has its roots in 1960's radicalism, is the view that Western society has for centuries been dominated by what is often called "the white male power structure," or "patriarchal hegemony." . . .
    [P.c.] includes a powerful environmentalism and, in foreign policy, support for Palestinian self-determination and sympathy for third world revolutionaries. (Bernstein 1990)

The goal [of p.c.] is to eliminate prejudice . . . the grand prejudice that has ruled American universities since their founding: that the intellectual tradition of Western Europe occupies the central place in the history of civilization. (Adler 1990)

[A] position is so "obviously superior," so "obviously correct," and its opposite is so "obviously out of bounds" that they are beyond discussion and debate. Indeed to hold the "wrong" opinion, one must be either mentally imbalanced (phobic—as in *homophobic,* irrational, codependent, or similarly afflicted), or, more likely, evil. (James Davison Hunter, *Before the Shooting Begins,* quoted in Devine 1993, 28)

[A]n attempt to put relativism to work for nominally progressive political purposes. (Devine 1993, 28)

[P.c.] is a wonderfully concise indictment that says that a group of unscrupulous persons is trying to impose its views on our campus populations rather than upholding views that reflect the bias of no group because they are common to everyone. (Fish 1994, 8)

Political correctness, the practice of making judgments from the vantage point of challengeable convictions, is not the name of a deviant behavior, but of the behavior that everyone necessarily practices. (Ibid., 9)

First of all, [p.c.] implies the introduction of politics into an area (often called the life of the mind) where politics doesn't belong; and second, it implies that this intrusion of politics is itself politically organized, the result of design and coordinated activity. (Ibid., 54)

Most of these attempts do not constitute "definitions" in any objective sense, since virtually all of them are political, p.c. seen from one or the other position.[6] Also noteworthy is the frequency with which these writers borrow all or part of their definitions, as if seeking to avoid responsibility or throwing up their hands in despair or disgust. For a term on everyone's lips, p.c. remains remarkably elusive. One suspects that rather than attempting objective definitions that would clarify the term for a neophyte, these writers are using definition-making politically.

THE RISE OF P.C.

If words are "just rhetoric," p.c. passes the UAT (the Undue Attention Test) with flying colors. Perhaps the most interesting aspect of the history of the term over the last couple of decades is its rise and decline. A search through the Lexis/Nexis News database (the only one that goes back so far) finds the first use of the term in its current sense in 1983, in an article in the *New Republic* that seems a bridge between its Old Left and New Right acceptations: "Politically 'correct' [note punctuation] judgments now dominate reviews of painting, movies, books, fashion, even restaurants" (Denby 1983).[7] The history of usage continues:

1983	3 uses (all in the article cited above)
1984	3
1985	ca. 30
1986	ca. 30
1987	ca. 50
1988	ca. 60
1989	ca. 200
1990	ca. 450

The increase from year to year (especially toward the end) is striking. Partly it is the result of an idea catching on, writers picking up the Zeitgeist from one another. Neilson provides another explanation for the proliferation: a 1984 memo "written for the Smith-Richardson Foundation in which Roderic R. Richardson argued that, to facilitate its educational agenda, the right needed to aim for the rhetorical high ground (a goal achieved in the subsequent PC debate, where the left were totalitarians, the right defenders of liberty)" (1995, 70).

The thread can be traced after 1990 in two more databases, MAGS and NEWS. The results are tabulated below:

MAGS

	by subject	*by title*
1990	0	4
1991	30	55
1992	79	51
1993	72	47
1994	53	41
1995	58	32
1996	27	28
1997	36	20
1998 (6 mos.)	9	11
TOTAL	364	289

NEWS

	by subject
1991	8
1992	30
1993	68
1994	68
1995	33
1996	18
1997	24
1998 (6 mos.)	11
TOTAL	260

While the different databases yield somewhat different results, the overall conclusions are similar. The term picks up steam around 1990, peaks between 1991 and 1995, and appears to subside after that. It continues in heavy use but has gone from being the subject of articles, or appearing in their titles, to throwaway uses like that in the cited *Chronicle* article.

The rhetorical thrust of the discussion remains consistent over time. Almost all of the perspectives are rightist (with exceptions, for instance, Fish 1994 and Neilson 1995). Of the popular articles often cited as sources, Bernstein 1990 and Adler 1990, the first is distinctly conservative, the second moderate-liberal.

A brief survey of some characteristic examples shows both change and remarkable consistency over time. Before it became a household word in 1990, p.c. made an appearance in an article on AIDS discourse in the *San Francisco Chronicle* (Shilts 1989), still in the Old Left mode of self- or intra-group ribbing:

> A helpful glossary of politically correct terms was handed out to reporters at the most recent international AIDS conference. . . .
> To outsiders, all this may sound somewhat arcane. Yet in the world of AIDS, woe to those who violate the linguistic regulations imposed by the AIDS Word Police.

While Shilts is speaking of people with whom he is in basic sympathy, his vocabulary ("politically correct," "word police") is shared with the right, as they are quoted in several articles in 1990 that attempt to pin down this new phenomenon. An influential article in the Paper of Record (Bernstein 1990) echoes the conservative slant: "a stifling example of academic orthodoxy"; "Stalinist orthodoxy"; " 'liberal fascism' "; "a growing intolerance, a closing of debate, a pressure to conform to a radical program or risk being accused of . . . thought crimes"; "a hidden radical agenda"; " 'The idea of candor and the deeper idea of civil discourse is dead' "; "the dubious connotations of a politically correct orthodoxy"; " 'politically correct discourse is a kind of fundamentalism.' " Some of these terms are attributed to others and/or enclosed in quotation marks; but reiterated again and again is the theme: p.c. is the goose step of the totalitarianism to come. Thus, according to T.R.B. (Michael Kinsley) in the *New Republic* (May 20, 1991), "the *Wall Street Journal* claims that 'we are far worse off now as regards the threat to intellectual freedom, the pressures to conform ideologically, than during the McCarthy era.' " [8] (Even as the right critiques the "orthodoxy" of p.c., the critics use remarkably similar vocabulary throughout the discourse, establishing or adhering to an orthodoxy of their own.)

As the controversy boils to a head, *Newsweek,* in an article by Jerry Adler (1990), assesses the scene. As Adler's definition, cited earlier, suggests, his is an even-handed position. Unlike most media commentators, Adler can see the conventional assumption of Western superiority in all things as a "prejudice," however "grand." At the same time, he says that the proponents of p.c. are 1960's radicals who no longer have to take to the streets because they have achieved power on campuses and can use "when they have the administration on their side—outright coercion."

Perhaps I work at an unusually conservative campus, but I can recall few—actually no—instances of "coercion" by old Sixties radicals in my twenty-five-year tenure at Berkeley. Indeed, I would describe the majority of my colleagues as moderate to rightist, on the basis of voting patterns in the Academic Senate. While the humanities and social sciences are further to the left than the rest of the faculty, they comprise, here as at most large research universities, a small minority of the voting faculty. The administration is demonstrably even further to the right. I can think of several kinds of decisions we liberals might have liked to "coerce," but we never stood a chance.

In many media reports, it is difficult to tell whether a particularly argumentative and nasty phrase is quoted or paraphrased from a neoconservative source, or represents the writer's own perspective on things. Thus Adler comments that "opponents of PC see themselves as a beleaguered minority among barbarians who would ban Shakespeare because he didn't write in Swahili." Is the reader to infer that "who . . . Swahili" represents an interviewee's hyperbolic utterance, rather than reporting an event that actually occurred? Or is the clause to be read as the writer's own observations—that he, a reporter for a national newsmagazine, has actually observed faculty members who want Shakespeare "banned"? (Not "slightly de-emphasized," but "banned"—there is a difference.) The danger is that nervous, or careless, readers will jump to the former conclusion, and the hysteria will spiral still further out of control.

The same stories are trotted out again and again—the Vincent Sarich case at Berkeley; the notorious "water buffalo" incident at the University of Pennsylvania;[9] the disciplining of a (black) student at the University of Michigan for insisting in class that homosexuality was immoral. But there is a distinct urban-folklore coloration to many of these tales: they often turn out to be third-party anecdotes ("my brother's friend heard from someone who teaches there . . . ") that, when tracked down, either cannot be verified, are much milder than reported, or involved additional factors that explained the "unreasonable" p.c. stance. Thus in the Sarich case, it was not merely that Sarich had, as Adler reports, written "in the alumni magazine that the university's affirmative action program discriminated against white and Asian applicants." He had also, in an undergraduate course required of physical anthropology majors, asserted the intellectual inferiority of blacks and women, roughly equivalent to my asserting in a similar course in linguistics that Chinese is an Indo-European language. When a faculty member makes unsupportable statements like these to students without the sophistication to evaluate them, education suffers. Sarich continued to teach or team-teach the course for the next few years after the report (1990), until his retirement.

Anecdotes are distorted to prove points. As T.R.B. reports in the column cited above,

> To support [Dinesh D'Souza's] peculiar assertion that racism is less prevalent at universities in the South, he reports that white fraternities at the University of Mississippi raised money to help "repair" a black fraternity whose "house was vandalized," as he puts it. In fact, the black fraternity house was completely destroyed by arson, an episode that apparently has no bearing on the question of race relations.

Moreover, while the anti-p.c. contingent grouses about the "incivility" of the discourse introduced by the radical hotheads, their own is hardly emblematic of cool reserve. Adler tells a story about Duke political scientist David James Barber, a self-described liberal who "stalked into the political-science section [of the campus bookstore] . . . and turned on its spine every volume with 'Marx' in its title—about one out of seven by his count, a lot more attention than he thought it warrants—and angrily demanded their removal."

Often the opposition's characterizations of p.c. seem overdrawn. Their repeatedly cited descriptions of the phenomenon suggest something much more threatening than is actually the case: "The new McCarthyism," "thought police," "Orwellian," "Fascist," and "totalitarian," among the favored terms, conjure up a *Nineteen Eighty-Four* world of inexpressibility, constriction, and savage repression. But reports of the alleged worst cases are vague, using passives and impersonal expressions ("some people," "things could happen," "it is claimed") to dodge responsibility. Thus, an article in the *San Francisco Examiner* states that "some worry that freedom to speak on the American campus has been chilled by pressures to be politically correct. Professors hesitate to review facts fully and fairly, and that concerns some of the best scholars in the land." The article goes on: "'I would think very carefully about my opening lecture (on Columbus),' [U.C. Professor Austin Ranney] observes. 'There's the danger of a truth squad monitoring my class. If I said the wrong thing, there could be anonymous phone calls, slashed tires, and worse'" (Irving 1991).

Reading this article fills me with dismay. It paints my university as a much more exciting place than I experience it as—clearly I am missing out on all the fun. How come none of these "truth squads"—presumably clad in snappy uniforms for ready identification—ever visit *me?*

Or, conversely (and more plausibly), how come I've never been asked to be on one? I get asked to be on committees all the time—why not a fun one like a "truth squad"? But if we read more closely (and more seriously), the terror is mitigated by the generality of expression, the expression of a future threat rather than a present actuality: there's *the danger* of a truth squad, not any actual one. There *could be* anonymous phone calls—but no evidence that there has ever been one. And "worse"— what could that mean but the Gulag? Ranney's tactics, rather than those of p.c., are the ways of the Thought Police and the McCarthyites: the anonymous smear, the whispered innuendo, the hinted-at menace.[10] When you get a direct quote, it is either anticlimactic or a misrepresentation. Thus, again in Adler, the story of Barber continues with his attempt to institute a chapter of the conservative National Association of Scholars at Duke, whereupon Stanley Fish characterized the N.A.S. as "racist, sexist, and homophobic." Adler comments: " 'That,' notes one of Barber's allies [as often, nameless], 'is like calling someone a communist in the McCarthy era.' " No, it isn't. (And the N.A.S. claims to be committed to rational discourse.)

Reading the anti-p.c. attacks one often feels that the pot is calling the kettle black. The right characterizes the other side as using the tactics of the Red Guard—public shaming and discrediting, humiliation, threats of, or actual, removal from positions of prestige, demands for self-abasement and re-education. I know of no cases where members of the p.c. contingent actually succeeded in accomplishing these aims. But the other side did, in the case of Sheldon Hackney, president of the University of Pennsylvania during the "water buffalo" incident, who was shortly thereafter nominated to chair the National Endowment for the Humanities, a position requiring Senate confirmation. For his role in that ruckus, Hackney was denounced by the right for capitulating to the forces of p.c. When he appeared before the Senate, several of its more conservative members, aided by conservative newspaper columnists, engaged in an orgy of public humiliation (Neilson 1995, 82). To save his appointment, Hackney prostrated himself, admitting he had been wrong and cowardly, denouncing p.c. and postmodernism, praising his adversaries as "nonideological," and generally genuflecting to the right. He was then confirmed, but the gauntlet he had to run bears more than a superficial likeness to what dissidents suffered under the Cultural Revolution.

When the right isn't representing p.c. as a threat to the Republic, it is making it the butt of jokes. These strategies might seem contradictory:

if it's ridiculous, it can't be very threatening. But the ultimate aim of the rhetoric is to distance *them*—those liberals—from *us,* the neutral and normal. First, they are represented as the enemies of *us,* a danger to *us.* Then they are shown as silly—something nobody wants to be. If you have any sympathy for them, you are equally risible. The important thing is not so much to preserve the Republic from "fascism," but to maintain control of language at all costs. Considered from this perspective, the two tactics merge into one consistent strategy. This rhetorical turn shows up especially with respect to the appropriation of the right to name ("blacks," "women," etc.). Alongside of "physically challenged," the neocons offered "follically challenged" (bald), "vertically challenged" (short), and "morally challenged" (corrupt). The effect was to make renaming and reclaiming ridiculous, without having to offer reasoned arguments against them.

HATE SPEECH: HOW THE RIGHT
CAME TO LOVE FREE SPEECH

The jewel in the anti-p.c. crown is the First Amendment, newly claimed by the right as its own. Historically the First Amendment was a thorn in the conservative side: it offered protection to nonmajoritarian views, lost causes, and the disenfranchised—not to mention, of course, Communists and worse. From the Sedition Act of the Adams administration to continual attempts to pass a constitutional amendment banning flag-desecration, conservatives have always tried to impose sanctions on free expression, while liberals have tried to keep the "marketplace of ideas" open to all traders. For most of this century it has been the liberal wing of the Supreme Court that has struck down constraints on expression, from Nazi marches to antiwar protests, and the conservative wing that has tried to keep them in effect. But when the shoe is on the other foot and language control is passing from them, conservatives rethink that position. If p.c. can be framed as an attempt to wrest from *us* our historical right to use whatever language we want, whenever we want, to whomever we want, its proponents can be made out to be opponents of free speech and—voilà—we are metamorphosed into all-American defenders of the First Amendment against the infidel Hun, or the p.c. professoriate.

No one is expressly demanding the right to make use of hateful slurs. As Mari Matsuda notes, those with media access, the educated upper classes, need not stoop so low: "The various implements of racism find their way into the hands of different dominant-group members. Lower- and middle-class white men might use violence against people of color, whereas upper-class whites might resort to private clubs or righteous indignation against 'diversity' and 'reverse discrimination'" (in Matsuda et al. 1993, 23). So a member of a higher caste might never actually be exposed to virulent racist or sexist language among his associates, and therefore might be able to claim that it didn't exist any more or need not be taken seriously (because *we* don't have to encounter it in its more distasteful forms). And while there do exist epithets to be hurled at males and whites ("phallocrat," "honky"), they lack the sting of slurs against women, blacks, Latinos, and Asians. That is because, according to Matsuda, "racist speech proclaims racial inferiority and denies the personhood of target-group members. All members of the target group are at once considered alike and inferior" (36).

But a proclamation of inferiority is meaningful, or even possible, only if it can piggyback on an older stereotype of one race (or gender) as inferior: the "Snark Rule" cited in the last chapter, which states that repetition makes a statement "true." Judith Butler defines hate speech as working through the repetition of similar prior speech acts: "hate speech is an act that recalls prior acts, requiring a future repetition to endure" (1997, 20). So if your group, or you as an individual member of that group, have never been subjected to epithets in the past, no words directed at you, however irritating, can have the full noxious effect of true hate speech. That is not to say that such language is benign. But if you are not a member of a historically submerged group, "you just don't get it," since you don't have a visceral understanding of the harm such speech can do. So it's relatively easy for you to see racist and sexist language and behavior as "just kidding" or "childish horseplay" and not demand a remedy for it.

Those who don't have personal reasons to feel that hateful epithets are damaging and who at the same time feel that any challenge to the right to use such speech is a serious threat to the First Amendment are apt to feel not only permitted but obligated, as a sacred duty, to oppose any attempts to legislate language control—at least those that come from the other side and attempt to constrain *our* preferred linguistic possibilities. Laws that might constrain *theirs* are still unproblematic. Hence the right's continuing attempts to outlaw flag-burning, and the loud ruckus on the right that followed the 1989 five-to-four Supreme Court decision (*Texas v. Johnson*) that flag-burning constituted permissible expression under the First Amendment.[11] And hence the rather convoluted dance of Congressman Henry Hyde.

Hyde, a staunch conservative and antiabortion advocate, was outraged by campus speech codes as violations of the First Amendment. In 1991, at the height of the hysteria, Hyde was cooperating with the American Civil Liberties Union (ACLU) to pass a bill to curtail campus speech codes by extending the scope of the First Amendment to private universities (it is already in effect in public ones). Yet at virtually the same time, Hyde was enthusiastically supporting a May 1991 Supreme Court decision (*Rust v. Sullivan*) that forbade medical personnel in hospitals or clinics that received any government support from so much as mentioning abortion to their clients, even to answering affirmatively if asked whether abortion was legal. In 1996, Hyde was a strong supporter of the Communications Decency Act, which would have kept information about such "indecent" topics as breast cancer, birth control, and abortion off the Internet.[12]

THE RIGHT TO HATEFUL SPEECH

To listen to some born-again First Amendment advocates, you would believe that its guarantee of free speech is and has always been absolute. But that is far from the case. Courts have always recognized the validity of competing claims: "clear and present danger," "falsely shouting 'fire' in a crowded theater," imminent threat, "fighting words," national interest, libel, threats, subornation of perjury, perjury itself, and others. Even some speech rights we consider uncontroversial today—including the right to provide birth control information or the right to protest the government's involvement in a war—were guaranteed only after arduous struggles. Even if hate speech regulations were to be enforced, that would not be the first curtailment of the absolute right to say anything, under any circumstances. In pondering the need for legislation against hate speech, the first question to address is the validity of competing interests. Does the right to enjoy speech that is as free as possible outweigh the right to "the equal protection of the laws" guaranteed to each of us under the Fourteenth Amendment, or vice versa?

This argument pits supporters of the Fourteenth Amendment (Critical Race Theorists and anti-pornography feminists like Catharine MacKinnon) against the odd couple composed of card-carrying ACLU liberals and conservative First Amendment supporters. Everyone agrees that hate speech is deplorable, and no reasonable person would ever indulge in any form of it. But the sides differ on what is to be done and on the consequences of what is done. Is racism so pervasive across this country and on college campuses, and other remedies so ineffectual, that speech codes must be enforced to guarantee to all the equal protection mandated by the Fourteenth Amendment? Or is the problem exaggerated—are there other ways to combat it, and does the need for preserving the First Amendment outweigh the responsibility to enforce the Fourteenth?

As a card-carrying ACLU member who is also a member of a couple of historically targeted groups, and as a member of a profession that abhors an unqualified statement, I naturally straddle the line. Others are more decisive. The CRTists tend to see hate speech as deeply pervasive, an increasing "epidemic" that can only be stopped by the immunization of speech codes. In the introduction to *Words That Wound,* its four authors argue that "Incidents of hate speech and racial harassment are reported with increasing frequency and regularity, particularly on American college campuses, where they have reached near epidemic proportions" (Matsuda et. al. 1993, 1).

Since no figures are given, it is difficult to assess the accuracy of the claim. Even reports of an increasing number of acts of hate speech on college campuses would not necessarily show that hate speech had reached "epidemic" proportions—and might not even be an unequivocally bad thing. First, the larger numbers might merely be the result of more such acts being reported, a sign that minorities are being listened to more and taken more seriously than they used to be and that they now feel safe enough to complain. Even if there actually are more acts committed, that might merely mean that the presence of more minorities and women in places where they previously had not had entree creates more readily available targets, and arouses more resentment. But even if the authors of *Words That Wound* have identified a real problem of endemic racism and sexism in America, the remedy is still not obvious: to some it is not even apparent that any remedy is needed, much less what remedy will work and occasion the least interference with freedom of speech.

LANGUAGE: THOUGHT OR ACTION?

Once again language is the problem. We don't know how to legislate hate speech, because we don't really know how to classify any kind of speech, which we would have to do before we could safely legislate against it.

We are pretty clear on other kinds of human activity. Most of us would agree that thought cannot be an object of legislation and should not become one even if science could develop ways to peer into our minds. On the other hand, overt actions are always subject to control by law, and we would agree that they have to be, if we are to live together more or less peaceably in a state of civilization. We may argue about what kinds of actions should be punishable, and how, but punished bad actions must be. Language is intermediate between thought and action: it is thought made observable. It straddles the line between the abstract and the concrete, the ethereal and the corporeal. Which of its aspects—the ethereal or the physical—should be the basis of our legal understanding of the capacity of language to do harm? Is language inconsequential and therefore immune to legislation? Or is language equivalent to action—world-changing and so capable of harm—in which case legal notice must be taken of injurious linguistic behavior?

We teach our children the proverb "Sticks and stones may break my bones, but words will never harm me." Do we offer this saying as truth or as wishful magic: believe it and the pain will go away? Probably we would not be so quick to teach our children these words if we did not fear that the opposite was true. In our natural desire to save our children from pain, we encourage them to deny their feelings. But denial doesn't make it so.

We have only recently become a psychologically conscious society. Only in the last hundred years or so have we talked about psychic *wounds* and mental *diseases*. We are never sure whether we mean those expressions as literal descriptions or metaphors. We know that an autopsy on someone suffering from psychic trauma would reveal no physical evidence of that "wound." Yet there now exist physical interventions in the form of drugs that "cure" these traumas, and this possibility of physical "cure" argues for the physical reality of the symptoms.

When our legal system was established, it seemed clear that words were not deeds, so only physical misbehaviors were legally actionable. The legal systems of all societies specify punishments or remedies for physical harm. The wound is visible; witnesses may have observed exactly what occurred. There may be disagreement among the parties about the interpretation of the events: Did the victim do anything to provoke the act? Did the perpetrator perform it intentionally? Did he mean to do harm? To do as much harm as he did? Are there other extenuating circumstances? But all participants can agree that something took place that changed the physical world.

But what about "words that wound"? Is that expression even meaningful? Are those who feel verbally wounded describing a real interaction with real and adjudicable consequences, or are they merely oversensitive souls who should grow up and take it like a man? If outsiders can't observe the damage, how can anyone prescribe a legal remedy for it?

If observers can agree on the amount and kind of force employed to make a physical wound, they can agree on the amount of damage probably sustained by the victim: their conclusions are based on scientifically demonstrable physical laws. But words mean different things to different people in different contexts: a word that would shock and intimidate a woman uttered by a strange man on a dark street at night might be a delightful expression of intimacy between her and someone she loves and trusts. African Americans can call one another "nigger" with relative impunity under specific conditions, but a white person cannot do the same. Language by nature is ambiguous and sensitive to context. The law by necessity strives to be precise and decontextualized. There is a discontinuity between the two words in the expression "language crime." Yet the law recognizes several: threats, defamation, offers of bribes, and perjury, for example. To make these concepts workable, we need to reach a formal understanding of language and its relation to action.

SPEECH ACTS: "ONLY THEORY" OR REALITY?

Relevant here is the discussion in Chapter 1 of J. L. Austin's theory of performative speech acts. Austin concluded that language was equivalent to action, in that all utterances were performative and all performatives were world-changing—that is, actions. That theory has had important consequences for several academic fields: philosophy and linguistics (naturally), as well as literary theory, anthropology, and education. As long as it is confined safely within academia, it is mere theory that applies only to ideas, with few actual consequences. But in recent years, it has been incorporated into the discourse of the law, by both legal scholars (as in several papers of Peter Tiersma [1986, 1987]) and sociolinguists (see, for example, Shuy 1993). But nowhere does speech act theory have such concrete and far-reaching consequences as in the definitions of hate speech and its legal status.

Those who believe in Austin's formulation are likely to follow it to its logical conclusion: that linguistic misbehavior is a type of bad action and should be treated as such by the law, criminally and civilly. A strict

Austinian is likely to support speech codes. If problems of enforceability arise based on the vagueness or ambiguity of language, it is the job of the codifiers to rewrite their statutes clearly enough to solve the problem. Those who disagree with Austin are apt to treat words very differently from actions, beyond the reach of legal remedy in most or even all cases.

There are many mixed positions and evasions, depending on the ability to draw and maintain a distinction between those kinds of language that constitute action-equivalents and others that are closer to thought-equivalents. Since the 1920's First Amendment law has divided utterances along those lines: language that constitutes "expression" and receives a high degree of protection under the First Amendment, versus language that constitutes "conduct" and doesn't. A political opinion like "the Republicans deserve to win" will be counted in the first set and be protected, while a threat (even in indirect form) like, "I have a gun and I know how to use it" will under many circumstances be judged "conduct" and treated as a criminal action.

A crucial concept is that of "fighting words," as addressed in the 1942 Supreme Court decision *Chaplinsky v. New Hampshire,* which established the category of "fighting words" as unprotected action-equivalents. Chaplinsky, a Jehovah's Witness, got into a verbal altercation with the town marshal of Rochester, New Hampshire, in the course of which he used language considered very shocking in its time, calling the marshal a "Goddamned racketeer" and a "damned Fascist." [13] He was arrested and found guilty under the town's speech code, which prohibited "fighting words." The case was appealed up to the U.S. Supreme Court, which found for the state. In its unanimous opinion, the Court defined "fighting words": "There are certain well-defined and narrowly limited classes of speech, the prevention and punishment of which have never been thought to raise any Constitutional problem. These include the lewd and obscene, the profane, the libelous, and the insulting or 'fighting' words—those which by their very utterance inflict injury or tend to incite an immediate breach of the peace."

Significantly *Chaplinsky,* as well as later decisions citing it as precedent, locate the justification for the "fighting words" exception in the government's duties to prevent injury to citizens and keep the peace. The former has been essentially negated by later opinions, while the latter has provided appellate courts with an enduring can of worms. If the danger of "fighting words" is that the addressee is apt to lose control and breach the peace (the "breach" is accomplished, in this perspective, only via actions, not via the offensive utterance itself), why not hold the breacher, not the utterer, responsible? The Court's assumption is that some words are so very bad that on hearing them, an ordinary person *must* strike out (as reflexively as, when the doctor taps your knee with a hammer, you *have to* jerk your leg). No psychological or other evidence is cited in support of this proposition.

Chaplinsky would seem to suggest that verbal aggressors should pick their targets carefully. Persons with less testosterone are known to be less likely than those with more to react physically to provocation. So, presumably, insulting women is more likely to be constitutional under *Chaplinsky* than insulting men, and it's probably better to insult someone smaller than you (who will be less likely to "breach the peace") than someone larger. Scholars who try to justify speech codes these days, like the authors of *Words That Wound,* avoid the morass by thinking in terms of psychic rather than physical trauma. But the "fighting words" exception was not meant to cover psychic wounds, and even if it were, determining whether psychic trauma has occurred is—if possible at all—not the business of a court of law and a lay jury.

As fond as linguists are of Austinian doctrine (if words are actions, then what we linguists do is important), we must recognize that in fact words are not the same as actions. Most people given the choice between a vile epithet and a punch in the nose would opt for the former. Arguably this is because the second has immediate and obvious painful consequences, while the effects of the first take longer to emerge and are harder to link directly to their cause. If, as the judge said in admitting *Ulysses* into the country, no woman was ever seduced by a book, so no one was ever killed by a word. If language is world-changing, the way it works is different from that of direct action, and less accessible to legal investigation.

Franklyn Haiman, in *"Speech Acts" and the First Amendment* (1993), proposes that language is "mediated" action. Austin is not quite right, he suggests, in equating performativity with action. When I give an order, you have to perform the mental act of *deciding* or *willing* to obey me. Even in the clearer case of excommunication, the recipient must determine that the appropriate conditions are met and decide to behave as an excommunicated person in the future, for it to succeed. The words alone, Haiman points out, are meaningless: they derive force through the agreement by all participants on the nature of the real-world circumstances in which they find themselves.

But Haiman is not quite right to dismiss the word-as-action theory entirely. While words are not directly as world-changing as actions are, they are indirectly or psychologically world-changing. If I make a promise to you, that utterance forever alters our relationship and the way I think about it and behave toward you, and you toward me, in the future. To say that speech is not action is to fall into the logical error of drawing a sharp distinction between mind and body.

How we feel about hate speech and the First Amendment reflects our view of language itself. If we believe that words are not world-changing, we are apt to be comfortable with an interpretation of the First Amendment that permits much more freedom of speech than is permitted to action. But this leeway comes at the price, ironically, of devaluing language—seeing it as non-action, essentially harmless.

LANGUAGE, THOUGHT, AND REALITY (REPRISED)

This is another side of the enigma explored in Chapter 1: the extent to which we can, and the criteria we should use to, distinguish between "reality" and "fantasy." Memory, individual and cultural, is increasingly seen as a psychosocial construction, like identity, to which it is intimately connected. Likewise the culture tries to keep distinct—but finds it increasingly hard as we become psychologically more sophisticated or at least more involved—physical illness, arising from physical causes (germs, genes, hormones, and such), and psychological "distress," arising from psychological causes, like poor communication or bad parenting. The debate is continuing about the physical "reality" of a number of ailments, including Gulf War Syndrome, Multiple Chemical Sensitivity, and Chronic Fatigue Syndrome. Are these true "illnesses"—that is, physically caused and physically diagnosable and treatable—or problems of mind that are "just in your head"?

The answer might come from either of two perspectives. The traditional one is that psychogenic distress isn't "real" and the way to deal with it is not to get it at all, or at least if you do, to just get over it. This position is not sympathetic to demands for government intervention or compensation, or for government funding for research into the roots and treatments of the problem, since a psychological problem is seen as self-inflicted, if not imaginary or devised for the purpose of malingering.[14]

Others, particularly those who suffer from these syndromes, take the diametrically opposite position that these conditions have physical causation, are physical in nature, and require physical interventions to be cured. There are many theories about the origin of each, but government action (or inaction) figures in all. So the government (that is, the tax-payers, *us* to the sufferers' *them*) is called on to redress the wrong. A reasonable compromise might seem to be that psychological distress, while without physical causes, is as "real," as serious, and as deserving of prevention or treatment as its physical counterpart; and indeed as we come to understand mind and body better, we realize more and more that the traditional line we draw between the two is illusory. But the suggestion that the cause of these syndromes is any less concretely physical than that of, say, cholera or cancer enrages the sufferers; and any suggestion that they have a legitimacy equal to those "real" ailments infuriates the other side.

While this issue may seem irrelevant to my topic, it has parallels to the speech-act situation. The strong Austinian position that language and action are identical puts a believer in the camp of psychic trauma sufferers, recovered-memory believers, and others in some disrepute in claiming a link, perhaps a clear identity, between mind and body, saying that thought is reality and changes the world.

There is another link between these two disputes. In both, though for different reasons, groups historically without power form the preponderance of the "psychophysical connection" side. The fact that the less powerful people are associated with the less authoritative position impairs the credibility of both—not too surprisingly.

So the arguments on both sides of the First/Fourteenth Amendment competition connect with current struggles over the redefinition and redistribution of power via language. The Critical Race Theorists, frequently women or minorities, argue that speech has effects as serious as actions, and is thus indistinguishable from action. The Fourteenth Amendment guarantee of equal protection of the laws entitles everyone to the same degree of protection from oppressive actions—including those accomplished by linguistic means. Until that goal is achieved, the First Amendment guarantee of free speech merely serves to protect the interests of those who are already protected by the Fourteenth Amendment: those with traditional power.[15] For until all have equal protection, language will not have the same meaning for all. To protect the speech rights of some, the protection of others must remain unequal. And as long as inequalities exist, the First Amendment does not equally protect the speech rights of all: the weaker are apt to have fewer options for expression and (as we have seen) are less likely to be listened to and taken seriously. And a slur from stronger to weaker has more clout than it does coming from the other direction. The claim from the other side that *we all* benefit from the strongest possible interpretation of the First Amendment falls on Critical Race Theory's deaf ears. For them the harm that hate speech does to individuals and communities outweighs the value to the community of unconstrained speech.

For CRT, to invoke the First Amendment in protection of hate speech is to misunderstand the purpose for which the founders created it. As U.S. Supreme Court Justices Oliver Wendell Holmes, Jr. and Louis Brandeis suggested in a series of dissents during the late 1910's and the 1920's, democracy is meaningful only to the extent that citizens can choose among competing viewpoints in the "marketplace of ideas." [16] To create this marketplace, speech must be unfettered, or relatively so. (Just as there are laws against really dangerous merchandise in the literal marketplace, so it is reasonable to legislate against truly noxious expression.) But this rationale divides speech into two categories. Only speech that is political and ideational in nature is guaranteed full First Amendment protection. Other speech (e.g., advertising and pornography, which are not political; or "fighting words," which are not expressive of ideas) requires that there be no strong competing interest (the protection of morality, for instance, or the national interest) to be protected. From this perspective, "fighting words" and other hate speech, not being expressive of political ideas, do not come under the aegis of the First Amendment.

Some members of this, the civil rights side, argue that framing the discourse as a First-vs.- Fourteenth Amendment dispute has "advanced the cause of racial oppression and placed the bigot on the moral high ground" (Charles Lawrence, in Matsuda et al. 1993, 57), because the First Amendment (unlike the Fourteenth) occupies, in the American mind, an iconic position, as a kind of defining American virtue, so any diminution of its scope is seen as an attack on The American Way.

The opposite side, the uneasy alliance of conservatives and civil libertarians, believes, at least with regard to hate speech and speech codes, that the First Amendment trumps the Fourteenth and must be guarded against any erosion, however well meant. While hate speech is certainly deplorable, they say, it isn't as serious as hateful actions and does not demand analogous remedies. Speech is not action and does not have the potential for harm that action does. So remedies other than legislation—persuasion, education, shaming—are more appropriate. If slower and less certain, they are also less destructive of free speech. Further, speech codes are apt to be turned against the victims of hate speech, the weaker parties: in some of the infrequent cases in which campus speech codes have been enforced, they have been enforced against a minority person. Thus the student punished in the "water buffalo" case was a Jewish foreigner; in the Michigan case, the student who was censured for calling homosexuality immoral was black. Chaplinsky was a Jehovah's Witness, and the case with which Adler leads off his article (cited above) concerned an Asian-American woman.

But speech codes and other linguistically restrictive legislation are seldom enforced, because their necessary vagueness makes them unenforceable. It is impossible to provide a list of forbidden expressions, and without such a list, it is impossible to apply any law or code fairly. An early version of a University of California Berkeley speech code illustrates some of the difficulties.[17] Paraphrasing *Chaplinsky,* it attempts to define "fighting words":

> "Fighting words" are those personally abusive epithets which, when directly addressed to any ordinary person are, in the context used and as a matter of common knowledge, inherently likely to provoke a violent reaction whether or not they actually do so. Such words include, but are not limited to, those terms widely recognized to be derogatory references to race, ethnicity, religion, sex, sexual orientation, disability, and other personal characteristics.
>
> "Fighting words" constitute "harassment" when the circumstances of their utterance create a hostile and intimidating environment which the student uttering them should reasonably know will interfere with the victim's ability to pursue effectively his or her education or otherwise to participate fully in University programs and activities.[18]

This statement is both about as clear as it could be and full of murk. Who is an "ordinary person"? Who defines the "context"—speaker, addressee, or uninvolved third party? Whose knowledge is "common knowledge"? Under what conditions is a "violent reaction" likely to occur? We know that people of different genders, ethnicities, and ages are apt to make very different judgments on these issues.

Who decides what the "circumstances" of an utterance are? Is "we were just kidding around" a reasonable defense to a charge of harassment? And no matter how complete your list, it could not possibly include all cases that someone might find problematic. A particularly interesting example surfaced at the NAACP convention in 1992, according to an article in the *San Francisco Examiner.* Speaking to the group, third-party presidential candidate Ross Perot told them: "Now, I don't have to tell you who gets hurt first when this sort of thing happens, do I? You people do, your people do. I know that; you know that."[19] Perot, who was looking for support, certainly had no intention of alienating his hearers through the use of ethnic slurs or fighting words. Yet his choice of the expression "you people/your people" offended many in his audience. The article goes on to say that H. Ron Brown, Democratic National Committee Chairman (and an African American) "said Perot's use of the expression 'demonstrates a lack of sensitivity.'"

"You people" is not even a fixed expression or phrase. It can hardly be characterized as "fighting words." But used by a white speaker to a black audience, it can sound patronizing, a speaker moralizing at an audience he considers his social inferiors. There is nothing in the overt content of "you people" that creates that interpretation; it's just suggestive of an attitude that members of the minority group have encountered too often in the past.

In an article entitled "Only When I Laugh," Linda Ellerbee (1990) asks a related question: when are jokes are funny, and when do they cross the line to become offensive? She starts out by considering a cartoon by John Callahan showing "two Ku Klux Klansmen, draped in their bed sheets, setting out in the moonlight to commit some atrocity. One turns to the other and says, 'Don't you just love it when they're still warm from the dryer?'" According to Ellerbee, the cartoon got Callahan into a lot of trouble. "People said it glorified the Klan," but, notes Ellerbee, "glorifying" is not what it does; rather, it humanizes the Klan, makes its members out to be regular people just like us—even more dangerous. Ellerbee suggests that such jokes are *both* funny and offensive, and we should tolerate—and enjoy—them. But the degree to which they are "funny," versus the degree to which they are "offensive," is probably in the eyes of the beholders, depending on the role the Klan has played in their lives. If we were to adopt a "cartoon code" or "humor code," who would be the gatekeeper?

In a position paper the ACLU offers several arguments against campus speech codes. While acknowledging that hate speech has been a problem on many campuses, the ACLU argues that speech codes are not a good way to attack it. For one thing, the university's mission is education. That means, first, that it should discourage hate speech through education, via courses and other forums for discussion. Additionally, as an educational entity, the university requires extensive freedom of speech to do its work. Furthermore, the ACLU takes a strong anti-Austinian position: "We're not talking about choosing between the First Amendment and the Fourteenth Amendment. We're talking about choosing between regulating speech and regulating action. Murder is illegal. Talking about it isn't."[20] Well, yes and no. Persuading someone to commit murder, or offering them money to do so, is illegal. The line is, as usual, fuzzy. But that's all the more reason why we need to explore routes other than the one-size-fits-all solutions that are the province of the law.

More sophisticated arguments in favor of a strong First Amendment are presented by the authors of a book published under the auspices of the ACLU, *Speaking of Race, Speaking of Sex* (Gates et al. 1994). In one article Robert C. Post (124ff.) gives a number of arguments against the CRT position. In the first place, the First Amendment is the basis of democratic government. So any erosion of it necessarily is antidemocratic. Yet it is not quite so simple. There is a fundamental paradox: to achieve full communication between individuals and their government (a prerequisite for democracy), it is necessary to erode, to some degree, the sense of community among these individuals. This is because the robust and uncensored communication that is necessary to achieve democratic consensus must offend someone, must violate civility—must, in other words, run up against the Fourteenth Amendment when power differences are involved, as in any human society they must be.

Further, race, gender, and the other considerations invoked by the Fourteenth Amendment side of the debate are socially constructed (as postmodern theorists in many fields have been arguing for some time now), and that construction is accomplished via discourse. That discourse works best and role-construction is most open and unfettered (as CRT would wish it) when there is the least amount of legal interference with the public discourse process. It is true that a strong First Amendment would permit members of more powerful groups to offer opposition to nonconventional role construction (for example, by members of the gay community). But in that confrontation, possibilities would be explored and arguments tested and strengthened.

And finally, Post argues, the CRT argument turns on its creators. If the aim of the Fourteenth Amendment supporters is to legislate away the incivility of hate speech, is that not accepting the purported neutrality of the groups in power? The traditionally powerful determine what styles of discourse are "appropriate" or "civil." To create a legal opening for determining what kind of utterances are "civil" and what is to be done about those that aren't is to give still more meaning-making power to those who have too much of it already.

Another argument is offered by Ronald Dworkin. He distinguishes between *instrumental* and *constitutive* justifications for freedom of speech. The first is represented by the arguments summarized earlier: free speech enables democracy to function; it is valuable because it furthers other goals that we consider valuable. Constitutive justifications suppose "that freedom of speech is valuable, not just in virtue of the consequences it has, but because it is an essential and 'constitutive' feature of a just political society that government treat all its adult members, except those who are incompetent, as responsible moral agents" (1992, 56). And because free speech makes us more fully human, it enables us to be the most that we can be.

Instrumental arguments can be overcome by more pressing instrumentalities. Thus the civil-rights side argues that, as good as free speech is for democracy, full equality is even better. But a constitutive argument, if accepted at all, cannot be controverted in this way. If free speech is a necessary precondition for full humanity, we have to have it. Maybe we have to have equality as well, but the deal has to be both-and, not either-or.

THE STRANGE BEDFELLOWS OF
THE FIRST AMENDMENT

Basically, then, the fight is between two schools of liberal thought over which of two liberal doctrines is the more important. The most curious aspect of this debate is the alliance between the civil libertarians and the conservative right, never in the past particularly friendly. Almost never has the right taken the First Amendment side in a debate. As noted above, it was nearly unanimous in condemning the Supreme Court's decision in *Texas v. Johnson*. It strongly favored "McCarthyism" when it was being practiced by Joe McCarthy rather than "campus radicals." Its representatives stood on the sidewalks during protest marches against the Vietnam and Gulf Wars howling "America: Love it or leave it!" at marchers. And it is the conservatives, spearheaded by Henry Hyde, who are urging the enactment of "decency" statutes for the Internet. So what brings them into the First Amendment fold? Have they joined the ranks of the "card-carrying ACLU members" derided by George Bush in his 1988 campaign?

It is not that the right has joined forces with the left in this battle (perish forbid!). Rather, the left has joined forces with the right. The rhetoric of the right seems to have seeped into the writings of at least one member of the ACLU forces—as an African American, a particularly improbable borrower of traditional elitist rhetoric. The crossover illustrates the twists and turns occasioned by an argument that is not about what it seems to be about. In his paper in *Speaking of Race, Speaking of Sex* ("Critical Race Theory and the First Amendment"; 1994), Henry Louis Gates, Jr. attacks the proponents of CRT and the Fourteenth Amendment in a style that sounds familiar, since we have encountered it in the mouths of traditional white male conservatives. While many of Gates's statements are sensible and insightful, the way in which he makes his arguments is noteworthy.

His tone sometimes moves into the conservative realm: reductive, sarcastic and dismissive.

> Something, let us agree, has gone very wrong here. In arguments of this sort, the pendulum has swung from the absurd position that words don't matter to the equally absurd position that *only* words matter. Critical race theory, it appears, has fallen under the sway of a species of academic nominalism. (54)

But Charles Lawrence, whom Gates is specifically singling out for criticism here, isn't saying that *only* words count, merely that words count *a lot*. Gates's comment about "academic nominalism" manages to be both antiacademic and obscurantist, borrowing from new allies like George Will and William F. Buckley. Gates attacks the Critical Race Theorists in rhetoric that comes straight from the conservative, traditionalist perspective: he attacks them as participants in the "cult of victimhood" and as members of the "recovery movement." Their claims are "therapeutic"— a sneer.

> For beyond the wrangling over particular statutes and codes lies an encompassing vision of state and civil society. Moreover, it is one whose wellsprings are to be found not in legal scholarship or theory, but in the much more powerful cultural currents identified with the "recovery movement." At the vital center of the hate speech movement is the seductive vision of the therapeutic state. (48)

Finally, then, it is time to answer the question posed earlier: what brings these strange bedfellows to share their strange bed? Why do Henry Hyde and Henry Louis Gates, Jr. bring out similar arguments, employing similar rhetoric, against similar targets? To answer that, it is necessary to inquire into the function served by referring to the First Amendment. Its two groups of defenders use it for different, not always explicit, purposes.

The civil libertarians are concerned about the preservation and continuing strength of the First Amendment. Since the founding of the ACLU, they have demonstrated their adherence to it steadfastly, even supporting unpopular decisions like *Smith v. Collin* (the Skokie decision) and *Texas v. Johnson.* You can argue about whether the First Amendment deserves the paramount status they give it and whether that status should continue unexamined and unaltered in an increasingly pluralistic society; but you cannot fault their adherence to principle.

The conservatives' newly hatched First Amendment advocacy demands more scrutiny: Why the sudden support for the First Amendment? Why now of all times? How to reconcile their concern over erosion of the First Amendment with regard to speech codes with their nonchalance about its weakening in their support of *Rust v. Sullivan* and their rage over its strengthening in *Texas v. Johnson?* Most of us—including the staunchest civil libertarians—believe that the government has, and should have, the power to prohibit or punish actions that harm others and interfere with the calm maintenance of the social contract and our ability to live together peaceably as the social species we are. So to exalt the First Amendment in all or most circumstances over the Fourteenth is to avow, as many civil libertarians like Haiman and Post have, that language is *not* action or at most is an attenuated form of action without action's capacity to do harm. Words are "mere words." Language isn't a serious concern—a perspective that returns us to the days when "grammar" was the business of the schoolmarm, not to be taken seriously by real men, whose bad grammar was the badge of their virility.

Members of groups that know viscerally that meaning-making is power and are watching their unilateral and absolute access to meaning-making erode have a couple of options available—Viagra for their new impotence. They can try valiantly to keep *them* from attaining equal status, by legislation, threats, rhetoric—whatever it takes. But if that fails, and it is failing (as we shall see in later chapters), the only recourse is denial, that favorite premillennial elixir. They must diminish in their own minds, and the minds of others if possible, the importance of language. That is easy enough for those who have never been targets of true hate speech. For the wounding message of hate speech goes beyond the "mere words" that are slurs and fighting words. Hate speech in any form both presupposes and re-creates a narrative in its very utterance: the story of who has had power over whom, and how that power is maintained, and what will happen to anyone who challenges that power. As long as the narrative continues uninterrupted and unquestioned, language can be used (at whatever level of consciousness) by those with language-making power against those without it: to remind *them* that they are *them* but we are *us;* and to let them know by words that we can do actions that harm, by that utterance doing word-harm. So word and action merge in narrative meaning-making, allowing covert control because the story need not be told in so many (or any) words. The status quo is maintained. Control of the story is control of history (words that are etymologically related). To belittle the importance of language, however high-minded the excuse, is ultimately to magically restore power to those who in fact are losing it, by denying that the lost power matters. If they can persuade enough of the rest of us that that is true, well then, it is true. Then the conservatives' newfound enthusiasm for the First Amendment is not so much a vote of confidence in freedom of expression as it is a last desperate attempt to hold on to their power by denying the potency of language at the moment when the right to control it is slipping from their grasp. It's a version of sour grapes: "Well, if I can't have it for myself, I'll make it seem as worthless as possible."

The struggle over hate speech and p.c. was the opening battle of the language war. While the fury over this issue may have abated, it remains as the continuo while an increasingly complex melody plays above it. The next movement of the symphony is the 1991 Anita Hill / Clarence Thomas hearings and their aftermath, which I turn to now.

MAD, BAD, AND HAD

The
Anita Hill / Clarence Thomas
Narrative(s)

PROLEGOMENA TO A CIRCUS

The movie everyone was going to see, and heatedly discussing, in the summer of 1991 was *Thelma and Louise*. In it two women (played by Susan Sarandon and Geena Davis), one a harried waitress and the other a put-upon wife, go off together without their partners for a couple of days' vacation. They stop off for dinner; Thelma, the younger and prettier married one, is hit on, responds positively, drinks too much, and is helped outside for some fresh air by the guy she has been flirting with. He proceeds to try to rape her, at which moment Louise appears with Thelma's gun and, when he insults her, shoots him dead. They take off in a panic, with Louise gradually evolving a plan to get to Mexico. In the course of their flight they are harassed, threatened, taken advantage of, and variously mistreated by virtually every male with whom they come in contact. They kill a couple and disable a few others. The plan is thwarted by Thelma's irresponsibility, and they end up (in all probability) committing suicide by driving off a cliff to avoid capture.

This picaresque plot is not unfamiliar to Hollywood audiences, yet the movie was shocking: instead of guys (who can be expected to behave this way), it was two *women* who take off by themselves to have fun, mouth off to the opposite sex, and take no guff from anyone. Critics and audiences were split about how to take the story. Was it right to show women responding to adversity with violence? Even though the protagonists (probably) got killed in the end, did the movie send women the wrong message? One thing was striking: women tended to respond much more positively to the action than men; and at each scene in which the women turned violently on their harassers, the female members of the audience responded with lusty cheers.

If *Thelma and Louise* did nothing else, it brought up in the most graphic and unavoidable way, on the big screen where it couldn't be avoided, the fact that too many men treat women as children, sex objects, or possessions. It brought the topic of sexual harassment into sharp focus as a subject of impassioned arguments between and within the sexes, and presented the possibility of retribution (if not necessarily of exactly this kind). The popularity of the movie, and the reactions of audiences, made it clear that harassment and other gender-related mistreatment were neither a dirty secret in which the woman was at fault nor something that only happened to *you:* it universalized the problem, presenting it from a female perspective, and gave us a language, visual and verbal, in which to discuss it. Of course, it was just entertainment, a summer flick, and the excitement would simmer down as the weather cooled off. Nothing to worry about, really.

Inside the Beltway, matters of greater moment were detonating. In June Thurgood Marshall, the only African American on the Supreme Court and a strong liberal, announced his retirement. With a presidential election coming up in 1992, the Bush administration realized that Marshall would have to be replaced by another black jurist. They naturally preferred a conservative. The ideal nominee would be young, so as to be able to serve for many years, and not have a record (a "paper trail") that might complicate his confirmation. Not many candidates fit this description, but finally one was found: a forty-three-year-old Federal appellate justice, former head of the Equal Employment Opportunity Commission (E.E.O.C.) named Clarence Thomas.

The candidate's selection had little to do with professional distinction or civil rights background. There was immediate protest, both from legal circles concerned about his competence and from civil rights and other liberal groups concerned about his worse than lackluster record. But the administration persisted, and Senate Judiciary Committee confirmation hearings began on September 10. While Thomas proved an uninspired choice, the Democrats on the committee were reluctant to question him too closely, and the chairman, Joseph Biden, seemed more concerned with establishing himself as the American Demosthenes than with learning about the candidate. On September 27 the committee split 7–7 on whether to recommend Thomas's confirmation to the Senate as a whole. The hearings were officially concluded.

Meanwhile, other problems with the nominee were slowly oozing to the surface. A former subordinate of Thomas's at the E.E.O.C., Anita Hill, a law professor at the University of Oklahoma, had earlier that summer after the nomination was announced discussed her history with Thomas. On numerous occasions, she alleged, Thomas had asked her out on dates; rejected, he had spoken to her in his office several times using graphic and often disgusting sexual terminology. Twenty-four at the time she took the position, conservatively reared in rural Oklahoma, Hill had found the assaults so distressing that she had at one point been hospitalized with gastrointestinal symptoms. Eventually she had left to take a position at Oral Roberts University. But she had remained on the job, without making any formal complaint, for a few years (though she had spoken of the incidents with distress to a couple of friends), and had kept in contact with her former boss, calling him once a year or so on professional business.

Exactly how Hill's allegations made it to the Judiciary Committee is still not clear.[1] Reluctant to be brought to public attention, she agreed only under pressure to testify if called. If, in fact, the head of the E.E.O.C. —the government office charged with investigating and dealing with sexual harassment complaints—was himself a harasser, that was no trivial matter. And if a nominee to the Supreme Court had knowingly behaved illegally (since sexual harassment is illegal), that in itself might constitute grounds for disqualification.

As awareness of Hill's allegations swirled through the media, pressure mounted on the Judiciary Committee to reopen the hearings to allow Hill to testify. The full Senate was scheduled to vote on the nomination on Tuesday, October 8; reporters meanwhile were besieging Hill to come forward before the vote was taken. As reports of Hill's claims became public knowledge, anger began to be expressed by all sides against everybody: by feminists against men as harassers and the Judiciary Committee as unconcerned with the issue; by conservatives against unnamed "special interests" who had allegedly leaked the information on Hill to the media; by black male civil rights leaders against Hill for not standing by a black man, whatever he might have done. As one black woman writer put it shortly thereafter in the *New York Times Magazine:* "Hill confronted and ultimately breached a series of taboos in the black community that have survived both slavery and the post-segregation life she and Clarence Thomas share. Anita Hill put her private business on the street, and she downgraded a black man to a room filled with white men who might alter his fate—surely a large enough betrayal for her to be read out of the race" (Bray 1991).

The Judiciary Committee was in a quandary. To reopen their hearings would be extraordinary, perhaps unprecedented. But if they let Hill's allegations go unexamined, they risked antagonizing everybody—both those who wanted the nomination scuttled and those who wanted Thomas honorably confirmed. At first Senate leaders thought of holding closed hearings, but media and public pressure quickly made that a nonviable option. It appeared that if new hearings were not held, Thomas lacked the votes for confirmation. So Biden announced that televised hearings would be held starting Friday, October 11, three days later.

If Hollywood offered one contextualization for the Hill / Thomas fracas in *Thelma and Louise,* Washington itself provided another. The bitterness surrounding the efforts to derail the nomination or bring it to fruition went back over fifteen years, to the Watergate debacle that brought down the Nixon administration. Previously, although the major parties not infrequently disagreed, Republicans and Democrats in Congress tended to behave toward one another with at least a veneer of civility. At least for public consumption they assessed opponents' motives charitably; they referred to one another in terms of orotund flattery: "my esteemed friend on the other side of the aisle," "my worthy opponent." And while the nice talk fooled no one, at least it gave the impression of a government whose members could work amicably together toward common goals. Senators and congressmen frequently served for generations; because choice committee assignments and chairmanships were given out on the basis of seniority, those in power knew each other as friends and were aware of one another's foibles and misbehaviors—which kept them cooperative. Since they expected to serve for many years, they generally considered it impolitic to make deadly enemies of their colleagues over any one piece of legislation—they might need their cooperation another time. Compromise was the rule; legislators went along to get along.

Watergate changed all that. First and most obviously, it created bitterness and suspicion between Republicans and Democrats. The Democrats were horrified at the discovery of the break-in and all that that implied, equally distressed at the idea of Nixon's "enemies list," and upset too at hearing people in the Oval Office plotting like common thugs. The Republicans felt that the whole business was overblown for political purposes, careers deliberately destroyed to gain control of government. The rift brought about by the public downfall of a president (admittedly one few personally liked) left mistrust on both sides and a thirst for revenge on one.

Watergate also left in its wake the desire to reform a system that had almost proved unable to cope with demonstrable governmental malfeasance. Changes were made in the running of Congress. In particular seniority was dispensed with, so that key positions now went to neophytes favored by the party leadership. That brought in new blood and fresh ideas, but removed from power legislators with a long view of history and a familiarity with the way Congress optimally ran. After Watergate there was no longer a shared memory of common purpose, civil discourse, or compromise. Since then every action has been framed as a move in a game of revenge, a quid pro quo, me vs. you.

Nor was Watergate the only irritant in the autumn of 1991. The Republicans remembered the rejection of Supreme Court nominee Robert Bork in 1987. A Reagan nominee, Bork was so right-wing that his opinions distressed even some conservatives. Bork's nomination was defeated by a coalition of civil rights, civil liberties, and feminist groups. Since presidents had until then ordinarily had carte blanche in Supreme Court and Cabinet appointments,[2] Republicans, still smarting from Watergate and its sequelae, saw the undoing of the nomination as a betrayal unique enough to occasion the creation of a verb "to bork," meaning "to subvert a political appointment by stealth." The creation of the word in turn legitimized their feeling that the failure of the nomination was something unprecedented and illegitimate. The Bork defeat was enmeshed in Republican minds with Watergate, as a conspiracy by "liberal special interests" to destroy them, and they itched for revenge, and so were particularly tenacious over the Thomas nomination: to be "borked" so soon again would cap the victory of the sinister (in both senses) forces that were out to get them.

The controversy over language rights (see Chapter 3) was coming to a head around the same time. That had heightened suspicions on both sides, creating a world increasingly polarized into *us* and *them,* who not only did not speak the same language but were fighting over the right to decide whose language would be spoken and what it was to mean. In a direct sense these prolegomena were unrelated: Watergate and Bork were inside-the-Beltway politics that were of little concern to most of us; the p.c. battle was fought mostly among the intelligentsia; and *Thelma and Louise* was only a summer film. But all contributed to the social climate and the discourse it created.

So as the Judiciary Committee assembled in the Senate Caucus Chamber, and all of us gathered before our television sets, on October 11, a sequence of events had come together to produce a narrative into which the hearing and its outcome would be fitted.

THE CLIMATE OF THE HEARINGS

Both sides construed the hearings as Custer's Last Stand, *patria o muerte*. While according to Biden the proceedings were to be nonadversarial, comments from Republican committee members suggested otherwise. It became evident early on that rather than informational "hearings," the events of the weekend of October 11 were more like the opening gambits of a trial, without the appropriate safeguards for witnesses normally part of an adversarial proceeding. Participants were pushing the envelope before the reopened hearings even began, with an astonishing statement from one member of the committee, Alan Simpson, ordinarily a genial if sharp-tongued senator. Speaking to the media on Tuesday, October 8, Simpson said of Hill: "She will be injured and destroyed and belittled and hounded and harassed—real harassment, different than the sexual kind—just plain old Washington-variety harassment, which is pretty— pretty—unique in itself." [3]

This is an extraordinary statement on a couple of counts. In her September 1997 "Dateline" interview, Hill says that she saw Simpson's utterance as "a threat," an interpretation that is perfectly reasonable under the circumstances. To be sure it isn't *explicitly* a threat, since Simpson doesn't say, "I threaten you," and in fact doesn't even state that if Hill goes ahead with X, he will do Y—the typical "threat" formula. But like apologies (see Chapter 1), and for similar reasons, threats are often issued in non-canonical form. Ironically, the greater the power of the issuer to make good on the threat, the more likely the threat is to be expressed indirectly—precisely because the speaker knows that the target will be able to derive the "I will" from context. Simpson, as a powerful Senator and member of the Republican leadership, as well as a member of the Judiciary Committee who will be questioning Hill, is clearly in a position to make good on his promise (and as events later demonstrated, he did his best to do so). In keeping with his powerful status, Simpson's meaning is couched in a syntactic form favored by those seeking to avoid explicit responsibility for troublesome speech acts, the agentless passive ("She *will be injured,*" etc.).

For a threat to be effectual, its utterer must have the means to carry it out and want the addressee to act otherwise than would be the case without the prompting of the utterance. Then, once a speaker is seen by the target to be in such a position of power, any utterance forecasting negative consequences to the addressee, even if not framed explicitly as involving the utterer's own behavior, can be reasonably understood as a threat. (Just as its converse, a promise, can be put into effect under the same conditions, without an explicit statement of promising or explicit first-person reference by the speaker; and just as an apology can be transmitted without any of the explicit material required for its understanding as an apology: in all of these, the context invites these inferences.) This is how we make sense of remarks by movie Mafiosi that contain no overtly threatening material. "Tonight you sleep with the fishes" is not taken as an invitation to sleep over at the speaker's house in the room with the aquarium; the horse's head found by a character in *The Godfather* in his bed is not interpreted as a generous gift ("The Godfather knows how much I like horses, and while he couldn't afford the whole horse . . ."). So while technically Simpson's words could be construed as a kindly warning or a simple prediction, the fact that Simpson was in a position to make the prophecy come true and had a motive to do so makes them interpretable in this context as a threat.

That is pretty astonishing in itself. Here is a prominent U.S. senator, about to act as a juror in a quasi-trial proceeding, threatening a witness! In a normal trial, such behavior—on nationwide TV, no less—would occasion at the very least his removal from the deliberative body and perhaps criminal sanctions. Even if we accept Biden's declaration that the proceeding is only a nonadversarial "hearing," a threat by a member of the fact-finding body is an infraction. The purpose of a hearing is to find the truth through sworn witness testimony. Anything that is likely to interfere with this aim should be subject to penalty and render the proceedings null and void, just as, in a real trial, it provides grounds for a mistrial. Threatening a witness is an obvious way to discourage truthful testimony and therefore could readily be seen, since witnesses at Senate hearings are under oath, as suborning perjury—a criminal offense.

Even more seriously, Simpson appears to be prejudging a very important part of the testimony he is to hear. A lot hinges on the decision: what is sexual harassment, and how seriously should it be taken? Juror-equivalents should be entering the proceedings with an open mind on these questions. Yet Simpson refers to "real harassment, different than the sexual kind," a statement that makes the presupposition that the "sexual kind," the kind Hill is alleging, isn't "real." So even if her charges should prove to have a basis in fact, at least one member of the committee has announced his verdict in advance. "Verdict first—evidence afterwards," as the Queen of Hearts put it in *Alice in Wonderland*.

INTERPRETATION, META-INTERPRETATION, AND NARRATIVE CONTROL

When an event changes our understanding of our world, ourselves, and each other, its meaning is never fully apparent as it unfolds. The story itself is intelligible and available for discussion: it has meaning in and of itself. But that might be called "raw meaning," unprocessed, not reflected upon, without depth or texture. You could see the American body politic as similar to a cow's in having several stomachs, into each of which fodder travels and through each of which in turn it must go in order to emerge, at the end, fully digested—understood and given a generally agreed upon meaning. Typically a galvanizing event (like Hill/Thomas, or the O. J. Simpson trial, to be discussed in Chapter 6) achieves its complete meaning only in the fullness of time, after it has been evaluated and reevaluated by a variety of commentators and meta-commentators (people commenting, as I am here, on the commentators). So the final understanding of Hill/Thomas, should that ever occur, would be an amalgam of five levels. Level 1 is the original happening itself (as experienced by all but the immediate participants via newspaper transcripts and live TV coverage). Level 2 occurs with contemporaneous newspaper accounts, both news and editorials, which synthesize and abstract the gist for readers, and thus provide a first digestion of meaning. Level 3 includes weekly magazines with a longer lead time in which to reflect on what the story is about and what is important about it. At Level 4 are monthly magazines with still longer lead times, which can publish long articles or groups of articles that provide a broad and deep view of the events. Finally, Level 5 comprises scholarly journal articles and the like, reflecting (often years later) on the meaning of the event and the effects it has had on our lives.

The construction of an event's meaning is a collaboration between the actions of the participants themselves, later interpreters, and finally, all of us, both makers of meaning (in that we choose our media and may accept some takes and reject others) and receivers of it. And just as the interpretations we assign to events are outgrowths of our culture and made

through its perspectives, so these events—the ones that pass the UAT—
contribute to that culture, altering, enriching, and complicating it.

THE HEARING PROPER (BUT NOT ESPECIALLY)

It may have seemed to the typical American television viewer, switching
on the tube to catch the Hill/Thomas hearings the weekend of October 11-13, 1991, that the format itself, the Senate Judiciary Committee
Hearing, was without any meaning of its own, merely a means of providing interpretive spin for one side or the other. Congress has been holding hearings for two hundred years; surely within that time it must have
evolved a canonical form for these events. But that is not the case. The
form the hearing took, indeed, its very identification in terms of discourse
genre, remained malleable throughout, with problematic consequences
for many participants and observers.

The *hearing* is a distinct form with its own rules of procedure, unlike
a trial in both function and structure. Formal discourse types (like both
of these) make use of their formalisms to protect both weaker and
stronger participants. This is essential in adversarial trials. But it is perhaps even more important that hearings be conducted according to
strictly laid out procedures, since one of the protections afforded com-
batants in courtroom trials is notably absent here: the active participation of an attorney. It is true that Hill had attorneys present at all times
during her testimony. But they were not permitted to act like lawyers
at trial: they could not deliver opening statements or closing arguments,
make objections, or examine witnesses. Thus Hill was essentially unde-
fended. But (as discussed by Wiegand 1996) that was only the first problem caused by the committee's confusion about just what kind of discourse they were engaging in.

If both parties in a contest are of equal strength, genre crossing may
not be a problem. But in these hearings, Hill was pretty clearly in a
weaker position (despite claims to the contrary by Thomas's partisans).
For one thing (as was perhaps not realized immediately, but became clear
as the hearing progressed and opinion polls were taken), her side was
sociopsychologically less defensible. In a struggle that was played as feminism vs. civil rights, race trumped gender. In theory, both women and
blacks are equally disadvantaged in late-twentieth-century American society, so each was equally deserving of special consideration. But events
proved that Hill's champions, the Democrats, were terrified of being cast

as racist, a fear both Thomas and his defenders hastened to exploit. Thomas on a couple of occasions referred to the proceedings as a "lynching"; he and the Republicans regularly emphasized his race and the disadvantages that that had exposed him to in life, playing "the race card" for all it was worth. On their part, the Democrats were unwilling or unable to place corresponding emphasis on a "gender card." Or perhaps there is no "gender card." Certainly the Republicans didn't worry about sounding sexist.

As a nominee for Supreme Court justice, Thomas had an edge on Hill. Anyone in that position, photographed standing beside a beaming president, enjoys a heightened status, as demonstrated by early polls among both blacks and whites favoring his confirmation—despite the tepid approval, at best, of both the American Bar Association and the NAACP.[4]

The two sides had achieved very different degrees of organization in preparation for the fight. While the Democrats held a majority in the Senate, and therefore on the committee, which was also chaired by a Democrat, the Republicans acted and voted as a bloc, while the Democrats were split: Senator Dennis DeConcini, a Democrat, voted with the Republicans to recommend Thomas for confirmation, creating the 7–7 tie. Thomas had a strong advocate in Senator John Danforth, while Hill had no personal champion. And while all the Republicans on the committee expressed strong partisanship in their questioning in favor of Thomas, the Democrats were scattered and ineffectual. Senator Edward Kennedy, injured by his own personal sexual indiscretions, played virtually no role in the proceedings. Joseph Biden was still laboring under an accusation that he had plagiarized a speech by a British Member of Parliament and perhaps as a result was given to perorations as relentless as they were irrelevant, as if to prove that he *was so* a terrific orator in his own right. A conservative Democrat, Howell Heflin of Alabama, was selected to lead the questioning of Hill as a sympathetic partisan. But reading the colloquy between him and Hill in the hearing transcript, it is difficult not to see him as a fifth column, his questions undercutting Hill and offering the Republicans an opening wedge. The Democrats seemed uncertain what to do with Hill. Rather than guide her through her story and work with her to make a powerful and compelling narrative, they left her on her own to twist slowly in the wind. That nonetheless she created a spellbinding story and made a persuasive case attests to her sincerity and personal strength. Thomas, on the other hand, had been coached heavily from the moment of his nomination; had three months' time to prepare, as opposed to Hill's scant three days; and was questioned with much more support and sympathy by Republicans, and much less hostility by Democrats, than was the case for Hill (mutatis mutandis).

Finally, Thomas was a long-time Washington insider. That meant not only that he had friends inside the Beltway, but that he knew the ropes, was conversant with the procedures of the Senate, and was familiar with members of the media. Hill, aside from her brief stay in Washington many years earlier, was an outsider, with little support and not much knowledge of how things were done on Capitol Hill. And since those who come into a discourse with greater power tend to amass still more power, Thomas's initial advantages snowballed once Hill began her testimony.

The obscuring of genre lines creates a fertile soil for abuse of the less by the more powerful participants in a discourse.[5] As onerous and constricting as formal rules may be, they keep interactions from degenerating into screaming matches or kangaroo courts. The precisions of the courtroom, the careful adherence to rules about who may speak, when, to whom, and of what and in which way, at least partially protect defendants from being bulldozed by representatives of the state. Constitutional guarantees—the right to confront and cross-examine witnesses, the presumption of innocence, the requirement that guilt be proved "beyond a reasonable doubt," the exclusion of most hearsay testimony, the presence of a neutral judge to arbitrate—help to deflect a jury's natural rush to judgment, its desire to "solve" the crime by finding the defendant guilty. As we are too well aware, sometimes these safeguards fail. But more often they work to bring about a reasonable semblance of justice.

When lines are crossed, when the properties of two kinds of discourse are confused, problems arise. Even when the discourse types are aesthetic categories—such as fiction and memoir, as discussed in Chapter 1 —confusion and suspicion arise. But when fiction gets puzzling, the reader can put the book aside with no harm done. Things get more serious when the discourse is world-changing—has consequences for at least one of the participants, generally the defendant in a criminal trial. If that person's ability to affect the course of the discussion is unfairly interfered with, injustice results. The outcome may be greeted with glee by the community (which can justify abuse as allowing the punishment of miscreants who might otherwise have "gotten off on legal technicalities"), but misuse of language with world-changing consequences is corrosive to the meanings we construct and the social contract we live by. Just as lying is dangerous because it diminishes the trust of a language-using species in language, so obfuscation of the boundaries between discourse genres makes us less willing to abide by the conventions human societies have created to ensure their survival.

But the biggest problem may have been that the chairman of the Judiciary Committee, who was responsible for the conduct of the hearing, was never quite sure how to define the procedure that he was overseeing. He had some ideas to be sure about what it *wasn't:* it was not a forum about sexual harassment in America, and it was not a trial. It was, he said vaguely, "a hearing convened for a specific purpose, to air specific allegations against one specific individual, allegations which may be true or may not be true" (Anita Miller 1994, 10). But Biden failed to keep his committee even to that level of specificity. Thomas, in particular, was allowed to range wide of the mark. Biden went on:

> Because this is not a trial, the proceedings will not be conducted the way in which a sexual harassment trial would be handled in a court of law. For example, on the advice of the nonpartisan Senate legal counsel, the rules of evidence that apply in courtrooms will not apply here today. Thus, evidence and questions that would not be permitted in a court of law must, under Senate rules, be allowed here (10).

This statement seemingly allows for anything anyone wants to introduce, as proved true in the Republicans' questioning of Hill. For instance, Biden let Arlen Specter "speculate" at length, as would never be permitted a witness or an attorney in a trial.

SEN. SPECTER: [to witnesses] But can you women shed any light on the possibility that Professor Hill might have had an attachment or a feeling which would have led her to think about these things?
          Senator Hatch yesterday put into the record some speculation, and that is what we are doing here, pure and simple. (342)

The presence of an attorney who could make objections might have prevented such flights of fancy. But since the process was defined as non-adversarial, the assumption was that none was necessary. Yet the procedure clearly was adversarial from the start—as Senator Simpson's veiled threat made perfectly clear. And while Thomas's proponents were permitted great latitude in questioning witnesses about Hill's character and mental health, Thomas was allowed to exclude all "personal" topics— such as his reputed interest in pornography, a claim that bore directly on Hill's charges. Nancy Fraser (1992) suggests that the differential treatment of Hill's and Thomas's personal privacy reflected a gender-based distinction: since women can't control their privacy, it was relatively easy to introduce private matters about Hill into the public record; men, on the other hand, traditionally assume the right to determine which aspects of their lives are to be kept "private," a privilege implicitly granted to Thomas. Because this differential treatment was based on presupposed gender stereotypes, it seemed "normal," rather than perversely skewed.[6]

Although in most ways the Republicans were prosecutorial, in one way they crossed over and behaved toward Hill as a defense attorney in a criminal trial would act toward prosecution witnesses (further confusing the discourse). A trial is the creation and testing of a narrative: how the crime came to be committed. It is the job of the prosecution to create this narrative, and the job of the defense to undermine its purported coherency. But in questioning Hill the Republicans acted like defense attorneys, trying to demolish her narrative. On the other hand, Thomas provided no narrative beyond "it never happened," a claim never vigorously contested by the Democrats.

Erica Verrillo (1996, 73) says that Hill was "powerfully aided" in the making of her narrative by Democrats Biden and Patrick Leahy, who directed her through questions like, "Can you lay out the sequence of events that brought you forward?" or asking her to "walk through" those events. But her narrative's coherency was promptly challenged. When his turn came, Arlen Specter (a state attorney general in his prior life) tried to dismantle its logical sequence and thus discredit it, suggesting that her recollections were the products of fantasy and expressing incredulity that a woman who had been harassed *could have* followed her harasser to a new job or maintained cordial relations with him after she left his employ. Since Thomas provided no narrative of his own for the Democrats to attack, the effect of discrediting Hill's was to weaken Hill's disproportionately. Competent lawyers look out for their clients' interests. But Hill's putative defenders often seemed to be doing just the reverse, especially Howell Heflin. According to Timothy Phelps and Helen Winternitz (1992, 292), the Democrats chose Heflin as a principal questioner because of his reputation as a savvy interrogator, and because, as one of the most conservative of the Southern Democrats, if he played a prominent role he might bring other conservative Democrats, and even Republicans, to their side. But Heflin seemed to be illustrating the phrase "you just don't get it." His questioning of Hill rehashed misogynistic stereotypes which, once brought up, could be and were eagerly made use of by the Republicans.

SEN. HEFLIN: [to Anita Hill]: Now, in trying to determine whether you are telling falsehoods or not, I have got to determine what your motivation might be. Are you a scorned woman?

MS. HILL: No.

SEN. HEFLIN: Are you a zealoting civil rights believer that progress will be turned back, if Clarence Thomas goes on the Court?

MS. HILL: No, I don't—I think that—I have my opinion, but I don't think that progress will be turned back. I think that civil rights will prevail, no matter what happens with the Court.

SEN. HEFLIN: Do you have a militant attitude relative to the area of civil rights?

MS. HILL: No, I don't have a militant attitude.

SEN. HEFLIN: Do you have a martyr complex?

MS. HILL: No, I don't. [Laughter.] (Anita Miller 1994, 66)

Whatever Heflin believed he was doing here, his questions raised suspicions about Hill that the Republicans could capitalize on later. The "Snark Rule" is at work—the more times it is alleged that someone might be telling "falsehoods," the harder that accusation will be to dislodge.

Covert presumptions affecting senatorial and public perceptions of Hill and Thomas receive other kinds of differential treatment. Racial stereotyping—the myth of the hypersexual and threatening black male—is explicitly explored and thus at least partially defused as a threat to Thomas; but many stereotypes of women, black and white, are invoked without explicit examination: women as liars, fantasizers, hysterics, and malleable dupes. Typically, Hill is damned if she conforms to one of these stereotypes and damned if she doesn't (because if she doesn't, she's not a good—i.e., normal—woman).

As "the other," women, like blacks, are readily generalized.[7] It is easy to see them en masse, without the individual traits that evoke empathy and understanding. Because they are not us, we find it difficult to identify with them and understand their complaints. And as them, women are subject to interpretation on our part—we make sense of them, and not vice versa. Thus when Thomas makes long speeches telling his audience how life is, and who he is, and what everything means, the audience considers this normal, since he has become an honorary member of us for these proceedings. But Hill is not permitted to interpret: interpretations are made of her, which means that she will be perceived as aberrant (since interpretation is concerned with what is strange, not what is normal): she is, as Heflin suggests, either a "scorned woman," a "zealot," a "martyr," or as others are to suggest, a fantasist or a dupe—bad, mad, or had. As a woman speaking in public, Hill is marked—anything she says will sound odd and inappropriate.

The blackness of Hill and Thomas is treated and mythologized in different ways. We project out onto them traits we detest in ourselves or hope we do not possess but fear we do. In this society (astonishing as it may seem in an age of exuberant sexual expression) we remain afraid that sexuality reduces us to animality and deprives us of rational control. So for a very long time the culture has situated uncontrolled "hypersexuality" in *them*—both women and blacks.[8] The awareness of this country's horrible history of attributing hypersexuality to black males and punishing them for it by lynching made many Democrats wary of finding a black man guilty of an apparently sexual offense.[9] It is less well appreciated that black women are also the victims of white sexual stereotyping (but see Fiske 1996, 75ff., and Fraser 1992, 604, for insightful discussion of the point). John Fiske (1996) suggests that the Republicans, anxious to desexualize Thomas, worked to hypersexualize Hill. (Ironically, while the Republicans were representing themselves as the party of civil rights, in their insistence on black hypersexuality in *one* of the participants they were representing and modeling one of the viler racist myths of the culture.)[10] So the Republicans deliberately flogged "pubic hair" in order to play down "Long Dong Silver," attributing the former to Hill's hypersexual "fantasies." And since pubic hair is grosser than a penis, she comes out doubly the loser.

And Nancy Fraser (1992, 604) notes that, at the same time the white committee has created her as the representative of black female hypersexuality (a stereotype that has permitted white men to make use of their female slaves and other black female subordinates on the pretext that they enjoy it), Hill is construed by the black community as a renegade, "functionally white." To appreciate Thomas's repeated references to "lynching," the hearer must imagine the woman whose assault justifies the lynching. The only woman available to us is Hill. But lynching was only done to avenge injury to a white woman. So . . . Hill must be white! And since, to many in the black community, she participated in the sexual disgracing of a black man before an all-white tribunal, she can no longer be black—she must be not merely white, but a traitor to African Americans.

HE SAID, SHE SAID, SEZ WHO?

The events of October 11–13, 1991, unfolded within preordained meanings and understandings, intended and otherwise. Within the scope of these interpretations, what the participants said, what they could say, and how their utterances were framed by the speech of other participants made meaning—that is, formed the basis of what we now know as "Hill/ Thomas." The images are graven in our imaginations: how Thomas and Hill sat in the Caucus Chamber, how they regarded their questioners, their voices, their dress (Hill's turquoise suit, "prim" yet elegant, has become iconic). The totality, verbal and otherwise, creates the narrative we remember as Hill/Thomas.

In theory the question before the committee was: who's telling the truth? But for many participants a more crucial question was: who's in control? Both sides recognized early the importance of maintaining control over the Q-and-A, although the Republicans recognized it better, or acted on the recognition more effectively. It was important to let certain questions get asked and answered, others not; important to enable or force each speaker to present him or herself in a particular way, so as to come across as sympathetic or not, truthful or otherwise. Their stories had to be represented as coherent and hence plausible, or chaotic and therefore lies or fantasies. Much depended on the management of the dialogue by the questioners.

In many kinds of talk, to ask a question is a sign of weakness, of needing something—information. Therefore the one who provides the answers tends to be the speaker in control. In a classroom, for instance, questions from students are permitted only at specified points and are answered directly or tangentially, in whole or in part, or dismissed. In other kinds of talk there is more balance. At a news conference, the president can call on reporters or not; can answer in as much detail as he wishes and as many questions as he wishes; can end the whole colloquy at his will. But reporters can, once recognized, ask anything at all, and the president's failure to answer a potentially embarrassing question adequately can guarantee its appearance and detailed analysis on the evening news. There is a standoff between the two sides, an adversarial symbiosis.

Hearings, trials, and other truth-seeking procedures assign most of the power to the questioner. Typically the respondent is there at the behest of the questioners and is not free to dismiss questioners or to refuse to answer, and if the answers are not satisfactory, the questioners may persist until they get what they want. As I have noted, in a trial, witnesses and defendants are safeguarded from being forced to answer prejudicial or otherwise unfair questions through objections by counsel and rulings by the judge. But since a hearing is defined as nonadversarial, no such protection is provided, beyond wrangling among committee members about whether specific questions may be asked or need to be answered. Because the committee chair is in charge of these determinations, it might at first be thought that the Democrats, and Hill, enjoyed an advantage. But since Biden proved largely ineffectual, the Republicans got away with much broader and deeper questioning of Hill than the Democrats had in interrogating Thomas.

The Q-and-A of the hearing was the first, most concrete level of meaning-creation. It matters greatly whether the principal witnesses were treated similarly. Two conversation analysts who have studied this aspect of the hearing reach radically different answers to the question: who won?

Norma Mendoza-Denton (1995) interprets the dialogue to argue that Hill was sandbagged by the committee. She provides evidence that Thomas enjoyed much freer rein in the construction of the discourse than Hill and that Thomas's answers were treated with more respect than Hill's (thus conveying to the larger audience, as well as to the respondents themselves, that he was being taken more seriously). Thomas was permitted significantly greater gap length between the end of his statements and the next utterance by a committee member than was Hill (1.386 vs. 1.046 seconds). Temporal space is metaphorically equivalent to physical space: you "give space" to those you respect; you crowd in on people who don't matter or whom you wish to intimidate. (In a courtroom a judge may instruct a cross-examining attorney to step back in order to avoid intimidating a witness by mere physical proximity.) While the numbers given and the difference between them may seem trivial, pauses and gaps in conversations are highly constrained: this culture is very averse to silence, and a gap of much over a second will be felt as an aberration. Moreover, control over conversational space belongs to the person who holds the floor—the speaker—from the moment his or her utterance begins until the moment the next speaker starts a turn. So by leaving more space after Thomas's turns, the committee gave him more control over the conversation as well as giving him the appearance of power—neither of which options was offered to Hill.

Questions addressed to Hill took the form of tags more frequently than did those to Thomas. A tag is a sentence type that has both the form and function of a combined declarative plus question. In form, a tag is a declarative sentence with a question appended at the end; in function, a tag both asserts information and questions it. Some typical examples are (the "tag" part is italicized):

John's your brother, *isn't he?*
You didn't eat that, *did you?*
Tomorrow is Wednesday, *right?*
We should do that, *don't you think?*

Or, to take a case from the hearing transcript:

SEN. SPECTER: Professor Hill, you testified that you drew an inference that Judge
Thomas might want you to look at pornographic films, but you
told the FBI specifically that he never asked you to watch the
films, *is that correct?* (Mendoza-Denton 1995, 56).

Tags have been of great interest to linguists over the last thirty years,
both for their complicated formal syntactic properties and for their
equally intricate functional behavior. An argument can be made that the
only reason that a grammar would contain a complicated rule like tag
question formation is that tags represent extremely complex and diverse
communicative functions. Until well into the 1970's we were unable to
comprehend the prevalence of ambiguity in language, and if we talked
about the function of tags at all, we tried to assign all of them a single
function. For example, I suggested in the early 1970's that tags represented a strategy of the conversationally less powerful. The user of a tag
was giving information with one hand and removing herself from that
authoritative role with the other. Tags might also be a favored mode of
questioning for the less dominant because they demanded a response,
where a normal yes/no question could be ignored.[11]

But it was soon apparent, as we started to develop functional theories
of grammar, that ambiguity was much more common in language than
had been assumed: not a rarity, but almost a typical situation. The complex structure of tags encourages their use in diverse contexts. So one
might use a tag in case one was pretty sure, but not absolutely certain,
of getting an anticipated answer; or as a means of providing information
without looking pushy; or as a way of eliciting responses from reluctant
interlocutors, whether powerful or bashful, even if answering might go
against their interests. In the last use, a tag emphasizes the power of
the questioner to force a response. Particularly if a questioner wants to
highlight the inappropriateness of a woman speaking in public at all, let
alone making accusations against a man, the use of tags to her (and not
to him) would suggest her weakness and incompetence: she has to answer, but she must be prompted to do so. Mendoza-Denton notes that
Thomas was asked significantly more simple yes/no questions than Hill

(53 percent vs. 37 percent of total questions), and that Hill got significantly more tags (27 percent vs. 17 percent of the total). The 27 percent figure is particularly remarkable since tags are relatively infrequent, especially in formal circumstances. Most of the remaining questions to Hill were declaratives functioning as questions, as in the following interchange, cited in the same passage by Mendoza-Denton:

SEN. SPECTER: That's something he might have wanted you to do but the fact
                is flatly, he never asked you to look at pornographic movies
                with him.
MS. HILL: With him? No, he did not.

As Hill's response shows, she correctly interpreted the declarative as a question requiring an answer. Like tags, these types signal the power of the speaker over the addressee: "I can compel you to answer even without having to resort to the apparent weakness of asking a real question."

Thomas was permitted a number of authoritative devices that Hill was not. Thus Thomas was asked many questions that permitted terse responses: "yes," or "no," while Hill was encouraged to go on at length. While on the one hand a longer response can be a sign of power, terseness—especially in cases in which a response could be damaging to its speaker—can signify control, the ability to mete out just as much information as the speaker sees fit and to hold the floor for only as long as the speaker deems necessary. Also, a simple "yes" or "no," under these conditions, suggests truthfulness and an absence of guile. But many of the questions asked of Hill involved complex presuppositions and other backgrounded matter, which Hill had to deal with—refute or explain— before she could provide a meaningful "yes," or "no." Such answers tended to make Hill look to some as though she were prevaricating, or fuzzy-minded.

Speakers in control of the dialogue typically expect to get their responses acknowledged by interlocutors, if only by a "yes" or "mm-hm." Some of us remember teachers or parents who insisted on full verbal responses to their questions or requests—as a sign of attention and respect. So it should not be surprising that Mendoza-Denton found that Thomas's answers were acknowledged explicitly 50 percent of the time, whereas with Hill, her responses were followed 46 percent of the time by explicit *non*-acknowledgment—a total change of topic. Additionally, Mendoza-Denton says, Thomas was allowed to exploit a variety of black discourse styles (what Smitherman 1995b refers to as "testifyin, sermonizin and signifyin"), while Hill was not. That both gave Thomas authority and power (since these styles are rhetorically potent) and further allied him to the black community and severed Hill from it.

Denise Troutman-Robinson (1995) makes the opposite claim: by making implicit use of black speech patterns, for which the all-white committee members were unprepared, Hill achieved control of the discourse. For instance, in the first round of questioning Hill manages to interrupt even her most persistent antagonist more than he could interrupt her: she interrupts Specter 69 percent of the time (in nine turns), while he interrupts her only 31 percent of the time (four turns). Troutman-Robinson suggests that Specter and his colleagues, expecting Hill to behave like a polite white woman, who is much more apt to relinquish the floor when challenged, were unable to cope with a black woman who assumed the same discourse rights as a man.

Troutman-Robinson suggests that Hill gained power by using an "agonistic" style—a form of "learned assertiveness"—common among black speakers, male and female, but unfamiliar to the larger community. African Americans traditionally had only language with which to empower themselves and had to use it cleverly to straddle the line between empowerment and endangerment. So Hill's "calm, formal" style not only was more appropriate than the emotional style some commentators retrospectively urged on her, but was one to which the committee found it difficult to respond without losing power themselves.

Troutman-Robinson's arguments are attractive, but they fail to explain why Hill's testimony received unfavorable reviews, not only from members of the majority community (e.g., Noonan 1991 and Thernstrom 1991), but especially from black women (cf. Bray 1992; Crenshaw 1992; Grier 1995; Hare and Hare 1992; Jackson 1992; and Malveaux 1992). When we look at the discourse of the hearing as a whole, we find many ways in which, intentionally or otherwise, her interrogators forced her speech into a format that would show her in a less attractive and believable light and encourage the perception of Hill as crazy or dangerous.

For one thing—a common problem for women—overinterpretation of her performance took language out of her control, denying her right to make public meaning. She was relentlessly described, often in terminology that went beyond the mere recitation of physical traits and moved into psychological and characterological attributions. An article in *The New York Times* (Dowd 1991) exemplifies the way in which she was treated. Although the article contrasts Hill's and Thomas's testimony, Thomas receives almost no description other than a brief summary of his speech style: "After a day in which Judge Thomas succeeded in cow-ing the skeptical Democrats on the panel, blasting them with a gale of words about a bruising process. . . ." But Hill and her testimony receive a lengthy analytical description:

> In trying to discredit Anita F. Hill, Clarence Thomas and his supporters have portrayed many faces of the Oklahoma Law School Professor.
>
> Indeed, they painted so many pictures that some of them seemed contradictory. She was said to be malleable enough to become the tool of special interest groups or, on the other hand, so strongly opinionated that she would stomp out of meetings if she did not get her way. His supporters have suggested that she was a troubled woman who fantasized about a relationship with him that did not exist, and, on the other hand, that she was an ambitious woman with her eye ever on her career. . . .
>
> One witness described her as stridently aggressive; another as reserved. They all called her aloof; yet J. C. Alvarez . . . suggested that she might want to turn her experience before the Senate into a book or a movie, saying she wanted to be "the Rosa Parks of sexual harassment." . . .
>
> While one witness, Phyllis Berry, gave her theory, without illustration, that Professor Hill might have had a crush on Judge Thomas, Ms. Alvarez said that the two were not romantically interested in each other at all.
>
> A third, Nancy Fitch, . . . suggested that . . . perhaps Professor Hill was engaged in "transference."

It's the same old story: mad, bad, or had. And although these characterizations, as Dowd suggests, appear contradictory, their creators seem to have no problem entertaining them all. And in a larger sense they are not contradictory. All are ways of characterizing a woman who is speaking out of turn, where she has no right to be. Such a person is simply an aberration, and the particular form that the aberration takes is not especially relevant. The important thing is that she be discredited as an uppity woman, a credit neither to her race nor her sex. Each of the descriptions, although superficially contradictory, works with the others to establish this point. Similarly, Hill is described by her detractors both as lesbian (Simpson's allegation of "proclivities") and as heterosexually voracious (John Doggett's testimony that she pursued him). These claims, too, may seem logically contradictory. But they are not, if by "lesbian" and "voracious heterosexual" we understand *a woman whose sexuality is deployed for her own pleasure, not that of men.* The very fact that she is continually being subject to the descriptions of others (the witnesses; the senators; reporters like Dowd) rather than being allowed to describe herself or not, as she sees fit, mark her again as a woman (and so automatically out of line in playing the role she had chosen).

The other participants seem uncertain even how to address or refer to her. While Thomas is addressed and referred to almost exclusively as

Judge Thomas, she receives a great variety of names. While the Senators generally address her as "Professor Hill" (a title equivalent to Thomas's "Judge"), they refer to her variously as "Miss Hill," "Ms. Hill," and "Anita Hill." Thomas in particular finds it almost impossible to call her by her honorific title. Even when he is prompted by a senator referring to her as "Professor," he generally responds with either "Miss Hill," "Anita," or "Anita Hill." She always refers to him as "Judge Thomas."

When Thomas speaks, he is permitted to define the scope and nature of the discourse, as well as to instruct the committee (and the audience) about who he is and how he feels about the situation. She remains calm and measured; his typical response is one of outrage. Students of human emotions, from Shakespeare ("Methinks the lady doth protest too much") to psychologist Paul Ekman, note that a show of anger, particularly if it is outsize or inappropriate, may be a cover for guilt.[12] If so, Thomas wins the contest hands down; yet his explosions are seldom cited as indications of guilt or as inappropriate at all. Hill's responses are usually specific and to the point, directly responsive to the question asked. Thomas's are general, bombastic, and moralistic: the prerogative of the powerful person with public meaning-making rights. Generalization and moving outside the topic at hand are good strategies for the untruthful, occupying time and discourse space without saying anything risky. Thomas is sullen, resentful, supercilious to his questioners, the embodiment of smug virtue assailed. Hill is quiet, composed, unfailingly polite and modest.

In his opening statement to the committee, Thomas refers to his "hurt, pain, [and] agony." "My family and I have been done a grave and irreparable injustice." "This is not American," he says. "This is Kafka-esque. It has got to stop. It must stop for the benefit of future nominees, and our country. Enough is enough" (Anita Miller 1994, 16f.). He feels put upon: "Little did I know the price, but it is too high." "There is nothing this committee, this body or this country can do to give me my good name back, nothing." He sets the rules, an unusual power for a witness: "I will not provide the rope for my own lynching, or for further humiliation. I am not going to engage in discussions, nor will I submit to roving questions of what goes on in the most intimate parts of my private life or the sanctity of my bedroom" (17f.).

Thus within the first few moments of the hearing Thomas takes control: *he* speaks for "our country," which his reticence is shielding. He quotes a common proverb, the embodiment of familiar and trustworthy folk wisdom. He demands reparation even as he denies that redress is possible. He sets up an adversarial situation between himself and the senators and warns them not to transgress (or they will be branded as racists: the "lynching" metaphor). And he explicitly specifies what he may be asked and what he may not. *And no member of the committee takes him up on the challenge.*

INTERPRETATIONS OF EVENTS;
OR, DIFFERENT TAKES BY DIFFERENT FAKES

Some critics of Hill and her performance suggest that she orchestrated her own downfall by being genteel, polite, and calm. Especially combined with her failure to act strongly to stop the harassment when it first occurred, her gentleness now conveys not rationality and reasonableness, but "aloofness," primness, unengagement—a lack of involvement that could only mean the events never took place. She is transformed into a representative of the elite, deserving of the contempt of real Americans. Thus Peggy Noonan (1991) sets up a distinction between "normal" —that is, working class, truthful—people, and Hill and her allies, who are neither normal nor credible:

> I believe I perceive a total perceptual split between the chattering classes . . . and normal humans, people who work in laundromats and oddly enough weren't invited to the hearing room—a class division, in a way, between clever people who talk loudly in restaurants and those who seat them.
>
> You could see it in the witnesses. For Anita Hill, the professional, movement-y and intellectualish Susan Hoerchner, who spoke with a sincere, unmakeupped face of inherent power imbalances in the workplace. For Clarence Thomas, the straight-shooting, Maybellined J. C. Alvarez. . . . Really, it was no contest. Ms. Alvarez was the voice of the real, as opposed to the abstract, America: she was like a person who if a boss ever sexually abused her would kick him in the gajoobies and haul him straight to court.

Noonan came into public prominence as the Great Communicator's Great Communicator. A perusal of the above makes clear how she achieved her effects. As she did for Reagan and Bush, she sets up a split between the "normal" hardworking *us,* the working class, and the "clever," restaurant-patronizing, and otherwise dubious *them,* the middle class. Curiously, this piece appeared on the Op-Ed page of the *New York Times* —hardly the reading of the masses. It's hard to know whom Noonan is appealing to here, but certainly the reader is cajoled— or gajoobie-kicked—into disowning any affiliation with the "clever" or "chattering classes" who form the Anita Hill entourage. There are shocking juxtapositions and transposals. We read of Susan Hoerchner's "sincere, unmakeupped" face" and think: That's good! Sincerity is good! But then it turns out, contrary to our belief system (and therefore both superficially profound and memorably shocking) that the one in the makeup, "Maybellined," is the *really real* one, the one who is direct, physical, and not "abstract," that is "intellectualish." [13] (Anti-intellectualism was always the first refuge of the Know-Nothing.) Somehow, Hill's dirt-poor lower-working-class background has been transmogrified into the "chattering class" that talks too loudly in restaurants; Thomas, on the other hand, along with Noonan herself, is good old working class. (Can you be a White House speech writer, or head of the E.E.O.C., and a member of the working class? If you can mythologize fast enough, you can.)

As for "kick[ing the boss] in the gajoobies," that sort of comment is frequent on the anti-Hill side. Why did she put up with it? Why didn't she say something definitively crushing,[14] or retaliate physically, or haul the bastard into court? The possibilities make tasty fantasy fodder, but they ignore the real reality of the workplace and the justice system. An article in the *Los Angeles Times* by Laurie Becklund (1991) relates several experiences of real women and considers their options, among which are included neither lawsuits nor kicks in anyone's gajoobies. Sometimes they solve the problem with forceful language; sometimes, when they complain, they are fired or told they are just being "childish." But there's no way to tell in advance how things will work out.

Why didn't Hill take her harasser to court? Quite aside from the fact that the defendant was the head of the agency that would normally have been involved on the plaintiff's side in any litigation, myths outrun realities about the working of the justice system. It was essential in the early 1980's—more than now, thanks in great measure to Hill—to have an utterly ironclad case, involving at least one of (1) nonconsensual physical assault; (2) demotion or quid pro quo; (3) repeated verbal assaults in the presence of witnesses. Otherwise no sensible lawyer would have taken the case, and most trial judges would have thrown it out on a summary judgment. It would have been almost impossible to convince a typical jury that he wasn't "just flirting," or that she wasn't an exaggerating hysteric. Even if we discount these realities, civil cases normally take years to come to court. Could Hill have tolerated the situation that long? And in suing, she might well have rendered herself unemployable in the future, as a troublemaker.

Suppose, for the sake of argument, that there does exist a plausible way to stop harassment without retribution. Even so, Hill should not be penalized for not using it. A point too little noted is that, if everyone is to have full workplace and public equality, then no one should be subjected to behavior that others are not; and no one should be *expected* to cope with mistreatment to which others are immune. So let us grant, again for the sake of argument, that it is always possible, and always admirable, to put a stop to harassment by one of the methods Noonan sanctions. Why should the victim of the harassment be expected to run further risks by taking steps to end it? Why is it her fault if, for reasons of upbringing or personality, she feels unable to do so? These interpretations are indulged in by people sitting securely in their homes, at their word processors, writing and reflecting in peaceful serenity. Often these critics are considerably older and more worldly than the then twenty-four-year-old Hill, barely out of law school and just a few years away from conservative Oklahoma, where women don't talk back to their male bosses. The clever retorts a forty- or fifty-year-old woman can think of, and the poise required for delivering them effectively, are a lot to ask of someone in Hill's position. And we know all too well "l'esprit d'escalier"—the tendency to think of the perfect cutting riposte when it's too late to deliver it. Sure, all of us can come up with le mot juste in the privacy and comfort of our homes. But how many of us could do so at the moment of impact, in the boss's imposing office, as he looms over you? Unless you're absolutely sure you could actually do what Hill could not, the word on the street is *Put up or shut up.*

Other second-guessers more charitably see Hill as truthful but undermined by her self-presentation. To them, she failed to fit her testimony into the style of the stereotypical wronged woman: angry, tearful, pleading for redress. In this view, a woman who has suffered as Hill has must act in a particular way—must be "womanly" before she can be credible. There may be a grain of truth in this argument: that we make sense of one another via stereotypes, and however unfortunate it may be, we have to act a part, the part expected of us based on the kind of persons we are, if we are to appear believable. Of course, every time someone gives in to this argument, they strengthen the hold of the stereotype on our minds and make it harder for the next person to step away from it.[15]

But the argument is more dangerous than that. We have become a nation of amateur psychoanalysts. We *think* we can read others. Jurors are told to infer intention from demeanor; the rest of us do so as a matter of course. Too often, when jurors are questioned about a guilty verdict after a criminal trial, they tell the reporter that one factor in their decision was that the defendant, sitting there in the courtroom day after day, didn't show "enough" remorse. That in itself is troubling. How do you know when someone feels remorse? "Enough" of it? And how can a defendant who is innocent sincerely express remorse? But jurors have seen enough soap operas to be experts in this judgment.[16]

We all behave differently, based on the usual suspects: gender, ethnicity, class, age . . . In some cultures, it is considered appropriate to wear your heart on your sleeve, weep, tear your hair, and snuffle in front of strangers. In others, that would create the presumption that you were out of control and perhaps had something to hide; a good and rational person is one who maintains face by keeping a stiff upper lip. In Hill's case, some analysts have pointed out that many southern black families teach their children—especially their daughters—to maintain a calm, unreadable demeanor in public. Since black women are doubly subject— as women and as black—to interpretation by others, it is safest to offer observers as little as possible to work with. And one trait typical of middle-class mores in European cultures, distinguishing them from the working class, is unemotionality among strangers. For those who have been brought up within the middle class and feel securely ensconced there, this restraint becomes less essential. But if you're outside trying to get in, your demeanor is the ticket of admission. Hill's interpreters, mostly members of either the white or the black middle class, may well have misread her imperturbability; and black viewers might have misinterpreted it as literal and "true" uninvolvement, rather than a superficial and conventional representation adopted in order to preserve "face."[17]

There are other reasons why taking outsiders' advice might have backfired on Hill. If she had shown anger, she would have been seen as a "bitch." Thomas's supporters did their best to portray her this way anyway, calling her "aloof," "arrogant," "argumentative," and so on. It was hard for the viewer to connect these descriptions to the patient and humble woman giving testimony; anger would have made it much easier, further eroding her believability. (Credibility depends at least as much on being likable as on being judged truthful, especially in the absence of hard evidence.)

Thomas, on the other hand, ran no risk in showing anger and received only positive notices for it. It seemed to enhance his credibility, despite Ekman's claim that anger often masks lying. Anger makes a man more manly, a woman less womanly, and thus enhances the credibility of the former, but detracts from that of the latter.

What if she tried another tack—suppose she broke down and cried, became inarticulate, overwhelmed by the horror of her memories? Then

MAD, BAD, AND HAD: HILL/THOMAS / 144

she would have triggered the other discrediting characterization: she would have been seen as "hysterical," out of control, and the argument that the whole accusation was the "fantasy" of an "erotomaniac" would have received added support.

Geneva Smitherman (1995b), an African-American sociolinguist, comments that Thomas's credibility was enhanced, and Hill's diminished, by the language each chose to use. Grammatically, lexically, and phonetically both spoke Standard American English (another indicator that both had positioned themselves within the middle class). But in terms of rhetorical style, says Smitherman, Thomas made frequent use of AVT (African-American Verbal Tradition), while Hill used traditional white public style, LWC (Language of Wider Communication). According to Smitherman, Thomas "signifies" and "sermonizes": he engages in verbal jousting with interlocutors, and he uses the style and intonational contours of the Black church. He "personalizes," making reference in public discourse to his family, his pain, his personal life. Hill does none of this. In making these choices, Thomas took a calculated risk: the white members of the committee, and the predominantly white audience, might have rejected his style as alien or inappropriate. But since he established himself from the start as a proud black man, his adoption of AVT served to enhance and fit that image. Hill, on the other hand, lost all identification: she was white, yet not-white; black, but not black—her ambiguity giving weight to the charges of insincerity.[18]

However Hill had presented herself, some of her audience would have constructed an unfavorable image of her. Thomas had much more latitude: less, probably, than a white man in his place would have, but more than a woman, and certainly a black woman, would receive. Finally, Hill's credibility suffered because many came to judgment biased against her and interpreted her testimony and demeanor so as to support their original decision.[19]

Whatever else can be said about Hill/Thomas, it passed the UAT. The amount of media (and public) attention given to the hearing was extraordinary. By contrast the Bork hearing several years earlier had attracted only lackluster attention from the public beyond the Beltway, as would be expected in a nation a significant percentage of whose citizens cannot name a single Supreme Court justice. The first (pre-Hill) round of questioning had garnered only minimal attention. So it wasn't the simmering resentments left over from Watergate and Bork that sparked the attention of the populace. In part it was the "sexual" nature of Hill's charges. Sex always sells. But it took more than mere titillation to keep people glued to the TV that weekend and discussing it heatedly for months thereafter. The Watergate-Bork residue drove Washington insiders to heights of rhetorical excess; but the people stayed tuned for other reasons. For many Americans, *Thelma and Louise* had brought the issues examined in Hill/Thomas to fever-pitch intensity. The movie established the topic of sexual harassment in the collective public mind, so that when Hill came to tell her story, it seemed familiar and reasonable. But the response to the movie, too, did not arise out of nothing. *Thelma and Louise* would not have been a hit—perhaps could not even have been made—had the social climate not been receptive. New ideas were in the air, seeking expression in celluloid. The political correctness debate that reached its apotheosis around the time of Hill/Thomas had accentuated and illustrated the political dividedness of the nation, making it easier for the media and their audiences to understand what Hill/Thomas was about and why winning was crucial. So as with other topics that pass the UAT, the significance and persistence in the American psyche of Hill/Thomas arose from many prior and contemporary events, and the case itself contributed to and altered our understanding of those prior circumstances as well as subsequent events.

UAT cases reach public awareness in two major ways. Some begin with a galvanizing event identifiable at the moment of impact. The narrative takes off from that initial flashpoint. Its salience begins to subside after a few months or a year, but the story still lingers in the group memory, retrievable for many purposes. It is an assertion of new information no longer, but has become part of our background knowledge about who we are and what we believe. Hill/Thomas is of this type.

The other kind starts slowly, simmering imperceptibly for a time. It is impossible in retrospect to assign it a definite starting point. Interest may flare up with the publication of a popular article or the occurrence of a relevant event, but it feels not so much like a new idea as like one that has been around for a while and been given a fresh "buzz." For a time it effervesces through the media and only gradually diminishes. But it remains, like the first, as an undercurrent in our conversations. The p.c. debate is a topic of this kind.

THE MEDIA MAKE THEIR MESSAGE

The amount of media attention devoted to the story was astonishing. Besides the huge television play, major newspapers gave it an extraordinary

amount of space. The NEWS library database has 364 listings of Hill/
Thomas for the period between October 1 and December 31, 1991. The
preponderance (319) appears at the epicenter of the quake, between Sunday, October 6, and Sunday, October 20. That makes about 64 stories
per paper over the two-week period, or over five a day per paper. *Newsweek* and *Time* had cover stories on the hearing in their issues of both
October 21 and October 28, each occupying a hefty amount of space (in
Newsweek's October 21 issue, twenty-one pages; in *Time*'s, nineteen).
The monthly popular magazines weighed in next, and thereafter, more
specialized popular and then scholarly journals (MAGS, the database for
both popular magazines and scholarly journals, has 150 listings for the
period from October 12, 1991, to December 1992). Several of these pe-
riodicals produced issues devoted largely or wholly to Hill/Thomas during 1992 (for instance, *The Black Scholar; Ms.; Tikkun; Political Communication;* and *Journal of Applied Behavior Science*). Though still a hot
topic, attention to Hill/Thomas was dwindling by the end of 1992. A
MAGS search for articles from 1993 to 1998 produced only fifty-six
titles. But there have been retrospectives. On television, *Dateline* devoted
long segments to it on September 29 and 30, 1997. There have been
a number of books by participants (Hill [1997] and Thomas's mentor,
Senator John Danforth [1994], in particular) and by reporters (including Mayer and Abramson 1994 and Phelps and Winternitz 1992); as
well as collections of readings (e.g., Smitherman 1995a).

The first newspaper treatments of Hill/Thomas provide mostly summaries of events, although there are also evaluative articles, among them
the one by Becklund (1991), which includes interviews with several
women discussing their own experiences of workplace harassment, and
those by Ronald Brownstein (1991) and Felicity Barringer (1991). The
newsmagazine coverage likewise includes both straight reportage of the
events and some analysis: speculations about future effects (on the workplace and the 1992 elections), discussions of the "gender gap" in the understanding of harassment, evaluations of the relative weights of race vs.
gender, and so on. Later and more intellectual takes on the topic theo-
rize: why Thomas won, how the discourse was created, the roles of race
and gender. The narrative thus takes its eventual shape through the five
levels described earlier in this chapter.

One pervasive response to the whole affair was the slogan that arose
out of it: "You/They Just Don't Get It." Even more striking were the fe-
vered responses to it by "you/them." The phrase had not been newly
minted for the occasion, but was a gripe privately muttered by women,

perhaps forever, which suddenly, like sexual harassment itself, burst into the public domain to serve as a rallying cry. So traditional men hated it on two grounds: first, it was public language that they had no hand in creating; second, it was a public attack on them, by people who had had until recently neither the means nor (as far as men could tell) the desire to criticize their betters. But that was far from the worst of it, some of the more astute came gradually to realize as the phrase gathered momentum. The slogan itself was about the making of public meaning—and by suggesting that it was women who were the makers of a meaning that men not only didn't create but *couldn't even understand,* it captured the fear that was already surfacing in the p.c. debate.

That fear may explain the wailing and teeth-gnashing that ensued over these few small words. On November 18, 1991, five weeks after D-Day, Daniel Seligman unleashed all the forces of desperation in an article in *Fortune,* "On Getting It." The piece begins: "As is well known, the National Organization for Women (N.O.W.), the Women's Legal Defense Fund (W.L.D.F.), the Fund for the Feminist Majority (F.F.M.), and their ever eager collaborators in the media have been laboring overtime to make They Just Don't Get It the cliche of the day." It's an amusing conceit: all these big, powerful organizations uniting (with "collaborators," no less—there's a war on!) to push a phrase. He slathers the slogan with opprobrium: it's a "tiresome phrase" that "lurks in 38 news stories and articles published in the three weeks beginning October 1." A bit odd is the embedded presupposition that the use of the phrase in the news stories is "collaboration," rather than reportage. Women who are in cahoots are bitches. They have *"belabored* a certain dull-witted sex"; law professor Kathleen Sullivan's *Newsday* piece is a *"tirade. "* (Italics are mine.) Worse yet, male turncoats have contributed to the flood. Only a few holdouts, like Seligman, see the truth and dare to tell it. It couldn't possibly be that women and other media commentators are on to something, that the slogan recognizes and gives voice to a formerly unspeakable reality. No: when something unpalatable is said, it must be the result of conspiracy.

Conspiracy is in fact the only explanation some on the right can produce for the whole Hill/Thomas affair. In an article in *The New Republic,* Abigail Thernstrom (1991) suggests that the hearing itself was the result of a well-orchestrated "conspiracy" of the left, "the nation's most organized thought police, the civil rights establishment." (Thernstrom's hyperbole is clearly borrowed from the anti-p.c. campaign.) She can't believe that Thomas could possibly be guilty as charged: "I met him once and found him to be immensely articulate and forceful." The article implicitly links Anita Hill's supporters in the media, or the media as a whole, with the "state-control press in Eastern Europe" which "fed the citizens nothing but Communist garbage." The right has to decide: the left is either McCarthyite or Communist; it's difficult to be both,[20] unless the implication is that both prevent *our* side from exercising its First Amendment right to free speech. It's remarkable how much media space is occupied by right-wingers whining about their loss of freedom of speech (see Chapter 3).

Common to articles like Seligman's and Thernstrom's is a lot of gleeful crowing (amidst the whining). When these pieces appeared, it looked as though the forces on the right had a lock on things. Thomas had been confirmed, polls supported him, President Bush's approval rating was in the high 80s, the Democrats were visibly in disarray. Yet the right still saw a dangerous conspiracy behind Hill's testimony and was never criticized for this view, despite all the evidence to the contrary.

"Extreme feminism is now a state religion in America," grumbles Barbara Amiel in the *National Review*. "People are being disentitled to their own sexuality. . . . Meanwhile, about the only relevant argument Professor Hill might have made was that anyone crazy enough to ask her out is not fit to be a Supreme Court Justice" (1991). In this passage, Amiel displays either remarkable ignorance of what Hill's testimony was about (not "courtship," "compliments," or "the occasional pass") or demonstrates a willful desire to distort it. Her conclusion shows the regrettable female tendency to attack other women on a personal basis. The hearings had nothing to do with whether someone would be crazy to go out with Hill. To say so is to do what Thomas, and harassers generally, are guilty of, erasing the line between public and private, making it impossible for women in the public sphere to cordon off their private lives. It's inadvisable for a woman in the public eye (such as Amiel) to play into that set of assumptions, however tempting the rhetorical cheap shot: what goes around is apt to come around.

I find the right-wing obsession with conspiracy on the left particularly curious in view of more recent events. In 1998 Hillary Rodham Clinton suggested that she and her husband were being hounded by special prosecutor Kenneth Starr as a result of a right-wing conspiracy. She was jeered at for months. Yet the evidence for that claim is at least as strong (see Chapter 8) as any claim that the disorganized Democrats and white male–dominated media had orchestrated a radical feminist left-wing conspiracy with Hill/Thomas. That claim, made forcefully and repeat-

edly by many rightist commentators, has remained impervious to critique or ridicule.

While the p.c. controversy showed a nation split in two, between the
traditional *us* and the new *them*, Hill/Thomas created, or rather brought
into focus, the more complex divisions that were splitting the left, the uni-
fied *them* of the p.c. debate: between male and female; black and white;
black female and white female; traditional vs. feminist men; "womanist"
vs. feminist black women. Conservatives have also seen in Hill/Thomas
a dangerous opening wedge of a "feminization" of America and its discourse.[21] They have tried to forestall this cataclysm by any means necessary—for instance, by linking Hill's testimony with ways of talking that
we feel negative about. According to Florence King (1991), Hill's flaw
was her "womanly forbearance." "Women swallow their pride and remain silent for fear of losing their jobs," she says sarcastically (although
Becklund's article showed that that is often the literal truth). We are all
becoming dangerously feminized: "Few Americans use declarative sentences now." Aside from the total lack of evidence in support of this hyperbole, what's so wrong with hedging your bets or your opinions when
there might be room for disagreement? Polarization makes no contribution to understanding, nor does it do anything to repair the rents in
the social fabric that so concern conservatives,[22] and more can be gained
from a dialogue in which parties can acknowledge as rational positions
other than their own. King goes on,

> I submit that last month's sexual-harassment World Series was only inciden-
> tally about sexual harassment. It was actually about our national dread of get-
> ting mad and throwing a fit.
>   We dread tempers for three reasons. The first has to do with the primacy
> of psychiatry in our national life, and the insidious potential danger it poses
> to us all.

It's puzzling to find this attack in the writing of one whose partisans—
the side she *isn't* criticizing—practiced more than their share of psychiatry without a license, from charges that Hill's claims resulted from
"transference" to claims that they arose out of her "erotomania." It was
reported (Clymer 1991) that the Republicans had a psychiatrist, Park
Dietz, ready to testify to Hill's erotomania sight unseen, though fortu-
nately saner minds prevailed. It's also unclear how a reluctance to speak
up against sexual harassment is connected to a purported national over-
dependence on psychiatry. When logical connection is lacking, propagandists often rely on linkage via similarity of emotion: fear = fear.

Why would a rational person consider Anita Hill, feminism, and psychotherapy not only connected but "insidious dangers" to the American people? All represent the possibility of historically weaker and voiceless parties acquiring autonomy and the power of speech. Good therapy encourages clients toward autonomy by enabling them to explore their identities. Psychiatry can be (though it too seldom actually is) subversive of traditional values, showing that these values may arise for neurotic reasons or can serve to mask illicit power relations.

Hill's testimony connects with psychotherapy in a more problematic way. Hill was rehearsing events remembered from nearly a decade earlier, as Thomas was vehemently denying that they had occurred. Could their memories be accurate? How can anyone know? By 1991, psychotherapists had for some time been encouraging clients to "remember" memories of abuse that had been repressed in childhood. The recovered memory movement made it difficult to dismiss out of hand charges by women against men about long-ago events. Anastasia Toufexis (1991) connects Hill's and Thomas's reported recollections with theories about the reliability of recovered memory, weighing the claims on both sides of the debate. "I find it highly unlikely that someone who can remember what pattern was on the wallpaper and that a duck was quacking outside the bedroom window where she was molested by her father when she was four years old is making it up. Why in the hell would the mind do this?" says Jill Otey, a Portland, Oregon, attorney. On the other hand, "Our memory is not like a camera in which we get an accurate photograph," says psychologist Henry Ellis of the University of New Mexico. Elizabeth Loftus and Ulric Neisser, both academic psychologists and noted experts on memory, suggest that either or both Hill and Thomas might be remembering truthfully, or might not. Psychology allows for both readings.

If traditionalists have no use for Hill's testimony or what it represents, feminists (generally white and female) have equally little patience with Thomas and the "ultimate white men's club" that was then, and largely still is, the United States Senate. They have tended to see Thomas's partisans acting out of a white male conservative agenda that would return us to "business as usual." They see Hill's story as corroborated by their own experiences; what males see as problems in her narrative (the long time during which she didn't report the abuse; her continued cordiality to Thomas) they identify as normal, necessarily arising out of the power imbalance between men and women in the working world, corroborative rather than suspicious. Hill's demeanor during the hearing also resonates as truthful and understandable in terms of the situation Hill was in and the double, or multiple, standard under which she was forced to testify.

The question—who is telling the truth?—is typically framed as a polarized either/or: *one* of them must be lying. But I see a plausible middle ground. Perhaps both are reporting their memories accurately, as they existed in 1991, years after the events in dispute. Her recollections are in accord with what actually happened. (Links to *The Exorcist* and such aside, I find it implausible that Hill could have or would have made up these tales. Would any woman willingly sit in front of a hostile audience talking about such topics, having her life dissected before her eyes? What, other than the need to tell the truth, would have brought Hill to Washington?) Thomas is telling the truth *as he remembers it.* To him, the interchanges seared so painfully into Hill's memory are just idle chitchat, joking around, the kind of small talk that no one remembers five minutes later. Who recalls the topics of conversation from a dinner party ten years ago?

This interpretation is not intended as exoneration. It is troubling to see a nominee to the U.S. Supreme Court as a person of such insensitivity. If the court is to interpret the law we all must live by, surely its members may be expected to have the capacity to empathize even with people with whom, demographically, they don't have much in common. Thomas's truthfulness might pose a more serious threat to his qualification than his lying would have.

Black women found themselves painfully torn during the hearing and its aftermath. Many black women are reluctant to identify with the causes or rhetoric of white, middle-class feminism. Some identify themselves as "womanist," meaning that they see themselves as black first and female second; and that they support values of home and family against the professionalization that is often associated with the goals of white feminism. Some of these women supported Thomas either because they mistrusted Hill and her white supporters or because they acknowledged that Hill's story might be true but saw it as irrelevant to the goal of confirming a black Supreme Court justice. They felt racial solidarity trumped gender solidarity.

Other black women identified as feminists. Some expressed outrage at the interpretations being made of Hill, black women, and women generally by black (and other) men. For instance, Harvard sociologist Orlando Patterson (1992) suggested that Hill's recollections might be true, but her reidentification as middle class had caused her to misunderstand Thomas's intentions: his talk, suggested Patterson, was exemplary of "Judge Thomas's down-home style of courting." Other black writers, male and female, expressed outrage at Patterson's suggestion that black men were and had the right to be as gross and obscene in the name of "courting" as Thomas was alleged to have been. Some black feminists saw Thomas's behavior as analogous to the misogynistic rant of rappers like Ice-T and Snoop Doggy Dogg, and saw no reason to tolerate that treatment. They questioned whether it was a good idea, even in the name of black solidarity and political progress, for women to cover up their mistreatment by black men.

Black men divided as well, between those who supported Thomas on all grounds, those who thought he was guilty as charged, but with an explanation (or that it didn't matter), and those who agreed with black and white feminists.

In Hill/Thomas we have to deal with an irreparably frayed and fragmented cultural narrative. There is irreconcilable disagreement on all sides about every aspect of the story: whether the events in Hill's story happened; why Hill behaved as she had, both before and during her Senate testimony; whether the harassment, if it did occur, was significant enough to disrupt Thomas's confirmation; what the uproar was really about; what relations between the sexes, and the races, in the workplace and elsewhere, are really like in the late twentieth century; who "won" Hill/Thomas and why. The last question is open to several answers.

Argument A: The Right Won

According to this view, the right maintained its dominance. Thomas was, finally, confirmed; the polls, at least initially, supported his confirmation.[23] That was what it was all about, wasn't it? But if they had won so resoundingly, why were right-wingers like Noonan, Thernstrom, Seligman, and Amiel endlessly apoplectic about the hearing and its aftermath? If they had won, why couldn't they let it go? And why hadn't the issue of sexual harassment melted away as the triviality conservatives claimed it was?

Argument B: The Left Won

According to this view, the right won the battle but not the war: it was a Pyrrhic victory. By forcing the issue of sexual harassment into public notice via the Thomas nomination fight, the right gave women a more prominent public voice and made it clear that many women had opinions different from those of the majority of men. By late 1992 the polls had changed significantly (according to the *National Review* of November 2, 1992, the same percentage believed Hill as Thomas: 38 percent—a switch the magazine attributed to the fading of memories).[24]

The laws on sexual harassment have changed, undoubtedly as a result of the public interest aroused by the hearings. More harassment lawsuits were filed, and more were successful. In May of 1992 there was a prolonged inquiry into "Operation Tailhook," in which a group of male Naval aviators were charged with indecent conduct toward female colleagues at their yearly conventions. Although complaints had been made fruitlessly for years, that year there were hearings, dismissals, and demotions in rank. Perhaps most significant was the election of 1992. Not only did Bill Clinton win resoundingly over George Bush (an outcome deemed impossible just a year before), but 20 women were running for Senate seats, of whom 4 succeeded, 150 for the House, of whom 47 were elected. The "ultimate men's club" was a little less of one.

The new respect accorded the concept of sexual harassment culminated in two Supreme Court decisions in June 1998 (*Burlington Industries v. Ellerth,* and *Farragher v. Boca Raton*) which defined relatively precisely the responsibilities of both employers and workers in preventing harassment and specified the circumstances under which employers could be found liable. One important aspect of these rulings is that they accord full legal status to sexual harassment, equating it to other civil torts like breach of contract or negligence and removing it from the vague category of social misbehaviors like "just fooling around" or "getting fresh," which can be (and had always been) dismissed as matters of "he said/she said," rather than adjudicable offenses.

Argument C: Nobody Won

In some ways, nobody won or everyone lost. Some have suggested that the current widespread public disenchantment with and cynicism about government was accelerated by the opportunity to watch the Judiciary Committee come apart on television (even as widespread distrust of the justice system may have been engendered, or given a boost, by the televised Simpson trial). Even if this is true, it's not necessarily a bad thing. If watching our lawmakers in action provokes cynicism, that seems less a problem arising from the televising of government process than a critique of the performers of that process, a realization that could conceivably bring this country closer to a more fully responsive and competent government.[25]

SEQUELAE, EPIPHENOMENA, AND
META(META)NARRATIVES: WHAT IT ALL MEANT

If one aftereffect of Hill/Thomas was to divide the sexes in the work-place more obviously than had been so before, another was to heighten interest in close encounters of the adulterous kind in high places, like the military, Congress, and the Oval Office. It came as no surprise to most Americans over the age of consent that sex, even of the illicit variety, occurred in those locales. There had always been gossip. Even the sainted JFK and FDR had in the recent past had their presidential philanderings brought to light. Stories about current officeholders, like Bob Packwood, were legion; and even the short memory of the American public encompassed the shenanigans of presidential candidate Gary Hart and Donna Rice on board the aptly named *Monkey Business* in 1988. But Hill/Thomas made sex more titillatingly discussible in public: Hill's use of "penis" on the Senate floor and its subsequent necessary reiteration on TV news broadcasts made it acceptable public fare, along with sundry related topics. The Tailhook scandal brought into focus the questionable behavior of military men toward female subordinates or colleagues and with that, demands for redress and legal protection. And while the public might be split on whether Thomas had actually done what he had been accused of doing, and whether it mattered, there was wide recognition that such behavior was no longer to be construed as "just fooling around." Actions and words that had formerly gone beneath the radar were now out there on public display, and claims had to be either credibly disposed of or acted on by those in positions of power.

The scrutiny reached the White House during the 1992 presidential primaries. Early in his campaign, Bill Clinton was accused of consensual, but adulterous, dalliance with a television news reporter, Gennifer Flowers. In the sensitized post-Hill/Thomas atmosphere, it looked as though Clinton's candidacy, like Hart's four years earlier, might be torpedoed. But the Clintons made an appearance on *Sixty Minutes,* snuggled on a couch, and together convinced the public that while they might have had (unspecified) problems in their marriage, they had worked through them and put them behind them. His ratings rose.

But the stories didn't go away. After Flowers was disposed of, Paula Jones came forward to claim that Clinton, when governor of Arkansas, had exposed himself to her in a hotel room. There were suggestions of probative anatomical irregularities, and the possibility was dangled before the American people, that, should the case come to trial, the First Organ might be displayed nakedly on television to a worldwide audience. As the Jones case began to recede from view, there were new allegations that the president had received oral sex from an intern, Monica Lewinsky, under the desk in the Oval Office (see Chapter 8). Other allegations, by present and former White House staff members and others in Clinton's past, followed.

Hill/Thomas has had lasting effects on the cultural, as well as the sociopolitical, climate. Just as the hearings are parenthesized on one end politically by Watergate and Bork and culturally by *Thelma and Louise,* so the political parentheses on the other end are provided by the discoveries of adultery in high places, the election of the Congressional "class of 1992," the Tailhook scandal and its aftereffects, the 1998 Supreme Court decisions, and the impeachment of President Clinton (a twofer: it functions both as payback for Hill/Thomas and as a media event dependent on the prior hypersexualization of the airwaves, via Hill/Thomas and later stories, to achieve media discussion at all). The cultural right parenthesis is David Mamet's play *Oleanna,* itself a successful entrant in the UAT.

Oleanna was first performed in Cambridge, Massachusetts, on May 1, 1992—less than seven months after Hill/Thomas—and was an immediate sensation. Audiences left the theater fighting. Many productions organized well-attended post-performance discussions between audiences and cast, and sometimes the local intelligentsia. The play is short and simple. In it, a university professor, John, has an unsatisfactory verbal encounter with a student, Carol, in his office. John is up for tenure and about to buy a house—on the verge of success. Carol (like John) is a member of the working class, awed at her presence in this prestigious institution. John befuddles her with his fluent academese. He drops a few potentially ambiguous casual remarks in the course of a rambling autobiographical statement intended to show Carol that he is like her and understands her problems. He says he "likes" her and makes some explicit sexual references (which he intends figuratively, but she takes literally), and offers to give her an A if she keeps coming to his office. She feels bewildered and insulted by the conversation, because she can't get hold of the meaning: she feels he is ignoring her worries and talking down to her. He is communicating as academics will, obliquely and ironically. But she, not a member of the institution, has not learned its code. Feeling degraded, but not clearly grasping how or why, she talks to some feminist friends, who hear her report of John's ramblings as sexual harassment, and arrange for him to be brought up on charges, with the eventual result that he is denied tenure.

Mamet intended the play as an attack on political correctness, and more specifically on feminists who illegitimately use sexual harassment as a weapon against innocent men. Unlike much of Mamet's work, *Oleanna* as Mamet directed it is remarkably without nuance. The characters are cardboard, especially Carol, of whom we know virtually nothing other than her gender and class. The plot is melodrama—good vs. evil, John-the-hero vs. Carol-the-dupe of feminism-the-villain. John is well-meaning, totally and unfairly misunderstood, done in by a dumb student, witchy (though offstage) feminists, and a politically correct administration. Like all melodrama, the play is enjoyable for the moment— it gets the juices flowing—but leaves nothing nutritious to chew on.

Mamet may have written *Oleanna* as a response to Hill/Thomas and its sequelae. He is a fast writer, and *Oleanna* is a short play. He could easily have started to write in October 1991 and had a version of it ready for production by May 1992. Whether or not this chronology is accurate, it is safe to say that the timing of the play is fortunate: if it had not so closely followed Hill/Thomas, it would not have been the resounding success that it was. The movie version a couple of years later was unsuccessful, a sign that the incandescent moment had passed.[26]

The farther away the precipitating events, the less interesting the play becomes, particularly when performed as Mamet intended. The essentially propagandistic piece loses its power to stir as the events that drove Mamet to write get resolved and fears of a feminist *putsch* subside. I think the play can be partly saved by a reading that focuses on the dangers of institutionalization—that is, becoming a member of a profession or an institution.[27] In the case of *Oleanna,* the university is John's institution, doctrinaire feminism Carol's. Institutions are essential in a complex society. But to achieve their ends their members necessarily develop their own languages and their own ways, which create impenetrable boundaries for outsiders. By the time academics reach the point of tenure (at least six years from employment as an assistant professor and minimally ten years from entrance to graduate school, where the socialization begins) they have been so thoroughly institutionalized that they are unable to communicate in normal language with outsiders or even to realize that they are unable to do so.

So John unintentionally befuddles and patronizes Carol, because he talks to her in academese, a language she does not know. She therefore misunderstands his intentions at several levels, a fact that contributes to her frustration. She realizes that, in some sense, she has been "harassed" by John, although his harassment is not "sexual." But the law is such that sexual harassment can be punished, whereas John's kind has no name and is not illegal. So, with the help of feminists, she reframes her mistreatment in sexual terms—because that has a name that allows her to make sense of what happened and because that allows her to seek redress.

It is legitimate to ask whether John's punishment fits the crime—he was only doing his job, being a good professional.[28] On the other hand, miscommunication should bring reprisals, if only to encourage us to try to do better. In this interpretation, the accusation of *sexual* harassment is unjust, but John did use language to harass Carol, unwittingly or not. Since the university has in its rule-book an official rule against only *sexual* harassment, Carol may be justified in using it, since the other kind is "business as usual" at the academic institution.

The final parenthesis to Hill/Thomas, its most significant aftermath, is that it opened up discourse options for women (and African Americans), continuing the process that began with the p.c. debate and leading to the further extensions that will be explored in the next chapters, on the role of Hillary Rodham Clinton as First Lady, and that of the jurors and other participants in the O. J. Simpson trial, as well as the Ebonics controversy of 1997. Before Hill/Thomas, women played a negligible role at best in the making of public language at the highest levels. What most horrified traditionalists at the hearing was not that Hill used the word "penis" in the sanctum sanctorum of the Senate Caucus Chamber (although some of them later tried to make out that that was the sticking point); or even, as in Hill's (1997) own interpretation, that she had brought the concept of sexual harassment into the open and forced America to deal with it. The most important aftermath of Hill/Thomas is that it gave women and others the interpretive power they had lacked and gave it to them publicly in front of everyone at the very highest level of public discourse. Anita Hill forced us to accept not merely the term "sexual harassment" and what it implied, but also the right of women to define male behavior for everyone and to give that definition legal standing. The potency and permanence of the slogan "They just don't get it" attests to this. Because of Hill's testimony, women can now contribute fully to the decision about what *it* is and how you *get* it.

HILLARY RODHAM CLINTON

What the Sphinx Thinks

VERY FUNNY

Bill, Hillary, and Al Gore are riding in Air Force One when it crashes and all are killed. They find themselves in heaven, and are directed to a large room, at the far end of which is God sitting on a majestic throne.

Al Gore approaches first. "And who are you?" asks God.

"I'm Al Gore, sir. I was the Vice President of the United States."

"Well, that's very impressive!" says God. "Come here and sit on the chair on my left."

Then Bill Clinton goes in. "And who are you?" "Sir, I'm William Jefferson Clinton. I was President of the United States."

"Well now, that's even more impressive! Come on over here and sit on the chair to my right."

Then Hillary comes in. "And who are you?" asks God.

"I am Hillary Rodham Clinton, and what are *you* doing in *my* seat?"

Bill and Hillary are driving around Arkansas and stop to get gas. The attendant and Hillary recognize each other and go on reminiscing together for a while.

Then Bill and Hillary drive off. "Who was that?" asks Bill.

"Oh, that was Fred, my first boyfriend in high school. We went together for a few years."

"Just think," says Bill, "if you'd married him, you'd be living behind a gas station, not in the White House."

"No, dear," says Hillary. "If I had married him, *you'd* be living behind a gas station, and Fred and I would be living in the White House."

These jokes, in many versions, are endemic on the World Wide Web, which lists some 17,000 sites dedicated (wholly or in part) to the First Lady. The student of contemporary political discourse must explain why there are so many jokes about both Clintons, why the First Lady continues to preoccupy such a large swath of the public's attention in her own right, and why the jokes, and the attention, take the multiple and often contradictory forms they do. Why does this First Lady—and this First Couple—pass the UAT so spectacularly?

To answer that question, we have to examine the first lady's role. During most of our history the first lady's job description has been vague, if the role was thought of as a job at all. During our first century, Americans didn't have an official title for the president's spouse. Martha was called "Lady Washington." Later, as populism replaced the Hamiltonian quasi-monarchy, titles like "Presidentress" and "Mrs. President" were tried out but didn't stick. It wasn't until 1870 that the title "first lady" came into use (Caroli 1987). The role itself is more problematic than the title. It has no constitutional status, no official duties or privileges. But unofficially, over time a complex if tacit web of expectations has become connected to the role (one can hardly call it an "office"), and even more so, to the woman who inhabits it.

TELLING TALES OUT OF SCHOOL

In the two previous chapters, I examined two recent cases in which language rights had come into sharp competition, provoking undue attention. In Chapter 3, the linguistic artifacts involved were small and concrete: words and phrases. In Chapter 4, there was a mixture: some of the language under dispute was like that in Chapter 3, small and concrete units: the meaning of "sexual harassment." More often the investigation had to move to higher levels: the functions of complex syntactic structures like tag questions; the interpretation of speech acts like threats; the distribution of conversational turns and its consequences; the uses of black and white traditional discourse styles. Finally the analysis moved to a still higher level: the competition over the meaning of the events of Hill/Thomas themselves: who got to make the story at the end.

In this chapter, the narrative will be my major focus. To my mind the most shocking thing about Hillary Rodham Clinton is the fact that, as a woman, she has found ways, either direct or subversive, of retaining control over her own narrative, her own meaning. But there has been from the start hot competition from many sides within the media and the Beltway for that right. We are eager for the story-making rights because we want to construct her, and through her ourselves; but she eludes our narrative grasp.

Some readers may feel a disconnect at this juncture. I have been representing myself as a linguist (I would be a card-carrying member of the LSA if they gave out cards). As long as I mind my business, keeping my attention focused on the minutiae of language (words, sentences, maybe even speech acts), I am safely within my allotted boundaries. Linguistics retains its historical definition (of great comfort to many of my colleagues). But in reaching out to the vastnesses of narrative structure, of stories and meta-stories, of narrative-making rights and their subversions, some readers may wonder if I'm still being a "linguist." Or, if I'm not, whether I retain the authority to speak.

Linguists study language; literary critics study text (including narratives). Once that division of labor made sense; once I obeyed it. But more and more that boundary seems like an artificial barrier that works to stop the flow of understanding. Language doesn't stop with the word or the sentence, or even the conversational turn; to understand its meaning, the analyst has to have the capacity to see it in its totality. Certainly the literary critic can find matter in stories that will be lost to me. Political scientists and historians will find stories here other than the ones I find worth exploring; communication theorists will look at these stories in different ways than I do, asking different questions. I think those notions are reasonable ways of drawing disciplinary boundaries nowadays: often different fields try to make sense of the same data, the same artifacts, but they do so in different ways and so arrive at different places that they call "answers." But I reject the older idea that disciplines are absolutely differentiated by the subject matter they may look at. For me, the linguist's job is understanding how language makes us human, and the answer to that question comes from looking at language in all its interlocking complexities, at every level. From each level of language —the sound, the word, the sentence, the turn—we learn something about who we are and how we work. From the higher and more abstract levels—the discourse, the narrative—alone do we learn about what we mean.

Narratives can be subjected to analytic techniques analogous to those used for lower levels of language. We can look at the choices of words, at sentence structure; at the presuppositions and frames assumed; at the speech acts that are chosen; at the levels of directness, or indirectness, the narrator chooses; at what is said, what is implied, and what is absent. All of these, and more, make the story what it is and allow maker and hearer to collaborate in a coherent meaning.

Perhaps more interesting still, at least here, is the meta-narrative: the story about or behind the story, the subtext. Why does the story exist in more than one version? What is *the one that wasn't told*—the other way to see a set of events? Always tellers have choices to make: in this case, how do those choices tell us what we want to make of our subject, and ourselves?

THE MAKING OF THE
HILLARY RODHAM CLINTON STORY

Just as presidents traditionally receive significantly more media attention than do ordinary men, first ladies get more coverage than average women (who until recently were admonished that a woman should get her name in the paper only three times in her life: when she is born, when she gets married, and when she dies). But while the amount of attention given President Bill Clinton is typical of presidents (although the quality of that coverage is not), since the start of her husband's candidacy in 1992 Hillary Rodham Clinton has faced virtually incessant media attention, much more and of a strikingly different type than have previous first ladies. Not only are her doings and sayings tirelessly reported. She is relentlessly interpreted. More significantly, she is relentlessly and deliberately *mis* interpreted.

Her media presence is ubiquitous: scarcely a day goes by without some report of her activities or some analysis of her psyche. And the fascination is endemic: in daily newspapers, newsmagazines, magazines of culture, Sunday supplements, radio talk shows, television magazine shows—everywhere. Images of her are remarkably diverse, ranging from strongly adulatory to ferociously critical; they represent her as a person of wildly different personalities, doing and saying what it is hard to imagine a single individual doing or saying. The coverage is unusual too for the deep psychological analysis of its target. While other first ladies have been covered largely on the basis of their observable actions, Rodham Clinton has been subjected to the ceaseless ministrations of amateur psychoanalysts: we seem more concerned with what makes her tick than with what she is doing. Also unusual is the fact that, while there are ups and downs in the level of Rodham Clinton's media attention, it has remained high. Ordinarily media coverage of first ladies has a predictable trajectory. When a man first presents himself as a candidate, there is interest in his wife, which increases when the husband becomes the party's candidate. After his electoral victory, interest in her continues for a while, turning now to the first lady's adjustment to her new role: her plans for redecoration of the White House; her moving into her White House office and selection of her staff; her family's integration into their new routine; and the selection of the First Lady Project. The latter is normally something decorative and uncontroversial: highway beautification, promoting mental health or literacy, teaching children to Just Say No to drugs. Then the first lady settles into relative obscurity, except for occasional photo-ops of her at work on her project or attending official functions with her husband, the president. Perhaps there is an occasional flurry of scandal, but it usually vanishes fast.

In Chapter 4 I described the levels of media attention given to Hill/Thomas: first the explosion of immediate impressions in the daily press and the electronic media; then the profusion of in-depth coverage in the weekly newsmagazines, followed by the more analytic commentaries of the monthlies. These had exhausted themselves by the end of 1991, a scant three months after the pivotal event. By early 1992, and continuing through that year, the more intellectual popular magazines, followed by scholarly journals, took over the business of analysis and prognostication in greater depth. By the end of 1992, the topic had retreated into obscurity, with only occasional forays back into public consciousness.

But the attention lavished on Rodham Clinton is different. Hill/Thomas was a momentary blip on the radar: the pivotal moment encompassed only the single day of October 12, 1991, the day of Hill's testimony to the Judiciary Committee (although the whole story has to include the penumbra from the resignation of Thurgood Marshall in May of 1991 to the confirmation of Clarence Thomas in late October). But the image catalogued in our minds under Hill/Thomas is one of Hill sitting before the committee, on that October day, in that turquoise suit, an image frozen at a moment in time.

Interest in Rodham Clinton, though, has extended over many years, waxing and waning. Long-term assessments and scholarly analyses of Rodham Clinton are significantly sparser than those of Hill/Thomas. While there have been a number of long analytical pieces in the intellectual popular media,[1] scholarly journals have contained relatively little discussion of the First Lady. One reason may be that Rodham Clinton's fifteen minutes aren't over yet, and academics prefer to concentrate on completed events. They're safer—you're less likely to be contradicted by what happens next. (And we are in this business because it's safe.)

The Rodham Clinton story develops gradually. She comes into public awareness in 1991–92, as her husband debates his candidacy and decides to run. It is clear from the start that she isn't like the other candidates' wives, even as her husband isn't like the other men: a new generation has come of age. For the male half of the couple, that means that a series of World War II–generation presidents (all of whom either served or had some reason not to or, in one case, allegedly believed he had served because he was in war movies) from Kennedy to Bush gave way to the Vietnam War generation, with its very different ideals, views of war, and social attitudes. Those changes make us nervous, but nowhere near as nervous as the change on what might once have been called "the distaff side."

Because Rodham Clinton was a curiosity, media and public attention focused on her; because she quickly became, like her husband but even more strikingly so, a symbol of the New World Order—the changing roles of women, the replacement of old mores by new—that attention was polarized from the start, either passionately positive or virulently negative. Clichés and stereotypes were tested, toyed with, fitted on her. Her refusal to fit into them was exhilarating to some, infuriating to others. Because she fits no pattern, the media flounder in their treatment of her. She slithers out of the analysts' grasp, resisting definition or categorization.[2] That both piques our interest and arouses anxiety and rage in many of us. Unlike any previous occupant of her position, she remains continually in the public eye, continually under scrutiny, examination, and reanalysis. She is the first first lady since Eleanor Roosevelt to pass the UAT.[3] When we examine her, we are trying to know ourselves.

The MAGS and NEWS databases provide a record of the ebb and flow of Hillariana over eight years:

	MAGS (816 total citations)	NEWS (2,152 total citations)
1991	0	2
1992	56	159
1993	152	410
1994	197	448
1995	89	271
1996	213	538
1997	71	214
1998 (through July)	38	110

High points occurred in 1993, 1994, and 1996. These dates are not random. The Clintons entered the White House in 1993, and Rodham Clinton was subjected to much more than the usual first lady scrutiny. The president soon appointed her to an unheard-of role for first ladies, the chair of a commission charged with reforming the country's health care system. The task itself was political dynamite; that a woman, and indeed a first lady, was to head it proved incendiary. The way in which she played that role attracted a great deal of media attention that continued unabated until the commission completed its task in 1995.

The rest of 1995 was relatively uneventful for Rodham Clinton, and media interest ebbed (although it still exceeded the attention normally given to first ladies). The great upsurge in 1996 was largely due to the publication of Rodham Clinton's book, *It Takes a Village*, which was on the best-seller list for many weeks, aroused immense controversy from all sides of the political spectrum (see below), and required the author's presence on interview shows and book tours. Again, interest subsided by the next year.

A LITTLE BACKGROUND NOISE

Why is Rodham Clinton endlessly fascinating? In large measure, like other UAT-passers, because she has come to represent something that makes us uncertain of who we are and what things mean—specifically, the new woman playing a new role. While Rodham Clinton is in many ways a representative of that novelty in her own right, her notoriety arises to a significant degree because, as first lady, she symbolizes the contrast between the old and the new, and especially because her predecessor, Barbara Bush, so perfectly represented the comfortable traditional woman and wife. Barbara Bush left Smith College in the late 1940's to get married, without taking her undergraduate degree. She had a large family and no career outside the home. The women's movement happened when Mrs. Bush was in middle age, a bit late for her to attempt to adapt, even if she had wanted to. The one book she wrote as first lady was a quasi autobiography of her springer spaniel, Millie—cute, charming, uncontroversial: the very model of first lady work.

Hillary Rodham Clinton was born about when Barbara Bush was getting married, in 1947. She graduated from Wellesley College in 1969 as a student leader, delivering a valedictory address that was featured in *Life* magazine. She went on to Yale Law School, where she met Bill. It never occurred to her not to have a career—the only questions were what career, and how, or whether, to combine it with marriage and mother-hood. Those were the difficult questions facing women of the baby-boom generation, as their male cohorts agonized over Vietnam. She served as an attorney on the staff of the Democratic members of the House Judiciary Committee's impeachment inquiry during Watergate. She followed Bill Clinton to Arkansas, taking a position at the University of Arkansas Law School. After Bill became attorney general, Hillary moved from law school to private practice at the Rose Law Firm in Little Rock.[4]

The Clintons were married in 1975; Hillary kept her birth name. Her refusal to change it was later blamed as the cause of Bill's failure to win reelection in 1980. The amount of vitriol expended on what in a rational world would be just a simple personal choice (but in Arkansas in 1980, clearly wasn't) was extraordinary. According to Connie Bruck (1994),

> One friend recalled standing next to her at a reception at the Rose firm in the late seventies, and seeing a man approach her, jab angrily at the nametag pinned to her blouse, and fairly spit out, "That's not your name!"

And, according to David Maraniss:

> During the 1980 campaign, one powerful member of the Arkansas House offered the opinion to Representative Ray Smith, Jr., of Hot Springs that "Hillary's gonna have to change her name and shave her legs." (1995, 399)

There is evidently a lot more at stake, in the minds of people like those quoted above, than a mere change in nomenclature, especially with the added injunction about leg-shaving (which in a reasonable universe would *surely* be None of His Business).

A RIDDLE WRAPPED IN A MYSTERY INSIDE AN ENIGMA

Who is the most feared and hated woman in America?
Tonya Rodham Bobbitt.

The multiple mystery is this: why does Rodham Clinton generate the amount, and kind, of attention that she does? Human nature needs to resolve mysteries: those that cannot be readily penetrated become objects of deep fascination. As a woman, Rodham Clinton's unwillingness or inability to be "penetrated" is itself contradictory. Women are meant to be penetrated and interpreted; a woman who resists is no woman. Of course, a woman who permits herself to be penetrated by strangers is no lady. But Rodham Clinton, even as she is no woman, is First Lady.

Since its inception, the presidency itself has been a locus of both symbolic and literal power. The president presides over the nation's business and executes its laws; uses his position as the bully pulpit, for purposes of persuasion; advocates for the passage of bills by Congress; utilizes veto power; makes appointments with the advice and consent of the Senate; and declares war. His literal power is relatively circumscribed by our system of checks and balances, the two-party system, and the limitation of his term of office to two four-year terms. His symbolic power is greater, and because its terms are never expressly stated, it becomes mysterious and like other mysteries generates fear. Among the symbolic powers, or roles, of the President of the United States is the expectation that he represents the current version of the ideal man.

To be sure, there is no single "ideal man" that we all agree on. We have different ideals in our minds for different purposes: the big moneymaker, the loving Daddy, the hunk, the competent worker, the creator, the athlete, the nice sensitive guy . . . But the president ideally plays at least some of these symbolic roles. Typically an older man, he is Father, or at least Daddy, of the country; he is a take-charge guy, he has stated opinions, he acts on them, he gets results. People listen to him and obey him. He is a good family man, faithful to his wife, loving to his children (but not overly attached to either: his work is his real life). He is Ward Cleaver, Ben Cartwright, Dr. Ben Casey, images of a time remembered (or encountered in reruns) as a golden age.

The first lady's literal role is virtually nonexistent. As a symbol—the totality of her job—the first lady serves as an ideal and role model for women. She must be the womanliest, the most feminine, of us all. That is not to say that she should be sexy: no man wants to be caught desiring Daddy's mate. So she should be feminine in a womanly rather than sirenly way. That means that she should be devoted to her man and concerned for his well-being; attentive to her (usually grown-up) family and its domestic animals; occupied in traditional kinds of good works and worthy projects; ladylike and stereotypically feminine (demure, submissive, compliant); well, but not flamboyantly, dressed; her home and family should be her life.

Because the first lady has no real role, her symbolic role becomes all-important. This is especially true because she defines contemporaneous womanhood, and thus (if she plays her part properly) serves as a standard and a source of instruction for all American women. Her propriety keeps us all in line. If the rest of us can grasp the first lady as a simple caricature or stereotype of ideal womanhood, then we control both the first lady and all women.

The first lady and the president thus perform similar symbolic tasks, and as a result are sharply differentiated by sex role stereotyping and polarization. First ladies who play by the rules are by no means exempt from criticism (thus Barbara Bush, an almost-perfect specimen, was needled for her amplitude and her white hair—there were comments about her looking older than her husband). But what there is, is rare and relatively mild.

Occasional first ladies overstep. Eleanor Roosevelt was described, if jocularly, by her husband as out of his control. Mary Todd Lincoln was seen as eccentric and demanding, if not an outright Confederate spy (mad and bad). Rosalynn Carter was dubbed "the Steel Magnolia" and chastised for attending her husband's cabinet meetings and otherwise meddling in affairs of state. Nancy Reagan caught criticism for consulting an astrologer for guidance in governance, meddling in the running of the White House, and extravagance in dress and in the purchase of White House furnishings. But Mrs. Carter and Mrs. Reagan staved off more severe criticism because they behaved in other respects like traditional ladies. Nancy gazed adoringly at her husband at all photo-ops, the prototype of proper wifeliness. Rosalynn spoke in a soft Southern drawl. By fitting the stereotype, a typical first lady allows herself to be readily interpreted and invites us to make of her what we will—the result will threaten no one. No wonder that the first lady always comes out high on the list of "most admired women."

But Hillary Rodham Clinton is the striking exception. Right up there with Mary Todd Lincoln, she kept her birth name. Even worse than Mrs. Lincoln, she tried at first to avoid using her husband's name at all. By so doing, she sought to maintain her own individual identity, one not defined in terms of her marital status. Hence, in the joke at the beginning of this section, it is "Rodham" that stands for Hillary Rodham Clinton, along with "Tonya" for Tonya Harding and "Bobbitt" for Lorena Bobbitt. "Rodham"—and all that that implies—stands for everything that makes her "feared and hated."

Her reluctance to change her name is only the most obvious and concrete sign of the threat Rodham Clinton poses as First Lady. The real problems are much deeper. She refuses to be interpretable, remaining contradictory and enigmatic; even as she is supposed to be a symbol of ideal womanhood, she changes the roles women play and our definitions of womanhood, and she does so at the very moment at which real roles for women are changing and resisting easy definition. The complexity and ambiguity distress not only many men, but women too, especially those who have come to maturity under the old regime. In fact women may be even more disturbed, since women writers have supplied the most vicious and undercutting critiques of the First Lady. An editorial writer in the *National Review* (March 30, 1992) quotes Kipling's line that "the female of the species is deadlier than the male." Especially to uppity females.

Here's Camille Paglia (1996), discussing Rodham Clinton as "Ice Queen, Drag Queen": she is high and mighty; she puts on airs; she is a "Queen" like all the Quota Queens and Welfare Queens of conservative infamy. She *looks* "glamorous," but it's just a ploy to get us into her clutches:

> A limousine pulls up and out steps not Hillary the shrewd lawyer or Hillary the happy homemaker but Hillary the radiantly glamorous movie star. Her blond hair is dramatically, seductively styled. She is wearing, quite improbably, a long black velvet coat trimmed with royalist gold brocade. Head high, she stalks grandly to the microphones and greets the press as if they were dear friends come to bid her well. Then, like Mary Queen of Scots on her way to the scaffold, she sweeps away for her grueling four-hour rendezvous with independent counsel Kenneth W. Starr.

It is not unreasonable to detect in Paglia's equation of Rodham Clinton with Mary Queen of Scots a threat or malevolent wish—*and look what happened to Mary!* (a point underscored by the reference to the "scaffold").

New York Times Op-Ed columnist Maureen Dowd has been on Rodham Clinton's case unremittingly since the start. One regrettable characteristic of Dowd's commentary is the way she combines the omnipotence of those born to the *Times*'s Op-Ed page with the age-old female ways of cutting down to size other women who aim too high: irrelevant comments on looks, style, clothing, and figure. The comments need not be explicitly negative to have the desired trivializing effect. At one press conference, Dowd (1996) notes that Rodham Clinton "wore pink." In a front-page article, Dowd (1994) describes her in the second paragraph: "But Mrs. Clinton, pert in a navy blue suit and a print scarf held with a gold frog pin, never looked weary for a moment."

Particularly vituperative is an article by Noemie Emery (1993) that makes explicit many of the deep anxieties that motivate much of the negative response from both sexes. Emery fears that the Clintons exemplify a move within the culture toward androgyny that started with "giving dolls to little boys and trucks to little girls, neutralizing the female as the movement pursues its real interest of negating and containing the male." [5] She is "a lot tougher" than he and, worse, has "made much more money"—proof positive that she is no real woman. "He insinuates. She orders. He seduces. She demands." This analysis is as fuzzy as it is weird: it's not clear whether Emery is seriously suggesting that the Clintons are at the vanguard of a feminist conspiracy to rob us of our gender, but if the article is ironic, you'd never guess it from its tone. It's peculiar to see medieval superstition and gullibility given a new life in the pages of an intellectually respectable magazine.[6]

I think, though, that it isn't so much either of the Clintons' actual gender indeterminacy (if such it is) that is troubling, as that that indeterminacy forecloses the possibility of certainty, of "pinning down" either of them. And if we cannot pin Hillary down, we cannot get control of her. Her insistence on defining herself makes her a new kind of woman—to some, not a woman at all. "[N]othing has been more conspicuous (or distracting)," says Bruck (1994), "than the barrage of changing images of Hillary." That obfuscation occurs in many aspects of the perceived character of Rodham Clinton. The repeated boomeranging between opposites suggests both a need to classify her via absolutes and the frustration and anger of the would-be classifiers.

She is poised between polar opposites: is she . . .

ICY OR EMOTIONAL?

She is often described as imperturbable under stress that would drive most of us to drink or mayhem. Indeed, it is her very unflappability that wins her epithets like "Ice Queen" or "Sister Frigidaire" (Bruck 1994). It would seem that her detractors are disappointed they can't get a rise out of her, because when they do, they can describe her as "out of control," "angry," or "depressed." " 'She has a temper like you would not believe,' a male former associate at the Rose firm said. 'It's not so much that she screams—it's more the tone in her voice, the body language, the facial expressions. It's "The Wrath of Khan" ' " (Bruck 1994).

COMPETENT OR INCOMPETENT?

On the one hand, when she was appointed to the Health Care Task Force in 1993, she turned in a stellar performance, according to early ratings.

Bruck (1994) quotes Lawrence O'Donnell, Jr., the Senate Finance Committee's chief of staff: "[A]nd what I had just heard were the most perfectly composed, perfectly punctuated sentences, growing into paragraphs, in the most perfect, fluid, presentation about what our problems in the field were and what we could do about them. . . . And then she held her position in the face of questioning. . . . And she was more impressive than any Cabinet member who has sat in that chair."

But when the Plan failed, she was blamed and widely savaged as incompetent:[7] she was too insistent on secrecy, the report was over a thousand pages long and impenetrable, she alienated congressmen with alternative but compatible plans, etc. The earlier raves were totally forgotten.

RADICAL OR CONSERVATIVE?

She is regularly denounced in the conservative media as a "radical" who kept her name, wants to allow children to sue their parents, wants the state to take over the control of your kids, and is in favor of reproductive rights. But there is also a chorus of opposition on the left, which scourges her for her conservative and un-feminist stands: for permitting the passage of the Welfare Reform Act; for preaching religion, chastity, and opposition to divorce; for failing to ensure the passage of health care reform; for the "therapeutic policing" Alexander Cockburn alleged she was advocating in It Takes a Village.[8]

FEMINIST OR SEXIST?

Here too it's all in the eye of the beholder. Conservatives see a "radical feminist" who kept her name when she married and as a married woman with a child, works outside the home as a high-powered attorney. But liberals, including many feminists, see a woman who has used a traditional female path to influence, marriage to a powerful man, whose feminism cracks under critique: she changes her name back to appease critics, dresses in pastels, apologizes abjectly when attacked, as reported by Marian Burros (1995): "Saying that she is eager to present herself in a more likable way, Hillary Rodham Clinton said today that she had been 'naive and dumb' about national politics and was to blame for the failure of the health care overhaul plan of last year." In It Takes a Village she expressed opposition to several tenets of feminist theory and practice, in particular the easy availability of divorce.

The criticism of Rodham Clinton for piggybacking on her husband's career might be apropos in a society in which a woman could hope to achieve influence and fully utilize her abilities by the same direct route available to men. When a female presidency has become unremarkable, we can sneer at career moves like Rodham Clinton's.

STRAIGHT OR LESBIAN?

And if the former, "*normal*" or *sexually predatory?*

Persistent rumors on the Internet and on radio talk shows have Rodham Clinton installing a coven of lesbian conspirators in her husband's cabinet; and, at the other extreme, murdering (or arranging the murder of) Vincent Foster to conceal the "torrid affair" she was having with him. The coexistence of both suggests that the troglodyte right either does not know what "lesbians" are, or does not know what a "torrid affair" is, or (as is consistent with Freud's characterization of infantile thinking) is untroubled by contradictions. On the other hand, perhaps (recall the discussion in Chapter 4) the contradiction vanishes if we understand the true meaning of the gossip. What lesbians and sexually predatory straight women have in common is that their sexuality is not intended for the pleasure of men. Thus both are equally outlaws, and both are "the same."

SAINT OR SINNER? (NAUGHTY OR NICE?)

The saint-or-sinner duality is repeatedly invoked—twice in *Newsweek,* once as the title of an article (Clift and Miller 1994) and once as the title of a cover story (Brant and Thomas 1996). The religiosity of the terminology is striking: one is reminded of Eve and her role in the Fall; it's always a woman's fault. The subhead of the 1994 story continues the theme: "Hillary: She wasn't all that greedy in Little Rock. But her pose as selfless public servant set her up for a fall."

Here as throughout, the dichotomization is striking. In our sophisticated age we seldom find it necessary to pin down our male public figures as "saint" or "sinner." The modern, post-Freudian consciousness recognizes and encompasses complexity. But when it is a woman under a microscope, we want an answer, a single answer, couched as "either/or," not "both/and."

To be sure, Rodham Clinton herself sometimes seems to be encouraging the confusion, creating ambiguity for the heck of it. She has often referred to the pleasure she takes in changing her hairstyle continually;

and she often reshapes her fashion image, now in hats, now headbands; in pastels, black, or bright colors. This is sometimes seen as a mark of indecision and fuzziness, the external counterpart to her husband's waffling in the politico-rhetorical sphere. But it could be another way she keeps control of her persona and her meaning: as soon as someone thinks they can predict how she'll look, she's onto something else. Now you see it, now you don't. And we don't even know what her mutability means: is she out of control? in control? So at the metalevel, she evades interpretation yet again. *We don't even know whether we know.*

BILLARY

Why won't Hillary wear miniskirts?
She doesn't want us to see her balls.

What does Hillary do after she shaves her pussy?
Sends him to the Oval Office to work.

The same ambiguity and indeterminacy exist between the First Couple. Bill and Hillary combine and recombine, mix 'n' match their characters and roles. Some refer to the aggregate as *Billary.* They bend gender. *He* is in many ways more traditionally "feminine": he is intuitive, he "feels your pain," he is warm and caring, he worries about his weight, he has fuzzy outlines: his hair is frizzy, his body is—well—a little sloppy. He used to parade before us in skimpy running shorts. All too often he exercises the famous female prerogative of changing his mind. He needs discipline: he eats junk food, he pursues trailer trash, he needs a "bimbo watch." He speaks in a southern accent, which Americans often associate with a feminine speaking (and thinking) style. He is, generally, *soft.*

She shares many traits with the stereotypical male. She is direct and precise. She is nonspontaneous, as Eleanor Clift (1992) reports: "[S]pontaneity has never been Hillary's style. She decided to become a blonde only after reading Margaret Thatcher's autobiography." She plans (or schemes), she is carefully controlled and seeks to control her environment. She is often perceived as cold or even icy, as by Paglia (1996): "The woman her classmates called 'Sister Frigidaire' has the 'mind of winter.' . . . This coldness is the brittle brilliance of Hillary's calculating, analytic mind, which at its most legalistic has a haughty, daunting im-

personality." Her clothes tend to conceal and cover, to shield her and define her boundaries precisely. Her hair, too, is a bit helmetlike: at least,
it is clearly differentiated from the surroundings. She has no discernible
regional accent. She is *hard*.[9]

The Clintons' image problems, then, include gender indeterminacy
and gender-bending, fuzziness and ambiguity of character and intention;
indeterminacy of role; and multiplicity of meaning. We have here the very
model of postmodernism. To an America that never even warmed to
modernism, this is a threat—certainly not something you would want
to find in your Chief Symbologists. The criticism is all the more potent
since many conservative critics have identified deconstructionism and
postmodernism (along with "radical feminism" and multiculturalism)
as the most pernicious of the evils destroying modern America.

The fears gain momentum from the observation, all around us, of the
erosion of the ancient, rigid (and to many comforting) divide between
men and women. In the very Paper of Record is a report that men are . . .
well . . . turning into women, even as women are turning into men. In
this article a therapist (worse yet—therapists are our new authority figures!) says:

> Our culture hasn't made sense of either the women's or the gay liberation
> movements, and as a result, the narcissistic roles are shifting between men
> and women. Traditionally, women have expressed their narcissism through
> sexuality, by being the identified objects of beauty. Men affirmed themselves
> through aggression, by gaining power and possessions. Now, not only have
> women gained much more power, but men are allowing themselves, in a way
> that wasn't possible 20, 10, or even 5 years ago, to display themselves pub-
> licly as sexual objects. Most men see this as both exciting and frightening.
> (Henderson 1998)

To many, this is scarier than a Stephen King movie. The article goes
on to describe men's preoccupation with their own beauty and perfec-
tion: workouts, face-lifts, manicures. "I've got to maintain my girlish
figure," says one—no doubt ironically, but that we understand it at all
is a sign of changing times, changing roles. And when the nation's Ideal
Couple themselves represent this fearsome switch, there is everything to
fear, including fear itself.

If the nation's highest symbolic office is (co-)occupied by a pair who
represent everything that many fear and loathe, Rodham Clinton in particular has become a symbol of all our fears: social change, intellectual
indeterminacy, loss of national purpose, loss of individual initiative and

morality, loss of parental control over children and male control over women. As a symbolic figure, she can only be dealt with by the construction of reductive, and destructive, images. As Paglia (1996) notes: "Like Judy Garland, Maria Callas or Madonna, with their excesses, heartbreaks, torments and comebacks, Hillary the man-woman and bitch-goddess has become a strange superstar whose rise and fall is already the stuff of myth."

Conservatives sometimes seem unable to pinpoint exactly what it is about her that drives them so crazy. They try to find character traits in her that anyone would despise. For instance, according to Henry Louis Gates, Jr. (1996): "'A lot of Americans are uncomfortable with her self-righteousness,' Arianna Huffington says. . . . Peggy Noonan . . . speaks of 'an air of apple-cheeked certitude' that is 'political in its nature and grating in its effects,' of 'an implicit insistence throughout her career that hers were the politics of moral decency and therefore those who opposed her politics were obviously of a lower moral order.'" Yes, self-righteousness is distasteful, and moral certitude and superiority unattractive. But the critique would sit more persuasively in the mind were it not from those who equate homosexuality with criminality and sin, abortion with murder. Rather than speaking, as Rodham Clinton does, in generalities, they are very specific about what you *may not* do in the privacy of your home, and what should happen to you if you do; and what I *may not* put into or take out of my body, and what should happen to me if I do. Huffington and Noonan should recall the old adage about pots calling kettles black.

MEETING THE PRESS

Predictably, the Clintons' obfuscations distress the members of the Fourth Estate. In part it's the same distress that affects many others; and the media reflect public opinion at least as much as they create it. But the level of rancor seems to demand more of an explanation. The media seem fixated on Hillary's negative poll numbers, and at each election offer up prognostications about how her numbers, lower than his, will hurt his chances of reelection. What is missing from this calculus is a realization that the people who claim to hate Hillary so much that her existence makes them "less likely" to vote for her husband (a very small percentage—14 percent in 1992) are unlikely to vote for him anyway (Carlson 1992; Corcoran 1993).

Media perceptions may not accurately reflect popular opinion. Katherine Corcoran notes that at a period when "at least 20 major publications had compared Hillary to Lady Macbeth," her favorable rating was at 56 percent, the same as Bill's. Corcoran discusses the attempts of the media to demonize and blame Rodham Clinton, and the refusal of the public to be swayed very deeply, or very long, as a result. She notes that some of the harshest critique came from female members of the press corps, all of whom when interviewed denied that they were being in any way sexist or unfair. Eleanor Clift of *Newsweek,* after writing an article quoting an "anonymous friend" of Hillary's to the effect that "[A]s bitchy as she comes off, he [Bill] really loves her," told Corcoran that "Hillary's views were covered for the most part by women reporters who were very sympathetic to her." If this is sympathy, I'd just as soon be tarred and feathered. But it's hard to explain this snideness among just the women who, logically, should be the most supportive of the First Lady—women very like herself, women for whom, in the eyes of traditionalists, she is a stand-in. All are women who could be (and undoubtedly are) seen, by the same people who fear and hate Rodham Clinton, as pushy feminists usurping men's traditional power and expressive rights.

One partial explanation is Rodham Clinton's own distrust of the press and open hostility to them (though the treatment she has received from them makes that a rational attitude). They may feel, too, that they have to bend over backwards to avoid the appearance of favoritism. But there was much less bending over in previous administrations. Possibly they see Rodham Clinton as keeping them from doing their job, interpreting her. If she makes interpretation impossible, must they not feel, at some level, that she is deliberately thwarting them, even making sport of the whole journalistic project? And, finally, their resentment against Rodham Clinton could conceal regrets about their having been forced to become "one of the boys" to survive. As Maurine Beasley (1993) says:

> Deborah Howell, Washington Bureau Chief for Newhouse Newspapers, confessed in the Media Studies Journal that she, as did many women of her generation, patterned herself after successful men. "I thought it was wonderful when a colleague said I was 'a credit to my sex.' To be 'one of the boys' or 'a man's woman' were compliments. . . .
> "I really had three categories of gender—men, women who are men, and women who stayed home."

If that kind of uncertainty and self-doubt is characteristic of women in the press corps, it could explain their coverage of the Clintons, and Rodham Clinton in particular, who (as a new woman) might seem to be having all the fun and none of the pain.

One more reason for ambivalence toward the Clintons, by the media and the rest of us, is their age.[10] Bill Clinton is our first president from the post–World War II generation. As a result, he not only lacks war experience, but also grew up in a period of changing mores and morals. Americans older than the Clintons might be expected to resent the takeover of everything by young whippersnappers. The President arouses anxiety as the most visible exemplar of the scary fact that they are aging and threatened with losing their jobs to younger workers, and at the same time the First Lady reminds them that, for the first time, women are competing for jobs with men on terms of relative equality. On top of that, the President's life style is one many Americans, especially older ones, view with suspicion if not outright loathing: his extramarital escapades (involving as they do kinky forms of sex), his tendency to prevaricate, his various *excesses*. While the First Lady herself seems above suspicion in these areas at least, if the First Couple blend together as Billary, some of the stigma might rub off on her.

LOVE AND HATE

Rodham Clinton arouses passion in almost everyone: love or hate, nothing in between. Over the last eight years the media and the public have veered wildly in their feelings about her. An article in the *New York Times* plots the swings in public opinion over time (Alvarez 1998). For most of the Clinton administration, her "favorable" ratings have exceeded the "unfavorable," at times (mid-1992) by as much as 35 points (45 percent to under 10 percent). At times (during the Health Care Initiative period and its aftermath, and after the publication of *It Takes a Village* in 1996) the negatives have jumped above the positives by as much as ten points. At the time the article was written, the ratings were 50 percent favorable to about 27 percent unfavorable.

The split is nowhere better demonstrated than in the reviews of *It Takes a Village* on the Amazon Web site by nonprofessional readers. Visitors to the site are encouraged to provide capsule reviews and award books one to five stars. With most books, both opinions and stars tend to cluster together: a book gets three to four stars, or four to five. For instance, the Bob Woodward book about the 1996 presidential election, *The Choice*, which was on the best-seller list at roughly the same time as the First Lady's, got only a few reviews, whose writers gave the book either four or five stars. But *It Takes a Village* got eleven reviews, an unusually large number. The site gives the "average" customer review as three stars, but that is the one rating not found. There are five single stars, four fives, and two fours. The first two reviews illustrate the schism:

> ***It takes a phoney!!!!** A pathetic attempt to show concern for others from a woman who has nothing but contempt for others, especially if those others stand between her and power! Along with her husband, she has no apparent sign of moral behavior, nor does she or her husband stand on or for any principles. COW-ARDS, COWARDS, COWARDS!!!

> *******Well written (and spoken on audio) and from the heart.** Hillary Rodham Clinton has written a wonderful, thought-provoking book. Obviously written from her heart and substantial knowledge of children's issues, it explores how each of us impact children's lives and ultimately our own. Mrs. Clinton has the ability and intelligence to see that and to verbalize it very well in an engrossing book that everyone of us should read. It is too bad that under the dissimulation of a review, some people have chosen to bash it based on their political stand instead of their literary one.

As the second reviewer suggests, the book itself seems the last thing on several of the (especially negative) reviewers' minds. One suspects some of them may not have read it too closely: a couple complain that she gives short shrift to parents, when in fact the roles and importance of parents are discussed on virtually every page. Reviewers here and in more conventional media also are prone to seeing "village" either as a euphemism for "state" and the book as a call for taking children away from their parents to be raised (presumably, in Gingrichian orphanages); or understanding the "village" as exclusive of the "family" or "parents," when in fact Rodham Clinton makes it clear she intends "village" to include the "family" and "parents" (as real-world villages normally include the families that compose them). Here as elsewhere, conservative critics betray their ignorance of much of what human adults normally know about the workings of ordinary language (e.g., frames and presuppositions) in order to make their points.

In fact Rodham Clinton's advocacy for children—which might offhand seem to be a moot point—appears to function as the red flag to many a conservative bull. Just as Eleanor Roosevelt's advocacy of black civil rights made many contemporary critics foam at the mouth, Rodham Clinton's discussion of the culture's inhumanities to children does the same now. Many reviewers barely hide their rage against children and against those who would claim that children—*any* children, *ever*—need advocates or protectors from adults. Some of the reviews express a panicky fear that our children are out to get us, that they are just lying in wait for the opportunity to report us to the Child Protection Agency for *no reason at all*. This alienation is not unrelated to the media's current preoccupation with children who kill. Taken together, both kinds of stories illustrate the movement, in our collective psyches, of the semantic concept of "children" from helpless figures in need of nurture to manipulative or downright hostile creatures we can neither understand nor trust. Thus in her review Jean Bethke Elshtain (1996) sneers at Rodham Clinton's encouraging people to "'help' people in various ways, whether the people in question have asked for it or not." Following in the footsteps of many conservative critics, Elshtain suggests that the purported "epidemic" of child abuse is much overrated. No statistics are given to support that implication. (The review also takes a passing slap at the "chattering classes" excoriated by Peggy Noonan [1991], a current favorite in the neocon slogan armamentarium. I keep wondering who comprises the "chattering classes" if not people who write for intellectual(ish) magazines like *The New Republic*.)

The arguments themselves are less puzzling than the rage that fuels their overheated rhetoric. It is true that presidents other than Clinton have been the targets of virulent anger. In the last fifty years, Lyndon Johnson and Richard Nixon certainly qualify. But that anger never extended to their wives, and in both of these cases, it was directed at the president's official actions and behavior: LBJ's and Nixon's escalation of the Vietnam War, Nixon's anticommunist smear campaigns, his documented Enemies List, Watergate. Absent from the screeds on the Web and in the media is any clear indication of just what the writers or speakers are so furious at the Clintons for. There are fulminations about lying, immorality, and among the wing nuts, murders and cover-ups, but as far as documented political misbehavior—nothing. (And—by contrast with the LBJ and Nixon administrations—no one today faces getting sent off to die in the jungles of southeast Asia.)

From other quarters come equally passionate defenses of the Clintons, whose source is just as difficult to document. The more scandals are exposed, the higher their popularity soars and the more money pours into his defense fund and the Democratic campaign coffers (Seelye 1999). It is difficult not to conclude that the Clintons are detested, when they are, and adored, when they are, not for what they do but for what they are, and in fact not even so much for what they are as for what they symbolize: changes in the allocation of power and authority from those who always had it to new groups, new rules or no rules at all—the threat of anarchy, a new style of public (as of private) discourse.

Those fears may explain the passion of conservatives. But many liberals, including feminists, have taken up the cudgels against both Clintons, and especially against Hillary, and in particular against *It Takes a Village*. On this side, the critique *is* based on the perception of real misbehavior and is fueled by the bitterness of betrayal. A lot of it is directed at Hillary, because no one with any political acumen saw Bill as the great liberal hope. It was clear from the start he was a member of that new breed, the Republocrat. But many thought she was the liberal in the family and, even more, that once they won their second term, her (and perhaps his) "stealth liberalism" would emerge. In that they were disappointed, and many blamed Hillary for the betrayal.

Two questions are often raised: Is she (really) a feminist at all or merely an opportunist who has taken advantage of the gains made by feminism to achieve power? And does she support the goals that "feminists"— whatever that may be—support? Several writers answer one or both of those questions in the negative.

If you are a feminist and you believe that Rodham Clinton is not adhering to what you see as a feminist program, what should you do? Criticize her or (since her symbolic role is more important than anything she actually accomplishes) keep quiet and be supportive? Opinions are divided.[11] In an article by Zelda Bronstein in *Dissent* followed by commentaries,[12] several feminists argue about the Rodham Clinton problem. Feminists, says Bronstein, might have "taken the First Lady to task for her leading role in the disastrous campaign to overhaul health insurance," a position Ruth Rosen blasts as being as "absurd as condemning Truman for 'losing' China." Bronstein addresses Katha Pollitt's suggestion that criticisms of Rodham Clinton's role are veiled attacks on feminism and strong women. On the other hand, she notes that other feminists, for instance Karen Lehrman, question Rodham Clinton's feminist bona fides for achieving power in the traditional male-identified way: through marriage to a powerful man.

Bronstein and other feminist critics are also scathing about the Clinton administration's welfare reform bill. But it's uncertain how much of this discredit ought to reflect on Rodham Clinton. It's not clear first of all that the Clinton administration, working with a Republican Congress, could have done much better; and by enacting the bill that was passed, they might have fended off something even worse. Even if this is not true, we just don't know how much influence on her husband's, and his administration's, decisions she really has. (There are plenty of rumors, but they are only that—rumors.)

Then there are questions (which might better be filed under "None of Our Business") about the marriage itself. Rodham Clinton famously, or infamously, said in an interview on *60 Minutes* in January 1992, that she hadn't chosen to be "sitting here, some little woman standing by my man like Tammy Wynette." Rather, she made the choice to stay with Bill because she loved him and believed in him, despite "problems" in their marriage. But (if we must be nosy) is that the best choice for someone who purports to be a role model for today's young women?

Well, if we must be nosy, let's think about it. In a strange way, Bill and Hillary have an ultratraditional arrangement: he fools around, she looks the other way or forgives. In the old days, wives did this because they had no alternative that was socially and economically feasible: to acknowledge unforgivable wrong on the spouse's part was to either see oneself as a helpless victim (intolerable to a woman of character) or necessitate a divorce. Divorce, back then, was social and economic death for a respectable woman.

Rodham Clinton, the thoroughly modern role model, may be refusing to acknowledge the seriousness of the problem for analogous if different reasons. For her, divorce would mean a loss of political influence dearly won. Would it make sense to have endured twenty-five years of "problems," only to lose the prize now that it is hers? So—like traditional wives—she can't acknowledge her anger and disappointment, for that would force her to be a pitiful victim or lose it all. In this view, she's doing the only rational thing.

Or maybe she just loves the big lug. (Smart women, foolish choices.)

Or maybe, conceivably . . . it really *is* none of our business.

CONSPIRACY THEORY 101A

In January 1998, Rodham Clinton suggested on a morning television program that the allegations against both Clintons emanated from a "vast right wing conspiracy." She was promptly excoriated and ridiculed from all sides. But the right has been alleging explicitly and continually that the Clintons themselves are part of any number of conspiracies.[13] These allegations of conspiratorial behavior of the most serious kind are, to my knowledge, unprecedented in commentary on First Couples prior to the Clintons. It is true, to be sure, that conspiracy theories generally have flourished mightily in recent years, encouraged by the Web (not to mention the movies of Oliver Stone). But the virulence and prevalence of the rumors about the Clintons still call for explanation.

Conspiracy theory is a way to make sense of the randomness of the universe. It gives causes and motives to events that are more rationally seen as accidents. By attributing motives to chance happenings, believers gain control of the uncontrollable, bringing the disturbing vagaries of reality under their control, enough to make accurate predictions and maybe even alter reality: omnipotence, or at least omniscience. But the control is always threatened, and the renewed fear is often replaced by anger, since anger is powerful and controlling, while fear is weak and helpless. In this strange and scary world, irrational rage and weird conspiracy theories coexist happily.

Those theories work even better if much of the evil in the world can be blamed on powerful parental stand-ins like the First Couple. As children, we *knew* our parents were omnipotent; whatever good or bad happened to us, it was their doing. So (especially for the not fully mature) finding the root of all evil in the White House is deeply satisfying. If the First Couple themselves, by the literal and symbolic changes in gender relations that they represent, are contributing significantly to some Americans' fears of obsolescence and impotence beyond the reach of Viagra, blaming them for more traditional and impersonal conspiracies—murder and financial double-dealing—is a way to avoid direct recognition of the real source of the fear. It is uncomfortable to admit that Bill Clinton's defense of gay rights or Hillary Rodham Clinton's assertiveness in public raises doubts about one's own manhood or womanhood. If those fears and doubts can be transferred to murderous conspiracies (which *should* be feared and brought to light), how much more comfortable life is!

Eleanor Roosevelt, whose real and symbolic roles are in many ways similar to Rodham Clinton's, attracted conspiracy theories too. Doris Kearns Goodwin (1993) mentions a couple:

> rumors (none of them true, of course) that Eleanor had created "Eleanor Clubs" for black maids who promised to get out of white people's houses and go somewhere else to work. "Whenever you see a Negro wearing a wide-brimmed hat with a feather in it," they said, "you know it's a sign of the Eleanor Club." There were warnings of "Eleanor Tuesdays," when black women were supposed to bump into white women in honor of Eleanor.

Bizarre as these rumors seem today, they have the same source as the modern Vincent Foster rumors: fear of change in the power structure. *Plus ça change, plus c'est la même chose.*

DELIBERATE MISINTERPRETATIONS

A similar anxiety underlies another peculiarity of the Rodham Clinton reportage, the way in which practically everything she says is at best overinterpreted, but more often deliberately misinterpreted. I say "deliberately," because commentators knowingly take her remarks out of context, misconstrue them, or go off on wild tangents that suggest they have not even bothered to find out what the First Lady actually said.

If Rodham Clinton causes distress by resisting interpretation and insisting on speaking for herself, then stark misinterpretations of her are not—as they might otherwise be—necessarily a sign of the interpreter's thickheadedness. *That* would be ordinary garden-variety misinterpretation; *this* goes so far beyond it, in its floridity, its closeness to self-parody, that it must be intentional, it must be accorded the dignity of purposefulness. If you can *choose* by your interpretation to decide what Hillary Rodham Clinton is to "mean," you can deny her the right to determine what she intended by her words. You score a preemptive strike, you co-opt. You take back the taking-back, you reassign the right to make meaning to those who have possessed it in the past. Deliberate misinterpretation is a daringly reactionary, excitingly business-as-usual speech act. That is one reason why it doesn't matter when Rodham Clinton or her supporters painstakingly explain what was really meant, when they put the remark back into its original context. It only makes things worse if she apologizes, since by apologizing she acknowledges their right to make meaning for her. She isn't seen as apologizing for the comment per se, but for commenting about anything, in any way, at all.

Additionally, the misinterpretations, painting Rodham Clinton in the worst possible light, serve to justify on rational grounds the fear and anger she has aroused. If you can use "her own words" to show what a bad person she is, and *how much she hates you* and people like you, you legitimize your anger. Deliberate misinterpretation demonizes its target and justifies its user. And finally, by smacking her with her own words, you punish her for speaking publicly, thereby warning women everywhere to shut up. Deliberate misinterpretation functions as punishment is meant to, as a deterrent to others.

This is one way to make sense of the ruckus over the "famous-cookies-and-tea-remark," as it has become known. The story is this: during the 1992 primaries, in response to a charge by rival Democratic candidate Jerry Brown that the Rose Law Firm had profited improperly from a partner's marriage to the governor, she was reported to have replied, "I suppose I could have stayed home and baked cookies and had teas." There was an immediate flurry: the remark was taken as a deliberate slur on all women who did not work outside the home.

On its own, the quoted statement can be read that way (among others). But, as Barbara Burrell points out, none of the interpreters paid any attention to the rest of the remark that immediately followed the quoted portion: "I chose to fulfill my profession, which I had before my husband was in public life. The work that I have done as a professional, a public advocate, has been aimed . . . to assure that women can make the choices . . . whether it's full-time career, full-time motherhood or some combination" (1997, 31f.). Now when you factor in the complete comment, the famous cookies-and-tea remark becomes much more readily interpretable, not as a putdown of women working in the home, but as first, a justification for her personal choice as an act of autonomy rather than a move toward corruption (that is, it was directed at countering Brown's charge, rather than intended as an irrelevant commentary on her choice vs. that of other more traditional women); and second, an attempt to express solidarity with women who have made choices other than hers: her choice, she suggests, supported the right and ability of women to make any choice they deemed right. (It's not clear to me how her choice of a career helped other women stay at home, but I guess it's the thought that counts.) It does seem extraordinary that the media, well-known for their passion for ferreting out every detail of anything that catches their interest, were virtually unanimous in ignoring the full intention and contextualization of Rodham Clinton's comment.

The treatment of It Takes a Village is similar. Many of its reviewers seem either not to have read the book at all or to have read a different book entitled It Takes a Village, by Hillary Rodham Clinton, than I did. One is loath to come down too hard on the amateur reviewers on Amazon for confusing politics with literacy, but it's surprising to find the same level of contempt for the written word in reviews by authoritative persons in serious publications. Years before the book's publication, one such writer is already putting the party line in place. Couched as a Bobbsey Twins parody (i.e., putatively from a child's perspective), his cover story opens with a riddle:

Question: What's the difference between a children's rights activist and a
pit bull?
Answer: You might get your child back from the pit bull (Olson 1992)

and goes on in that vein from there, pausing to sneer at Garry Wills's supportive article on Rodham Clinton in the *New York Review of Books*
("'I think he's sweet on her,' Freddie [the Bobbsey twin] scoffed"), and
stirring up the old fears that, given the "rights" Rodham Clinton champions, children will waste no time in hauling their innocent and ideal
parents into court. Elizabeth Fox-Genovese (1996), also in the *National
Review,* makes the typical misinterpretive leap in her review: "The appalling evidence of children's distress and alienation leaves no doubt that
a village cannot raise a child. It takes a family—ideally a mother and a
father—to raise a child, and the village's first responsibility is not to
hamper them in doing so." But what about when the family isn't doing the job right? Should the village ignore that? What about when the
family can't make ends meet? And the purposeful dichotomization of
"family" and "village" is a blatant distortion of Rodham Clinton's argument. Fox-Genovese sneers that the "cozy, confidential" tone of the book
"thinly disguises an engaged partisanship"—pots and kettles again.

Another case is discussed by Lizette Alvarez (1998). Questioned about
the hostility toward her and the president, Rodham Clinton replied, "I
think a lot of this is prejudice against our state. They wouldn't do this
if we were from some other state." The argument gains some point if
one scans the Clinton jokes on the Web: quite a few are barely retooled
"Arkie" or "hillbilly" humor. (Example: *How do you break Bill Clinton's finger? Punch him in the nose.*) But Republican Arkansans leaped
to misread her intent. Representative Jay Dickey growled: "It is sad and
unfortunate that Arkansas is depicted by the First Lady as a backward
state, worthy of ridicule and prejudice. It would be much better if the
First Lady would make a mature and responsible assessment of the situation and not blame Arkansans for their troubles." Of course, the First
Lady did not "depict" Arkansas as backward: she depicted her enemies
as depicting Arkansans (herself and her husband included) as backward.
It may be a small difference—"just semantics," the pundits like to say—
but significant.

As with most effective propaganda, these conservative misreadings
are wrapped around a scintilla of truth, to which they can retreat when
challenged. It's true that *It Takes a Village* includes institutions other
than the nuclear family in the child-rearing process. The cookies-and-tea

remark did get made, and in another context could plausibly have received the interpretation it was given. Urbanites have been known to belittle Arkansans. By suggesting that their targets are anti-family and anti–little guy (Arkansas), the propagandists forge an emotional and quasi-populist link with "regular" folks, placing their targets beyond human comprehension, cold snobs without empathy.

CYNOSURE OF ALL EYES

So Rodham Clinton gets subjected to continual public interpretation, reinterpretation, misinterpretation, and overinterpretation, because that is the best way to neutralize her. We *have* to solve the equation for "Hillary," because only by solving it will we ever be able to control what it stands for. But by its nature it is not solvable: it remains a paradox. Rodham Clinton passes the UAT with flying colors: she gets more attention than any previous first lady, probably more than most movie stars (or your average multiple murderess). But media attention is not all she gets. Because she cannot be pinned down in the normal, rational way, she is not only *mediacized,* but also subjected, in our desperation, to more invasive techniques: she is *psychoanalyzed* and ultimately *mythologized.*

THE INSIDE STORY: PSYCHOANALYSIS

Psychoanalysis has been with us for a century now, and functions for us variously as a medical subspecialty; a philosophical system; a quasi religion; a modernist object of postmodern critique; and a way to cut people we are afraid of down to size and render them harmless, while defanging any response from them. Camille Paglia (1996) invokes the last to deal with the First Lady Problem. Paglia spends a good part of her article venting spleen at her target. But to disguise the pure venom of her attack, Paglia claims the "objectivity" of science and medicine by couching it in psychoanalytic terminology (even as Freud legitimized misogyny by making it scientific).

> A hostility to conventional masculinity can be detected in both Clintons'
> past. . . . While she idolized her father and seems to have competed with her
> mother and siblings to be daddy's number one girl, Hillary also saw the psy-
> chic damage inflicted by his iron rule in their close-knit, secretive family. . . .
> In her book Hillary tells of an incident in grade school when an older boy . . .

chased her, threw her to the ground and kissed her. . . . The theme of male intrusion and contamination would recur. . . . [Paglia uses as her example Rodham Clinton's criticism, as Wellesley commencement speaker, of the invited guest, Sen. Edward Brooke.] . . . The sexual repressions and resentments of Hillary the snow queen would have long-reaching effects on policy when the Clintons arrived in Washington.

This is what responsible psychoanalysts would call "wild analysis," made worse by the fact that, as far as I know, Paglia has never met "Hillary" in person, much less been made privy to her innermost thoughts. Paglia's aim is not to cure, but to neutralize; to render Rodham Clinton harmless because she is not only "bad" but also "mad." Yet psychoanalysis has its positive uses. Our fascination with Rodham Clinton's psyche may represent our deep curiosity about Rodham Clinton as a role model at a time when we all are exploring new identities. We need to know what she is "really" like in order to determine what we want to be "really" like—not to hate her, but to emulate her. "I'm a Rorschach test," she has taken to telling interviewers. We psychoanalyze Rodham Clinton in order to try to see how she works, because that might be a clue to how we all will shortly work, or perhaps already are working.

HERE SHE IS . . . MYTH AMERICA!

Wild analysis at a distance cannot give us real control. We must examine not just the individual, but our culture. Before psychoanalysis, before even what we think of today as proper "religion," our species, just achieving consciousness, developed a tool to explain the world, themselves, and other people: mythology. We use it still, to try to account for the way things are, and predict the way they will turn out, by inventing stories about the way things came to be as they are. The cohesion of the narrative gives tellers and hearers a sense of control over the events it describes, even though the stories are fictional.

Thus we *mythologize* Rodham Clinton, as we never have any previous first lady. She becomes an object of awe, veneration, fear, and fascination. Walter Shapiro, in *Esquire* (1993), lays out some of the myths we have constructed to make her make sense:

Hillary has the sense of humor of Pat Nixon.
. . . And the common touch of Nancy Reagan.
Hillary takes her cues from Marx (and it ain't Groucho), and is at
   the core of a secret radical coven.

Hillary the Virtuous—the greatest feminist role model since Joan of Arc.

As Shapiro shows, all of these are false, although all have a grain of truth at their cores. But we are less concerned with finding the true Hillary than with constructing a mythic "Hillary Rodham Clinton." Accepting these myths gives us a superiority that allows us to dismiss her. When we need more depth, we try to pin her down by fitting her into a pre-existing plot. We borrow from familiar narratives, snipping and stretching them as necessary, in order to construct a plausible simulacrum.

LADY MACBETH

Over the last several years there have been an inordinate number of productions of *Macbeth*.[14] Just coincidence? I don't think so.

Recall the plot and characters of the play. The Macbeths—medieval Scotland's two-for-one power couple—lie, scheme, and kill to achieve the throne. (Already it sounds familiar.) Besides the blood and gore, the Macbeths serve as a worst-case marital scenario, a warning about what happens when the unnatural attains ascendancy, when boundaries are transgressed and the nonnormal becomes the rule. The play abounds in lines suggesting that *she* is the man of the family and *he*, not quite a man. (Queen Elizabeth I had died shortly before the play was written, to be succeeded by a man, a proper King, and the descendant of Elizabeth's hated rival, Mary, Queen of Scots.) Lady Macbeth plots and schemes. Her husband just follows orders. They gain the throne, but get little pleasure from it, in large part because (being unnatural and ambiguous in gender) they have no offspring to succeed them. Finally, the same supernatural forces that brought them to power snatch it away, and at the end *he* finally dies, as a man at last, and *she* reverts to true womanhood—madness, illness, helplessness, depression, and suicide.

Hmmm.

THE SPHINX

In ancient Greece there was a terrible she-monster with the head of a woman and the body of a lion. The Sphinx lay in wait for travelers and posed them a riddle. If they could answer, she let them go; if not she strangled them and ate them.[15] Until Oedipus, no one ever answered her riddle. She ate them up, every one. Sound familiar?

Well, not literally, any more than that the Clintons reign over medieval Scotland. But current paranoid fantasies create connections.

Like the Sphinx, Rodham Clinton is mysterious and enigmatic. You cannot know her, that is, answer her riddle; yet it is of the utmost importance that you do so.

She is voracious and deadly. She kills for sport.

She is not quite human, not quite female: a monster, half and half.

But most especially, like the Sphinx she *deprives men of speech*, or surpasses men at speech—asks them things they cannot answer, silences them, and thus kills them—renders them impotent. The Sphinx's M.O. was (as is true of cats) to bite the victims' windpipes shut so that they cannot breathe or make a sound. She cuts off their communicative capacities, as any self-defining woman does to men (or so some fear). There must be some connection between the Clinton administration and the Viagra craze.

AS THE WORLD TURNS: THE REHABILITATION
OF HILLARY RODHAM CLINTON

The Lady Macbeth/Sphinx image is not the last we have tried on the First Lady. In August 1998, the president admitted to an "improper" relationship with a White House intern, Monica Lewinsky. At once public perception of Rodham Clinton changed, from omnipotent controller to helpless victim of marital infidelity. (Again the pendulum had to go all the way.) Her popularity soared.

The visual representation of Rodham Clinton in the media underwent a concomitant and probably uncoincidental sea change. In the past, she had regularly been photographed in the most unflattering poses available: mouth open, silly hat, funny looks. Now she was depicted in a candlelit photo in the December 1998 *Vogue* (take that, Monica!) by celebrity photographer Annie Leibovitz, looking undeniably . . . glamorous. News photos suddenly showed her smiling and looking good. It was as if she had suddenly become a woman, indeed a desirable one, not because of any change in herself, but because she had been brought down: she was suffering, she was a victim. She was harmless, helpless, not in control: womanly.

The need for interpretation continued, now fixated on the First Couple's relationship. Tea leaves were endlessly scrutinized: Were they still partners? Was he in the doghouse? Was the marriage effectively over? Former detractors sound bemused, uncertain what course to take. Thus Arianna Huffington: "Well now Hillary has become the Wronged Woman and has the sympathy factor, which is something everybody is much more comfortable with than the strong, determined Hillary" (quoted in Clines 1998), although it's not entirely clear who "everybody" includes.[16] Grist is still required for the interpretive mill. Among the entrails regularly scanned are photos of the First Couple. It is noted that they rarely touch any more; in public at times when he attempts to take her arm, she unobtrusively brushes it off. In an article (Fineman 1998) that discusses Topic A at length, there is a photo that tells all. They are caroling at the national Christmas tree lighting ceremony. He has his arm around her shoulder—so far, so good. But . . . he is facing to his right (away from her), she to her left, in fact not only facing left but standing perpendicularly away from him. They are together but apart.

The tea leaves are compulsively stirred up. In his State of the Union message in January 1999, the President included a love note to his wife: "I honor her, for leading our millennium project, for all she has done for our children and for her historic role in serving our nation and in advancing our ideals at home and abroad" (*New York Times,* January 20, 1999). In the standing ovation that followed, Mr. Clinton ad libbed "I love you" *sotto voce.* The moment occupied the pundits for the next couple of days. What was he *really* saying? What was she *really* feeling?

The Big Question all America wants answered remains: What are they *going to do?* What is the state of the First Marriage? Rumors reach me from far-flung Buenos Aires: she has demanded a divorce in the immediate post-millennium; she had a tantrum while they were on vacation. And so on.

The story sets off echoes in the minds of the boomers and gen-X'ers of their own childhoods, the divorces of their own Mommies and Daddies. The Clintons—they are us. Like those children, we *want* to ask the Question, but (perhaps for other reasons now) we cannot bring ourselves to do so. So we frame another substitute question to satisfy our prurient curiosity: Will she, or won't she, run for the Senate from New York in 2000? At this writing (July 1999) Rodham Clinton has formed an exploratory committee, received the blessing of the man she would replace, Senator Daniel Patrick Moynihan, and embarked on a sort of pre-campaign "listening tour" of New York State. She has not officially announced her candidacy, but the eventual announcement is taken as a

fait accompli. Extraordinarily, out-of-state Republicans are already mo-
bilizing to "pillory Hillary" in an election still almost sixteen months off
(Van Natta 1999a). But for most, the question itself is titillating: will she
or won't she? Of course it's a tantalizing question in its own right . . .
but would we care as much if it weren't a stand-in for The Big One?

GLORIOUS DAYS OF YESTERYEAR

Our preoccupation with a woman in a high position may seem unique
in history. We may think that this is the first woman who has been in
such a position, and therefore the first woman who has ever received this
sort of ambivalent but most often malevolent treatment. It is true that it
is rare for a woman to achieve power via means other than divine right
and inheritance. But while such cases are rare, they are not unheard of. I
know of three historical parallels, all women who came to power through
marriage (and were excoriated on those grounds).

The first we know already, Eleanor Roosevelt. Rodham Clinton herself has often cited Roosevelt as a spiritual ancestor and role model, the
contemporary criticism of whom is similar to what she herself suffers,
and who, in historical retrospect, has largely been rehabilitated. According to the examples cited in Doris Kearns Goodwin's *No Ordinary Time,*
the most frequent, personal, and vitriolic attacks on Roosevelt came
from women; and the attacks intensified as Roosevelt was seen as empowering the historically powerless—particularly African Americans.

To take a few representative examples from Goodwin:

> Across the country, Eleanor's activism on behalf of blacks engendered scath-
> ing comments. "If you have any influence with the President," a New Jersey
> woman wrote Missy LeHand, "will you please urge him to muzzle Eleanor
> Roosevelt and it might not be a bad idea to chain her up—she talks too damn
> much." (1995, 164)

> "Mrs. Roosevelt," a woman from Kalamazoo wrote Eleanor, "you would be
> doing your country a great service if you would simply go home and sew for
> the Red Cross. Every time you open your mouth the people of this country
> dislike and distrust you more." (325)

> "I know, of course, you are bidding for negro votes for your good husband,"
> an "outraged" woman wrote Eleanor, "but isn't it rather a costly price to
> pay? . . . Would you have enjoyed seeing your daughter Anna being hugged
> by those negroes. . . . You are the most dangerous woman in America today
> and may I beg you to stop and think before you are guilty of such a thing
> again." (503)

At least Eleanor Roosevelt was never accused of outright criminal conduct. But that happened often to my second example, the wife of Augustus Caesar, Livia Drusilla. As with both Roosevelt and Rodham Clinton,
the age in which she lived, the late first century B.C.E. and early first century C.E., was experienced by contemporaries as frightening and dangerous—a time of radical social and political readjustment, of changing
values and new rules of conduct for all. While Augustus was a firm believer in family values (except of course for his family and especially himself) and an opponent of women's rights, it was generally acknowledged
by both contemporary writers and later historians that Livia had a great
deal of influence over him. The historian most influential in forming
posterity's opinion of Livia is the Greek author Dio Cassius, writing over
a century after the events he describes. He devotes nearly ten pages to a
speech Livia is supposed to have delivered to Augustus in bed (the an-
cients had no compunctions about "reconstructing" speeches that might
plausibly have been delivered). In it she sets out his foreign and domestic policy for the remaining ten years of his reign. "Augustus heeded these
suggestions of Livia," Cassius concludes (1906, 55:21). But Livia's influence came at a price. Elsewhere Cassius repeats traditional charges
against her: that she had too much power, which she misused; that she
committed high crimes and misdemeanors with impunity (causing the
deaths of people who stood in the way of her sons' and grandsons' ac-
cession to power, finally including Augustus himself):

> Livia, however, was accused of having caused the death of Marcellus because
> he had been preferred before her sons. (53:33)

> So Gaius resigned at once all the duties of his office and took a coastwise trad-
> ing vessel to Lycia, where, at Limyra, he breathed his last. Prior to his demise
> the spark of Lucius' life had also paled. . . . His death was due to a sudden
> illness. In connection with both these cases, therefore, suspicion rested upon
> Livia. (55:10)

> So Augustus fell sick and died. Livia incurred some suspicion regarding the
> manner of his death. . . . She was afraid, some say, that Augustus would bring
> [Agrippa] back to make him sovereign, and so smeared with poison some figs
> that were still on trees from which Augustus was wont to gather fruit with his
> own hands. So she ate the ones that had not been smeared, and pointed out
> the poisoned ones to him. (56:30)

A third example is discussed by Pierre Saint-Amand, in a paper entitled "Terrorizing Marie Antoinette." The author looks at the negative
representations in the media during the reign of Queen Marie Antoinette,
which contributed to the downfall of the monarchy and the coming of

the French Revolution. "The hatred trained upon Hillary Clinton during the last presidential election," says Saint-Amand, "was reproduced in the very same language as the discourse of infamy that sent Queen Marie Antoinette to the guillotine" (1994, 379). The author identifies three aspects of this syndrome: (1) the demonization and cloning of the woman's influence; (2) the accessibility of the woman's genitalia as the very organ of influence; (3) a seizing of the woman's body by way of sexual appropriation. The article describes in detail the pornography of the period, in which the Queen is represented as engaged in acts of sexual perversity and debauchery; the deliberate creation and dissemination of scandalous gossip about her, accusing her of lesbian and extramarital heterosexual activity; the attribution to her of undue influence over her husband, blaming her for the wrongs of his regime ("Let them eat cake!")—and connects them to Rodham Clinton's treatment in the contemporary American media. Both Rodham Clinton and Marie Antoinette, says Saint-Amand, "are victims of a backlash against the advancement of women in the public sphere, against their increased visibility and competition with men for participation in social institutions" (384). Women's influence in both cases "is seen as a form of hysterical persuasion" (385). And just as Rodham Clinton is denied the right to name herself, so Marie Antoinette is referred to in the literature of the Revolution as the "Widow Capet"—a title containing no name of her own or any she herself had ever used. Elsewhere her given name is diminutized as "Toinon" and "Toinette." Analogous to Marie Antoinette's detractors' use of her body and sexuality are the jokes about Rodham Clinton exemplified above.

While the political situations in Ancient Rome and in France at the end of the eighteenth century bear little direct resemblance to the scene in this country today, these parallels are intriguing. The three societies, different in so many ways, nevertheless find it essential to undermine the power of influential women and use remarkably similar means to do so.

Hillary Rodham Clinton's role in the making of meaning is—like everything else about her—complex and even contradictory. On the one hand, her action is negative: she subverts the attempts of traditional meaning makers to define her and control her by her ambiguity and ambivalence. On the other hand she is a positive and active maker of meaning, a woman who—at least sometimes—chooses her own words, makes her own meaning, speaks for herself. But that active and positive role is counterbalanced by her tendency to backpedal and apologize, to repackage herself in a more traditional form at any sign of controversy. Hillary Rodham Clinton herself, with her uncertainties, is one thing. The discourse about her, with its conflicting absolutes, is something else. It has taken on a life of its own.

There are good reasons why. The source is larger than life and arouses responses in us that go beyond our responses to people whose role is only literal. Hillary Rodham Clinton is who some of us want to be and want women to be, and who others fear that women have become. Therefore everything we feel about her is distorted and exaggerated. Responses to her are provoked less by her actual behavior and more by the symbolic function she plays and the narratives we wrest from her. The symbolic and largely imaginary "Hillary Rodham Clinton" was created out of the real Hillary Rodham Clinton and continues to be so created, by each of us, to serve our own particular needs, to galvanize us on one side or the other, to exemplify the major *angst* of the 1990's, the growth of women's power and influence. The ambiguity of both her current role, and her personality; and the indeterminacy of both Clintons in their roles as idealized gender representations—the postmodern co-presidency—encourage an ambivalent public response, as well as guaranteeing that the public will never be satisfied with any single media representation of Hillary Rodham Clinton. We may embrace Hillary Rodham Clinton's presentation of the feminine ideal of the 1990's; oppose it; deny her right to represent it; or attempt to undermine it. But it is always with us and will remain a part of our culture and our individual identities.

WHO FRAMED "O.J."?

THE STORY OF THE CENTURY

Sometime between 10:15 and 10:45 on the night of June 12, 1994, the plaintive wail of a white Akita dog named Kato sliced through the calm evening air of Brentwood, California. The calm has never been restored.

The story is still too familiar to merit detailed retelling. Kato's wails led a hearer to the condominium of Nicole Brown Simpson, estranged wife of football hero and movie semi-star Orenthal James ("O.J.") Simpson. In the front yard lay the mangled bodies of Nicole Simpson and a friend, Ron Goldman, stabbed multiple times.

By 11:45 that night O.J. himself had boarded a plane for Chicago, possibly with a cut on his finger but showing no other signs of involvement in a bloodbath. Informed by the police of his wife's death, the former superstar dutifully returned from Chicago the next day. Simpson was questioned at length, without an attorney, the day after that. Later in the week it was determined that he should be placed under arrest, but when the police went to collect him from where he was staying, he had vanished. He was located in a Ford Bronco being driven by his long-time buddy A. C. Cowlings.

The police provided an escort for the "low-speed car chase" up and down the L.A. freeways, as it played out over several hours. O.J. lay in the back seat, holding a phone to one side of his head on which he held conversation with the police, complaining about how he had been misunderstood and mistreated, and a pistol to the other side, threatening suicide. Every television network interrupted its programming to broadcast the "chase." Just about everyone in America watched at least some part of it—why? Something surreal and hypnotic, real-live-action yet slo-mo, real-life yet bizarre, kept us glued to the set as nothing happened, and kept on happening, and happened some more. Finally Cowlings and his police entourage pulled up at O.J.'s house, where Simpson was allowed to go inside, change clothes, and drink some orange juice ("O.J.") before being formally arrested.

All this was but preliminary to the main event, the Trial of the Century. The trial was televised live over nine months. Summaries of each day's doings occupied significant chunks of the daily news broadcasts, local and national, of the three major networks. Both defense and prosecution employed huge teams of eminent attorneys and experts (some sixty for the defense, forty for the prosecution; let no one say the Simpson case lacked redeeming social value: it functioned as a full employment act for the legal profession and the media in Los Angeles). The jury was selected from a panel of nine hundred. By July there was real fear that the court would run out of alternates, leading to a mistrial. At long last, on October 3, 1995, the largely female, largely African-American jurors returned a verdict after a four-hour deliberation: NOT GUILTY.

Everyone was watching: more people than had watched the Kennedy funeral, the moon landing, or the first day of the Gulf War.[1] The fascination with the crime, the dramatis personae, and the trial itself seemed to pale at that moment relative to the shock of the verdict. More shocking still, at least to members of the white community, were the different responses of blacks and whites as the verdict was announced. The black members of the audience cheered, hugging and high-fiving one another; the whites stood silent and separate, looking dazed and grim. For weeks, media second-guessing flowed like lava: why had it happened, what did it mean, what would the fallout be? The pundits pontificated away, and some of them still are at it.

Like me.

ALL ABOUT "ABOUT"

I keep coming back to the story because I can't quite figure it out: it keeps changing both its form and its meaning each time I scrutinize it, whenever I try to pin it down like a good social scientist, with a firm,

"It's about . . . " or "This is why . . . " The crime and its sequelae raise too many questions for Americans, questions we would rather not ask and prefer not to have to answer. The "abouts" have been discussed exhaustively, a litany of what makes us nervous about ourselves as individuals and as a culture:

- Our fascination with celebrity, and our tendency to either lionize or demonize the rich and famous; to let them "get away with murder" (as we say) or to keep an obsessive watch on them, moralistically clucking at their weaknesses.
- Our uncertainty about justice and its administration: Are the police honest? Is the D.A.'s office competent? Do our trial courts work? Do we provide "equal justice" to all?
- The relation between these first two items: Does a defendant like Simpson, wealthy enough to afford a "dream team" beyond the hopes of virtually any other criminal defendant, get to "get away with murder" as a result? Does the outcome of a trial of a wealthy defendant like this shed lurid light on the usual functioning of the justice system for everyone else? Could it be, just perhaps, that *only someone like O. J. Simpson could get a truly "fair" trial*—one in which the defense and the prosecution were evenly matched, or almost so?
- The effect of a verdict, if any. Will all of us be able to accept it and go on?

Thus the questions that shaped our discussions before the verdict formed in the interstices of fame, money, and justice. But as the "not guilty" verdict hit the air, new and more disturbing questions were raised: the trial, perhaps the crime itself, turned out to have been "about" more than we had thought.

Was the verdict "just"? Who can say? Justice must be similarly accessible to, and the same for, everyone in a society, or at least look that way: equal justice under the law, as our courthouses are wont to proclaim over their doors. But the different reactions of the black and white communities to the verdict, and their different perceptions of the trial and the crime itself, belied that myth. That a largely African-American jury provided closure to the story, gave the whole its "meaning," as jury verdicts are intended to do, forced us all to reflect: what did it mean that all of us could be privy, via the media, to the exact same series of events—

and one group understand what had happened, and see the role of "justice," so differently from the other?

Whites tended to see the story as a traditional sequence: crime, trial, verdict; a whodunit in which the mystery must be solved by finding the guilty person and the conviction and punishment of the latter brings an end to our public confusion, distress, and uncertainty about the ability of the government to protect us.

Blacks, though, including those on the jury, tended to see the story very differently. The white community whose distress had to be cured by the verdict was not *their* community, so that the "whodunit" interpretation of the task held less attraction for them. As *Newsweek* suggested in its post-verdict story:

> The Fuhrman factor evoked a powerful story in the African-American experience: of the black man fighting a system that's rigged against him. So when blacks applauded the verdict, many were cheering less for the literal event than its allegorical significance—for a different ending to the story. As legal scholar Lani Guinier . . . put it, "The rejoicing is not that someone got away with murder, but that somebody beat the system." (Whitaker 1995)

(Note the use of *story*.) Interpretations like this remind us that, for everyone, the aim of the game is to control the frame (as Johnnie Cochran might put it): to have the right to decide, for all of us, what pivotal events mean. The white reading "whodunit" seemed to many interpreters the unmarked or normal story, one that need not be justified. But this is nothing but exnomination. The notion of different legitimate stories in the excerpt is important. It is our continuing struggle for narrative rights that causes the Simpson case to pass the UAT: who decides what it is, or was, "about"?

In Chapter 2, I discussed the frame, the expectations we bring to our experiences that allow us to use them to construct an understanding of the way the world works, make sense of them and give them coherent and cohesive meaning. We use narratives as framing devices. We try to encode our experiences and observations as stories with beginnings and endings, predictable outcomes, rationales, logical conclusions. The more disturbing an event or series of events and the less it fits neatly into our preconceptions of a "good" story, the more it requires framing to bring it to reasonableness.

We can see our continuing preoccupation with this story as a struggle between two communities to provide the frame for it, the prism through which posterity will understand it. As with our other examples, the fact that the competition exists at all is shocking, the shock most palpable at the moment of the verdict, when the gauntlet was flung down: *We have the right to make sense of this, via the verdict: not you!* In this way the Simpson story is similar to the p.c., Hill/Thomas, and Hillary Rodham Clinton narratives, except that the struggle is starkly defined as black vs. white. And since this struggle remains unresolved and highly salient, the O. J. Simpson story easily passes the UAT. As the Clinton/Lewinsky saga played itself out (see Chapter 8), an increasing number of references within it—jokes, cartoons, even serious stories—linked it to the Simpson narrative, despite their great dissimilarity in all respects save their social disruptiveness. (For instance, a comment on the infamous "semen stained midnight blue cocktail dress": "If it's on the dress, he must confess," a takeoff on Johnnie Cochran's immortal line: "If the gloves don't fit, you must acquit.")

O.J.: THE JOKES

Like other UAT-passing events, the O.J. story contributed mightily to popular culture, in particular to the creation of innumerable jokes. This is hardly surprising. Freud saw joking as a defense against anxiety, manifesting itself at an individual level. But defenses can be used by whole cultures. What we cannot expel, ignore, or encapsulate we joke about.

The jokes are of many types and genres. Some are fairly innocent—for instance, plays on Simpson's nickname:

> What do the LAPD and Tropicana have in common?
> Both have O.J. in a can.

> Did you know that the Juice confessed?
> Yes, they squeezed it out of him.

Others link him to earlier notorious cases, in particular the Bobbitts (the connection, besides notoriety, is "cutting someone close to you"):

> John Bobbitt called O.J. last night—he wanted to tell O.J. that he knows how it feels to be separated from a loved one.

Some reflect on the (to many, including a significant number of the jurors) incomprehensible idea that a football star could be a murderer, turning on football terminology:[2]

> What was O.J.'s favorite play in the Bills' playbook?
> Cut left, then slash right.

But many of the jokes play on a darker theme, one studiously avoided in serious commentary: the attitudes provoked in the white community by Simpson's mixed marriage.[3] The jokes on this theme come in several forms, from relatively innocuous to downright scary (especially if you're black and male). Some comment on the interracial nature of the presumed marital relations:

> Why did O.J. make that trip in the Bronco?
> He knew it would be a long time before he'd get to take a ride inside anything white again.

But the nastiest jokes of this nasty genre work via the presupposition that Simpson will be found guilty and go to prison, and talk about what will happen to him there:

> O. J. Simpson will go down in history as one of the most versatile players in history . . .
> He entered the NFL as a running back . . .
> He entered prison as a tight end . . .
> And will leave as a wide receiver!

> Why won't prison be that different for O.J.?
> He will still have big guys opening holes for him.

It may be puzzling why so many of these jokes turn on the possibility of Simpson's suffering sexual humiliation and emasculation. But think about it as payback for taking a white woman, revenge of a historical kind. In the old South, the penalty for even the appearance of it was lynching, which as a rule involved sexual mutilation. So here we have—shades of Clarence Thomas!—the high-tech (via the Web, where the jokes are recorded on many sites) verbal lynching of someone guilty of the same crime.

Finally, there are a number of jokes that appropriate the joke ("just kidding") format to express out-and-out racism.

> Disney is making a new movie based on the life of O. J. Simpson. It's called "The Lyin' Coon." [cf. "The Lion King"]

> What's the difference between a paralyzed miner and O. J. Simpson? Well, the former is a numb digger . . .

OUR OWN PRIVATE (AND PUBLIC) IDENTITY CRISIS

Long before the verdict there was obsessive interest in the story. People watched the low-speed chase and discussed it, and its implications, for days on end; the media ODed on the story in virtually every venue (with the near-exception of the austere PBS *MacNeil/Lehrer NewsHour*). It was in play somewhere every day and every night. Even before racial reframing became an issue, the story was seriously big. The racial chasm alone cannot account for our tenacity.

Some would argue that the combination of celebrity plus murder equals public fascination. Certainly the story itself would merit a *frisson* or two over a few days. But by 1994, Simpson was no longer a mega-celebrity. His football heroics were long behind him; he was a man in his forties, crippled by arthritis. True, he had appeared in supporting roles in a few forgettable movies; true too, he had made a couple of very successful commercials for Hertz Rent-a-Car. Are those achievements alone sufficient to establish someone as the kind of superhero whose exploits, or travails, will keep All America glued to the screen? I don't think so.

Take a somewhat similar case. In June 1998, the comic actor Phil Hartman was shot and killed by his wife. Hartman was one of the stars of a currently well-rated (if not major hit) sitcom, *Radio News,* and had been a regular for several years on *Saturday Night Live.* He had thus had continuous weekly exposure to a great many people for years and so was arguably a bigger "celebrity" than the aging almost-has-been Simpson. This story also had the man-bites-dog angle that piques our interest: the woman killed the man. The story played on the TV news for a few days, in the print tabs for a little longer, and then went quickly and finally away. A few months later, I can hardly recall the broad outlines of the case, let alone the details. Why did we seize on one murder and not the other?

Again framing plays a role. What is tantalizing about the Simpson case is precisely its recalcitrance to framing, its resistance to being given the clear, unambiguous, and "satisfying" narrative structure that would enable us to thrust the story from our consciousness. The Simpson story contains too many loose ends that can't be shaped into a coherent narrative with a conclusive plot, causal connections, and a happy ending with a moral. We like our nonfiction to resemble our fiction in these ways, and when the story doesn't unfold like a romance novel or a whodunit, it nags at our minds, causing us to pick at it obsessively, going over the details again and again (with the help of the media) until (we hope) the verdict provides closure: the "happy ending" every exciting and disturbing story requires.

The fact that the verdict did just the reverse only made things worse, keeping the story alive far beyond its normal longevity. But even before the verdict, as we watched the trial each night on the tube, its resistance to neat packaging kept us coming back.

Heroes and villains were hard to distinguish, and roles often switched in unpredictable ways. O.J. had been a prototype Nice Guy—his post-football career depended crucially on charm. That niceness had all kinds of repercussions. Like Bill Cosby or Colin Powell, he was a black man whom the white community saw as nonthreatening, yet clearly black. Our ability and willingness to take him into our hearts, to see him (almost) as if he were white, made us feel good about ourselves, enabled us to deny our racism: "See? I love O.J./Cosby (or would vote for Powell). And he's black. So I must be unprejudiced." No one is more lovable than someone who can make us feel like wonderful human beings in the face of disturbing counterevidence.

Yet, as the story unraveled, O.J.-the-hero became increasingly hard to swallow. He was a convicted wife-beater. He spurned his own community (weakening his bridge-between-the-races image). His alibi was full of holes. His sex life was a swamp. There were even rumors of drug use (now *that's* not nice!).

It wasn't easy to find unambivalent sympathy for Nicole, either. On the one hand, as victim, and as beautiful blond mother-of-two, she wrung our hearts. She had the makings of a feminist icon, too: killed by a wife-abuser who had been let off too often. But there were complications in that simple and satisfying narrative.

Nicole Brown Simpson is in many ways the antithesis of the modern feminist (or even postfeminist) heroine. In life she was a passive participant: her victimhood is consistent with everything else. She went to live with Simpson (many years her senior) when she was fresh out of high school—before he was even divorced from his (black) first wife. She was the quintessential "trophy wife" and "lemon tart" of *Bonfire of the Vanities,* a type that repels sympathy because it depends so totally on youth and conventional good looks. She used those assets to snare a man, and that was her career. (And she wasn't even all that good at the game: he didn't marry her until 1985, eight years later, when she was pregnant with his child. Perhaps he felt snookered into marriage—the abuse escalated around then.) She never thought seriously about holding a job: even after their final separation, her thoughts about self-support got no further than chitchat with friend Faye Resnick about running a cafe with "really terrific teas." Despite Simpson's repeated abuse, she found it almost impossible to separate from him. All this is not to say that we should withhold sympathy from Nicole and not blame her batterer/killer. But it does make it harder to see her as the locus of unequivocal sympathy.

Witnesses on both sides displayed a disturbing tendency to elude pigeonholing. Kato Kaelin—was he just an amiable hanger-on, or an aider and abetter? Philip Vannatter and Mark Fuhrman—competent cops or liars and racists? Rosa Lopez—what was *that* about? They shifted like leaves in the wind.

Then there's the equivocal role of the various arms of law enforcement. Most Americans find it easy to believe in The Law, whether in the personae of the police, the D.A., or the judge. The Law is just; The Law is fair; The Law protects us from the scum out there. (I must have caught the bug from Johnnie Cochran.) Justice under The Law is, so we are told, Equal: it is meted out exactly the same to the rich and the poor. The policeman is your friend; the District Attorney wins cases by wrestling the truth out of the crooks; the judge deals out even-handed and sober justice in the courtroom.

It is not so easy to believe in these things any more. They were continually battered during the trial. The police turned out to be incompetent bumblers in the kindest interpretation, virulent racists in the worst. The prosecution made several mortal errors that (in hindsight, anyway) resist exculpation (the venue; the jury; the glove). The judge—well, what can be said about Lance Ito that has not already been said and is printable? It is enough to note that in the next set of highly publicized trials after Ito's, Simpson's civil trial and Timothy McVeigh's, the trial procedure of both judges (Fujisake and Matsch) could be summed up succinctly as: do as Ito didn't. Perhaps most telling is the fact that, in a case in which just about every participant and bystander produced a book (eighty-eight at last count, according to Amazon), there is none by Lance Ito. (There are no legal constraints on his writing one.)

During the trial there was continual rumbling about the effects of the outcome on the justice system. While there have been many other Trials of the Century since 1900, none of the others spawned as high a level of anxiety about the functionality of the legal system. What if there was a guilty verdict? Would there be riots reminiscent of those after the Rodney King trial? What if there was a hung jury and no closure? The smart money had it that the jury would hang, leading to suggestions (some since implemented) that criminal juries ought to be allowed to return nonunanimous verdicts and (more reasonably, I think) that jury sequestration should almost never be used. The jury seemed to many to have failed in its mission. By the end, nine months after their empanelment, eight of the original twelve jurors had been replaced by alternates, on grounds that ran the gamut from barely rational to lunatic. (She seems to be thinking about writing a book; he looked at me funny; she might have once been a victim of spousal abuse.) Most bizarrely, this highly atypical trial was used by critics as the exemplar of all that is wrong with the American justice system.

Money and celebrity always affect the administration of justice, although not necessarily in the way critics of the Simpson trial have suggested. In a typical criminal trial, many implicit advantages accrue to the prosecution; and since most of these reflect our normal assumptions, they have been invisible through exnomination. In California, the prosecution is named "The People" (as in "The People vs. Orenthal James Simpson"). Who is "the people"? *We* are. So the jury is under powerful implicit pressure, from the moment it enters the courtroom, to identify with the prosecutors as *we*. The prosecution is protecting *us;* the defense is merely defending some seedy-looking character, who (although jurors promise to remember "innocent until proven guilty") often *looks* stereotypically guilty. Besides, jurors feel a powerful desire to accomplish something, so that their days, weeks, or months of travail shall not have been in vain (the longer the trial, the stronger the wish). A guilty verdict solves the case; a verdict of innocence leaves it open, the threat to the community still out there. The jury may perceive a "not guilty" as a kind of failure. And finally, the prosecution has resources, financial and other, that are typically unavailable to the defense. The District Attorney generally has a significantly larger budget (and plusher quarters) than the Public Defender by whom the huge majority of defendants are represented;[4] the D.A. has links, official and sentimental, to the police department and other agencies of government, which can make their work easier.[5] And while public defenders are paid reasonably well, if not quite as well as prosecutors, the P.D.'s office (or even a private attorney) does not have the wherewithal to hire phalanxes of expensive experts to counter prosecution evidence.

HOW IT TURNED OUT THAT WAY

In the Simpson case, the rules were reversed. Because a majority black jury was empaneled, and because of Simpson's charm and celebrity status, it was natural for the jury to identify with him rather than the prosecution or the victims. While both sides spent huge amounts on the trial, the defense spent more: Simpson put his immense fortune at its disposal. The result was the "Dream Team," who managed to introduce enough "reasonable doubt" into the jury's minds to allow them to justify an acquittal, in their eyes at least.

From the perspective of many if not most members of the majority community, any attempt to justify a finding of reasonable doubt is ludicrous. The four-hour deliberation in and of itself puts the lie to any claim that nine months' worth of evidence was seriously considered. We were left trying to account for what the verdict meant—that is, how such a travesty could have come into being. Perhaps the interminable sequestration of the jury helped to distance it from the usual understandings of the daily world; perhaps Johnnie Cochran's silver tongue enabled them to ignore what was plain to see; perhaps they were so intent on sending a message that they seized on the shreds of "reasonable doubt" offered them and ran with them.

The defense, especially Cochran, devised strategies designed to be persuasive to a jury such as this. The shared experience of racism and voicelessness both created trust and loyalty in the jury for Cochran and his client and discouraged it from identifying with the prosecution or the victims. Cochran told the jury, in many ways, day after day: *We* understand the role of the police; *we* know the truth about the legal system— as *they* do not. The evidence the prosecution trots out so confidently before us is all the proof we need that *their* system is out to get *us*. The narrative of the trial created an essential unity between defense and jury via shared negative experience.

Cochran did something even more complex and ingenious. In addressing the jury, particularly in the closing arguments, he "spoke their language." He did not use the more obvious traits of African American Vernacular English (see Chapter 7). Its unique sounds, grammatical structures, and special vocabulary would have bewildered and antagonized the jury. Those forms belong to the casual home language of the black community, not to public speech in church or school, or especially in court—*their* place, where *we* have to make a good impression (even as we prepare their comeuppance). Rather, Cochran formed an identification with the jurors by using a uniquely black public discourse style— the dignified and eloquent language of the black preacher, familiar in the rhetoric of Martin Luther King, Jr. and Jesse Jackson. Typical of this style are allegorical references to Biblical subjects; repetitions; alliteration and assonance (as in, "If the gloves don't fit . . . "); marked variation in tempo, loudness, and pitch; invitations to the audience to respond (even if they were only rhetorical here).[6]

Cochran's counterpart on the prosecution team, Christopher Darden, could not have provided a clearer contrast. Also black, Darden almost became a parody of the ineffectual white pedant. He seemed to be trying to be as boring, unemotional, and uninvolved with his hearers as possible. His voice was flat; his style utterly impersonal. He sounded depressed: his pitch fell precipitately at the ends of sentences, and sometimes he seemed barely willing, or able, to articulate loudly enough to be heard. The effect struck me as familiar, typical of academese, which seeks to persuade by (ahem) the brilliance of the content, not the pizzazz of the package. Even in the classroom, that can put an audience to sleep. Its effect was even drearier in the courtroom. Although in sympathy with the prosecution, I found myself responding much more positively to Cochran than to Darden. Style counts.

Cochran's style also worked because it was lively and engaging, and, therefore, flattering to its audience. ("See the energy I'm using? That's because I enjoy talking to you!") It was effective because it made an implicit, emotional connection with the majority of the jurors. It was the kind of talk they viscerally knew, had heard from people like them. It was *our language*, the way *we* make meaning on important public occasions. In the whiteness of the courtroom and the system it represented, Cochran's talk was home, safety, and trust for jurors who had been sequestered in a strange place for nine months.

It is easy to call the defense rhetoric misleading and manipulative, and to argue that its reframing of standard operating procedures was illegitimate and led to an aberrant and unjustifiable verdict. To be sure, the acquittal violated the norms. Compared with a "typical" case, this one was unintelligible. Marcia Clark, the chief prosecutor, had had a stellar record (20–0); in general, around 85 percent of prosecutions in L.A. end in convictions (not counting the 90 percent of cases that are plea-bargained and so never come to trial at all). Surely in a case as prominent as this, as subject to media scrutiny, law enforcement would be on its *best* and most careful behavior, not unusually sloppy! Perhaps Clark's (and the rest of the prosecution team's) long experience (usually a plus) worked against them in this instance: their standard M.O.'s failed when subjected to the unusually close defense inspection and presented to the scrutiny of already suspicious jurors, who were unaware (like most of us) of the normal and unavoidable sloppiness of police procedures.

For whites, the most serious problem with the verdict is the implausibility of the defense arguments. While the defense could poke innumerable holes in the evidence and offer countless alternative interpretations, it is very hard to see any cohesion in their case—to believe that, rather than a series of normal random sloppinesses that probably meant nothing, the prosecution errors taken together were the result of a calculated conspiracy of, necessarily, dozens of people (none of whom ever told). From another perspective the series of prosecutorial errors and misfortunes does form an all-too-cohesive narrative (Murphy's Law), and a commonsensical jury might have seen that. This jury's verdict flies in the face of the injunction traditionally given medical students: "When you hear hoofbeats, think horses, not zebras": when there is a diagnostic ambiguity, go with the more likely explanation. The verdict was zebras all over.

Maybe there is a narrative, or metanarrative, that could make sense of the outcome for everyone. Suppose the defense is right in suggesting that the prevalence of errors, even innocent ones, should give pause to jurors sworn to consider reasonable doubt. Further, suppose that these errors are not unique to this case, but are present even in the strongest prosecution cases. But the defense seldom has the resources to bring these errors to light, much less use them to win over a jury. Then the Simpson case is one of the few in which justice has actually been done, that is, in which the defense had resources equal to the prosecution and could use them effectively. Could it be, just possibly, that there are many innocent people languishing in prison because everyone was playing by the rules of "business as usual"? Could it be that the D.A.'s vaunted conviction rate represents a miscarriage of justice because justice is seldom equal under the law?[7] These are the questions the new frame would force us to ask. Are we willing to contemplate American identity through this new frame? The ruckus over the verdict suggests that the answer is *no*.

From the standard, exnominated perspective, the trial was a fiasco: justice was not done, the whodunit not solved. The verdict, in some eyes, inflamed an already tense national racial divide; in speaking the unspeakable, the jury made the nightmare a reality. But if a nationally galvanizing, universally involving story has a conclusion that makes us question our cultural cohesion and the innermost efficacy and fairness of our system, we ought to know we are in trouble.

WHAT IS A TRIAL?

Not only does the Simpson case make us worry about ourselves and our society, but its pieces don't come together. There are two main snags in the coherence of the O.J. story: the difficulty of fitting the trial itself into our preexisting narrative frames (partly due to competition between defense and prosecution, black and white, over interpretive rights), and the disruptiveness of the moment that should have brought resolution, the verdict. Both of these are disturbing (to those of us whom they disturb) because they violate presupposed frames. They destroy their functioning by making them visible and non-"normal": we are forced to acknowledge, however momentarily, that there might just be another way to understand some very important things. A frame works successfully only as long as it is imperceptible to those who employ it.

An ideal murder trial lets us write the final soothing chapter of a distressing story. We want the moral of the tale to be that civilization keeps us safe. We have (as thinkers as diverse as Rousseau and Freud have pointed out) given up much of value in order to live under a system of laws; we have abandoned various means of quick gratification for the larger long-term benefits of security.

When a murder occurs, that security is disrupted. We no longer trust one another unquestioningly: anyone could have been the murderer or the victim. Without trust, we cannot live together. Up till the murder, we shared a coherent narrative, the story of *us*. But now that story is in shards; we no longer are sure of ourselves as individuals (since so much of our individual identity resides in our social membership), as we have lost faith in society.

Once upon a time, there was a simple solution. The family members of the victim figured out who the likely perpetrator was and exacted bloody revenge. Then, of course, the family members of the new victim figured out who must have done it, and exacted similar retribution. And so on . . . The trouble with such talion law is just that: it goes on and on, it is never settled, no one ever feels safe again. Society becomes increasingly incoherent. This is where government steps in and takes over the business of retribution, now in the name of "justice," cool and impersonal. The victims are excluded from any official participation in the process, because the mending of the narrative web and restoration of trust is seen as something we do for all of us, for society as a whole rather than one angry family. The jury's role is to function as representatives of the larger community, and therefore anyone who knows anything about the crime itself, or is in any way acquainted with any of those involved, cannot serve. Because they are uninvolved, we trust them to be fair, and we are able to accept their verdicts as valid. The story can have a close.

The social role of the jurors is complex. They are not the actual involved parties or even acquainted with them. But those parties themselves are members of *us,* and the jury represents that larger *us.* It is essential that the jury be perceived, in terms of its makeup as well as its final decision, as truly representative of ourselves, all of *us*—otherwise, their verdict will bring, not closure, but exacerbation of the original alienation. A good conclusion to a trial is a moment of collective meaning-making: the individuals who comprise the jury act as one (just one reason why a unanimous verdict is important) and in so doing speak with the voice of all of us. The jury makes meaning, restoring our confidence in the original frame. We normally accept their statement and our confusion ends.

That is exactly what did not happen here. In part because of prosecutorial miscalculation, in part because of Judge Ito's inability to stand up to the defense, a jury was selected that, ultimately, both *looked* and *behaved* like representatives of the non-majority. It's bad enough when this is the perception in a low-profile case that no one outside the courtroom ever hears about. But when everyone in the country is aware of it, that's a recipe for disaster—or social change.

To be sure, there have always been "runaway juries" and nullifications (which I will discuss, with reference to this case, later on). Often (as in the first Menendez trial)[8] these create an immediate flurry, some grumbling and blaming, and pressure for reform, but generally they have no long-term effect on the community's sense of cohesion. That is because the perceived misbehavior of the jury is laid at the feet of the jurors themselves, seen not as representatives of *us,* but as errant individuals. Such verdicts are not seen as the outcomes of society-wide battles over meaning-making rights, between communities at odds with each other, sharing only a long history of mistrust.

As long as only one group has the right to construct the stories, problematic jury verdicts like Simpson's will not arise. Often, to achieve the appearance of consensus, members of nondominant communities may be excluded from juries (as was the case in many jurisdictions for both blacks and women into the late 1960's). Their members have to accept the stories, and the justice, of the majority. But they will remember, and they will be embittered, and if the rights get reallocated, it will be pay-back time.

The word "payback" turns up frequently in discussions of the Simp-son case. Many critical events of the 1990's have been interpreted as payback for earlier ones, starting with the Simpson criminal verdict as payback for the Rodney King verdict in 1992, then the Simpson civil ver-dict as payback for the criminal. The thirst for vengeance seems bound-less: many other public decisions bear traces of blood lust going back to October 4, 1995. The amazingly protracted argument over Ebonics dur-ing the winter of 1996–97 can be construed, as I will argue in Chapter 7, as a struggle between majority and minority over the right to make pub-lic language. Many have suggested that the Welfare Reform Act of 1997, ending, as the catchphrase went, "welfare as we know it," is the major-ity reasserting its possession of real definitional clout. California's 1996 Ballot Proposition 209, destroying affirmative action (and its many imi-tators elsewhere) is more payback. While it's certainly not inconceivable that these events could have occurred anyway, their proximity to the ver-dict guarantees that they will be interpreted as payback, or payback for payback. The fact that, after more than four years, the white need for payback for the Simpson verdict seems not to have been exhausted sug-gests the traumatic nature of the verdict for the majority community, its need to restore cohesion by taking back the right to bring stories to their preferred conclusion. As Frank Rich (1995b) wrote presciently on the Op-Ed page of the *New York Times* on October 4, 1995, quoting L.A. lawyer Ben Stein, "When O.J. gets off, the whites will riot the way we whites do: leave the cities, go to Idaho or Oregon or Arizona, vote for Gingrich . . . and punish the blacks by closing their day-care programs and cutting off their Medicaid." Not precisely right, to be sure, but aw-fully close. You blacks wanna fight over meaning? Well, mean *this!*

WHAT THE JURY NULLIFIED

What is highly upsetting to the majority about the verdict is that the "message" it sent was not intended to apply only to this case. It went be-yond common garden variety nullification into something scarier, which we might for want of a snappier term call "metanullification." Nullifica-tion is a right as sacred to jurors as it is loathed by the system's profes-sionals, especially prosecutors (who don't as a rule trust jurors much anyway). The official rule is that the judge is the "trier of law," the jury the "trier of fact": the jury weighs the evidence to determine what happened; the judge instructs them on how to relate those findings to the laws.

The law wants to be one-size-fits-all, as decontextualized as possible. That is what we mean by "a government of laws and not of men"—regardless of who you are or whom you harmed, the penalty for the same crime will always be the same. Without this assurance, it would be common for the rich and well-connected to receive a preferential kind of justice . . . which as we have seen never happens here, thank goodness. Cynicism aside, we can be sure that without this ideal guiding our legal practice, things would be much worse than they are.

But juries often find the rigors of the system oppressive, forcing them to make decisions they recognize, in their street-smart way, as unjust because based on assumptions that run counter to the way they feel life really works. They decide to go with *fairness,* as opposed to the letter of the law as communicated to them by the personage in the black robe on the raised bench up front. These decisions are "nullifications."

There are two kinds of simple nullification. One occurs when jurors horse-trade during deliberations: you want first-degree murder; it looks to me like voluntary manslaughter; let's split the difference and call it second-degree murder so we can go home. Another, probably the prototype understanding of "nullification," occurs when the prosecution has presented seemingly ironclad evidence of guilt and the jury acquits, arguing that the laws they were instructed to use in this case ought not to apply although technically they do. In such cases, it is a single law that is nullified, and the denial of its appropriateness refers only to the trial in process, not to the legal system in general or the society as a whole.[9] Such verdicts may create momentary consternation, but that generally passes.

Several of the Simpson jurors, in their books and post-verdict interviews, insisted that they had not nullified at all: they had followed the judge's instructions, one of which stated that if the jury believed any witness to have lied, they were free to disregard the totality of his testimony, not just the part that had been proven false. They naturally applied this dictum to Mark Fuhrman, whose testimony about the finding of the glove and the blood on the Bronco were crucial parts of the prosecution case, although his demonstrated perjury only extended to his use of the word "nigger" (years before the murder). Therefore, they said, excluding Fuhrman's and other tainted testimony and problematic evidence, they had found reasonable doubt. But this justification is shaky because it would have been difficult for them to have sifted through and discarded nine months of evidence in the under four hours it took to produce the verdict. The shortness of the deliberations makes nullification the only logical interpretation.[10] The jury was encouraged by Cochran's persuasive summation to send a message rather than decide whodunit.

If that is the correct interpretation of its verdict, what the jury did was not simple nullification but rather metanullification. There was no law, or even set of laws, with which the jury took issue. They were not saying that, by some special definition, although Simpson had killed, he had not committed murder, or that murder should not be criminalized. In setting aside the evidence, they were saying that they were not really interested in establishing culpability for this or any crime. They perceived their most important role as messengers from the African-American to the majority community, saying: "We do not accept *any* of your laws or their underpinnings; we spurn your whole legal system. It has never worked in our interest (our people are either mistreated or ignored by your system), so we see no need to participate in it." And since the law is fundamental to social cohesion itself, the ultimate force of that message is: "*We* are not a part of *your* society, we do not have to follow your rules when they conflict with our needs. Take that."

Now *that* is shocking, even horrifying. At the very least, a large group of Americans explicitly and publicly has spurned *our* system, indicated its unwillingness to cooperate with us any more. As your mother would say, What if everyone did that? Not a happy thought.

Metanullification is the denial of the validity or applicability of the whole system. It is not the creation of the black community: generations of white juries in the south habitually metanullified by refusing to convict white defendants for crimes against black victims. It took the passage of the Voting Rights Bill in 1965 to change that practice by giving blacks access to the ballot box and including them on jury lists. Our society's chickens have come home with a thud to roost.

Metanullification denies the existence of any single narrative the whole community can share and thus denies the possibility of a shared language, in the wider sense of that term, and the possibility that we can collaborate on meaning together. It further asserts, on that basis, the right of minorities to make meanings for themselves and, when they can (as here), to impose their interpretations on the dominant community. Then what does "dominant" mean any more? Thus the O. J. Simpson verdict falls into place alongside political correctness, Hill/Thomas, and Hillary Rodham Clinton as an object of terror to those who believe that they naturally possess the right to make meaning for everyone. An examination of the pre- and post-verdict public discourse on the case shows how effectively that lesson was inculcated, yet how resistant we remain to it.

MORE BAD NEWS

It wasn't just the verdict itself, though that was bad enough. The alienation, and the message of nonacceptance of the majority narrative, based on the autonomy of the minority, was seconded and made completely clear by the different responses of blacks and whites on television. We often take the behavior of people depicted on television as a model for our own, to suggest how we should feel and speak about events. But what was the white community to make of *this?* We were excluded, segmented off into a quasi minority who didn't get it. How could that be?

It was not only the justice system that was compromised by the verdict and its sequelae. Other presuppositions about how the world works and how we understand it came under attack. Science, perhaps the most hallowed and trustworthy of all our contemporary institutions, also was scarred by the verdict and the jury's justification of it. That in itself is frame-shattering. In the late twentieth century, one of the two ultimate arguments for virtually anything is "Scientific studies show . . . "—the only competitor is, "It says in the Bible . . . " If you have done a study, if you can provide numbers, statistics, experiments—your claims are considered beyond reproach or refutation, at least by the majority community.

Judge Ito, encouraged by the defense, permitted the selection of a jury with virtually no post-secondary education and, in many cases, an active distrust of science. (It is astonishing that the prosecution, knowing the importance of DNA and other scientific evidence in the case, permitted this to happen.)[11] The results were predictable: the jury slept through several months of scientific evidence, allowing the defense to dismiss it all on the grounds that it had either been planted or misanalyzed. Several commentators (e.g., Bugliosi 1996 and Toobin 1996) sift through the DNA data to show pretty conclusively that, even granting mismanagement of some of the specimens, the number of the samples and variety of their sources make it very difficult to discard the results wholesale. At the very least, the jury should have spent a day or two evaluating and weighing the scientific evidence.

The jurors' refusal to address the scientific evidence can be taken as a sign of their laziness or ignorance, or of their overriding determination to "send a message" rather than decide whodunit, and both of these have some truth to them. But it can also, more disturbingly, be construed as a verdict on the purported objectivity and therefore race-neutrality of science. The jury, speaking for its peers, says to *us:* We don't believe in *your* science. It's just another form of subjectivity that makes you look good and us bad; that allows you to imprison and otherwise subjugate us. (The publication of *The Bell Curve* around the time of the trial supports that argument, even if the jurors were in all probability unaware of it.)

In itself that rejection is not necessarily deadly: groups are free to disagree about the relative importance or validity of discourses of all kinds. But the discourse of science has played a privileged role in our society for the last century. Belief in the objectivity, rationality, and value of science has united the majority of us at a time when the prior great unifier, religion, is losing that status. For the representatives of a particular community to assert that science is meaningless, useless, or untrustworthy is for it to declare its independence of a generally held and highly admired belief system.[12] As belief in "justice" is the great social unifier, so belief in "science" unites us cognitively. If both come into question, as they do here in one fell swoop, we could be in for a bumpy ride in the postmillennium.

MAKING SENSE OF DISSONANCE

It was left to the media to pick up the pieces and interpret their meaning to the rest of us, to provide some reassurance that things weren't as bad as they looked. They strove to extract both reason and hope from the post-verdict wreckage, to make meaning, even if that meaning was that there was no meaning. The *New York Times* took up fully half the front page on October 4, 1995, with Simpsoniana. The lead article reports the facts ("Jury Clears Simpson in Double Murder; Spellbound Nation Divides on Verdict," by David Margolick); a second page-one article, by Martin Gottlieb, covers the most salient story aside from the verdict itself: "Deep Split in Reactions to the Verdict." On the bottom of page one, a third article by N. R. Kleinfield discusses "The Day (10 Minutes of It) the Nation Stood Still." Continuations of these stories, and the wholes of several others, occupy four inside pages. There were also an editorial and two Op-Ed pieces.

The *Times*'s editorial (blandly entitled "The Simpson Verdict") is balanced and conciliatory. It points out that there *could have been* reasonable doubt based on police bungling, Fuhrman's racism, and messy investigation, and that Ito's dragging out of the trial only made matters worse. *Yet* the jury hadn't taken enough time to assess the evidence properly. "But in the end," it concludes, "this will be remembered as a case that was disrupted by the police."

In other words, the rules are still in effect, proper judicial procedure has been followed. There is no need to perceive the verdict as a miscarriage of justice, or a metastatement, or any other dangerously divisive communication. We are still one nation, indivisible.

The *Los Angeles Times,* on the other hand, confronts the problem. The headline of its lead editorial reads, "The Verdict Is In: A City Divided; The Simpson Trial Has Raised Questions of Police Propriety and Racial Antipathy." Los Angeles, says the writer, "is a city in a nation so divided that we cannot even agree on what we all see when we look at the same picture." But it, too, comes down hard on the L.A.P.D. and comments that the trial showed, "unsurprisingly, that a rich man can buy a better brand of justice than a poor man." By framing the verdict in this way, the *L.A. Times* is attempting to salvage at least a semblance of unity: at least all of us can agree on this. One can ask whether both papers are using the police to reunite us by giving all of us a scapegoat (if a highly deserving one) we can hate as one—a bit reminiscent of Big Brother's Two Minutes Hate in *Nineteen Eighty-Four,* designed to take the citizens of Oceania out of their individual miseries just long enough to bring them together in mutual hatred of a (fictitious) enemy.

The Los Angeles paper, not surprisingly, outdoes its New York counterpart on Simpson coverage, with thirty-five articles on the trial on October 4 alone, compared to a mere fourteen in the latter. On its front page, the *New York Times* attempts to salve the wound. While the Gottlieb article recognizes the "deep splits" between the black and white communities across the nation, based on their different responses to the verdict, below it the Kleinfield piece unifies us again. We were *all* brought to a halt waiting for the verdict; we were *all* moved by it, in one way or another. Kleinfield graphs "percent change from a week earlier in the volume of long-distance [phone] calls," in five minute intervals (the verdict was announced a little before 1:10 P.M. New York time). All through the time period from 12:50 to 1:20, call volume was significantly down. (The verdict had been announced for 1:00 EDT.) At 12:50 volume was down from a week before by only 20 percent but by 1:05, the falloff was

60 percent. (And *you* were there, contributing to that bar graph by *not making calls,* like everyone else.) So some quasi-editorial content ("it really isn't as scary as it looks—we are all in this together") is sneaked onto page one.[13]

The *Los Angeles Times* too has several articles on page one, representing diverse takes on the verdict and summing up the case. Writers speak of "A Ripple That Keeps Moving Out" (Robin Abcarian); "Mirroring a Deep Divide among Us" (Robert A. Jones); "Feeling Saddened by the Outcome." Other articles, throughout the paper, comment not only on the racial divide, but also on topics as diverse as: O.J.'s future life; the recoveries of the victims' families; jurors' views on the problems in the prosecution's case. In the lead article, by Jim Newton ("Simpson Not Guilty: Drama Ends 474 Days after Arrest; Verdicts: The Ex-Football Star Expresses Gratitude and Returns to His Brentwood Estate Where Friends and Family Celebrate . . . "), the twists and ambiguities of the case are nicely summed up in a quote from Steven D. Clymer, prosecutor in the Rodney King case: "I think it's a tragic irony that O. J. Simpson, a person who probably never suffered the kind of racism that Mark Fuhrman dished out, is a beneficiary of the claims of racism. . . . I feel it's a terrible result. I feel so bad for those families." A juror dismisses the whole of the prosecution case with a slogan out of Silicon Valley: "Garbage in, garbage out." (Technology, *sí;* science, *no.*)

Another page one story, by Lynell George (1995) suggests that "we" must try to bridge the divide that has been too painfully revealed by developing a way to talk across that divide.

> For Los Angeles, it is only the beginning in a search for language, frankness, forthrightness. In stirring up issues too often skirted, discussions often quickly silenced for fear of upsetting the careful, though invisible balance.
> We speak too many languages, without interpretation. . . .
> What has been difficult to separate, to explain, to understand, is that the prism of race does indeed affect perception. As does gender. As does class. . . .
> And is this a case about race?
> It isn't, but it is.
> It's that and so much more. The card universally played was emotion.

While this writer's take on "emotion" is sympathetic and universalizing, that was not the case in all quarters. The *New York Times* lead article (Margolick 1995) remarks that some critics felt the jury had been "manipulated." L.A. District Attorney Gil Garcetti grumbles in the same article, "This was not, in our opinion, a close case. Apparently their decision was based on emotion that overcame the reason." Comments like these explain a lot about why the verdict came out the way it did. Re-membering the gender and racial makeup of the jury, the age-old ten-dency of white males to patronize women and blacks ("half savage and half child," as Rudyard Kipling called the latter a century ago) as slaves to emotion and easily manipulated thereby to the detriment of "reason," attitudes like this, explicit or not, could have had a backlash. But Gar-cetti's comment exposes his own intellectual failing. In discourse gener-ally, but especially in court, emotion and reason are not antitheses. One underscores and makes sense of the other. Either, alone, becomes the weapon of the propagandist. To fail to understand this is to fail to com-municate appropriately to the context. Fiske refers to this strategy on the part of Garcetti and other apologists for the prosecution, attempting to defuse the bomb dropped by the verdict, as the "Oprahizing" of the jury —a way to "simultaneously Blacken and feminize the verdict" (1996, 272), thereby denying it is something *we* need to take seriously, a desper-ate attempt to restore control of meaning to its "rightful" owners.

WHO'S ON TRIAL HERE?

In the period from just before the verdict until the end of October, the media circled the case, competing for interpretive rights and deliberating over the proper take on what was to come or had just arrived. A lot of the discussion attempted to discover what the trial had been "about"— and more implicitly, who should have the right to make that determina-tion. There are several candidates for "about." Simpson himself—inno-cent or guilty—may seem the most obvious. But for many, that question had retreated to the background; whodunit became almost incidental. Foregrounded were questions raised by one side or the other or, increas-ingly, the media themselves. As noted above, the defense put the L.A.P.D. and its cohorts in the dock, and the jury's vote could be seen as against the police, not for Simpson.

Some media commentary had already emerged on the role of the me-dia in making the trial, and in the months to come there would be much more on this theme. Did the presence of the cameras change the way the trial unfolded? For better or for worse? Had the media framed the issues correctly, or were they too busy looking for, and accentuating, the shock-ing? The jury had been strictly sequestered since January; but they were allowed five-hour weekly unmonitored conjugal visits. It was generally assumed that some pieces—the most inflammatory and memorable parts, no doubt—of the media blitz had gotten through to the jurors via this route.

As the case began to recede from our lives, the media began to ruminate about who might be the real defendants, the real people responsible: not for the murder itself, but for the attention the case had drawn, not just here but everywhere.[14] From one perspective, the responsible party was all of us, Americans and America: our insoluble difficulties with race, gender, and celebrity. The media picked up on this and devoted a good deal of commentary to the question. In one way this answer was gratifying: it gave us a good reason for our obsession. It's not that Americans are consumed with lust for trivia to the exclusion of the important things in life (as the intellectuals would have it), but that we recognize what is really important. The more you think about it, the more depressing this conclusion becomes. We are fixated on race, gender, and economic inequity because we cannot solve those problems.

These questions are explored at some depth in the October 9 issues of the newsweeklies (*Time, Newsweek, U.S. News and World Report*). The weeklies were caught in a deadline bind. They go to press eight or nine days before the publication date on their covers. Hence, the October 9 issues actually went to press on September 30 or October 1, days before the verdict, yet they bear a post-verdict cover date; the October 16 issues contain the first post-verdict stories. All three October 9 issues devote considerable space to the trial, mostly prognosticating, as if they are trying to present the post-verdict perspective appropriate to their cover dates, but of course cannot literally do so. So they use the big picture, What It All Means, as a substitute or decoy for the verdict the cover date promises.

Newsweek's cover story, by Larry Reibstein, is titled, with appropriate ambiguity, "Judgment Day." Its page-and-a-half photo shows Simpson dabbing at his eyes. It almost explicitly assumes an acquittal and discusses the reasons for it: prosecutors "tried mightily" (the phrase suggests failure) "to wrest the jury back to the version of the evidence as they saw it," but "Cochran matched his rhetoric with some showmanship," and diners in the courthouse cafeteria "chanted 'We love you, Johnnie!'" The die is cast.

Time's cover story, by Richard Lacayo, hedges its bets a trifle, but its views on the outcome are very similar and pretty explicit. Just as *Newsweek*'s lead photo stressed tears, *Time*'s opening sentence tells us that "The impossibly tangled issues of the O. J. Simpson trial could best be understood last week by paying attention to the tears" of Nicole Simpson on a 911 tape, the Goldman and Brown families in the courtroom, and one of the jurors, during Cochran's summation. Virtually all of the stories in the issue talk about race and how any kind of verdict will worsen the gulf. While *Time* avoids making a commitment to either verdict, it gives more space to Cochran and his arguments than to the prosecution's.

Both cover stories weigh all the evidence and come down in the middle. While *Newsweek*'s story ends on a note of grim resignation,

> The jury gets to decide the case. Then the rest of us, the Other America, gets to talk about it. Forever.

Time tries for a note of hope:

> If they [the families of Simpson and the victims] can find common ground, maybe there is hope for the jury. And the rest of us too.

The grammarian might find it of interest that both stories end with sentence fragments. Fragmentation. What we feel.

U.S. News and World Report's cover story by Betsy Streisand starts out by comparing the trial to Vietnam as "an event of sickening revelation": "It has trashed what little faith many Americans may have left in lawyers, judges, police and, perhaps, each other." The story goes on to contrast the prosecution's "tag-team" approach with "the powerful theatrics of defense lawyer Johnnie Cochran." But unlike the other two weeklies, *U.S. News and World Report* spends most of its cover-article space contemplating the effects of the trial, whatever its verdict, on the justice system: judges' behavior, cameras in court, jury reform. It devotes little space to weighing verdict possibilities and their consequences.

By October 5, V-day-plus-two, the daily papers are already working on postdiction and epignostication (to coin words meaning the opposite of "prediction" and "prognostication"). The *New York Times* again has news stories on page one (and elsewhere), an editorial and an Op-Ed piece; on October 6, a page-one story, one on an inside page, and three Op-Eds on Subject A. The first article on October 5 is by Timothy Egan ("With Spotlight Shifted to Them, Some Simpson Jurors Talk Freely"). It is still looking backward, focused on why the verdict turned out as it did. Predictably, the jurors say they obeyed the judge's instructions, responding to "a matter of evidence": what there was had been "planted." While they minimized the force of Fuhrman's racism, they found him "not credible." One juror's response suggests that they had perhaps not fully grasped the meaning of "reasonable doubt": They didn't sift through "the 1,105 pieces of evidence or 45,000 pages of transcripts from 126 witnesses," because, she says, "[w]e based it on reasonable doubt. We had a lot of reasonable doubt from the beginning." But *reasonable* doubt can only arise properly out of the weighing of evidence during deliberations, at the end.

The next day's main story in the *Times*, by Stephen Labaton ("Lessons of Simpson Case Are Reshaping the Law"), as the title suggests, looks forward, assessing the Simpson trial as a bad example for judges and lawyers. The focus has shifted from the racial angle back to the courtroom. Likewise the *Times*'s October 5 editorial ("False Lessons of the Simpson Trial") focuses on the legal aspects of the trial, the fear that the conduct of the trial and the (presupposed) unpopular verdict will lead to bad changes in the legal system: restricting the rights of defendants and revamping the jury system. But since this case was "idiosyncratic," it would be an error to use it as a justification for sweeping changes.

An October 5 Op-Ed by Maureen Dowd finds another diversion from the glaring issue: "O. J. As Metaphor." If we can see the whole thing as a figure of speech, as not-quite-the-real-thing, we gain some distance from it, we achieve something close to plausible deniability (or denial). The verdict suits "this surreal case": "This made-for-TV case is the nadir of our fascination with celebrity, psychological compulsions, victimhood and redemption," an analysis that neatly squelches any urge to search for deeper meanings, managing (as *Times* personnel love to do) to deal a slap to L.A. in the process.

The October 6 crop of Op-Eds in the *Times* turns more anguished and more analytic.

> The answer to what the Simpson verdict illuminated—the black community's fundamental distrust of our system—cannot be to aggravate that distrust. Our aim should be to build trust: for everyone's sake. We do not, we cannot, live in different countries. (A. Lewis 1995)

> It is time for men and women of courage to assert themselves, to try to find a way to bring together people whose ignorance of one another is profound and whose hatreds are intensifying. Men and women of goodwill are also needed to begin reconstituting the disaster we call a criminal justice system.
> This is not work for the faint of heart or for people who need the constant affirmation of their peers. But it is work that needs to be done. Soon. (Herbert 1995)

> That does not mean we can respect the verdict. But it helps in thinking about how it came about—and whether we can end that certain difference, how, and when we get started. (Rosenthal 1995)

The single word found most commonly throughout these commentaries is "we," or its semantic equivalent ("men and women of courage/goodwill"). Its frequency seems almost an attempt to deny or defy the force of the verdict: "There is no 'we' here." It is not necessarily clear, in each of these examples, just who "we" are intended to be: The white community? The black community? (Herbert is black.) All of us together—if there is such a thing any more?

The newsmagazines devoted large chunks of their October 16 issues to The Case, The Verdict, and The Meaning. *Newsweek* dedicated forty-three of its eighty-eight pages to it, in four sections entitled "The Reaction," "The Verdict," "Looking Back," and "The Impact." The lead article, by Mark Whitaker ("Whites v. Blacks"), pictures first the Dream Team and their client; then a split audience hearing the verdict, blacks cheering, whites glum. It stresses the impotent rage of the whites. "'Do you know how to riot?' a white talent-agency executive called a friend in L.A. to ask." The irony is grim: the world is turned upside down, those with meaning-making rights (and therefore no prior need to "know how" to riot) suddenly are outsiders who need to acquire that underdog's knowledge. The fear and horror and bewilderment written on the white faces in the pictures is, finally, just about that: the rules have suddenly changed, and they don't know how to be competent any more. By the time the issue of October 16 had gone to press, about five days post-verdict, everyone knew that something fundamental had changed, for Simpson himself perhaps least of anyone.

The same article quotes N. Don Wycliff, the black editorial page editor of the *Chicago Tribune*: "White people are now feeling the same anger and frustration over the justice system that black people have felt for a long time. I fear the reaction will not be, 'Hey, *now* I see what the other guy has been saying all the time.' It will be, 'Let's get back.'" Clairvoyance, again. But the full realization had not sunk in. Another article in the same issue, written by Larry Reibstein, with reporting by Mark Miller, Donna Foote, and Tessa Namuth, is titled "What Went Wrong?", suggesting that the writers have not appreciated *their* point of view, still less identified with it, and even less than that moved toward erasing the boundary between *us* and *them*. The verdict is "wrong": unintelligible.

Practically from the moment of the crime until the verdict, the intellectual view was predominantly one of scorn. Interest in the trial was defined as characteristic of "popular culture," beneath serious investigation. Intellectuals were proud to "admit" that they paid no attention to the news on this subject. (Yet if you questioned them, they were always up on the salient points: the names and character traits of the dramatis personae, the latest rulings and rantings from the bench, current predictions about trial length and verdict.) But the moment the verdict was in, the serious media scrambled to analyze its message and offer diagnoses of the disease and prescriptions for its cure.

Several of the more intellectual magazines took up the scrutiny shortly after the verdict. The *New Yorker* of October 23 contains two articles on the case. Jeffrey Toobin's "A Horrible Human Event" sees the verdict as a disaster, from a white perspective, and examines what went wrong: the prosecution's use of Mark Fuhrman; the defense's relentless playing of the race card (and all sorts of other illegitimate tricks, aided and abetted by a complaisant judge); Marcia Clark's misplaced trust in black female jurors; the defense's increasing control of the courtroom. But ultimately, says Toobin, at least from Clark's perspective, there was nothing the prosecution could have done to change things; the speed of the deliberations proved that. By stressing legal incompetence and jury malfeasance, he keeps our focus on the white telling of the story. Now the whodunit moves up a level. While the original question remains at least technically unanswered, there is a new crime, a new whodunit: who lost the case?

A different view is that of Henry Louis Gates, Jr., in "Thirteen Ways of Looking at a Black Man." Seeing things from an African-American perspective, Gates begins by noting that commentary since V-day has moved from the verdict itself, to reaction to it, reaction to reaction to it, and so on. First there was the white reaction to the black jury's verdict, and then the black reaction to the white reaction. Thus Rita Dove, then Poet Laureate, "found it 'appalling that white people were so outraged.'" In counterpoint to a prevailing sense that a terrible injustice has been perpetrated, Gates states that

> To believe that Simpson is innocent is to believe that a terrible injustice has been averted, and this is precisely what many black Americans, including many prominent ones, do believe.

And to the same point a bit later, he quotes a saying of older blacks,

> When white folks say "justice," they mean "just us."

Gates sees this perspective as a counternarrative to the "official culture" white narrative, unheard in the white-dominated media and therefore a tremendous culture shock to the majority when it emerges, as here. Official culture, says Gates, gives no serious credence to the black perspective; when alternate narratives emerge (e.g., that the government caused AIDS to kill off the blacks; that the L.A.P.D. framed Simpson),

> they are given consideration primarily for their ethnographic value. An official culture treats their claims as it does those of millenarian cultists in Texas, or Marxist deconstructionists in the academy: as things to be diagnosed, deciphered, given meaning.

Thus *we,* in our kindly if patronizing way, continue to provide the meanings for *their* narratives.

Gates discusses the way in which "a communal experience afforded by a public narrative . . . was splintered by the politics of interpretation." The split itself is nothing new, to be sure: what is new, and shocking, and difficult for us to get over, is that the other side of the split was heard from and will have a highly significant role in the making of the final narrative, whenever that comes about.

Gates is ambivalent about the split narrative: true, it shows that the black community is willing to believe all kinds of implausibilities if that will make the story come out right; but then, it is a triumph to have that option at all, to be the interpreter rather than the interpreted for once. It's difficult to encompass Gates's and Toobin's perspectives within the covers of one magazine, just as it is hard to try to fit together, within the narratizing strategies of a purportedly single society, the two stories they represent. It is hard to believe in a single entity called *"The* O. J. Simpson Case."

The media mostly treat these ambiguities as something altogether new in the world, an unparalleled puzzlement. As we have seen, the same uncertainties over the meaning of events, or their very occurrence, help explain the persistence of several earlier stories, Hill/Thomas and Hillary Rodham Clinton in particular. But in those cases, the confrontation between the two (or more) communities, and the competition between their narratives, didn't surface at one extraordinarily public moment. Yet our failure to really settle the earlier cases, to determine what sort of culture we were and whose constructions counted, remained seething underground. And when the Simpson verdict and the responses to it surfaced, the confusion of the white community dredged back up our distress over the earlier events, which contributed to our unwillingness to confront this one and our inability to let it go.

Other writings with an October 23 publication date demonstrate the same flailing around as the double-take in the *New Yorker.* The press's job is to tell a story. But what story, or what stories, is it to tell?

Presupposing the verdict's "travesty of justice," Michael Lind in the October 23 *New Republic* uses it to argue for the abolition of the jury system: "The American jury system does not work to free the innocent and punish the guilty in an efficient and humane manner. It never has." Since the adversarial justice system and the juries that necessarily go with it have been a part of a particularly sacred American narrative about who we are and how great we are, to use the Simpson verdict as a means by which to demolish both is shocking: it has become necessary to destroy bedrock American self-definitions in order to preserve an even more potent myth: "one nation indivisible, *e pluribus unum*." That myth can only be saved if we are willing to agree that the Simpson jury not only failed in its job, but was no aberration: juries don't work. Three weeks post-trauma this article attempts to reconstruct a shattered narrative of cohesion. The possibility of cohesion still exists, but only if we are willing to undertake a profound revision of the way we work as a society.

In the same issue, an unsigned editorial ("Unreasonable Doubt") takes a more temperate position but likewise sees the verdict and its aftermath as aberrations, wounds in the body politic that must be healed. While the trial, and the verdict, pointed to abuses in the administration of justice by the L.A.P.D., that's not enough to justify any verdict in this case beside "guilty beyond a reasonable doubt." Rather than indict the jury system as a whole, the writer criticizes this particular jury and the way in which it was selected: "[T]he representative jury is fatally undermined when jurors in criminal cases are selected by attorneys for their ignorance and credulity and hermetic isolation from civil society. The Simpson jury looked not very much like America." But this is, *mutatis mutandis*, just Gates's point: to the black community, the jury looked like *their* America, not *ours*.[15] They were not isolated from civil society, but rather fully involved members in a different society, one of which most of us have been only dimly aware. Here, as in Toobin's article of a week earlier, one senses a desperate scramble to take back unequivocal narrative rights, without explicitly identifying that as what is being done (exnomination).

MULTINARRATIVITY TRUMPS POLYNARRATIVITY

The shock of the verdict was exacerbated by its destruction of the belief earlier parts of the case encouraged in our societal unity—by watching the low-speed car chase together, enjoying the "Dancing Itos" on the

Tonight Show, participating in the construction of a complex narrative in the media and around the office water cooler, sharing a familiarity with all the aspects of a discourse being created daily: Judge Ito; Johnnie Cochran; Marcia Clark and Christopher Darden; Kato Kaelin; Rosa Lopez; Mark Fuhrman; and the rest of the cast of characters, including the cryptic figure of the defendant himself, a perfectly blank slate in the courtroom, waiting for us to write on him. The verdict forced us to perceive our society not as "a" society, but as many: ex uno, plura. We did not share one narrative, but were trying to create at least two, both of which could not be right. We were engaged in *multinarrativity,* the creation and dissemination of conflicting meaning-making narratives.

The pain was all the greater because, up until V-day, our sharing of the Simpson stories created a potent belief in a communal *polynarrativity:* many stories one inside another, stories that enriched one another and together formed a cohesive whole, a set of concentric circles rather than conflicting and separate understandings. Until the verdict, the story felt like eight (or so) narratives enfolded in one another like Matryushka dolls starting from the innermost circle (not unlike the levels of narrative discussed in Chapter 4).

Level 1 is outside the narrative proper and in fact unknowable. It is the "real truth," what actually happened. The next, Level 2, is the story presented by the prosecution—and the alternate version offered by the defense, along with the deconstruction of the prosecution narrative by the defense. Level 3 is the jury's group narrative, their attempt to create a fusion between prosecution and defense scenarios, or reject one for the other. Thus far, these levels are part of any jury trial. But the succeeding levels come into existence only for notorious trials that attract media attention, and the highest levels (5–8), only for the several "Trials of the Century." Level 4 is the media commentary on the preceding levels. While this level has the appearance of objectivity, in fact the media are selective in what they choose to show and how they frame it. So Level 4 becomes a narrative in its own right, with a life of its own.

Level 5 captures the ripples extending from the first four levels: the media's gloss of its own role and assessment of its own importance in the meaning-making task. While superficially it sometimes appears to involve a lot of hand-wringing (the problematic role of cameras in the courtroom; the seepage of news to the sequestered jurors), in fact the real speech act comes pretty close to self-congratulation. (We are so important! Without us all of this could never have happened! We can make or break or spin a story—we don't make the news, we *are* the news!)[16]

At Level 5 comes discussion as well of the effect of all that coverage on all of us: Are we becoming knowledgeable about the law or merely cynical? More concerned about our racial divide or just more divided? Are we (as we tell the pollsters) sick of it all? Then why are we watching it so voraciously?

Level 6 is the media's post-verdict take on what its own obsessing (through Level 5) was all about and prognostications about the future of court journalism. Level 7 reverts to the people: our digestion of all of the above, our appreciation of its relevance, as demonstrated by the creation of popular culture takes on it: jokes, allusions in TV sitcoms, metaphors, Web sites devoted to analysis of the case.

And finally, Level 8 is the assessment of the meanings of Levels 1–7. This discussion is an example of Level 8.

LATER APPRAISALS

Nor is this the only one. In *Postmortem: The O. J. Simpson Case* (Abramson 1996b), a number of prominent writers reconsider the trial and its meanings. The contributors present diverse perspectives, from considerations of the courtroom dynamics to the racial divide and the feminist perspective. Two, Barbara Babcock and Diana Trilling, as well as Jeffrey Abramson (1996a) in his introduction, consider the possibility that, with the help of Judge Ito, the jurors misunderstood reasonable doubt. As noted earlier their apparent assumption (as reported in several jurors' memoirs and post-verdict interviews) that if a witness was found not to be credible on *one* issue, *all* his or her testimony could be discounted, might have enabled the jurors to dispense with virtually all the physical evidence offered by the prosecution.

Several authors offer interpretations of the blacks' cheering after the announcement of the verdict: to Diana Trilling, it is an event equivalent, in terms of its effect on the society in which it occurred, to the cheering of the crowd at the fall of the Bastille. Abramson sees it as much less ominous: "a proud instance of racial solidarity" in which a black jury "delivered a retaliatory blow against a pernicious system." A couple of contributors identify Johnnie Cochran's machinations as the force behind the verdict. Jim Sleeper sees him as an "impresario of racial theater" who won by creating a "false moral dilemma." As Abramson notes on the same point, Cochran "made [the jury] *want* to disbelieve the evidence."

Many popular magazines had retrospective articles in 1996, including Posner 1996, Thernstrom and Fetter 1996, and Trudeau 1996. In a more scholarly vein, the *Journal of Social Issues* devoted its Fall 1997 issue to Simpsoniana. Commentators included courtroom lawyers and cognitive, social, and clinical psychologists, on various aspects of the case and the trial.

WHAT IT'S ALL ABOUT

What, finally, are we to make of it all? Academics are tempted—indeed, expected—to rise above the fray, maintaining the appearance of objectivity and refusing to take a moral position. That is certainly tempting: there are too many ambiguities, too many arguments for and against too many moral positions. But if we are to make any meaningful statements from our Olympian heights, we have to make some judgments. For instance, which is more important for a society like ours: a shared belief in a trustworthy justice system that protects us all and treats us all as "equal under the law" or the right of each individual and group in a diverse culture to contribute to the making of meaning for all of us? Or is the first illusory without the prior existence of the second? If so, it seems to me, the choice is clear: as repugnant as it is to see a murderer go free, and as much as that outcome to a highly public trial erodes our faith in our government and one another, the jury did right. Until we can all place our trust in a government that treats us equally, we cannot share any narrative about "equal justice under the law." [17] The jury in the O. J. Simpson case took advantage of the defendant's celebrity and charm, the Los Angeles Police Department's and Los Angeles District Attorney's ineptitude and malfeasance, the ingenuity and limitless financial resources of the defense Dream Team, and the judge's mismanagement of the trial to make a statement more important, in the long run, than the punishing of one guilty person: that justice exists only if everyone can play a role in constructing the stories that frame it. The jury, finally, framed "O.J."

EBONICS—IT'S CHRONIC

"But 'glory' doesn't mean a 'nice knock-down
argument,'" Alice objected.

"When I use a word," Humpty Dumpty said,
in rather a scornful tone, "it means just what
I choose it to mean—neither more nor less."

"The question is," said Alice, "whether you *can*
make words mean so many different things."

"The question is," said Humpty Dumpty,
"which is to be master—that's all."

Lewis Carroll, Through the Looking-Glass, chapter 6

THE OPENING SALVO

On December 18, 1996, I was watching the local evening news programs on television, idly flipping from one to another. One story caught
my linguist's attention. It appeared that the Oakland School Board had
just passed a resolution that "Ebonics," the "primary language" of many
of its students, was a "Niger-Congo African Language," rather than a
form of English, being "genetically based." "Such languages," the resolution continued (it went on for about two pages), had been "officially
recognized" as "worth [sic] of study." Therefore this language was to be
used as a means of instruction in the Oakland schools ("the Superintendent in conjunction with her staff shall immediately devise and imple-

ment the best possible academic program for imparting instruction to African American students in their primary language").

The anchors and reporters had some discussion about what the resolution meant (we will see that their confusion was perfectly justified). Was the Oakland School Board (hereafter OSB) saying . . . unthinkable . . . that "Black English" was *OK?* Was to be taught in school? Was *not English?* I figured it for a couple of days' play in the local venues, no more.

As I bent over to pick up my *San Francisco Chronicle* the next morning, my eye was caught by a typically florid *Chron* top-of-page-one headline (Olszewski 1996):

OAKLAND SCHOOLS OK BLACK ENGLISH
Ebonics to be regarded as different, not wrong

Worthy of note is the presupposition in the subhead: the *normal* way Ebonics is "regarded" is as "wrong": what's newsworthy is the OSB's proclamation that it is only "different." (From? We don't even need to mention the standard explicitly.)

The other major local papers weighed in the next day (along with just about every other paper in the country). The tone was generally similar: raucous and incredulous disapproval. Shocked, *shocked.* There were some more measured assessments. The headline in the *Oakland Tribune* on December 20 read merely, "WAGING WAR OF THE WORDS: OAKLAND GROUND ZERO IN EBONICS CONTROVERSY." In other words, the issue had erupted in under two days into a national brouhaha. The *Trib* helpfully provided some definitions in a box (Bazeley 1996):

HOOKED ON EBONICS

Linguists trace the origins of Black English or Ebonics to the Gullah language that slaves in Georgia and the Carolinas developed when their Niger-Congo language came into contact with English. Experts say it has its own syntax, verb forms, and grammar. Some examples:

- The verb "to be" does not exist in Niger-Congo languages. Speakers say "he be rich" instead of "he is rich."
- The absence of the "th" sound at the end of words, which results in "wif" instead of "with."
- Use of stressed "bin," as in, "She bin married," for "She has been married for a long time."

THE PROBLEMS WITH EBONICS

The *Trib* was only trying to be helpful, but practically every word in the box is misleading or incorrect, like much of the OSB's statement. Likewise, most of the outraged responses in the local and national media were misleading or incorrect. Very little effort seems to have been made, over the six weeks or so that the debate (if that is what it was) raged, to get clear statements from authoritative sources about just what the ruckus was all about: "Ebonics," "Black English," "AAVE," "Pan-African Communication Behavior," or whatever. It seemed from the start that the aim on all sides was to achieve conflict rather than mutual understanding or consensus. "Experts" are always, as here, referred to, but it's seldom clear who they are. And whoever gave the *Trib* the information that fills the box is, for sure, no "expert."

1. While AAVE (African American Vernacular English—the currently preferred term among sociolinguists)—does have "its own syntax, verb forms, and grammar," so does every form of any language: the Queen's English, Brooklynese, or Valley Girl. By "its own" I mean here variants that are intelligible to other speakers of English, rather than forms like those of (say) French or Hindi, which are so different from those of English that a monolingual speaker of English could not understand them. And "grammar" subsumes the other two: "syntax" and "verb forms" (morphology) are parts of "grammar." Moreover, AAVE has other distinctive forms, for instance in its nouns and pronouns. The *Tribune*'s explanation should have read, "has some grammatical rules that differ from those of Standard American English (but most of its rules are the same as those of the standard)."

2. The first example given is not of a sentence that lacks *be,* but one with "invariant *be.*" The latter exists not only as one option in AAVE, but also in many other English dialects past and present, standard and nonstandard. Think of Puck's "What fools these mortals be!" and the common legend on old maps, "Here be dragons." Sentences without *be* are also an option in AAVE, as well as being the norm in some Niger-Congo languages, but there is no copula (the verb *be*) in many languages throughout the world. Classical Latin, Greek, and Sanskrit—as Indo-European as you can get—had the option of so-called "nominal sentences," that is, sentences without *be.* Modern Russian has no copula in the present tense. Oh, and it's improbable that a monolingual speaker of any Niger-Congo language would say *either* of the sentences given. But let's not nitpick.

3. While it's true that Niger-Congo languages lack the *th* sound, so do the majority of the world's languages: it's highly marked. Therefore it is unsurprising that in many nonstandard English dialects including New York and Cockney it is replaced by the similar segments *f* or *t* (and the voiced equivalent by *v* or *d*). Indeed, Cockney, exactly like AAVE, substitutes *f* and *v* for voiceless and voiced *th*. John McWhorter (1998) suggests plausibly that most of the traits of AAVE that differ from Standard American English were borrowed from the nonstandard English dialects of the whites the slaves came into most contact with: overseers (remember Simon Legree?) and indentured servants. And *th* turns to *f* (or *t*) not only at the ends of words, but anywhere in them.

4. While it is possible that the use of "bin" to indicate distant past time is a semantic borrowing from a Niger-Congo language, there are other plausible explanations. In any case, one or two borrowings from Niger-Congo do not a Niger-Congo language make. If it were that simple, we'd all be speaking French and/or Latin. (Who says it's so hard to learn foreign languages? Spaghetti. Ketchup. Ginger. Now I speak Italian, Malay, and Tamil.)

But the *Oakland Tribune* cannot be made to bear all the blame, since the OSB's original resolution was a blooming, buzzing confusion. A few representative paragraphs should give the flavor of the statement:[1]

> WHEREAS [it begins], numerous validated scholarly studies demonstrate that African-American students as part of their culture and history as African people possess and utilize a language described in various scholarly approaches as "Ebonics" (literally "Black sounds") or "Pan-African Communication Behavior" or "African Language Systems"; and
>
> WHEREAS, these studies have also demonstrated that African Language Systems are genetically based and not a dialect of English; and
>
> WHEREAS, these studies demonstrate that such West and Niger-Congo African languages have been officially recognized and addressed in the mainstream community as worth of study, understanding or application of its principles, laws, and structures for the benefit of African-American students both in terms of positive appreciation of the language and these students' acquisition and mastery of English language skills; . . .
>
> NOW, THEREFORE, BE IT RESOLVED that the Board of Education officially recognizes the existence, and the cultural and historical bases of West and Niger-Congo African Language Systems, and each language as the predominant primary language of African-American students; . . .
>
> BE IT FURTHER RESOLVED that the Superintendent in conjunction with her staff shall immediately devise and implement the best possible academic program for imparting instruction to African-American students in their primary language for the combined purposes of maintaining the legitimacy and richness of such language whether it is known as "Ebonics," "African Language

Systems," "Pan-African Communication Behaviors," or other description, and to facilitate their acquisition and mastery of English language skills.

Well, you get the idea. No sooner did the fecal matter hit the ventilation machine than the OSB did two things: (1) hire a PR firm; (2) revise its statement. But the first was taken as a sign of malfeasance (hiring a PR firm, like taking the Fifth Amendment, is popularly interpreted as an admission of guilt), and the second was too little too late. The revision was just as orotundly impenetrable as the original, and the battle had already been joined.

In the few paragraphs cited above, the seeds of the controversy are apparent: the gauntlet has been flung. The majority community's statements on the matter generally represented its dismay as caused by the subject of the resolution, ostensibly the (not well specified) use in the Oakland public schools of some version of AAVE. But there is reason to suspect that that isn't the real cause of public outrage. As reported in the *San Francisco Examiner* on December 22 (Wagner 1996), Los Angeles had had a similar plan in place in thirty-one schools for six years, with no controversy at all. And it's incredible to me that a huge swath of the American mass media, and their audience, could remain fixated for several weeks on a minor decision by a school board of a small Western city—each of the above points generally being sufficient to doom any potential news item to oblivion. So there was something about the OSB's resolution—both the form it took and the fact that the resolution was made at all, in any form—that caused this bit of ephemera to pass the UAT. To see what that something was, let us look closely at the resolution, first considering specific details of form, and then going on to the larger question: who gets to decide publicly what *is* and what is *not* a "language"?

RESOLUTION FOR THE HELL OF IT

The red flag waved in front of the majority bull was inflammatory both in style and content, but the style rankled more and provided an "in" for hostile commentators, a justification for ridicule, satire, and bemused incomprehension. Many members of the linguistic profession, which (liberal souls that we largely are) would normally have been supportive, hesitated to get involved or straddled the line, because the statement on its face contained so much arrant nonsense.

Some apologists for the OSB argue that, with a little bit of exegesis, it's possible to ascertain what the resolution was intended to mean and discover that that intended meaning is actually reasonable. My exegetical enthusiasm is the equal of anyone's, but I can't agree. There is a time and a place for exegesis. When you make a statement that you suspect may have controversial aspects; when you make this statement publicly; when you are a member of a minority community; when you represent "education"—it is incumbent upon you to be clear and precise; to use words in their ordinary acceptations, in accord with the practice of the community whose "scholarship" (a word used entirely too often in the resolution) you are appropriating. You cannot claim to be "misunderstood" (as the OSB was quick to do) when your explicit, written statement is laden with obfuscations, baroque pomposities, and idiosyncratic usages. While understanding is a two-way street, the writer probably bears more of the responsibility than the reader for creating shared meaning—the more so in the case of public resolutions. Let's look at just a few of the resolution's thornier problems.

"Numerous Validated Scholarly Studies"

At the risk (again) of revealing a pedantic streak, there is scholarship and scholarship. I'm not sure what a "validated" scholarly study is, exactly. The phrase is repeated at several points, like a mantra, and indeed it is used as a mantra—to reassure its users and hearers that all is well, to induce a trancelike serenity. A "validated study" normally is one that has been replicated, and the results of both original and later research published in a recognized and refereed journal within a relevant professional field. But *no* studies meeting those criteria ever demonstrated, or claimed, what the first cited paragraph says "validated scholarly studies demonstrate." Indeed, research by all of the best-regarded workers in the field has concluded without exception that AAVE is a dialect of English. It is not a "language" in its own right, although it is a variety of one language—English.

Ebonics, Pan-African Communication Behaviors, African Language Systems

Linguists do not use terms like "Ebonics" (which would not in any case literally mean "Black sounds"), "Pan-African Communication Behaviors," or "African Language Systems," even for indisputable African languages. Most of these terms convey nothing but an attempt to enforce one's claims to authority by ponderousness: if you can create impenetrable and mysterious terminology, you have to be taken seriously. Scholars in a field create its taxonomy for the purpose of expressing their ideas unambiguously. Paleontologists who discover new fossil species today still use the Linnaean system of classification devised over two hundred years ago, because doing so enables any other paleontologist reading a report of a new find to understand immediately where it fits into the established scheme of things. Naming is narrative: it furthers the story by connecting what is newly named with what is already known. To go outside of established procedure and create your own taxonomy can be fun and empowering. But it puts you outside the "validated scholarly" discourse and, to the insider, marks you as an interloper. So in making use of terminology not standard in the relevant field, the OSB managed to alienate the world at large, because of their pomposity, and linguists in particular, because the Board refused to play by the rules of linguistics, while borrowing its prestige and authority.

The OSB could claim that it wanted no part of the games the (very largely white) world of professional linguistics plays. Fine: we can take it. But then they shouldn't piggyback onto the respectability of "scholarship" and "validation," or invoke in a virtually self-parodic way a twisted variant of the field's taxonomic conventions. You can't have your cake and eat it.

"Genetically-Based"

This statement above all others created anger and consternation on all sides. Despite the OSB's insistence on its "scholarly" credentials and bona fides, the term was used in a way that bore no relation to professional linguistic practice. We do speak of "genetic relationships" among languages. We might say, for instance, that many of the structural and lexical similarities between Spanish and English are "genetically based," meaning that they exist because Spanish and English share a common source, Proto-Indo-European. In the same way we could say that there is a "genetic basis" for the similar noses of Third Cousin Harry and Great Aunt Elvira. In the latter case, we use "genetic" literally: "resulting from shared genes." In the former case, "genetic" is metaphorical, since languages don't have biological genes. But the analogy is perfectly apropos and has been part of the discourse of linguistics for a couple of centuries.

We can use "genetic(ally based)" in isolation when discussing heritable biological traits: *Mary's tendency to obesity is genetic(ally based).*

We can use the same phrase metaphorically: *The inflectional character of German is genetic(ally based).* But in both examples, it is a *trait,* not its bearer, that is "genetic(ally based)." We can't say, for instance, **Mary is genetic(ally based),* or **German is genetic(ally based).* Such statements would not be considered biologically, or linguistically, incorrect. Rather, they are nonsensical and meaningless. So linguists were dismayed and bewildered at the language of the statement, purporting as it did to be derived from "validated scholarly studies."

Non-linguists were, if possible, even more nonplused by the wording. To them, "genetically based" suggested that Ebonics was not, like all other human language forms, learned, but rather innate, like animal cries. Certainly this was far from the OSB's intention, but in the absence of any other plausible interpretation, it suggests itself.

The OSB, as noted, was quick to attempt damage control. By December 23, according to Sarah Lubman (1996), writing in the *San Jose Mercury-News,* OSB President Jean Quan was explaining that the proposal's author

> didn't mean genetic, she meant passed down orally through the family.
> The next day, the school board put out a clarification that said the phrase "genetically based" was "used according to the standard dictionary definition of 'has origins in.'" It is not used to refer to human biology. A district spokeswoman explained that what the board really meant to say was that Ebonics "has its origins in Africa."

The reader is referred to the epigraph at the top of this chapter.

Once again, you can't have it both ways. If you want to secure your authority with "scholarly" undergirdings, you must play the "scholarly" games, using words as they are used by respected sources whom you cite by name (the OSB never does this either). If you deviate from conventional practice, you must explicitly indicate your awareness of the changes you are proposing to the scholarly armamentarium, citing sources again, and explaining what you are changing, and why the change is necessary. Yes, in a free country with a robust First Amendment, legally you *can* use words to mean whatever you want them to mean. But then you're on your own, with no supportive institutions to back you up—and you take the consequences. One is that readers and hearers will make what they will of your usage (if you can freelance, so can they). Moreover, you cannot fall back on new authorities—"the dictionary," again unsourced—because no dictionary defines "genetic" as "having origins in" without requiring a noun following the preposition. And if, as the spokeswoman asserts, "genetic" is not being used in

its biological sense, and if, as I have said, it is not being used in its linguistic sense, in what "sense" is it being used?

"And Not a Dialect of English"

For one thing, the use of "and"—that is, the explicit semantic linkage of
"genetically based" and "not a dialect of English"—is difficult to parse.
I suppose this confusion could be used to argue that the ex post facto
"meaning" the OSB tried to impose was in fact the one they intended
in the first place: if they had *meant* by "genetically based," "genetically
based in an African language family," or something similar, then the
conjunction would make sense. But since, as we have seen, "genetically
based" by itself cannot be read this way, the conjunction becomes un-
interpretable.

Here is another sticky point, perhaps the most controversial phrase
in the document. On what basis does the OSB claim that Ebonics is "not
a dialect of English," and how does their argument relate to the ways in
which "scholars" establish that two forms of expression are or are not
dialects of one language? As with so much that involves language, the
answers that have to be given are less definite and precise than might be
ideal. Linguists have a pat definition: two forms are dialects of the same
language, rather than separate languages, just in case they are "mutually
intelligible," that is, a speaker of one can understand a speaker of the
other without special study (although sometimes a fair amount of attention and goodwill is necessary).

But some forms that are traditionally called "dialects" are in actuality separate languages. Mandarin and Cantonese, for example, are not
mutually intelligible in oral speech. But because the Chinese writing system, unlike ours, is not phonetically based, these two forms can be *written* so that speakers of both can understand the same written form. In
that narrow and special sense the two might be called "dialects." On the
other hand, Swedish and Norwegian are mutually intelligible, with perhaps some difficulty—but no more than that required, say, of a Californian listening to a Cockney. But because geopolitics has established national borders between Sweden and Norway, we think of their forms of
speech as distinct "languages," although by strictly linguistic definition
they are dialects of a single language.

Another problem lies in the notion of "mutuality" so crucial to this
question. Speakers of nonstandard dialects—those that, like AAVE or
Cockney, are spoken by people without political or cultural power, and

therefore on whose dialect the literate form of the language is not based —generally can understand speakers of the standard without much trouble. Sometimes they can code-switch at will—speak in the standard on formal occasions, in the home dialect in folksier circumstances.[2] On the other hand, speakers of standard dialects often are unable to understand the "thick" or "heavy" dialects of nonstandard speakers, and generally don't do a good job of imitating them. That makes sense, since nonstandard speakers *have* to at least understand the standard: it's the language of all public life. But there is little impetus for standard speakers to make the adaptation to the nonstandard.

Leaving these cavils aside, though, we linguists do have a pretty good idea of when two forms are languages and when they are dialects of a single language, based on similarities and differences at all levels of the grammar: sounds, words, sentence structure, and discourse structure. Again, though, we are operating with continua rather than either/or absolutes. All languages share *some* similarities, because the brains of all human beings are similarly structured and wired. Languages that are genetically related (go back to a common source) share many similarities, just as members of human families do. The closer the genetic relationship and the more recently the forms have split from the common source, the greater the similarities. French and Spanish, having diverged from a common source (Latin) not much over a millennium ago, are much more similar than Spanish and English, whose common source is the protolanguage (Indo-European) itself. On the other hand, while genetically French and Spanish are equidistant from English, because of the Norman Invasion English borrowed a tremendous amount of vocabulary from French, making English seem superficially more similar to French than to Spanish, or perhaps even German, to which English is much more closely related genetically. But if we were to examine the grammars of each of these languages at all relevant points, English would emerge as much more similar to German overall, and French to Spanish, than French to English. Even so, the complexities involved in these decisions show how hard it is to make absolute statements about linguistic relationships.

So how can you determine whether AAVE/Ebonics is a language in its own right or a dialect of English?[3] And how can you tell whether it is more closely associated with (genetically related to) English and other Indo-European languages, or "West and Niger-Congo African languages"?

Most obviously, there is the criterion of mutual intelligibility. Every speaker of AAVE can understand Standard American English (SAE); and generally speakers of SAE can understand (with occasional difficulty) even the most divergent forms of AAVE. Many speakers, if not most, of AAVE can switch into the standard. On the other hand, without special training, no speaker of English (including speakers of AAVE) can understand any of the West African languages of the Niger-Congo subfamily of Niger-Kordofanian languages, including (among many others) Ewe, Swahili, and Zulu. On that basis alone, AAVE is a form of English and not a "West or Niger-Congo African language."

As discussed briefly above, a number of proponents of "Pan-African Communication Behaviors" have tried to argue for the existence of a relationship between Ebonics and Niger-Congo languages on the basis of shared features. Robert Williams, the inventor of the name "Ebonics," provides a list of shared traits that might argue in favor of the hypothesis:

> The absence of the double consonant: Consonant blends do not occur in the final position. *West, best, test, last* and *fast* are pronounced in Ebonics as *wess, bess, tess, lass,* and *fass.* . . . .
> The lack of possessives: Daddy car, Bob house. . . .
> The lack of pluralization: Two boy, three girl. . . .
> The zero copula or the absence of the verb: "We busy," "You full?" and "You tired?" . . .
> Double and triple negatives: "I ain't never going nowhere with you no more." . . .
> A good deal of Ebonics is found in the pronunciation of words: sandwich-samich, shrimp-swimp, Saturday-Sadday, before-befoe. . . . (1997, 211f.)

Many of these forms are found in other nonstandard English dialects and speakers of Ebonics over many generations in this country are likely to have come into contact with speakers of these nonstandard English dialects time and again. That contiguity would have encouraged the creation and retention of these forms in AAVE. But contact with Africa and its indigenous languages was severed with the end of slave importation early in the nineteenth century. Hence, even if the forms Williams cites exist in African languages, nonstandard English dialects are a more probable source for them in AAVE.

Another reason to question the Niger-Congo connection is that, with respect to the properties Williams lists, AAVE behaves much more like a dialect of English than like an independent language. As William Labov (1972) has shown, it is seldom the case that nonstandard features of a dialect are used by all speakers of that dialect, all the time. On the other hand, if these are features of the language as a whole, all speakers are likely to use them all the time.

Thus, while many nonstandard dialects of English use multiple (actually, it can even be "quadruple" or more) negation, they don't necessarily use it with perfect consistency. It depends on linguistic and social context. But if multiple negation is the rule in a language (as in Russian), all speakers will use it all the time. Likewise, if a language does not possess final consonant clusters, they will never show up in words of that language. If speakers borrow into that language a word with a final cluster, it will be simplified (as happens, for instance, to English words borrowed into Japanese: *instant* becomes *insutano*). But many AAVE speakers sometimes simplify final consonant clusters, sometimes not. So the cases that Ebonicists use to argue for their position are, looked at in terms of systematicity, not very persuasive, since the dialect-of-English position explains the differences much better.

It's true that AAVE has borrowed a few words from various West African languages: *tote, goober, okra,* and *jazz* are the ones most commonly listed. But even borrowing wholesale from a language (as English did from French and Latin) does not make the second language into a version of the first.[4] English is neither French nor Latin.

ENOUGH BLAME TO GO AROUND

The OSB committed a serious tactical error in allowing its resolution to be made public in the form it took. But the errors were hardly confined to one side. As soon as the dispute erupted, the anti-Ebonics faction, including some African Americans, weighed in with all kinds of equal absurdities. And while the OSB's errors were innocent and not meant to do harm, their antagonists' often have the aroma of a covert, and so especially dangerous, form of racism.

While the critics often made use of the Board's pomposities and obscurities to justify their attacks, the ferocity of those attacks cannot be accounted for by the resolution's style or content alone. It is always a favorite game of the powerful to pick on the linguistic usage of their inferiors, but it's considered bad form to keep at it as the media did for over a month. A strong motive is needed to explain this departure—so un-p.c.—from conventional etiquette. And much of the critique ignored the specific statements of the resolution and certainly misunderstood the intent of the OSB in putting it out. The nature of the criticism suggests that the aim of the critics was not so much pedagogical—to discourage the Oakland schools from using Ebonics as a teaching aid—as political.

The OSB's resolution seemed to many of its critics a cry of defiance: they had been dissed. It was read as a demand, not only that Ebonics be incorporated in some undefined way into the Oakland school curriculum, but that (1) students be *taught* AAVE as a second language (bizarre, since presumably they already knew it!); and that (2) AAVE be recognized by the larger community as a valid communicative form (the intent, I think, behind a lot of the huffing and puffing about "validated scholarly studies," "Pan-African Language Systems," and the "West and Niger-Congo African languages [that] have been officially recognized and addressed in the mainstream public educational community as worth[y] of study"). A lot of the yelling in the media was directly addressed to this claim: specifically, the often-repeated (by many black commentators as well as white) argument that AAVE was "slang," "street talk," or "bad English." Just as the OSB's discussion of AAVE as "genetically based" and a language distinct from English demonstrated one form of ignorance, so the equation of AAVE with "slang" demonstrated another, the more appalling because of its racist tinge. And while plenty of commentators from the majority community savaged the OSB's errors, most left those of the mainstream commentary strictly alone.

The tendency to let the well-spoken and well-connected get by isn't unique to this case by any means. In *Pygmalion,* George Bernard Shaw remarks that a shopgirl or lady's maid needs better English than a duchess, because the former will be scrutinized by her betters and suffer if she doesn't measure up, while the latter has very few betters and enough clout to be forgiven for any linguistic sins. For the same reason language maven William Safire (1998) can offer up genuine boners like the following in the august pages of the *New York Times* Sunday Magazine, and emerge unscathed: "The present third-person singular of the verb 'to be' [is] comes from the Latin *esse,* as in Bishop George Berkeley's *esse est percipi,* 'to be is to be perceived.' It's a short jump from *esse* to *is.*" As the students in any introductory linguistics course can tell you, *is* is neither derived from, nor borrowed from, any Latin word: *is* and its Latin equivalent *est* (not *esse,* the infinitive) are cognates. They come from the same original source, but English (unlike French, for example) is not derived from Latin. Safire's remark displays many of the same features as the OSB's: easily avoided errors, pomposity, irrelevance of the troublesome topic to the real matter at hand (in Safire's case, President Clinton's equivocation around the present tense—the identity of the verb itself being beside the point). Yet the column did not unleash torrents of scathing abuse from all sides. Just as Shaw's duchess gets away with poor English, Safire's linguistic gaffe goes unchallenged. Only the powerless get clobbered.

The well-spoken and well-connected got away with a lot of nonsense about Ebonics. Sarcasm and jokes at the expense of Ebonics and its speakers abounded from the start: references to "Moronics," "Ivoronics," "Hebonics," "Ebonics—no Thonics," and so forth. (Just try that with any other language name!) Then there are the jokes on the Internet. While many are putatively "about" the language itself, it doesn't take much exegesis to detect a racist subtext: speakers of Ebonics are ignorant, sexually promiscuous, and criminal. "Aesthetic" critique masks racist subtext.

FROM: ELEVEN RULES ON HOW TO SPEAK EBONICS
. . . 3. Omit forms of "do" from most of your sentences.
EX. "What you say about my mama?"
4. Use the same form of a noun for singular and plural.
EX. "One joint, two joint, three joint."
5. Disregard verb tense in your sentences.
EX. "I know it good shit when she tell me."

FROM: EBONICS HOMEWORK ASSIGNMENT
Leroy attends an Oakland high school where they teach Ebonics as a second language. Last week he was given an easy homework assignment. All he had to do was put each of the following words in a sentence. This is what Leroy did . . .
7. Rectum: I had two Cadillacs but my ol' lady rectum both.
8. Hotel: I gave my girlfriend da crabs and the hotel everybody.
9. Odyssey: I told my bro, you odyssey the jugs on this hoe. . . .
Needless to say, Leroy got an A. God bless America.

FROM: EBOLYMPIC GAMES
Opening Ceremonies
The Torching of the Olympic City
Gang Colors Parade

Track and Field
Rob, Shoot & Run
9MM Pistol Toss
Molitov [sic] Cocktail Throw
Barbed Wire Roll
Chain Link Fence Climb
White Peoplechase
Monkey Bar Race [5]

More "serious" commentators weren't too far behind. In the daily press, there was an effusion of cartoons, columns, and editorials, almost without exception strongly negative. A cartoon in the *San Francisco Chronicle* of December 20, 1996, by Tom Meyer depicts a classroom. The students, black and white, are labeled "Oakland Teachers." One black student, reading from a "Black English Dictionary" is raising his hand to ask, "How do you say: 'Are you nuts?'" On the same day the *San Francisco Examiner,* in an unsigned editorial headed "'Ebonics' Be Gone," sneers at AAVE as an inadequate form of communication:

> Try getting a job by listing your language as "Ebonics."
> Try getting into college by saying, "I be well qualified."

True enough, but beside the point. Job and college interviews aren't places where AAVE is spoken.

Ellen Goodman (1996), a usually liberal voice (as with p.c., liberal and conservative whites came together on this issue) argues: "By fiat they [the OSB, of course] have transformed black street talk into ebonics and put ebonics on a par with French or Chinese. They have made 'I be' the linguistic equivalent of '*je suis.*'" Actually, "I be" *is* the linguistic equivalent of "*je suis.*" But the metamessage is plain enough: French is "good," Ebonics (note Goodman's lower-case) is "bad," unworthy to be considered in the same breath.

A cartoon by Mike Luckovich, printed on January 1, 1997, in the *San Francisco Chronicle* and reprinted from the *Atlanta Constitution,* shows Beavis and Butthead in a classroom, characteristically going "Huh-huh, huh-huh, huh-huh . . . " A white teacher standing by says to a black colleague, "I say the school board should recognize it as a distinct language." Beavis and Butthead are paradigmatic jerks whose humor derives from their oafish incapacity to communicate. To make the implicit equation with AAVE in the cartoon is to equate B & B with speakers of Ebonics.

A black editorial writer in the *New York Times,* Brent Staples (1997), compares the OSB's position to Leonard Jeffries's Afrocentrism. Both positions, he argues, are fatally flawed.

> Defining broken English as "black English" is particularly galling, given that black poets, writers, and musicians have made eloquent contributions to the culture for at least 200 years. Gospel, blues, and jazz to name just three forms, have swept beyond national borders and become important on the world stage as well. To equate degraded English with Frederick Douglass's speeches, Mahalia Jackson's gospel or Duke Ellington's suites is beyond absurd.

There is some sense to this, but as with so many of the well-meaning liberal grumblings, it misses the point. Speakers of AAVE would normally switch into the standard if they were making public speeches. I'm not sure what the connection is to music. And as should be perfectly clear, AAVE is not "broken English" (ironically, a term usually used for the attempts of nonnative speakers) or "degraded English."

Egged on by the professional journalists, letter writers to all the local papers weighed in heavily against Ebonics and the OSB. "I am absolutely thrilled at the Oakland school district's choice of ebonics as the language of choice in the classroom," says one, in the December 21 *Chronicle*. "I expect that very shortly we will see New York punks being taught in Brooklynese, Georgia rednecks in Ya'allonics, Valley girls in Bimbonics, chronic nerds in Siliconics, and farm boys in Rubonics. But what most of us need to keep up with the bureaucrats is a thorough understanding of Moronics." It pains me to report that the writer is from Berkeley.

The Ebonics debate was fought daily, in the newspapers and on television and radio.[6] In the electronic media, it became a favorite whipping boy of both conservative talk shows and "liberal" news telecasts. In general, the appropriate take on the topic was determined early and reiterated often: how dare the OSB try to palm off street slang and bad talk as legitimate language? The only questions had to do with motive: stupidity or cupidity? Many conservative commentators accused the OSB of using Ebonics in order to shunt federal funds intended for bilingual education to its inner-city black clientele. (Many of these same pundits strongly supported California Ballot Proposition 127, outlawing bilingual education, in the next election.) The OSB strongly denied this.

Pretty soon the TV talk shows, with their nanosecond attention spans, turned the examination of Ebonics into occasions for hip-hop teens to strut their stuff and barely veiled racists to excoriate "Ebonics" as low and dirty talk by people who don't know any better. No one had a chance to provide a definition of "slang," or explain why Ebonics, or AAVE, wasn't it.[7] When official real linguists got on radio or TV news or talk shows, they often found that nobody wanted to hear what was probably our prevalent, if pedantically intermediate, position: AAVE (rather than "Ebonics") was neither a language in its own right nor "slang" and "street talk." It was a nonstandard dialect of English and therefore, as is generally the case with nonstandard forms, appropriate in casual and private contexts (at home and with friends), and speakers of these dialects had to be able to switch into the standard for public speech. People got to talk only if they either took the OSB's position, in which case there was always some "authority" on hand to lambaste them; or if they took the "bad talk" line, in which case they won the host's approval, but sometimes got slapped down by callers or members of the studio audience. Anyone attempting a serious explanation got cut off after a few seconds or left to die on the cutting-room floor.

It was odd that many of the same people who, in other contexts, were continuing to bemoan the p.c. that kept them from speaking freely about "sensitive" issues, were happy to express themselves at length about the defectiveness of a "sensitive" group's language skills, and were seldom if ever criticized for their remarks. Of course p.c. (or, as some might say, common decency, or "c.d.") kept them from making the sorts of comments that were tolerated half a century ago about nondominant groups, playing on their presumptive physical ugliness, intellectual backwardness, and moral turpitude. But somehow the totalitarian and ubiquitous p.c. police didn't point out that language is an intrinsic part of individual and group identity and to demean the language of a group, or excoriate a group for its characteristic language, is as harmful and as reflective of bias as any other form of prejudice.

There was a silver lining. Suddenly it was socially advantageous to be a linguist. We were the people of the hour: *everyone* wanted to hear from us.[8] (More accurately, everyone wanted to *tell us* what they thought: they wanted their opinions heard, but not critiqued, by professionals.) We were the stars of the holiday parties, breathless circles formed around us. It was very heady. Alas, it was fleeting.

So fleeting that the usual sources of extended and more thoughtful analysis barely got to weigh in before it was over. While several of the topics of earlier chapters achieved weight and depth in their passage through the daily, weekly, and monthly media, the Ebonics issue had scarcely reached the newsweeklies, with their week-long publication lags, before it ran its course. For the magazines with longer trajectories, the whole thing was over before they had a chance to cope with it, for the most part. Most of the later discussion adds little, either in content or clarification or cooling-down, but just summarizes the newspaper accounts or provides points of view similar to those already encountered. In *Newsweek* Ellis Cose (1997) both makes fun of the OSB and argues more seriously that inner city kids don't need to have their self-esteem bolstered by the belief that their language is of African origin as much as by a sense of achievement that comes from the development of skills, including the ability to use the majority dialect competently. "Students already at an educational disadvantage should not be provided with false pride in the misuse of language."

In the *New Yorker* another subtext emerges. Louis Menand (1997) suggests that the OSB's resolution was "a reminder that linguistics has often been as much about ideology as science," without recognizing that most linguists considered the resolution well outside current thinking in linguistics. A bit later he does a little linguistic exegesis of his own:

> It's easy to see, in each case, how politics march right alongside the "scientific" conclusions. The notion that African-Americans speak an underdeveloped form of the speech of Southern whites who emigrated from England connotes racial condescension; the notion that they speak an independent dialect connotes racial pride; and the notion that they speak a distinct language connotes cultural separateness. Everything seems to turn on which explanation you prefer.
>
> But nothing turns on it. The thesis that something useful can be learned about people from the origins of the way they talk is a myth. It makes not the slightest difference whether the colloquial speech of twentieth-century inner-city African-Americans is traceable to the speech of eighteenth-century English immigrants, to slave-boat pidgin, or to West African languages.

Menand makes some reasonable points, and an intelligent reader could easily feel sympathy with his position. But as so often in this dispute, even reasonable arguments conceal dubious presuppositions—here, among others, what a "linguist" is and does; and what "makes a difference"— a phrase with no expressed indirect object. Before we can properly analyze it, we need to know, and cannot, "makes a difference *to whom?*"

What is a "linguist"? The word was thrown around a lot. Often, as apparently here, the OSB's vaguely cited "scholars" are taken to include, or be included within, the category of "linguist." I have tried to explain why the majority of linguists, by my definition of the term,[9] would take exception to large parts of the resolution, as much as they might be in sympathy with many of its aims. The options Menand offers likewise include none that most "linguists" would accept. We wouldn't call AAVE an "undeveloped" form of English—that is not what is meant by "nonstandard." Linguists have been demonstrating, methodically and continually since the 1960's, that the grammatical structure of AAVE (like that of any nonstandard dialect of any language) is equal in logic and expressive capacity to that of the standard.[10] To call AAVE "nonstandard" is, therefore, in no sense condescending—it merely captures the obvious fact that the linguistic variety of those who have little political clout will be considered "nonstandard" for that reason alone.

I don't know what Menand means by an "independent" dialect. Of course AAVE is *distinct:* all dialects are distinct from one another, but not "independent," if that means unrelated to other dialects of the same language. Why should this realization enhance racial pride? In the usage of linguists, to say that AAVE is a nonstandard dialect of American English is not to make any sort of political statement at all—it's just a definition. Menand sets up an opposition between the first and second "conclusions" he mentions in the quote above, but in fact (shorn of the word "undeveloped," which has no meaning in linguistics) the two statements are very similar: AAVE is, as McWhorter has suggested, a dialect of American English that developed from nonstandard British dialects.

To call AAVE a separate language from English would connote cultural separateness, but to linguists that isn't the problem. And although to Menand the distinction between the first two "conclusions" and this third one may seem trivial, to us it isn't. Not because of politics, but because the decision is based on what we think languages are and contributes to our knowledge of how human beings make and use them. To determine whether a variety is a dialect of a language (in the linguistic rather than the geopolitical sense) or an independent language requires close and careful study of the complete grammatical systems of both objects under comparison. It isn't a decision that turns on political expediency.

I find it odd that intelligent and well-informed people, people capable of reading the linguistic literature and talking to professional linguists, come to these conclusions again and again in the course of the Ebonics debate. It's not too dismaying that the yahoos on radio talk shows shoot their mouths off with no knowledge and no concern that they have no knowledge. But when people who elsewhere demonstrate a capacity for thoughtful intellectual consideration come to Limbaugh-like conclusions, something must be interfering with their normal thought processes. Especially disturbing is linguist-bashing like Menand's with no understanding of what a linguist is and does, only the fuzzy idea that it's "linguists" behind the scourge. It gets even worse in a piece by Jacob Heilbrunn (1997) in the *New Republic*. Like Menand, Heilbrunn lumps together as "linguists" a very disparate group, alluding sarcastically to "a rich corpus of academic work" that is not merely "amateur crackpotism," but "professional crackpotism":

> The linguist Robert L. Williams coined the term in his 1975 book *Ebonics: The true language of Black folks* by combining the words ebony and phonics.

Williams and his fellow Ebonologists—who include John Baugh, John R. Rickford, Peter Sells and Tom Wasow of the Stanford University Linguistics Department, William Labov of the University of Pennsylvania, Ralph Fasold of Georgetown University, Walt Wolfram of North Carolina State University, Geneva Smitherman of Michigan State University, Lisa Green of the University of Texas at Austin and Orlando Taylor of Howard University, who is a consultant to the Oakland school board—trace the origins of Ebonics to African languages such as Yoruba, Ewe, Fula, Igbo and Mandinka. The consensus among these linguists is that black English is a legitimate linguistic system with a highly complex grammar and syntax that can be identified as coming out of Africa and the Caribbean.

Well, some of this is right, some is sorta-right, and much of it is, frankly, actionable. Many of those named above are people that any linguist, in the sense in which I use the term, would recognize and esteem highly as colleagues. A few are more peripheral. It is the more peripheral members of this list who have made the statements that are causing all the trouble.

All of the people named above have contributed to the study of AAVE, though most have done many other things within various fields of linguistics as well. Baugh has done important studies of the grammar of AAVE. Labov is probably the person principally responsible for our current understanding of the formal properties of AAVE (not to mention his enormous contributions to the entire field of sociolinguistics). Fasold and Wolfram are eminent sociolinguists whose work encompasses the study of many nonstandard dialects, of which AAVE is only one. Rickford is a major creolist who has also worked on AAVE.

All those I have mentioned would subscribe to the first part of Heilbrunn's "consensus," that "black English is a legitimate linguistic system with a highly complex grammar" (syntax, as we know, is just one part of grammar). But I am pretty sure that none of those named in the last paragraph would agree to the second, that it "come[s] out of Africa and the Caribbean." Indeed, all of their work demonstrates that AAVE is a form of English, most of whose grammar is identical to that of Standard English. While their descriptions naturally concentrate on the differences between the standard and nonstandard, any serious linguist would agree that the great majority of the traits of dialects of the same language are shared—necessarily so, or speakers would not find them mutually intelligible. Ridicule and parody are potent weapons in the hands of the powerful, ways to force the undecided to take a stand against less powerful opponents whose views diverge from the exnominated norm. That helps explain a comment by John Leo (1997) in *U.S. News and World Report:*

The nationwide roar of laughter over Ebonics is a very good sign. Talk shows, cartoonists, Internet surfers and famous comedians have all chimed in. A Jewish friend has sent along a primer on "Hebonics," the Jewish-American language in which "W" is pronounced as "V," an extra "T" is placed at the end of many words . . . , and questions are always answered with other questions. . . .

Compare this upbeat, satirical commotion with the reaction to the last Ebonic outbreak—the somber silence in 1979 when an imaginative federal judge in Michigan concluded that lack of respect for black English is a form of educational bias. . . .

The other big reason for all the chuckling over Ebonics is the decreasing public tolerance for the politically correct notions lurking in the shadow of this debate—identity politics, victimization and self-esteem theory. . . . To the PC-minded, what most of us call the mainstream is known as "the dominant culture". . . . Standard English is "establishment" language or "standard" English (in quotes to show contempt. . . .)

Hmm. Here all the big guns are brought to bear on Ebonics—the guns that were built to deal with p.c., Hill/Thomas, Hillary Rodham Clinton, and the Simpson verdict. Contempt for AAVE and its speakers is expressed in the now-familiar coded language of the dominant—sorry, "mainstream"—group in the form of references to p.c., identity politics, victimization, and self-esteem theory. The writer defines the members of what most of *us* call the mainstream by their opposition to those (discredited by us) ideas. But is it such "a good sign" that the "mainstream" is getting a laugh at the expense of an inner city minority school board? Has it once again become permissible—nay, clever—to make those in inferior positions the butts of your jokes?

Leo mentions his Jewish friend's primer on "Hebonics." Pretty amusing, but suppose we make a slight change in his story to read:

A Catholic friend sent along a primer on "Hebonics," the Jewish-American language . . .

Suddenly it's not quite so side-splitting, is it? And the fun at the expense of the OSB was made largely by whites.

THE LSA RESOLUTION

The high-water mark of the controversy happened to come at the time of year at which many scholarly professional societies hold their annual meetings, the Linguistic Society of America among them. It made use of

the coincidence to schedule a discussion about Ebonics.[11] From this discussion there emerged the following resolution:

> Whereas there has been a great deal of discussion in the media and among
> the American public about the 18 December 1996 decision of the Oakland
> School Board to recognize the language variety spoken by many African
> American students and to take it into account in teaching Standard English,
> the Linguistic Society of America, as a society of scholars engaged in the sci-
> entific study of language, hereby resolves to make it known that:
>
> a. The variety known as "Ebonics," "African American Vernacular En-
> glish" (AAVE), and "Vernacular Black English" and by other names is sys-
> tematic and rule-governed like all natural speech varieties. In fact, all human
> linguistic systems—spoken, signed, and written—are fundamentally regular.
> The systematic and expressive nature of the grammar and pronunciation pat-
> terns of the African American vernacular has been established by numerous
> scientific studies over the past thirty years. Characterizations of Ebonics as
> "slang," "mutant," "lazy," "defective," "ungrammatical," or "broken En-
> glish" are incorrect and demeaning.
>
> b. The distinction between "languages" and "dialects" is usually made
> more on social and political grounds than on purely linguistic ones. For ex-
> ample, different varieties of Chinese are popularly regarded as "dialects,"
> though their speakers cannot understand each other. But speakers of Swedish
> and Norwegian, which are regarded as separate "languages," generally under-
> stand each other. What is important from a linguistic and educational point
> of view is not whether AAVE is called a "language" or a "dialect" but rather
> that its systematicity be recognized.
>
> c. As affirmed in the LSA Statement of Language Rights (June 1996), there
> are individual and group benefits to maintaining vernacular speech varieties
> and there are scientific and human advantages to linguistic diversity. For
> those living in the United States there are also benefits in acquiring Standard
> English and resources should be made available to all who aspire to mastery
> of Standard English. The Oakland School Board's commitment to helping stu-
> dents master Standard English is commendable.
>
> d. There is evidence from Sweden, the US, and other countries that speak-
> ers of other varieties can be aided in their learning of the standard variety by
> pedagogical approaches which recognize the legitimacy of the other varieties
> of a language. From this perspective, the Oakland School Board's decision to
> recognize the vernacular of African American students in teaching them Stan-
> dard English is linguistically and pedagogically sound.[12]

While I would replace "usually" in the first line of paragraph (b) with
"often" (the Chinese and Scandinavian cases represent the far ends of the
continuum, and in most cases the dialect/language decision has much
less political involvement), the statement makes good sense, and is especially noteworthy for evading the problem of what the OSB was actually

saying, in favor of making its own interpretation of what they *meant,* and supporting that.

WHAT'S ALL THE FUSS ABOUT?

That brings us back to the question raised earlier: why did a minor decision about language by the school board of a small Western city create a six-week furor? The Ebonics debate passes the UAT—but why?

The answer should be familiar by now. The majority community is struggling to maintain its right to control language: in this case, to determine what form of the language is "good" English, the form that is suitable for public discourse. Since the powerful have always had the right to make their form of language—the standard—the only publicly valid form, the converse must also hold true: if you can maintain your form of language as the only one that is valid, right, logical, and good, then you will legitimately continue to hold power.

Why can't the powerful compromise and admit the propriety of nonstandard dialects for informal use? Fear of being overwhelmed by a newly powerful group makes compromise unattractive. All-out victory becomes the only option imaginable. That fear may stem from an equally irrational belief that if AAVE is judged permissible ("worthy of study," "positive appreciation of the language," "cultural and historic basis," "the legitimacy and richness of such language" in the OSB's resolution being a few of the red flags), then the standard automatically becomes "nonstandard" and bad, and its speakers are automatically demoted from *us* to *them.*

This analysis may help explain a mystery (to me at least): since this argument so clearly revolves around language, why wasn't the opinion of linguists (e.g., in the LSA resolution) given more weight? It would make sense to have done so. We live in a culture of expertise. We lead our lives, or try to, according to what "scientific studies show": eat oat bran, quit smoking, pop vitamin pills because the experts cited on this evening's network news shows—the doctor in the white coat, the lawyer flanked by law books, the scientist tapping at a computer, all the badges of trustworthiness—have told us to do so. So if a current controversy can be given enlightenment by a certified class of experts, why not utilize that resource? While the field of linguistics is relatively new and arcane, we have amassed some knowledge about how language works and how to think of Ebonics and the OSB's resolution. Why was attention not paid? The OSB relied on advice from the uncredentialed; the other side made use of its own prescriptive judgments and visceral prejudices. It makes no sense.

Unless the discussion was really not "about" language at all. In that case, linguistic opinion would have been irrelevant. If, as I am suggesting, the fight was not about what kind of language is valid, but about who has the right to certify its own form of language as valid, then it makes perfect sense that we were largely ignored.[13]

This wasn't the first time that fear of linguistic appropriation by African Americans played a role in the making of the news. According to David Remnick, in the early 1960's the black heavyweight boxer Cassius Clay (now Muhammad Ali) was coming into prominence. At the time, the boxing columnists in major American newspapers and magazines were mostly middle-aged white men. Most heavyweight boxers were black. While boxing experts and fans had abandoned the "great white hope" that a white man would regain the heavyweight title, they clung to certain expectations about black heavyweights: they were slow-moving brutes who won by slugging and taking blows. They were either inarticulate or (like Archie Moore) floridly expressive in nineteenth-century prose style—suggesting that he had deferentially absorbed the best his white betters had to offer. Slow and stolid, they were not sexual threats to white men. They reassured whites of their superiority by fitting an "animal" stereotype.

Clay was completely different. He was graceful, lithe, and fast—almost balletic in his movements, although a large man. That was bad enough—like the Impressionists or the Imagists, he violated current critical presuppositions about what X (art, poetry, boxing) should be. In so doing, he deprived commentators of their vocabulary. Suppose you're a late-nineteenth-century art expert. All your life, you've done well with "chiaroscuro" and "perspective." Now along comes Claude Monet or, even worse, Pablo Picasso. What can you say? Can you still be a critic? No wonder you get mad. The boxing experts had no descriptions available for Clay—he defied description. Worse, he himself was dazzlingly articulate, and not in a deferential way. He spun rhymes, in-your-face anthems to his own prowess. As Remnick says, "Clay was a talker, and they resented that. Language was *their* property, not the performer's. Jim Murray, of the Los Angeles *Times,* remarked of Clay that 'his public utterances have all the modesty of a German ultimatum to Poland, but his public performances run more to Mussolini's Navy'" (1998).

We like to think that we have made great progress in race relations since that time, and in many ways we have. But the majority is reluctant to bring down the last hurdle, the language barrier. We still expect linguistic deference from *them,* whether it is literal silence as in the case of Clay or acceptance of the majority's linguistic standards and linguistic superiority by the Oakland School Board. Just as Clay violated the taboo and incurred years of opprobrium, so the OSB went against the unwritten rules and reaped the whirlwind. Majority resentment was exacerbated by context: the scars of the Simpson verdict had barely begun to heal over, and a decade of payback-for-payback kept the competition for control of societal meaning very much alive. "Good" language could no longer be presupposed to be the exnominated standard. The Language War was moving toward its Armageddon.

THE STORY OF UGH

LIFE AND DEATH IN THE CULTURE WAR

The ordinary acceptation of words in their relation to things was changed as men thought fit. Reckless audacity came to be regarded as courageous loyalty to party, prudent hesitation as specious cowardice, moderation as a cloak for unmanly weakness, and to be clever in anything was to do naught in anything. . . . The hot-headed man was always trusted, his opponent suspected. He who succeeded in a plot was clever, and he who had detected one was still shrewder; on the other hand, he who made it his aim to have no need of such things was a disrupter of party and scared of his opponents. . . . To get revenge on someone was more valued than never to have suffered injury oneself. And if in any case oaths of reconcilement were exchanged, for the moment only were they binding; . . . but he who, when the opportunity offered and he saw his enemy off his guard, was the first to pluck up courage, found his revenge sweeter because of the violated pledge than if he had openly attacked. . . .

The cause of all these evils was the desire to rule which greed and ambition inspire, and also, springing from them, that ardour which belongs to men who once have become engaged in factious rivalry. For those who emerged as party leaders . . . by assuming on either side a fair-sounding name, the one using as its catch-word "political equality for the masses under the law [democracy]," the other "temperate aristocracy [oligarchy]," while they pretended to be devoted to the common weal, in reality made it their prize; striving in every way to get the better of each other they dared the most awful deeds, and sought revenges still more awful, not pursuing these within the bounds of justice and the public weal, but limiting them, both parties alike, only through the moment's caprice.

Thucydides, *History of the Peloponnesian War*, 3.82.4–8

The Peloponnesian War, as chronicled by the historian Thucydides, was partly a culture war. It has many of the attributes of a prototype war: standing armies, deadly weapons, territory changing hands. But the antagonists, Athens and Sparta, represented diametrically different ideas about how to be human, and perhaps more saliently to them, how to be Greek. For Athenians, *enjoyment* was a key word: of pleasures of the flesh, of art, of discourse. For Spartans, the good word was *duty* to the state and the gods. The less talk, the better; the less hedonism, the safer everyone was. The Spartans took cold showers, the Athenians hot baths. So when the two city-states found themselves locked in interminable combat in the late fifth century B.C.E., while technically territory and political domination were the objects to be won, the war was bitterer, and surrender less imaginable to either side, than might be the case in a normal war: this was a war for hearts and minds.

Culture war provokes rancor because the sides don't, and don't want to, understand each other's values. The battles are over abstractions— identity, lifestyle, self-esteem—our very selfhood. "Better dead than Red," said the conservatives at the height of the Cold War. Liberals sneered, but there was something to it. Pretty scary, that *Nineteen Eighty-Four* scenario, everything gray and grimy and slimy and cold, and no conversation to speak of.

So the horrific situation Thucydides describes in ancient Athens is business as usual in a culture war, a war about territories of the mind, heart, and soul. And the struggle whose individual skirmishes I have been describing in the last several chapters is part of a culture war. As Thucydides shows, in such a war language is both a deadly weapon and an early victim—naturally, since the disputed turf includes who has the rights to make, and make sense of, the narrative. It has been said that in any war the victors get to tell the story. Never is this more true than in a culture war, since the victors are the ones who get exclusive rights to make and shape the language in which the story is told. Culture war is language war.

Thucydides didn't mean that words changed their meaning completely, but rather that their presuppositions switch: behavior formerly considered bad becomes good, and vice versa, while the word for the behavior remains constant (as in the case of "ambition" that I discussed in Chapter 3). That is dangerous because language is part of the social contract that enables humans to live together. The relation between object and word exists because we will and wish it to, because we agree, as speakers of English, that the string of phonemes /buk/, which we represent in standard orthography as *book,* will mean the object you now peruse. If I decided that that string of sounds was hitherto to mean "flowerpot," and you decided it would mean "run for your life!" we would be unable to communicate, and there would be no possibility of trust or intimacy between us. The shifting Thucydides describes is more subtle, and therefore even more insidious: it isn't obvious that it is occurring, and no one needs to take responsibility for it.

Such a situation is both an invitation to engage in culture war and a guarantee that, without extraordinary goodwill and efforts on all sides, the war cannot ever end, because there is no way to make a truce. We have reached a point where we mistrust one another's use of language and cannot respect one another's need to achieve some meaning-making power.

In earlier chapters I contrasted the traditional communicative haves and the have-nots. I suggested that the unilateral right to make meaning and control language was being renegotiated, to the distress of the haves. After some thirty years of skirmishes, no clear winner has emerged, and none of these struggles ever ends. Rather its antagonisms and unresolved jealousies are carried over into the next fight: from p.c. to Hill/Thomas to Hillary to O.J. to Ebonics, the continuo never changes even though the melody may shift. Each one has forced some changes in language, and thereby occasioned ever deeper mistrust and factionalization. Just before the millennium, we arrived at what could have been the mother of all language battles. Not merely the most rancorous of all, nor the one where the most was to be won or lost, this one was also the most complex. In the others, there were essentially two sides: men vs. women, whites vs. blacks, conservatives vs. liberals. All of these sides were operative here, openly or covertly. Additionally the most explicit and confusing battle for narrative rights was divided among three bodies that had not been in such open, internecine competition before: the government, the media, and the people.

THE ROAD TO GATEGATE

"Take care of yourself!" screamed the White Queen, seizing Alice's hair with both her hands. "Something's going to happen!"

Lewis Carroll, *Through the Looking-Glass,* chapter 9

Abruptly, at the end of 1998, Americans found themselves at what the media persistently referred to as a "historic" moment: the House of Rep-

resentatives impeached President Bill Clinton. It might seem to the bemused onlooker that the crisis had arisen out of nowhere and merely reflected the continual rise in partisan politics during the 1990's. In fact it
started at least thirty years ago and encompasses several upheavals, some
more evident than others: one genuine prototype war (Vietnam); a culture war, arising in part out of the Vietnam War; a war of revenge, starting in the mid-1970's with Watergate; and two separate but intertwined
language wars.

The national disruption of Vietnam in the late 1960's had not come
out of nothing. Perhaps we can trace its origins to the 1950's, when rock
and roll and the new teen culture aroused in adults a new fear and suspicion of the youth, and in the young, disaffection from their elders. In
the early 1960's the civil rights movement pitted old ways against shocking new ideas, often forced by young activists into the attention of their
elders. President Kennedy's assassination in 1963 created in the minds
of many young people a deep disillusionment with the power of their
elders. If the president could be assassinated, virtually before their eyes,
and the assassin himself assassinated, literally before the eyes of most of
us, then those American institutions we had assumed would keep us safe
were suddenly as vulnerable as we ourselves were. The young had to
create a world of their own. Vietnam added force to the argument. Sex,
drugs, and rock and roll—the epitome of the 1960's—drew the prover-
bial line in the sand between the new, daring, and dangerous and the traditional, comfortable, safe, and boring old. The Culture War was on.

The civil rights struggle unleashed other changes, directly and indirectly: it gave voices to blacks and (in time) women, unleashing one arm
of the language war. First blacks reclaimed "black," then women reclaimed "woman." After relative quiescence through most of the 1980's,
the backlash burst into public with the p.c. debates late in that decade
and—seriously disrupting the delicate new consensus—Hill/Thomas
in 1991.

These cultural battles had their effect on politics in Lyndon Johnson's
decision not to run for another term and Richard Nixon's hair-thin victory in 1968 at the head of the self-proclaimed "silent majority." His
polarizing win further alienated those who had never trusted "Tricky
Dick." As evidence began to emerge that in the summer before his 1972
re-election he had colluded in a break-in of Democratic Party head-
quarters, there was little goodwill and still less personal charisma to
break his fall. He was forced to resign to escape impeachment. Republican diehards saw his fall as a plot orchestrated by those on the other

side of the Sixties culture war. They vowed revenge. And a war of revenge we had for the next twenty-five years. As Iran-Contragate gathered steam in the mid-1980's, Republican bitterness grew worse. There was minor retaliation through the Republican unseating of Jim Wright as House Speaker, but that was neutralized by the Democrats' derailment of the appointment of Senator John Tower as Secretary of Defense. Republican frustration reached its apogee with the rejection of Judge Robert Bork for a Supreme Court seat. The revenge war had created a timoriocracy—government of, by, and for revenge. All Revenge, All the Time could have replaced E Pluribus Unum on the national coinage. And we were ripe for the denouement that I am calling Gategate (rather than any of the many other names it has been given—Monicagate, Sexgate, Sexygate, Tailgate, Zippergate, and so on)[1] to underscore its role as the Armageddon of the Watergate-instituted revenge war.

THE TWO LANGUAGE WARS

So by the 1990's four separate, increasingly uncivil wars were being fought: a culture war, a revenge war, and two language wars. One of the language wars is the one I have been discussing: the struggle of the formerly voiceless to achieve parity in the making of cultural and societal meaning. It can be viewed as the inevitable outgrowth of one aspect of the culture war: the linguistic emancipation of women and blacks. Other nondominant groups followed suit: Asians, the disabled, Native Americans, and many others, adding their voices to a cacophonous yell. The stridency gave rise to complaints by the traditionally empowered of "special interests" and so forth, ignoring the fact that all interests are special (but one is more special than the others). The new demands seemed strange and raucous because their speakers intentionally broke the comfortable old rules for public discourse. And because those now speaking had been silent so long, their voices were harsh and strident; they didn't know, or didn't feel comfortable with, the genteel language the majority had made to transact their gentlemanly disputes. The interests of those who made up the majority were similar enough to allow them to make use of tacit understandings. The new speakers didn't understand those understandings, so some shocking things were said. Theirs was a new language with a new etiquette.

So the new language was scary to many, and unpleasant to most at least some of the time. You had to unlearn old habits and learn new words. It was sometimes annoying, though not nearly as bad as the propagandists on the other side made it out to be. It wasn't the novelty of the language, it was the novelty of who was making it, that rankled those who were rankled.

As divisive and strident as this language war has seemed, its aim is positive: equality in the creation of our national discourse. It is unifying in intent: once we resolve our confusion and dismay, we can forge a single language that we all can adopt as our own.

The other language war posed a more serious problem, one with no solution through time and tolerance alone, the battle Deborah Tannen discusses in *The Argument Culture* (1998). This is the rancor both President Clinton and House Minority Leader Dick Gephart warned about immediately after the impeachment, the "politics of personal destruction." This, too, was the outgrowth of the 1960's culture war, and the revenge war of the 1970's, a deadly mixture. It also gained impetus from the first language war. Because we had come to realize that we all speak different languages, that there are innumerable separate interests demanding satisfaction, that communication has become painfully complicated, the lines dividing Democrats and Republicans grew harder to cross. The culture war added personal fear and bitterness to the mix, setting up a battle line between two sides, the I-Wannas and the Thou-Shalt-Nots. Each side not only was politically opposed to the other but feared that the other was out to get them at a personal level: their children, their marriages (or non-marriages), their relationships, their religious beliefs, and their ability to make personal choices. Earlier in this century political battles focused far from daily life, over foreign policy or economics, where their effects appeared to be indirect and too complicated to permit close attention. Now each side sees the other penetrating into their homes via the law, television, or the Internet.

This is a more negative war, not an attempt to make communicative opportunities more available to all, but to keep them from those on the other side who didn't deserve them. The powerful brandish their age-old weapons of sarcasm and condescension. But they aren't working, thanks to the first language war. In the 1990's funny things started to happen on television. On interview shows panelists began to interrupt one another, and when they were shamed out of that, camera operators learned to catch smirking, head-shaking, and eye-rolling "reaction shots." In Congress, debate got more directly and hurtfully personal: private vices, real or alleged, became part of the public dialogue.

Meanwhile, because of Hill/Thomas and other titillations of the early

1990's (the Bobbitt affair; Tailhook; Kelly Flinn; Paula Jones), the specifics of sexuality had become not only permissible, but normal, on the nightly news. In the 1970's there had been earnest debate about whether it was seemly to say "breast" on television in the open discussion about breast cancer initiated by Betty Ford. By the early 1990's "penis" had entered everyday public speech; by the late 1990's, references to alternative sexual practices were the stuff of prime time. As the debate got more acrimonious, it also got more sexually explicit, which allowed public to penetrate private (and vice versa) and allowed attacks and allegations to be more hurtful because they could be more intimate.

Still another path on the Road to Gategate was taken from a rallying cry of the women's movement: The personal is political. In the 1990's it acquired new meaning. The personal is political, and the political is personal. Public is private and private is public. (And fair is foul and foul is fair.) Commentators often contrast the ugliness of current discourse with the golden age of FDR or JFK. Both of these revered leaders were known to Fool Around rather prodigiously. And yet no one said anything, the secret stayed secret. Why . . . how?

For one thing, because there was no way to talk about it in public. You couldn't even say any of the relevant words on radio or television or write them in a family newspaper. And if you can't talk about it, it didn't happen.

Another change was the new role of women after Hill/Thomas. As long as women are objects who cannot speak for themselves, without the power or the right to give or withhold consent, male sexual predacity is "just having some fun," or "boys will be boys." Whether the woman was pressured or harassed was not, until very recently, an askable question; and sympathy for the "fallen woman" was unlikely. A woman in that position wisely kept her mouth shut to save her honor and was not apt to surface on TV or in the tabloids with her story, to institute a lawsuit or write a tell-all book.

Because this war is a take-no-prisoners business, and because it threatens private life, compromise seems out of the question. And since we no longer speak the same language, there isn't even a way to negotiate a compromise. So as the 1990's waxed on, the various wars of the last four decades intersected with each other. The stakes grew higher and higher. Resentments on both sides grew ferocious. There *had* to be a showdown at High Noon.

And so there was.

WHAT IT'S ALL ABOUT

The expense of spirit in a waste of shame
Is lust in action; and till action, lust
Is perjured, murderous, bloody, full of blame,
Savage, extreme, rude, cruel, not to trust,
Enjoy'd no sooner but despised straight,
Past reason hunted, and no sooner had,
Past reason hated, as a swallow'd bait
On purpose laid to make the taker mad;
Mad in pursuit and in possession so;
Had, having, and in quest to have, extreme;
A bliss in proof, and proved, a very woe;
Before, a joy proposed; behind, a dream.
All this the world well knows; yet none knows well
To shun the heaven that leads men to this hell.

William Shakespeare, Sonnet 129

The epigraph is too obvious a choice only if "lust" is understood in just its sexual reference. Construing the concept more broadly, both sides have been lusting pretty lustily, even as they assure us that "this" isn't "about" (or "just about") "sex." Certainly sex and its epiphenomena play a role in the attention Gategate has received, and in its reluctance to go away. How else could we explain how a midnight-blue semen-stained dress led to an impeachment, when Whitewater, Travelgate, Fostergate, and File-gate came to nothing? Yet, at the same time, sex isn't the whole story.

Perfumers know that their products (not unrelated to Topic A) do not work by scent alone.[2] However delicious, however alluring, the odor of a perfume will dissipate almost on application by itself. It is necessary to include in the formula a *fixative:* a liquid that is itself odorless, but enables the scent to linger on the skin.

In Gategate, sex is the fixative, but the perfume is narrative rights, that is, language rights. Everyone really needs to know what the story is "about." But with a story as full of ambiguities as Gategate, there is no simple answer to the question. We have to construct (horrible, but true) a *metastory,* a story about the story: how the story came to be as it is; what it is; who gets to determine what the story *is,* who the characters are, what style is appropriate to tell it in, what the genre is, how it ends, and therefore what kind of story, at last, it is. As with so many gripping tales, sex provides the cement that both holds the story together internally and glues the reader to the page. But it isn't the real point, the moral of the tale that is Gategate.

WHOSE STORY IS THIS, ANYWAY?

Leading the list of aporias (unresolvable ambiguities) is a metaquestion: who actually is making the story, who has the right to narrate it? Narratives of the same event may differ in every significant detail depending on the perspectives of individual narrators (the *Rashomon* paradox). If we can't determine who has the right to tell the story, through whose eyes we will be seeing its events, then we can't have too much confidence in the validity of the story itself, let alone its moral, or meaning. And, just to make matters more bewildering, in Gategate two fights are going on over narratizing rights: one, between government and media; the second, within government, between the two parties. On the sidelines, the people, the hearers of the tale, are also demanding construction or at least interpretation rights.

Traditionally, the government made the story, the media told it, and the people received it and decided what to do about it. Reality was created at both ends, not in the middle. But now the middleman, the information entrepreneur, wants to act as both maker and consumer of the product. The media are becoming the creators of our reality, not merely its conduit.

Media control over the making of reality burgeoned in the 1970's and 1980's, an outgrowth of the inchoate science of the sound bite. Once politicians spoke directly to us. In its infancy television continued this direct relationship, transmitting political speeches without editorial interference. But TV time grew increasingly precious, and viewers' attention spans increasingly attenuated. Out of this exigency was born the sound bite. Television news editors snipped off ever-smaller segments of speeches as "newsworthy," co-opting the making of meaning in the name of efficiency. Politicians learned to counter their manipulations with sound bites of their own embedded in their longer speeches, controlling the controllers. In turn the media got more ambitious: Why simply create the news event? Why not create the news itself—produce the discourse that they themselves can then dissect?

The race became more urgent as the media were pressured by their own exponential growth. Network television has to compete with cable; print media are increasingly scooped by the Internet. Just as the story of the Gulf War was made by cable rather than network news, Gategate has been goosed along by the Net, in particular Web gossipmeister Matt Drudge, who rescued the original Monica story from *Newsweek*'s circular file, and some of the new online mags, especially *Salon,* which broke the story of Representative Henry Hyde's long-term infidelity. The problem for the traditional electronic and print media is not merely the increase in the number of competitors, but the diversity of types, luring audiences into turning away from their accustomed habits. They have had to become hotter, faster, noisier.

Though the media cannot literally make events themselves, they can put a spin on events to make them newsworthy (that is, to enable them to pass the UAT). The fact that a story gets relentless coverage *makes* it interesting, even as the stories so selected have "legs" because they are about more than appears on the surface. Because their business is language, the media take special notice when language drives events and narrative becomes the creator of reality.

This metastory is disturbing because it makes it clear that the media gave the story life rather than merely helping it grow. Despite regular complaints from both the supply and demand sides for the story to go away, the media kept it going. They seemed rather proud of their "independence," talking endlessly about how nobody wanted them to talk about it.

One reason for their insistence was the bitter competition between and within print, TV and radio, and Web venues. As in the golden (or yellow) days of print journalism, when a dozen daily newspapers might compete in a major city, the scoop became all-important. None dared let Gategate go because someone else could get the glory, or more important, the ratings. Because something peculiar was going on: as much as the people derided the story when polled, whenever a particularly juicy bit surfaced, ratings rose. Like everyone else, The People lie about sex.

Another factor was a lingering case of Watergate envy among journalists themselves. In *All The President's Men,* one ordinary ink-stained wretch was transmogrified into Robert Redford at the height of his golden glory, and another into Dustin Hoffman, one of America's most distinguished actors. The prizes were too tempting to ignore. Even the *New York Times* had joined the baying pack early on, egging the Republicans on.

So it seemed natural, as the House geared up for the Big I, for the media to inflate the importance of the story they had made. The word on all tongues was "historic," although "hysteric" might have been more apt. The decision of the media so to dignify events is telling. Normally time determines whether an event is "historic" and what history will make of it. But this one was declared "historic" even before it had actually happened. I am reminded of events just a century ago, when William Randolph Hearst, to boost his papers' circulation, flogged the public into flogging the government into starting the Spanish-American War, by creating and exaggerating incidents. Once war was declared, one of Hearst's papers ran a banner headline: HOW DO YOU LIKE THE *JOURNAL*'S WAR? Well, how did you like the media's impeachment?

In this vein, one curious thing about Gategate is the playing of the Name Game. It has been hard to attach a single name to the case. Earlier "-gates" were usually given a name that stuck early on: Watergate, Iran-Contragate, Koreagate, Filegate, Travelgate, and so on. Here, many names were bandied about, with no consensus. One reason is that the possibilities are juicier than usual and lend themselves to puns (in part because of our deep recognition of the unseriousness of the whole affair). And there is dissension over the name because naming is one aspect of meaning-making, and the rights to that are up for grabs. The proliferation of names reflects both our inability to pin Gategate down and our struggle to take control of it by naming it.

THE NETWORK BATTLE OF
THE HYPOCRITES VS. THE TRIMMERS

Adding force to this competition is the one within government between the parties, manifested in battles over the words used to describe the indescribable. It is no mere triviality, not "just semantics": each choice of words we adopt to give form to Gategate makes different sense of it. The language we use structures the events it describes. Because that structuring takes place largely outside our consciousness, we don't realize how much events are made for us by phrase-makers.

On the Republican side, words were used to create an *absolute* view, either-or, black vs. white. If you fell on the wrong side, you were a swine. One by one, in the House, Republicans stood up to declare that their vote was forced on them by *duty;* with deep reluctance, they moved to support *the rule of law;* they made it an issue of *conscience.* The apotheosis came courtesy of Henry Hyde, who actually invoked the absolute of absolutes, the Holocaust, arguing that the Rule of Law must be preserved because without it, we would end up at *Auschwitz,* according to a report in the *New York Times:*

"Have you been to Auschwitz?" Mr. Hyde asked. . . . "Do you see what happens when the rule of law doesn't prevail?"

One of the few living persons who could answer both questions authoritatively, Elie Wiesel, expressed both outrage and incredulity at Hyde's insensitivity and ignorance:

"My God, how dare he!" [he said]. . . . "It *was* the law to put Jews in concentration camps, to kill them." (Haberman 1998)

But Hyde's hyperbole was simply the far end of an absolutist rhetoric which almost inevitably ends in comparisons with the Holocaust.[3]

On the other side, the Democrats offered imprecision and relativism. The President's behavior had been *deplorable,* they chorused as one . . . *But* it had to be taken in *context.* Lying about sex wasn't like lying about criminal behavior. We all do it, at least some of the time. Not exactly lie, maybe, but . . . exaggerate, mitigate, circumlocute. It's normal.

But one had to maintain a sense of proportionality. Suppose we grant the President had "sex" and "lied" about it. But that wasn't one of the "high crimes and misdemeanors" the Founders had had in mind when they wrote the rules for impeachment into the Constitution. If we throw this president out of office for this . . . this peccadillo and dismissal from office is the worst the Constitution provides, then what will we do in the future when a president (God forbid!) does something *really* bad? The punishment should fit the crime, and bad behavior is relative, not absolute.

Coincidentally or not, the division recapitulated a familiar argument between the two sides, between the "moral relativism" of the liberals and the "absolutism" or "extremism" of the conservatives as these terms applied to lifestyle beyond the political arena.

THE PLOT THICKENS

After we determine (or don't) what the story is "about," we have to figure out how it goes, construct a plot, a trajectory that gives the events a cohesion and thus a single meaning. As with everything, there are different versions of the plot of Gategate.

One possibility, much favored by both the media and the Republicans, is the Morality Play. Clinton is a sinner. How shall he be punished? That depends on which of two morality plays you think you're watching.

One is labeled "Bad Behavior (Especially of the Sex Kind) Never Goes Unpunished." In this scenario, Clinton's misbehavior was unforgivable and will not be forgiven. It is an affront to all Americans; it lowers us in the world's esteem. He must be driven from office by hooting crowds (which annoyingly failed to materialize). He must be forced to wear a scarlet letter, embroidery floss not supplied.

The second is entitled "Pride Goeth before a Fall." Clinton is guilty of hubris, overweening pride. He thinks that, since he is president, he can get away with things that the rest of us could not. Well, guess what, buddy? This is a democracy! This is the third strike: yer out!

But the electorate mostly seemed unwilling to read the story as a morality tale. Nobody reads *Pilgrim's Progress* any more. A complication in the untangling of the story is that not only are media and government in competition; not only are the parties in competition; but whites and blacks, men and women are also in competition for narratizing rights, just as we would expect from the events of the foregoing chapters. And while white men are apt to construe the tale in one of the ways listed above, blacks are more apt to see Clinton's story as a version of *their* story, the "DWB (Driving While Black)" narrative. In this story, the powerful are always out to get you, especially if you seem to be overreaching (have a nicer car than *you ought to,* are in a nicer neighborhood than *you should be*). In this mini-drama, Clinton is one of the Outsiders (see below), who is being made to suffer because he looks and acts different from *us* even as he tries to look better than *us*. He must be put in his place.

It has often been commented that women—whom one might expect (by tradition or as "feminists") to view the president's sexual irresponsibility harshly—are more supportive of him than men. Women may see the story in meta-terms: not as about "Bill-and-Monica," but about "Getting-frantic-about-'Bill-and-Monica.'" Women understand the use of sexualization as a means of control. Like blacks, women see the attack on the president as motivated by the powerful wishing to hold on to their power. Women reject morality plays in favor of another scenario: "French Sexual Farce Marries Jacobean Revenge Drama." In this plot (by Feydeau, perhaps), behavior that is more risible than dangerous, more suited to gossipy titillation than high affairs of state, somehow, phantasmagorically, becomes enmeshed in a seventeenth-century melodrama of revenge (say, by John Webster), in which innocent if thoughtless deeds lead inexorably to horrible conclusions, ever more hideous revenge crimes with still more dreadful punishments, and no end in sight.

Several prominent conservatives have lambasted feminists for not lambasting the president. Not only was this a problem for those seeking solidarity in outrage, it was scary precisely because women weren't docilely falling in line. *Women were speaking for themselves, thinking for themselves, acting in their own best interests.* Brrr.

Women persisted in creating their own narratives. Everyone agreed that Clinton had acted badly, but the behavior was, by the accounts of both participants, fully consensual. Conservatives tried to morally browbeat feminists into abandoning the President: why, they asked, couldn't women see this as Hill/Thomas *redivivus?* It was just the same, wasn't it?

By that argument conservatives showed that they still, so many years later, *just didn't get it.* Hill/Thomas is about consent: the ability of a woman to give and withhold it. It was clear that Monica Lewinsky had not only consented, but by her own account had been the instigator.[4] That didn't make the President smell like roses, but the story couldn't be filed under "H" for "harassment."[5]

One thing that made it hard for many feminists to fall into place behind the conservatives was that they had never before been women's helpers or defenders. They—often, the same people now demanding feminist support—had been highly critical of Anita Hill and had done what they could to demolish not only her story, but its narrator, in the ugliest and most traditional ways we have to destroy women (see Chapter 4). They had had sarcastic things to say, many of them, about women who had sued for sexual harassment. Had they suddenly seen the light? Yeah, sure.

Other disturbing facts surfaced about our would-be allies. Prosecutor Kenneth Starr tended to pick on women, to hound them, to prey on their weaknesses and insecurities, to use them without regard for their own future vulnerabilities. The list of victims is long: not only, of course, Lewinsky herself, but her mother and aunt, as well as her friends, totally innocent but forced to "cooperate." Linda Tripp (to be sure an eager co-conspirator), encouraged to act illegally in ways that may come back to haunt her (yes, so we hope). Kathleen Willey, forced to testify publicly about humiliating events she had preferred to keep private; Betty Currie, Clinton's secretary, incurring huge legal bills for doing her job. Susan McDougall, jailed for contempt for almost two years, made to appear in public manacled and with her feet chained, like a convicted and dangerous felon. I won't even mention Hillary Rodham Clinton, who might have escaped public humiliation were it not for prosecutorial zeal.

The *New Yorker*'s "Talk of the Town" section of September 28, 1998, contains two articles juxtaposing two strikingly opposite points of view. The lead article by Rebecca Mead asks "Who really exploited Monica Lewinsky?" The answer, she says, must be Starr. Monica was not "the victim of sexual opportunism at the hands of her boss," so much as the victim of "sexual abuse" and "metaphorical mugging" by Starr. Mead's paraphrase of the Starr/Lewinsky relationship makes the rape analogy clear: Starr "drives Lewinsky to bare herself to him, pressuring her with months of intimidatory leaks, threats, and proxy roughings up. . . . He ransacks her computer . . . for evidence of her private thoughts. . . . He rifles through her closet. . . . And he compels her . . . to speak with a specificity somewhere between the pornographic and the gynecological."

On the other hand an article by Hendrik Hertzberg, "Wind from Washington: Old White House Type: Railsplitter. New White House Type: Hairsplitter," goes on attack against Clinton, "our hapless, intern-diddling, lame-excuse-mongering, oops-I-made-a-boo-boo, come-to-Jesus President." Striking here is the open contrast between female and male takes on events. Mead feels less outrage at Clinton's behavior, seeing it as not so much misogynistic as merely adolescent, and more at Starr's controlling of women through brute force and threats of harm to reputation, attacks on their privacy for his own self-aggrandizement, and (the metaphors suggest) sexual gratification. We can forgive oafishness from someone we feel is on our side . . . but we recognize, and detest, Starr's power tactics, for we know how they have been used against us for millennia. Hertzberg, on the other hand, sees things from a male perspective. To him, as to many men, Clinton is despicable because he has gotten away with what many have fantasized, but few get to do.

GENRE BENDING

These ambivalences make a precise definition of the story as essential as it is impossible. Because the story is so confusing, we are desperate to endow it with a sense of familiarity: to see it as not unlike other stories, familiar, predictable in its course. To that end we try to control it by placing it within a narrative genre, fictional or not, whose parameters are known, whose ending is foreordained, whose style is familiar. For in many ways this tale is disturbing and scary, and like children who enjoy ghost stories, but only if they know they will come out well in the end, we have to find the right narrative genre to characterize Gategate, lest it assume an unpredictable and dangerous life of its own.

There had been scandals before, and there had been big stories out of Washington, but never had so many media commentators tried so hard to play what's-the-genre. (In part, this is due to the fact that never before had media commentators been so involved in self-analysis. Genre analysis is a kind of self-analysis, signifying as it does: what do I/we make of this?) Yet there was little agreement. The ambiguities resisted disambiguation, not surprisingly since the story changed with every teller. For some analysts, the narrative proper was the Monica-and-Bill story-within-a-story; for others it was the enveloping saga of Clinton-vs.-Starr. For some the analogy was to the classics of the eighteenth or nineteenth century; for others, contemporary ephemera, print or electronic.

Stephen Greenblatt (1998) notes that the Starr report offers the reader many of the pleasures of classic fiction: the narrator's apologies for a lubricious tale; time-honored plot devices (the lovers find each other first through mutual eye contact, as in Ovid or Petrarch); the moves of the skilled novelist—Balzac, James, or Eliot—as evidenced in the "plausible characters; the patient unfolding of linked events; the building of suspense; the intertwining of desire, fear and reproach in the doomed lovers; the intervention of a host of lesser characters; the intensification of pressure as the implacable pursuit grows hot and the lovers' mutual pledge of secrecy begins to crack—and finally their public exposure and shaming."

Tempting as this comparison is, Greenblatt resists it. For him the Starr report mixes genres, from comedy to pornography to tragedy. Finally he separates out what, for him, makes the Starr report unique: the nausea provoked by the details, found elsewhere only in a genre based on "cold, clinical accounts of humans stripped of all the protective covering with which we contrive to cloak our nakedness," namely the documentations of the witchcraft trials in Medieval and Renaissance Europe and sixteenth- and seventeenth-century Massachusetts. In these documents, prosecutors, certain that the end justified the means, since the accused were guilty of horrific evil, "violated every principle of equity, respect, ordinary common sense and decency." [6]

Going to the opposite (I suppose) extreme, Time, in an unsigned article entitled "Calling Grace Metalious" (1998), suggests that the right analogue is Peyton Place, the emblematic trashy novel of the 1960's. The article provides a checklist comparing aspects of Gategate against both Peyton Place and Watergate. Gategate and Peyton Place share all the items; Watergate shares only a few with them. Which is the better match?

	Watergate	Peyton Place
Were there smoldering glances?	No	Yes
. . . Passionate embraces?	No	Yes
. . . Illicit sex?	No	Yes
. . . Ingenues taken advantage of by cads?	No	Yes
. . . Silly gifts?	No	Yes
. . . Shared secrets?	Yes	Yes
. . . Lies?	Yes	Yes
. . . Betrayals?	Yes	Yes
. . . Treachery by false friends?	Yes	Yes
. . . Could key parts in the drama be played by Mia Farrow and Ryan O'Neal?	No	Yes

While all three share interesting similarities, Gategate is closer by the numbers to cheap 1960's fiction than to political (i.e., real-life) high crimes and misdemeanors.

Other commentators endow the case with the complexities of a canonical novel. In the *New Yorker,* Adam Gopnick (1998) sees the Starr report as "a classic story about adultery," one that is "vaguely eighteenth century" (à la *Pamela*) "in the constant references to a higher piety that nobody believes in." He identifies the genre as "pornography for Puritans." In the same vein, James Wood in the *New Republic* (1998) sees the report as a "literary confection," a narrative that "clings to the shape of the nineteenth-century novel of adultery, as we know it in *Effie Briest, Madame Bovary, Anna Karenina,* and *Thérèse Raquin.*" In these novels, as in the Starr report, "secrecy becomes narration. . . . [T]he adulterous woman is more serious than the man [and so] . . . she must disappear. . . . Such books abound in heavily symbolic detail, both of the titillating and moral kind." Both Emma and Monica, for instance, make use of their lovers' cigars. Just as the novelist introduces seemingly irrelevant detail to make a moral (or aesthetic) point, so does Starr: "the couple defiled Easter"; the first breach occurred during the government shutdown, the public chaos of which somehow led to, or turned into, the president's private chaos. As in *Lady Chatterley's Lover,* the man is crippled—in Clinton's case, on crutches (another gratuitous detail in the report) during the first sexual encounter. Wood concludes that Starr's novelistic skills may have worked against him: "Instead of prosecuting a case, his narrative enacts a drama, and makes sympathetically banal what might have been merely illegal."

Finally, Cynthia Ozick (1998) in the *New Yorker* argues that, despite all the foregoing, the Starr report is not novelistic after all. Literature is complex; this is not. The report "may reflect the passionate symbolism of myth or cautionary wisdom of fable. But a novel? No. All the characters are flat [that is, according to E. M. Forster, they] 'are constructed around a single idea or quality.'" But Ozick is overstating her case. While the Starr report can't be confused with *great* fiction, or even *serious* fiction, in the flatness of its characters, its sexual obsession, and its swollen length it resembles nothing more than the modern airplane read.

Why have all these culture mavens produced such impressive exegetical efforts? To make an analogy with fiction is to deny that this story—the tawdry initiating episodes, the tawdrier investigation, our own most tawdry of all response—is real. That is a great comfort, a good way to wriggle free of responsibility for any part of it.

Another reason why analysts are eager to attach the narrative to a traditional literary genre is that literary genres, different as they are, share several traits: characters whose motives are determinate, or at least only ambiguous, as opposed to vague and indeterminable; a clear plot line with a happy ending or at least a logical one; actions that are consistent with the characters who perform them, and which work to further the coherence of the plot; in short, characters, motives, and actions that each make sense in their own right and work logically together. But nothing about this story follows that outline. It just doesn't make sense. Here's Bill Clinton: Rhodes Scholar, Yale Law graduate, highly successful governor, obviously a man of intellect, foresight, and perseverance. Yet he engages in repeated assignations with women whose attractions are mysterious to most of us, even though he knows the "bimbo eruptions" are under scrutiny and could end his career. Here are the Republicans, cagey politicians, engineers of the 1994 Republican takeover of Congress: savvy, ambitious, farsighted. Yet they pursue the spectre of impeachment, though it will almost certainly fail in the end and may well lose them both Congress and the White House in the election of 2000. Here's Kenneth Starr: man of probity, sober as a judge. Yet under his aegis is produced a report swollen with the epiphenomena of kinky sex, making him the butt of every late-night TV monologue. What kind of plot is that? What kinds of characters are these?

One thing we needed to know—How does this lurid tale end? Is this story *Madame Bovary* or *Pamela?* Will the characters live happily ever after or come to a bad end? Is Monica a chaste young woman striving to protect her virtue from a vile seducer or a floozy destined to destroy herself and all around her? Is the president that vile seducer or a hapless slave to passion? Is Ken Starr a brave man risking all to save society from evils of Satanic provenance or an Inspector Javert, crabbed and obsessive, pursuing a quarry of no interest to anyone but himself (and a few other perverts)? The longer the story spun on, the further off any answers seemed.

WORDS, WORDS, WORDS

The language, or style, of a narrative provides clues to its audience or readers about its meaning. Is the language heavy and plodding or ironic and playful? How much work must the reader/viewer do to understand it? Is making meaning to be the task of the author alone or a collaboration between author and reader?

Those fighting over narrative rights in this case have made use of language to mark their territories: *historic, duty, context,* and so on. Within the tale itself as well, language plays a highly significant role, and the difficulty in parsing it constitutes a major twist of the convoluted plot. Gategate touches on some of our touchiest words, words we don't like to use outright, words to which we necessarily assign vague meanings, words we find ways around: *sex, lie, apologize.* The absolutists insist that these, like all words, have single, decontextualized meanings: everyone knows what each of these words means, everyone knows what constitutes an instance of each of their referents. Language is fixed. Meaning is certain. Santa Claus comes down the chimney at midnight on December 24.

The linguistic complication is that while many of us profess to believe the foregoing, no sane person really does, nor could humans operate in a world in which it was true. Gategate is the story of Everyman dealing with Everytalk—Bill Clinton is Us, trying to adapt the hard edges of language to an indeterminate universe; and at the same time, the Republicans are Us, trying desperately to fix meanings that can't be fixed. Humpty Dumpty is our prototype, insisting that a determined speaker can control the meanings of words.

"The question is," said Alice, "whether you *can* make words mean so many different things."

"The question is," said Humpty Dumpty, "which is to be master—that's all." (*Through the Looking-Glass*, chapter 6)

But understand H.D.'s predicament: he's a big egg on a high narrow wall, waiting for a fall he cannot prevent. No wonder he needs control.

The words around which Gategate revolves are just those that resist definition most tenaciously, for social rather than cognitive reasons. Most of us try hard to be inexact about "sex": who's doing it, what it is, how much we're getting. Hardly any other word in English (I venture to say in any language) has so many euphemisms and slang terms attached to it as do those about sexual activities. By euphemizing we mislead ourselves as well as others. And we tend to be even more euphemistic, and generally fuzzy, about our own sexual behavior than other people's.

Hence it's not too surprising that both Clinton and Lewinsky are in their various ways on record as off record about it. Both insist that it isn't "sex" unless it includes genital penetration—until you've "gone all the way," past all three bases, in the parlance of the Dark Ages. And yet it isn't really "not sex" to do all of the other kinds of things that anyone with imagination can do short of the transcendental It. But at what point is the line crossed? For all their harrumphing, the Republicans didn't make that clear either.

If the nation's Solons couldn't even agree on what a relatively simple word like "impeachment" means, how could they possibly find it risible that the president couldn't be precise about the meaning of one of the hardest words there is? Some say that "sex," like sex, is simple, and "impeachment," like impeachment, is hard. But it's just the reverse.

Then there's "lie." That word, too, is laden with complexities both cognitive and social in origin.[7] In fact there is an odd connection between sex and lies: during the heyday of the Hayes Commission, established by the motion picture industry after the Fatty Arbuckle scandal to make the movies family entertainment again, most words having to do with sex (not only the obvious ones, but even including "virgin"), were barred from use onscreen. Alongside of those, "lie" was also proscribed, unless said with a smile. To some arbiters, then, talk of sex is on a par with accusations of lying.

As with "sex," most intelligent analysts don't see "lying" as all-or-nothing. There are absolute lies, utterances anyone would condemn, just as there are behaviors anyone would identify as sex. But after that it's a jungle.

Some people insist that they "never lie." But offer them the following hypothetical: they're on the phone, they want to get off, but have no really good reason to. What do they say? "I've *got* to go," not, "I *want* to go." I bet that's as true of Henry Hyde and Trent Lott as it is of me. Yet, by a strict definition, it is a lie: a knowingly told untruth, uttered to gain advantage.

Then did Bill Clinton "lie" when he said he and Monica had not had a "sexual relationship"? Well, first, there is the confusion about "sex." Then, there is the uncertainty about "lying." Is it a "lie" to knowingly lead another to infer what you know to be untrue—as opposed to telling the untruth with your own tongue? A song from 1961, "Sad Movies Make Me Cry," frames the problem starkly. In it the singer sees her boyfriend and her best girlfriend making out together in the movies. She starts to cry, leaves the theater and goes home,

And Mama saw the tears and said, "What's wrong?"
And so to keep from telling her a lie,
I just said, "Sad movies make me cry." [8]

Even if her answer is literally true, it is misleading: that isn't why she's crying *now*, so the answer is not properly responsive to the question. In giving that answer, has she kept from lying to her mother? Different people will give different answers. If you feel she didn't lie to her Mama, then you should also feel Clinton didn't lie to us. [9]

We now have located linguistic ambiguities at two levels: the "locutionary act," that is, the naming of an action ("sex"); and the "illocutionary act," that is, what the speaker is seeking to accomplish in making an utterance ("lie"). Additionally there is a problem at the level of the perlocutionary act, the effect the utterance will have on others and future relationships between them and the speaker, as located in the third problem word ("apologize"), to which we turn next. [10]

In Chapter 1 I talked about the problems, and pleasures, of apologies and offered reasons for the current spate of public apologies for bad behavior which apologizing public officials did not commit nor their audiences suffer. I also discussed why it is dangerous for those whose power to accomplish things grows directly out of their personal authority to apologize for their own behavior. An apology is designed to place its speaker at a moral and political level below that of its addressee, somewhere no personage of importance can afford to be. For such a person, an apology is almost self-contradictory: it takes away the power that gives the apology its potency.

A deeper problem for important speakers about apologies arises out of their perlocutionary effects. It is rare for a speaker to deliver an apology in its full canonical form: "I apologize for X." But other options, as we saw in Chapter 1, create ambiguity. How can hearers tell whether an apology is "sufficient" or "sincere"? Not by its ambiguous form alone, and not by the speaker's future actions, since there may be no specific actions that would mark the apology as sincere. Recipients of apologies sometimes complain about a lack of "enough remorse." But how much is "enough" and how much is "too much" in Gategate? Would tears have been enough? Would rending of garments, dressing in sackcloth and ashes be too much? Were there words, a formula, that should have been said, but weren't? It wasn't clear what was wanted or if anything would have been satisfactory. Almost certainly nothing would have been satisfactory to everyone. The President has apologized to us all again and again, but his words never create the closure that marks a felicitous speech act of apology, a show of forgiveness from the injured party. In fact, the repeated demands for Presidential apologies were themselves infelicitous because their speakers had no intention of doing their part no matter what the President said. So their demands were analogous to orders from one human being to another that the latter jump off the kitchen table and fly around the room: the speaker knows the conditions cannot be fulfilled.

THE DRAMATIS PERSONAE

Its characters above all make a story compelling: we identify with some, shudder with revulsion at others. Most intriguing are those to whom we can't marshal a simple response. Those are the bases of serious literature. If that is the test, Gategate is pretty serious. The protagonist himself has almost as many twists and turns as Milton's Lucifer; his antagonist is equally hard to pin down.

It is clear that the two great divides running through the national psychological landscape these days are those of gender and race. Once it was fairly easy to think of these as necessarily embodying antitheses, lines that were not crossed except to create perversions and confusions. (Hence there have been laws on the books prohibiting line-crossings of both types: miscegenation and cross-dressing, for instance.) But contemporary thinkers know better. It is evident that *race* cannot be thought of as an either/or proposition, if it can be thought of as a meaningful construct at all. As for *gender*, we are coming to realize that it, too, is constructed psychologically and socially to a significant degree, and as a result, that it is a gross oversimplification to think of human beings as one or the other, in every way, all the time. Rather, as with race, gender occupies a continuum, with *masculine* and *feminine* as the polar opposites, but most of us, in many ways, falling in between.

But that is controversial. Conventional culture lags behind, with conservative thinkers declaring that the old assumptions are right and good, and it is merely the evil of "postmodernism" that creates these alleged confusions. These critics fail to understand the difference between complex reality and simplistic stereotype, finding the latter aesthetically pleasurable perhaps because unambiguous, just as less sophisticated readers prefer airplane novels wherein good characters are clearly distinguished from evil and prevail in the end.

If we are agonizing over our understandings of race and gender, and if many of us are resisting a more complex view of them, then it is natural that we would prefer our ideal leaders to represent the ancient simplicities. We can tolerate a RuPaul or a Michael Jackson *in their place,* where they titillate by being mildly scary but not really dangerous. But the President of the United States? That's another story.

I spoke in Chapter 5 about the sexual ambivalence of this First Couple, singly and together. I also discussed there the special role of the first couple, as our gender ideals: as the first lady must be an ideal woman, the president must be the epitome of a manly man. That is not only because we need to have a strong masculine image in mind for our leader, but also because (especially now that they are threatened) we want reassurance of certainty and determinacy, and we want our leaders to perform that symbolic role. Whatever else he may do, Clinton fails in this part of his job.

Let me count the ways:

He is indeterminate in gender, an indeterminacy implicit in Gategate. The double standard still exists. If we felt our President were all man, all the time, we might be more willing to overlook his sexual flings. But if he is, well, just a little bit of a woman, then we might be inclined to regard his promiscuities more harshly.

He is racially indeterminate, too. Absurd! you may say. Clinton is as white as anyone. Except that, according to some commentators, he isn't. Two black commentators, Toni Morrison (1998) and Orlando Patterson, interviewed by Phil Ponce on the *NewsHour with Jim Lehrer* (September 30, 1998), make the point that Clinton, as a southerner, is "culturally black." Besides, the way the media elites have hypersexualized Clinton, invaded his privacy, and entrapped him by quasi-legal strategies (DWB), reminds blacks of their own treatment, à la O.J., and encourages their identification with him. As Morrison notes:

> White skin notwithstanding, this is our first black President. Blacker than any actual black person who could ever be elected in our children's lifetime. After all, Clinton displays almost every trope of blackness: single-parent household, born poor, working-class, saxophone-playing, McDonald's-and-junk-food loving boy from Arkansas.

And Patterson says:

> He's the first president in the history of the nation to have African-Americans in a circle of friends. Secondly, the president is actually culturally very Afro-American. This ironically is true of a lot of southerners, but he's unusual in that, unlike other white southerners, he doesn't hide the fact.

What might make the situation even scarier to white, especially Southern, conservatives is that the President has "outed" himself, refused to "pass"; and by so doing, he threatens them with exposure: if he's black, or even "black," they might be too. Their condemnations of Clinton's behavior recall the grumblings of whites about the indecorously raucous behavior of their black servants, which work to remind everyone that *we* are not *them*.

Other ambiguities in the President's character and deportment underline his race and gender indeterminacies.

He is the Great Communicator, but he is also Slick Willie. Like Ronald Reagan, he can talk birds out of trees, touch our hearts and our imaginations. At his best, he uses words like a poet and makes us believe the story he is spinning about himself and us. But then, inevitably, he does something sneaky, even tawdry, and in so doing he uses language in a way we hate to admit we do too, to not-really-lie. Then, when we realize that, it casts his Great Communication in a new lurid light. Was that also mere prestidigitation? Were we snookered rather than legitimately persuaded? Rather than blaming ourselves for our naiveté, we turn on him. If he were *only* Slick Willie, it wouldn't be so bad; we'd discount it, see it as a kind of degenerate charm. But it's the other half of the equation that makes us uncomfortable, and the fact that both of those communicative selves are out there, all the time. You never know what you're getting.

He is both Insider and Outsider. The president has to be the nation's #1 Insider; but someone from Little Rock cannot by definition be an Insider. The outrage of the in-group is "out"-rage: rage against those who are or ought to be *out* yet are adopting the prerogatives (including both high honors and bad behaviors) traditionally reserved for *us*, the "ins." The Clintons are "outies." They are not from inside the Beltway. That in itself is not deadly, but if you are a Washington outsider, it's much better to be from an "in" place, like Hollywood (which made the Reagans OK though technically outies). But . . . Arkansas? Get outta town! (Literally.)

Arkansas is simply not a place serious people can come from. Arkansas is designed, in the view of the Beltway innies, as an opportunity for sneers and jokes. For instance. . . .

> Why is the F.B.I. having trouble reliably identifying the semen stain as Clinton's?
> Because everyone in Arkansas has the same DNA.

And you simply cannot have a president who is trailer trash. In this way, too, Clinton creates ambiguity or aporia. The president is supposed to be the greatest and the grandest. He is supposed to be our ideal, better than we are. Innies identify their distress as being purely over sexual shenanigans, because hand-wringing in this area is appropriate, as American as apple pie if not quite as tasty. But the grumbling conceals a deeper dissatisfaction, one which members of the classless society are not allowed to voice aloud: he is not (as the president should be) better-than-us because, at least behaviorally, he is infra-middle class. The Rail-splitter and log cabin dweller may have been OK a century and a half ago, but we don't like roughhewn any more. (Even in Lincoln's day, proper Washington society and the media elites didn't approve.) Clinton is president. But he is a hillbilly. How can this be?

Ambiguities pile on each other. An article by Sally Quinn (1998; the insider's insider, wife of former *Washington Post* editor Ben Bradlee) published the day before the 1998 election captures the attitude very well.[11] From the beginning, says Quinn disapprovingly, Clinton aligned himself publicly with those outside the Beltway: rather than trying to insinuate and ingratiate himself, he drew lines in the sand. Quinn reminds us of what Clinton said in his first inaugural address, that in Washington, "Powerful people maneuver for position and worry endlessly about who is in and who is out, . . . forgetting those people whose toil and sweat sends us here and pays our way." (Characteristically, the new president wanted it both ways: *they* maneuver for power, but at the same time *we* are here. He tries to be both *them* and *us* at once, thereby managing to alienate or at least confuse both sides.) Quinn sees this as Clinton's declaration of war on the Washington elite. The outsider now gets his comeuppance. Washington is hardly a place of stern monogamy. The insiders are mostly sophisticates: they have affairs with one another, they hobnob civilly with their exes and their exes' exes. So why the howls of outrage when the President tries it? "Their town has been turned upside down," wails Quinn. Washington is "their home," and the Clintons are interlopers from the wrong side of the tracks. "He came in here and he trashed the place," Quinn quotes media doyen David Broder, "and it's not his place." The President of the United States as trailer trash.

Other commentators in the article throw around words like "affront," "unacceptable," "sordid." One has a sense of having fallen through a time warp into a Henry James, or Jane Austen, novel, except that one has retrieved Quinn's article via Lexis-Nexis. Its level of fury—Quinn's article is 3,660 words long, packed with quotations in the same spirit—is hard to account for unless nervousness about presidential ambivalence piled on ambivalence plays a role. And if Clinton is not only from outside the Beltway, but sorta-black and sorta-female too . . . well, that *is* unacceptable.

He symbolizes our current uncertainties about the distinction, if any, between public and private. He talks on national television about his underwear. He reveals details about his personal misbehavior on *Sixty Minutes.* On the one hand we eat it up, we revel in it: it's exciting to be taken into the confidence of the Great and the In. The problem is that the president is a public person, our #1 public person, and in public you're supposed to maintain a certain decorum. The conflict surfaces in current discussion about the disgracefulness of the First Shenanigans in the White House, *our* house. What you do in the privacy of your home is, many have said, your own business. But the White House is not Clinton's private home: he's Doing It, in effect, out in the street and scaring the horses.

He is both Daddy and CEO. The problem of presidential non-privacy goes beyond the difficulties of the current incumbent. It arises from a confusion about the nature of the presidency itself, one our founders, usually so wise and so attuned to symbolism, overlooked. This confusion drives otherwise reasonable people to despair assessing the Commander in Chief's shenanigans. On the one hand they're repulsed; on the other, bemused at their repulsion. They know that America has become the laughingstock of sophisticated Europeans, who can't see why we make a big deal of a little peccadillo. But Europeans don't understand our confusion because their systems of government are different from ours. In ours the president has two major roles: on the one hand, the nation's CEO whose job is to keep us strong against the competition and protect the bottom line. As long as he does that, he's OK. But we also expect our president to represent our ideal male, husband and father. Father-president must fulfill our *private* fantasies even as CEO-president expresses *public* power. He must be strong, charming, articulate, potent —but virtuously monogamous.[12]

Even in terms of the second role alone, we don't really know what we want. While we *want* (we say) an Ideal Man, we *like* a rogue. It has been said of the modern postfeminist woman that she claims to be looking for sensitive, caring men, but the ones who turn her on are the louts. Is America a smart woman who makes foolish choices?

He is smart but he is dumb (as noted above).

So is the president a *scapegoat* or a *scapegrace?* After seeing Republican congresspersons one after another coming on television with heads bowed to acknowledge their "indiscretions," it is logical to wonder: are those who are most ferocious in their railing using the President as a scapegoat, hoping to load on him the blame for all their moral failings? Do all of us—not only the Christian Right—have to realize that you can't have everything? Can we claim to have high ideals, believe in marriage, fidelity, all the trappings—yet have urges for something else? Are we putting the blame on Clinton for all our moral ambiguities—so that, like the Biblical scapegoat, we can drive him out and our sins with him (and we can go forth and, newly cleansed, sin some more)?

Or is he merely—to resuscitate an old-fashioned word—a *scapegrace,* a rascal, a nogoodnik? He doesn't, on this reading, represent what we hate in ourselves, but just what we quite properly despise. In this view, our outrage is valid and punishment appropriate. But if his misbehavior has nothing to do with us personally, why are some of us so angry?

CLINTON AND STARR: SEPARATED AT BIRTH—
TOGETHER AGAIN?

Making the struggle even more confusing is the relationship between the main antagonists: the White House champion, Bill Clinton, and Congress's, Kenneth Starr. They have layers, an apparent surface and below it, murky depths. Clinton and Starr are superficially about as opposite as two people can get, in their lives, their looks, their styles. They are, respectively, Charisma and Anticharisma, and like matter and antimatter, when these forces meet, the result has to be explosive, a millennial Armageddon. There is a tragic irony here that perhaps explains Starr's bitterness and intransigence. You know how the battle has to end: the race is always to the charismatic, and the noncharismatic know this and resent it.

Ken Starr is the kid your mother made you invite to your sixth birthday party, maybe because his mom was your mom's friend or your dad worked for his dad. He shows up with a really dorky present (as you knew he would), like socks. He won't eat the ice cream and cake, telling everyone loudly that his mommy says they'll make your teeth fall out, and later you catch him cheating at Pin the Tail on the Donkey.

Bill Clinton is the kid you invite, and you hope he'll come but you're afraid he won't. He shows up late, explaining that he "had to" go to five other parties first. (But yours is the one he *really* wanted to come to!) He brings you a really great present and compliments your mom on the food (and eats several portions). But the next day in school, he doesn't remember your name.

Though diametric opposites, they are eerily similar beneath the surface. For instance (perhaps because they're both lawyers), there's the way they play with language. Just as Clinton waffles on "sex," Starr, in his testimony to the House Judiciary Committee, is inexact on his staff's treatment of Monica Lewinsky. Yes, he acknowledges (although he can't be certain: he has no idea what his staff is doing), his people did apprehend her at a shopping mall and held her for questioning for eleven hours. But during that time she was not held incommunicado, she was under no compulsion to answer their questions, and "she was free to go," although they would not let her consult her lawyer, ridiculed her for wanting to talk to her mother, and told her that if she didn't cooperate they could put her in prison for twenty-seven years (with the specter of the incarceration of Susan McDougall to underscore the seriousness of the threat). Starr is playing as fast and loose with "voluntary" as Clinton was with "sex." Yes, she *could* leave, the door was not locked and she was not shackled; but did she see herself as free to leave, or free not to speak? Maybe. Maybe not.

Both antagonists are spun by the spinners in parallel ways. Each, before his testimony is made, or made public, is alleged to be bizarre and unsympathetic. Clinton is "angry," "petulant," "uncooperative." Starr is "sex-crazed," "fanatic," "obsessed." Yet in the flesh, or at least on television, both come across as reasonably cooperative and calm. But would each have seemed so self-possessed and competent had we not been led to expect much worse?

The diametric opposites have other things in common. Both are very, very interested in sex. Their interests take very, very different forms, but underneath—well, sex is sex (when it isn't "sex").

Their covert identity suggests a final fictional analogy. I think the novel that Gategate most closely resembles is Vladimir Nabokov's *Lolita*. Some commentators have drawn a facile comparison between Mo and Lo, but it is unpersuasive. While Lewinsky is nearly as junior to the president as Lolita was to Humbert Humbert, she's no nymphet, in either age or physical attributes. Nymphets are slight and childlike; Lewinsky is ripe and juicy. The real analogy links Clinton and Starr to the protagonist and antagonist of the novel, Humbert and Clare Quilty.

Humbert and Quilty, like Clinton and Starr, share the same obsession, differently realized. Quilty uncannily picks up a number of Humbert's linguistic tics (the puns, allusions, figures of speech), as Clinton and Starr share evasiveness. And at the end of the novel, as Humbert confronts Quilty in a death struggle, they seem, almost, to become each other, to blend together:

> All of a sudden I noticed that he had noticed that I did not seem to have noticed Chum [Humbert's gun] protruding from beneath the other corner of the chest. We fell to wrestling again. We rolled all over the floor, in each other's arms, like two huge helpless children. He was naked and goatish under his robe, and I felt suffocated as he rolled over me. I rolled over him. We rolled over us. (272)

The narratives share another similarity, an unreliable narrator. In *Lolita,* the unreliability is a carefully crafted game the author plays with the reader. In Gategate, it occurs because there is no single narrator. There are multiple wannabe narrators competing for meaning-making rights. It is not clear that there will ever be a single story everyone agrees on.

The story continues to trickle on, almost out of sight but never quite. Like all UAT stories, it never fades away completely but moves away from the center to the periphery, while we wait for the next candidate to appear. The news programs go back to normal: reports from Kosovo and stories about the life and death of John F. Kennedy, Jr. The President gives a triumphal State of the Union address, while Republicans in the audience sit on their hands and grimace during the rounds of applause and standing-O's. House members of both parties go off on a weekend retreat to Hershey, Pennsylvania (home of chocolate kisses), to see if they can recapture civility (they couldn't). Monica, in tasteful décolletage, is the toast of the Oscar-night party in L.A. Hillary and Bill are together again—but at the same time Hillary and Chelsea are in Egypt (home of the Sphinx).

ENDINGS

So the ending, like the rest of the story, must be inconclusive, in part because as I write this no one knows how it will end. The impeachment attempt ended anticlimactically. But its effects go on—into the summer of 1999 as I write this sentence and almost certainly beyond. An article in today's *New York Times* (Van Natta 1999b) talks about the lingering role of the hearings on political fund-raising: "Fund-raisers for both the Republican Party and the Democratic Party have discovered that invoking the impeachment of President Clinton still dredges up raw emotions and motivates Americans to write checks to candidates seeking election in 2000." Even if Gategate ultimately reaches some conclusion, it won't end the story I have been trying to disentangle. We may never know just what kind of story we have been making together.

Maybe, as the media pundits darkly suggest, the end result will be tragedy: the protagonists, one, both or all, destroyed by their tragic flaws, and the rest of us remaining angry and vindictive. We will be unable to drag ourselves out of the "Argument Culture," unable to end the Culture War, and will remain mired in timoriocracy. One pundit (Alter 1998/99), foreseeing the possibility, finds his epigraph in Matthew Arnold's "Dover Beach":

And we are here as on a darkling plain
Swept with confused alarms of struggle and flight
Where ignorant armies clash by night.

Or maybe it will turn out to have been a comedy. Not particularly funny-ha-ha, but with a resolution in reconciliation and integration. We learn to appreciate our different voices, we all work together to make a new common language and a new understanding. We all win the language war, but we may have to go through a bad patch or two before this cheerful conclusion. Upon the millenarian prophecy of William Butler Yeats's "The Second Coming"

> Things fall apart; the center cannot hold;
> Mere anarchy is loosed upon the world,

we must superimpose the words of Jerry Seinfeld:

> Not that there's anything wrong with that.

Notes

INTRODUCTION

1. It has been suggested that non-Western cultures allocate the responsibility for meaning in the hearer rather than the speaker, or in a collaboration between the two. For consideration of this point see my discussion (Lakoff 1984) of "speaker-based" and "hearer-based" cultures, and Edward T. Hall (1977), whose concept of "low context" and "high context" cultures contains some of the same ideas.

2. See Chapter 8, in which breakdown of that agreement becomes highly problematic.

3. While this definition of "speech community" is rather simplistic, it will do for our purposes here. For discussion of the ways the term has been defined and used in sociolinguistics, see Hudson 1980, 25–30.

CHAPTER 1

1. As general semanticist Alfred Korzybski wrote years ago, "The map is not the territory." But we often forget this point.

2. To show briefly what I mean:

The name itself, "Christopher Columbus," is not in a one-on-one match with the person to whom we apply it, or at least it was not during his lifetime as it would be today. Today, the normal custom, at least among Western nations, is that we don't translate our names as we cross national borders. But during the Renaissance, someone named "Christoforo Columbo" when he was born in Genoa was referred to as "Cristóbal Colón" by Ferdinand and Isabella (more accurately, Hernán and Isabel) and was only called by the form familiar to us in English-speaking countries. So the immutability we attribute to our names, their direct link to our identities, was probably felt more weakly back then.

In using the verb "discover" as we use it in this example, the speaker is making a presupposition that what has been "discovered" was previously not known to anyone. The problem here concerns the identification of "anyone": who counts as human? Obviously there were plenty of indigenous people who were aware of the existence of the place Columbus came to, but the use of "discover" suggests that they are not part of "us."

As for "America," the name was imposed by the European explorers, rather than used by the indigenous dwellers. Normally we follow the convention that whoever gets to a place first has the right to name it. Again, the implication is that the inhabitants are not part of the "we" that has rights or competes for them—not fully human, that is. (Although a reasonable counterargument is that until some time after Columbus's landing there *was* no single name for the continent, and one was certainly needed.)

Moving to "1492," the date is obviously something imposed by the predominantly Christian culture of Europe in keeping with a particular event that they, and they alone, regarded as overwhelmingly salient (the birth of Christ). This form of naming time is of course not in use in the majority of cultures, so here again language allows us to express a dubious claim of universality.

And finally, the preposition "in" is one basically associated with spatial location. To extend the use of "in" (and "on" and "at" as well) to points in time is to make an implicit equation between space and time (as the language did millennia before Einstein). While this equation is found in many, and indeed the majority, of languages and cultures, it is not inevitable.

3. Conservative historians like Lynne Cheney (1995) wax virulent about this idea, their rancor suggesting that control over "truth" is an important aspect of the conservative agenda.

4. Is postmodernism in fact moving us into a culture of postliteracy? Literacy theorists (e.g., Goody and Watt 1972) argue that in the fifth century B.C.E. Athens moved within a generation from nonliterate to literate, from treating literacy as a special skill as we do computer programming, to considering it essential for all relevant people. This change necessarily engendered other redefinitions. One was a recognition of the distinction between "fact" and "fiction," "history" (as written by Thucydides or Herodotus) and "poetry," like the *Iliad*. With literacy, facts could be recorded in a specific form, which would remain constant over time, not subject to the frailty of human memory.

But over the last part of this century, the divide that has been in place for two and a half millennia is showing signs of erosion. As I will suggest later in this chapter, the literary works now considered most worthy of critical attention are those in which that line between fact and fiction is blurred, crossed, or ignored. Does that mean that the basis for the distinction, literacy itself, is becoming less relevant, maybe even an archaism?

The argument is intriguing. On the other hand, here I am writing this book.

5. Unlike linguists, particularly syntacticians, whose basic unit is the "sentence," a grammatically cohesive string of words unconnected to linguistic or social context, philosophers of language as well as linguistic pragmaticists use the "utterance" as their basis of analysis. While the term is used much more imprecisely than the syntacticians' "sentence," it can be generally defined as a gram-

matical string of words along with their speakers' intentions, hearers' understandings, and the social and linguistic contexts in which they occur.

6. The situation may be even worse for Austin's opponents. The performative and promissory sense of the first utterance is essentially synonymous with the performative sense of the second. By calling them "synonymous," I mean that the two forms share all important aspects of meaning. But the distinction between performativity and constativity is an important aspect of the meaning of an utterance. So we are left with a paradox: the forms are at the same time synonymous and not.

7. The current sense of "apology" represents a significant change over time. In Greek (from which it was borrowed into English, via Latin and French), the word means something in between "explanation" and "excuse." In making his *Apology*, Socrates was not acknowledging wrongdoing nor asking the Athenians for forgiveness. Rather, he was offering an explanation for the actions for which he was on trial.

8. In *Talking from Nine to Five* Deborah Tannen discusses the tendency of women to make apologies as a sign of empathy, rather than an acknowledgment of wrongdoing. But, she suggests, especially in conversations with men it tends to weaken the apologizer, since men often take apologies literally (1994, 44–51).

9. "President 'Apologizes' to Mrs. King," *San Francisco Chronicle*, October 23, 1983. (Note the quotation marks around "apologize.")

10. While some argue that the recent prevalence of such utterances is a sign of the feminization of public discourse (since women apologize more than men; see Tannen 1994), I think this argument is based on a confusion of women's "inappropriate" apologizing (from a male perspective) and these public "inappropriate" apologies (from a conservative perspective). While it is true that women say "I'm sorry" under circumstances in which men would not, it is probably incorrect to characterize these utterances as true apologies: they are intended to express sympathy and understanding in order to smooth over a difficult situation, not to express guilt and a desire for forgiveness. Not all "sorrys" are apologies. For example, when someone mentions a death in the family, a normal response is, "I'm so sorry." This is never taken as a true apology, i.e., a confession of murder.

The public un-apology is also, strictly speaking, infelicitous *qua* apology, and this shared inappropriateness may be the basis of the confusion of the two types. But what makes the latter type infelicitous is that neither speaker nor receiver is in an appropriate position for apologizing. At the end, as I suggest, the function of the public un-apology is to make the receiver equal to or higher than the giver in status; this is not true of the feminine quasi apology.

11. It should be noted that the clerics "beg for the pardon of God, and we ask the Jewish people to hear this word of repentance." This wording is rather reminiscent of Giuliani's, in that the wronged persons themselves are not directly apologized to, nor is it *their* forgiveness that is sought.

12. This cartoon was included in the Week in Review, *New York Times*, June 29, 1997.

13. I use the masculine pronoun here to reflect the observation that users of this form are almost without exception male.

14. The same problem, exacerbated by its contextualization in the Holocaust, has arisen over the alleged memoir by Binjamin Wilkomirski, *Fragments* (Schocken, 1996).

15. It may (or may not) be coincidence that just as identity becomes a thorny problem in intellectual theory, there has arisen a new category of crime, "identity theft," which has gotten a remarkable amount of horrified play in the media.

16. This argument was suggested by Andrew Lakoff (personal communication).

17. As discussed in an article in the *New York Times*, December 13, 1997, "Laying Claim to Sorrow beyond Words," by Samuel G. Freedman.

18. "Semantic bleaching," the weakening in the meanings of words, is hardly confined to these especially horrific cases, but is a normal process of historical semantics. For example, Modern English "starve" is derived from the same root as German "sterben," "die;" "nice" originally meant "ignorant."

19. "Glamour" is derived from "grammar": the ability to parse, to analyze language was seen, long ago when literacy and learning were scarce, as the ability to alter reality in mystical ways. "Glamour" first meant "enchantment," and only later developed its current meaning, one source of enchantment.

CHAPTER 2

1. Opponents of this position sometimes ridicule it by creating a straw man, in the manner of Camille Paglia (see Farber and Sherry 1997, 6–7: "Camille Paglia notes wittily that 'if there were no facts, surgeons couldn't operate, buildings would collapse, and airplanes couldn't get off the ground.'"). Witty this sally may be, but it is guilty of a semantic misconstruction. There are different kinds of "facts." There are the incontrovertible facts of nature: the earth goes around the sun, water boils at sea level at 212° F. No rational participant in this discussion has ever seriously suggested (to my knowledge) that these facts are created by consensus and thus politically sensitive.

I say "seriously" to exclude a partial counterexample. In 1996, physicist Alan Sokal published an article in the deconstructionist journal *Social Text* entitled "Transgressing the Boundaries: Toward a Transformative Hermeneutics of Quantum Gravity." (A perceptive editor's suspicions might have been aroused by the fact that the title contained altogether too many good words: *transgressing, boundaries, transformative,* and *hermeneutics.*) The article argued that the theory of gravity was socially constructed—just what I am saying never happens.

It shortly transpired that, in fact, the article was a hoax designed to exemplify the idiocy of postmodern theory. No sooner did the story emerge than all hell broke loose. The story escaped from the confines of academia first into the intellectual-popular and pop-intellectual press (*Dissent, Tikkun,* and *Lingua Franca*) and, by the summer of 1998, into the daily papers (including the *New York Times*), a trajectory perfectly illustrating the UAT. In any event, this case is only a partial counterexample to my claim: while it did get published in a respectable journal, it was intended as a spoof.

But there are other kinds of beliefs we often refer to as "facts," or by synonymous terms—*truths* that we hold to be self-evident: all men are created equal; the majority rules; an accused person is innocent until proven guilty. These are "facts," "truths," or "realities" only as long as the majority of us believe in them and act accordingly. Hence they are manipulable by language, and we must view all such purported facts with some suspicion, attractive as they may be.

2. An important and troubling example, in the field of law, is the reliability of eyewitness testimony. One persistent belief is that our memories get better under stress: witnesses to a crime are assumed to retain clear memories of it because the event was so traumatizing. But as Elizabeth Loftus (1979) and others have demonstrated, the more emotionally involved participants are, the poorer their memories will be for the details of an event.

3. A simple linguistic test to differentiate between cases like these is that in the normal-expectation type, we can link the two sentences with "and" but not with "but." In the second case, "but" would be more typical than "and."

4. For useful discussion of these concepts, see Tannen 1979, 1994.

5. To be precise, the last pair actually come from the same source, but have diverged so greatly in form over many centuries that most speakers don't recognize the fact.

6. In fact, in the early 1970's, as things were on the verge of changing, a very successful (that is, unguessable) riddle turned on just this point: A man and his child suffer an auto accident and are brought into separate emergency rooms. The surgeon who is operating looks at the child, and exclaims: "Oh my God! My son!" How can this be?

The answer seems obvious to us today (or should): the surgeon is the child's mother. But—incredibly, perhaps, but truly—people to whom this riddle was told back then *could not guess the "obvious" answer*. They would try all kinds of improbabilities: the child was the doctor's illegitimate son; the child was adopted, and the surgeon was his natural father; and so on. The hearer could understand the situation only by doing some violence to the "normal" meaning of the word *father:* the mere extension of an occupational category (*surgeon*) to include both genders was cognitively more difficult, even impossible.

7. English got into its current predicament by historical accident. Old English had two words, *wer* (retained in "werewolf") meaning "human being"; *man* meaning "male." But *wer* dropped out of the vocabulary, leaving *man* to carry both functions. So it is not exactly that *man* came by its present problematic dual meaning through the sexism of early English-speaking society. However, societal sexism made it seem normal for *man* to have both meanings, and the change was facilitated by the loss of *wer* for independent reasons.

8. The *American Heritage Dictionary* defines "catch a crab" as: "To strike the water with an oar in recovering a stroke or miss it in making one while rowing."

9. We are fond of reviling women in bad repute with the epithet "queen": quota queen, welfare queen, queen of mean. While there have been men who did equally opprobrious things, there is no comparable epithet for them. I suspect the "queen" epithet is effective because it captures our outrage at a woman who has usurped overweening power. A man who does that (compare Donald Trump with Leona Helmsley) isn't nearly so infuriating (since the behavior is "normal"), and therefore "king" would not pack the equivalent wallop. So both the fact

that only women are subject to this term of abuse and the popularity of the term itself are influenced by cultural frames.

10. There is an interesting reversal in Searle's argument. He equates the (actual and present) demand for a woman with a hypothetical demand for a *white* over a *black* candidate. If we follow without close scrutiny, we will be outraged, as he invites us to be: his hypothetical embodies the very essence of racism! But make the normal equation: woman: man = black: white, and much of the force of Searle's moral indignation is diminished. I attribute my colleague's reversal to a slip of the tongue in oral colloquy; but from such an example it's easy to see the technique of the propagandist.

11. I am also interested in Searle's statement that universities are "about" quality. Used by someone whose articulateness and precision of phrase are legendary, it suggests a degree of fuzziness about the concept, an inability to really determine what is meant. Can a university be "about" something, as a narrative can?

12. It is sometimes claimed by conservative critics (and, I think, implied here by Searle) that Shakespeare and Bugs Bunny are appreciated *in the same way* when both are used as texts, as equivalent high cultural icons. But while I am familiar with many courses in which one or the other is discussed, I know of no case in which a Bugs Bunny cartoon and *Hamlet* are treated as the same kind of aesthetic experience.

13. A new high, or low, may have been reached when Senator Dan Coats referred to President Clinton in a public speech as a "scumbag."

14. While occasional questions have been raised about the authenticity of this text, on the whole I don't find them persuasive.

15. For insightful discussion of the way our discourse has become polarized, why this is dangerous, and how to begin to remedy it, see Deborah Tannen's *The Argument Culture* (1998).

16. For some discussion of the history of the usage of "radical," see Lakoff 1997b.

17. Another instance of conservatives' conscious attempts to maintain control of language is the recent substitution of the adjective "Democrat" for "Democratic." I have not tracked the change formally, but would be surprised if it came into use before the 1970's. Currently, Republicans almost universally use the shorter form in public discourse, and I have even heard occasional Democrats doing so. Certainly the change started on the Republican side, and one may wonder why they did it: usually a shorter name is advantageous, and it hardly seems reasonable that the Republicans wished to confer a rhetorical advantage on the enemy. But there is a method to their madness: for Americans, "small-d 'democratic'" is an adjective with highly favorable connotations, while "small-d 'democrat'" hardly exists in the common vocabulary. So it pays to break any psychological connection in the voters' minds between the other side and "democratic" all-American ideals.

18. The Democrats' attempts to refashion themselves as "progressives" is reminiscent of the attempts of African Americans to find a term for themselves without negative connotations. Over the history of this country, words have

been introduced by whites—from "black" to "colored" to "darky" to "Negro" —to try to achieve respectability via language. Finally in the late 1960's blacks "took back" the original term "Black" (with a capital B). But this seems not to have been fully successful, since many members of the community have substituted "African American" for "Black." The two situations are parallel in that it is the peripheral group that has trouble controlling the connotations of its name. "Whites" remain unproblematically "whites."

19. Croce's piece provoked a great deal of media commentary; for examples, see Duffy 1995 and Rich 1995a.

20. Thus for instance in *The Daily Californian* columnist Max Boot (1990) (since moved on to greater things) characterizes "p.c." as "McCarthyism on campus." The worst (actually, only) case Boot can cite is the interruption of a lecture of Professor Vincent Sarich's anthropology class by demonstrators. I don't mean to suggest that stopping lectures is ever appropriate behavior. But Sarich went on to teach the rest of his course without incident, and team-taught the same course the next year.

The objection may be raised that, surely, *some* politically conservative assistant professors have been denied tenure for their views. This may very well be the case—the world is not fair. But there is an important difference between this situation, however regrettable, and what happened during the McCarthy period. At that time, many liberals were dismissed from their jobs on the basis of hearsay evidence or the refusal to betray confidences, and thereafter found it impossible to find appropriate employment for years, sometimes forever. On the other hand, there are plenty of universities, and even if someone fails to get tenure at one, he or she is quite likely to find a job at another. And even when claims are made that a denial of tenure was the result of political incompatibility (and by the way, liberal scholars sometimes get passed over by conservative departments, too), it is necessary to examine the case very carefully to make sure that the claim that the decision was politically motivated is not a smokescreen hiding old-fashioned incompetence.

21. An eloquent spokesman for this position is George Orwell, especially in his novel *Nineteen Eighty-Four* and his essay "Politics and the English Language."

22. A few selections, from the more accessible end: Dwight Bolinger, *Language: The Loaded Weapon* (Longman's, 1980); Robert A. Hall, *Leave Your Language Alone!* (Linguistica, 1950); Robin Tolmach Lakoff, *Talking Power* (Basic Books, 1990); Edward Sapir, *Language* (Harcourt, Brace, 1921).

23. The asterisk (*) is used by linguists to mark a form that is impossible, i.e., descriptively ungrammatical: something that would never be said, and therefore a form that prescriptive grammarians need never warn speakers not to say.

24. Answers to all the above: No, "their" would for aesthetic reasons be a better choice than "his or her" in informal speech (for discussion of the complicated history of personal pronouns in English, see Mühlhäusler and Harré 1990); if that is your choice, "floors" is probably the better option, since "everybody" is semantically plural if technically singular (the cavil about each of us having only one floor is irrelevant: we could certainly say, "We all got off at

our floors," although each of us still gets off at only one); the proscription of "get" went out in American English around the time I was in elementary school (long ago!).

25. Derrick Bell, Richard Delgado, Peter Gabel, David Kairys, Catharine MacKinnon, Mark Tushnet, and Patricia Williams are among those most closely associated with these movements.

26. A favorite whipping-boy (or girl) of conservatives is the purported claim of postmodern historians that there is no determinable historical "truth." This argument goes hand in hand with the canard referred to in note 1 to this chapter, that postmodernists doubt the determinacy of "everything," including the findings of the natural sciences. In a similar vein, most rational postmodernists would say that, while most attested historical events truly took place as described, the reasons for them and the interpretations of them are open to dispute.

CHAPTER 3

1. A closely related word, *ambitus,* usually meant *illegal* campaigning tactics: bribery, extortion, and overspending.

2. Thus during the 1994 election, Newt Gingrich provided Republican candidates with a list of words (compiled by Republican spin doctor Frank Luntz) that they should use, and others they should avoid. According to an article by Elizabeth Kolbert in the *New York Times* (June 5, 1995) Luntz advises Republicans not to use phrases like "cuts in projected growth" when discussing paring Medicare costs. "If it is phrased in those terms," he says, "Republicans lose the debate." Instead, he advises "reporters and Republican members of Congress" to say instead, "increase spending at a slower rate."

3. While these words have been around for a while in their literal sense, they have recently acquired the colloquial metaphorical meaning (usually applied to women) of "having (in)expensive tastes, needs, etc."

4. These terms are confined to descriptions by the right of the left's attempts at verbal control. But analogous attempts by the right seem exempt from naming and so from discussion. The use of "baby" rather than "fetus" to refer to the unborn has never been trivialized or demonized as "politically correct."

5. Hence the frequent characterization of the proponents of p.c. as McCarthyites of the left, Red Guard, Thought Police, and Fascists.

6. My dictionary, published in 1992, does not contain any definition of "p.c." or its equivalents.

7. Lexis/Nexis News indexes twenty-three hundred full text and over one thousand abstract sources, including U.S. and foreign newspapers, magazines, journals, newsletters, wire services, and broadcast transcripts. MAGS (discussed below) indexes articles from two hundred popular magazines and thirteen hundred scholarly journals, going back currently to 1991. NEWS (discussed below) indexes *The New York Times, The Washington Post, The Wall Street Journal, The Christian Science Monitor,* and *The Los Angeles Times.* The differences in the sources of each database may help to explain the discrepancies in the results. For instance, news articles would be discussing p.c. at the moment the term be-

gan to show up, while authors of articles in scholarly journals would typically wait a while to assess the trend. And the journals themselves typically have a much longer lead time between submission and publication than (of course) a newspaper or even a popular monthly magazine.

8. And yet extraordinarily, while writers who questioned HUAC's tactics during the McCarthy period were often subjected to virulent critique and loss of jobs and income, as well as threats of imprisonment, *none—not one—*of these current critics of p.c. has suffered in any way. Quite to the contrary: the media can't seem to get enough of them.

9. An Israeli student, angered by the talking of a group of African-American women students, yelled at them "Shut up, you water buffalo!" They interpreted this as a racist slur, and charged the student with violation of the university's speech code. His defenders claimed that, in Hebrew slang, "water buffalo" just meant a noisy or disruptive person, without any racist coloration. Nonetheless the Israeli student was censured.

10. David Mamet's play *Oleanna* (discussed in Chapter 4) is another example of the overreactions I am talking about here.

11. At this writing, an anti–flag desecration law has passed the House of Representatives and is considered likely to pass the Senate.

12. As reported on several Web sites, e.g. that of Brock N. Meeks (brock @well.com), March 21, 1996, and another on the Pacifica home page, Feb. 21, 1996.

13. Chaplinsky admitted making the basic statement, but said that as a Jehovah's Witness, he would never have uttered the d-word.

14. For discussion from this perspective, see Showalter 1997.

15. For more discussion on this point see MacKinnon 1993, 71ff.

16. Some of the principal Supreme Court decisions involved are *Abrams v. United States* (1919), *Gitlow v. New York* (1925), and *Whitney v. California* (1927).

17. This code has since been reduced almost to nothing and has never to my knowledge been enforced.

18. From the "Addition to Section 51.00, Student Conduct, *Policies Applying to Campus Activities, Organizations, and Students* (Part A)," from the section of the manual entitled Universitywide Student Conduct: Harassment Policy (University of California, Office of the President, September 21, 1989).

19. Examiner News Service, "Perot's Gaffe Bothers NAACP," July 12, 1992.

20. ACLU Answers: Issue: Racist Speech on College Campuses: "Why doesn't the ACLU support hate speech codes on college campuses?" (from the ACLU Web site, dated February 6, 1991).

CHAPTER 4

1. The story is summarized in Phelps and Winternitz 1992 and Mayer and Abramson 1994.

2. A tradition challenged, in recent memory, only during the first Nixon administration, over fifteen years before (and only rarely before that).

3. Shown on NBC's "Dateline," September 29, 1997.

4. According to Mayer and Abramson (1994, 175, 201), initial polls showed approval of Thomas by 49 percent (white) and 45 percent (black); by the hearings themselves, black support had risen to 65 percent.

5. For a discussion of this point, see Lakoff 1990, chapter 7.

6. If you don't find these differences in the treatment of Hill and Thomas startling, or convincing, try a thought experiment: imagine Thomas being expected to submit to examinations of his dating behavior, fantasy life, and video preferences, and his mental health becoming a topic of open discussion, while Hill could choose to deflect all such discussion, expressing anger that anyone would even *think* of bringing up her private life.

7. Discussed by Toni Morrison (1992a). See also the discussion of "Orientalism" in Chapter 2.

8. It is of course true that, at the same time, European culture traditionally desexualized "ladies," that is, "nice" women. But in religion, mythology, and literature, women are sexual predators and destroyers, evil temptresses always bringing good men down (think of Eve, Delilah and Salome—just for starters).

9. Sexual harassment is better seen as *harassment via the sexual channel* than as sexual behavior per se. If we could keep this in mind, we would find it much easier to take sexual harassment seriously, as it is intended: as a threat rather than as "just flirting." But since the word "sexual" is attached to the behavior, we permit ourselves to make a dirty joke of it and of those who are involved in it. If they could have seen sexual harassment as sexual merely in surface form, the Democrats might have been less leery of exploring the possibility that Thomas engaged in it.

10. An intriguing and unanswerable question is: would the outcome of the hearing have been different had Hill been white? Quite possibly, I think. The older "chivalrous" male senators might have found the image of Thomas harassing a *white* woman harder to overlook, and might have been reluctant to hypersexualize a white woman in this context.

11. The less powerful or authoritative still make much use of tags. For instance, they are common in the speech of teenagers in the forms "OK?," "y'know?," and "right?" as in: "So I went to see her, OK? And she was all—y'know?—'What're you doing here,' right?"

12. In an interview reported in the New York Times by Felicity Barringer (1991), Ekman "bet" that "although only one of them is telling the truth, neither of them is lying." He does suggest an alternative possibility, that "one of them in their mind knows they're lying to Congress and the American people. If so, the person who's doing that has to be terrified at being caught. Or they have to be very angry—angry at their opponent, angry at the world—to justify this. . . . From expression, voice, and gesture, I can read anger. The problem is, both people show it." Ekman, usually an astute observer of human expression, seems unaware here that while Hill may at times show anger (as would be almost unavoidable at the badgering she has to endure), her anger is both measured and appropriate to the eliciting cause, while Thomas's seems often to arise out of no provocation, indeed sometimes to be used as a deliberate means of deflecting questions and scaring off any opposition.

13. Noonan's use of the neologisms "movement-y" and "intellectualish" manages both to identify her with the inarticulate masses and hint at the aberrancy of the people so described—there are no "normal" words for them.

14. While there is a fair amount of suggestion in the anti-Hill commentary to this effect, there are few explicit modelings of exactly what a woman could say, in response to remarks about pubic hair on the Coke can or Long Dong Silver, that would hoist the perp on his own petard. One reason may be that there *is* no obvious, equivalent rejoinder. To respond with an equally gross sexual allusion is not to slap back, but to suggest that you're so low and degraded that you deserve even more of the same. In other words, vileness in a man's mouth can be dismissed as "boys will be boys." But a woman who talks like that is a "slut" who is "asking for it." Until the playing field is truly equal, i.e., the double standard nonexistent, equivalence is not equality.

If she were to complain, blush, or run from the room, it would show he had gotten to her—just what the harasser wants. If she were to say sweetly, "I don't like that kind of talk," she would be establishing herself, in most workplaces, as a prude deserving to be cut out of all future bantering, a decision that can redound negatively on one's employment potential.

Only a few possibilities have occurred to me. One is to say something that is as grossly offensive and horrifying to a man as remarks of this kind are to many women: talk graphically about your menstrual period. I have to warn the interested reader, though, that the effectiveness of this ploy may be diminishing. I saw a TV sitcom not long ago the plot of which revolved explicitly and at length around a character's menarche. Or perhaps, as suggested (in a personal communication) by Ellen F. Smith, you could politely say, "I'm sorry, I didn't quite catch what you said." That forces the perpetrator into his own trap. He must either deny he said anything, or anything of the sort, thereby making himself (a) a liar or (b) a person with an unreliable memory, that is either bad or mad himself; or must repeat it, out of context, where it will sound both asinine and crude.

15. See the similar point in Chapter 2 about the reasons for the relative credibility of Gennifer Flowers, Paula Jones, and Kathleen Willey.

16. Thus Louise Woodward, the British nanny accused in 1997 of killing the infant in her charge was criticized by jurors and other observers for not showing remorse on the stand. But she argued that, as a Briton, she had been brought up not to express emotion publicly. To reprise a question from Chapter 2: can juries be trusted to make cross-cultural determinations of "demeanor"?

17. For discussion of "face" and face preservation through conventions of public behavior, see Erving Goffman, e.g., *Interaction Ritual* (Doubleday, 1967).

18. The same difference played a significant role in the O. J. Simpson trial, in which Johnnie Cochran used AVT and Christopher Darden, LWC, choices which very probably affected the verdict (see Chapter 6).

19. I found the same process at work in post-verdict interviews I did some years ago with jurors in a capital case. In response to the question, "When did you decide the defendant was guilty?", many said that they made up their minds during the prosecutor's opening statement (i.e., before the presentation of any evidence). Those who had made that early determination tended to interpret the

defendant's demeanor and other ambiguous pieces of evidence as evidence of guilt.

20. In a similar vein, conservative black writer Thomas Sowell, in a syndicated column published March 24, 1996, explicitly equates Thomas and Hill to Whittaker Chambers and Alger Hiss, respectively, and feminism to Communism. One must have sympathy for the right: they clearly miss the convenience of the one-size-fits-all devil of godless atheistic Communism. On the other hand, the comparison has some validity. Feminism is a threat to the traditional American Way of Life—far more so than Communism, one might add.

21. Other examples (some of which have been discussed in Chapter 2) include: the "pinking" of the Olympic coverage in 1996 and of the rhetoric of the political conventions in that year; the "therapization" of disreputable behavior; and the rise of the talk show on television.

22. For insightful discussion of the dangers of polarization, see Tannen 1998.

23. See Brownstein 1991: "The *Times* Poll: Public Tends to Believe Thomas by 48% to 35%." This poll sampled 1,264 Americans on October 12 and 13. According to Mayer and Abramson (1994, 354) another (unspecified) poll taken in October 1991 showed a 47 percent vs. 24 percent split on the credibility of Thomas vs. Hill.

24. Actually, poll data in this case are notoriously hard to interpret. There were many polls, and many communities in which they were taken. So there are different results for black men, black women, white men, white women, and "all." Different polls ask different questions. A poll taken in October 1992 found that a majority of Americans still felt that Thomas should have been confirmed, but 44 percent of Americans believed Hill and only 34 percent Thomas.

25. And pigs fly.

26. It should be said in fairness that *Oleanna* is not cut out to be a good movie, being set in a single small office with two characters. The movie opened it up a bit, but by cinematic standards *Oleanna* remains claustrophobic.

27. In 1994, San Francisco's American Conservatory Theater performed a very successful version of *Oleanna* (directed by Richard Seyd, and dramaturged, whatever that is, by me) in an interpretation like this one.

28. It is equally legitimate to point out that the formal procedures by which John was deprived of his livelihood and his future are unthinkable at any "prestigious" university. Hearing procedures in such cases are typically skewed against students; much more, and much more significant, evidence of real misbehavior has to be presented; punishments, in all but really horrific cases (i.e., those in which nonconsensual sex has provably occurred) are minimal at most—mere slaps on the wrist. So it is fair to take the play as a parable about the injustices wrought by miscommunication, but not as a literal description of the way universities work.

CHAPTER 5

Parts of this chapter are adapted from Lakoff 1996b.

1. Notable examples are Bennetts 1994 and Bruck 1994.

2. Hence the frustration implied in Bennetts' title: "Pinning Down Hillary."

3. At least during her husband's term in office. Jacqueline Kennedy Onassis passed the UAT when she died in 1994, when more attention was lavished on her funeral, and on retrospectives on her life, than was given to Richard Nixon, who had died a couple of weeks earlier. But I would suggest that a good part of the attention given to Jackie was really a covert assessment of Rodham Clinton via the contrast between them: Jackie, who never spoke above a whisper, and Hillary, who is notoriously voluble; Jackie, who "never took a bad picture" and Hillary, whose photos are often uncomplimentary.

4. For biographical information on Rodham Clinton see Clinton 1996; Maraniss 1995; Woodward 1994, 1996.

5. As I suggest below, it would be more accurate to describe the Clintons as exchanging traditional gender stereotypes with each other, rather than blending them together, as Emery suggests.

6. Many things about this article put one in mind of Woody Allen's remark in *Annie Hall:* "*Commentary* and *Dissent* have merged to form *Dysentery.*"

7. Many commentators suggest that the failure was at least as much due to the administration's lack of support (it needed to reserve the heavy guns for NAFTA) and the virulent and well-financed opposition by the health care industry (i.e., the "Harry and Louise" commercials that played on television for much of 1993–94).

8. Mentioned in Bronstein 1997a.

9. I know this analysis sounds like Emery's, which I castigated above. But while Emery, as far as I can tell, is terrified about Clinton's sexual ambiguities, I find them kind of fun.

10. This problem was discussed on the *Charlie Rose Show* (PBS) on August 3, 1998, by David Gergen, Frank Rich, and Alan Brinkley.

11. While conservatives tend to see a monolithic "radical feminism" that thinks and acts as one, in fact the "movement," if any, includes a vast array of opinions about almost everything, the present case being only one example. On the other hand, the neocons seem to demonstrate extraordinary solidarity, down to their slogans and rhetorical style.

12. See Bronstein 1997a, and responses: Barkan 1997; Ehrenreich 1997; Jong 1997; Pollitt 1997b; and Rosen 1997; plus a reply by Bronstein 1997b.

13. A small sampling from the Web and elsewhere: Hillary Rodham Clinton arranged for the murder of Vince Foster to cover up their "torrid affair"; Bill Clinton had Commerce Secretary Ron Brown killed to cover up what Brown knew about illegal campaign contributions; Bill Clinton was responsible for the death of General Boorda, generally considered a suicide (no reason given).

Linda Tripp's televised allegations (on *Today* and the *Larry King Show)* that, by taping their conversations and handing them to Kenneth Starr, she saved Monica Lewinsky's life, fall into this category.

14. See Blumenthal 1998. Note also the comment in Corcoran 1993 cited earlier.

15. The word *sphinx* is derived from the same source as *sphincter,* and means "the strangler," or "the smotherer."

16. Huffington was to attain the "sympathy factor" herself almost immedi-

ately with the widely publicized revelation that her former husband, Michael Huffington, was gay.

CHAPTER 6

Some of the material in this chapter is adapted from Lakoff 1996a and 1997a.

1. According to the *San Francisco Chronicle* (borrowing from the *Boston Globe*) of October 4, 1995, the JFK funeral was watched by 93 percent of Americans; the moon landing, by 96 percent; and the first day of the Gulf War, by 84.5 percent. Although the Simpson verdict was viewed by only about 90 percent of the population, the increase in population since the earlier events makes its audience larger in pure numbers than either the first or the second, about 150 million viewers.

2. According to a pie chart in *Newsweek*'s October 16, 1995, issue, on *voir dire* questionnaires 75 percent of the Simpson jurors stated that they "believe O.J. unlikely to murder because he excelled at football."

3. Interestingly, while there was much discussion about black women's antipathy to Nicole as someone who had appropriated one of "their" prize males, I saw virtually nothing in the media about the converse: the resentment of white men toward Simpson for having taken one of "their" babes. Were white men singularly free of prejudice, or is this just another case of exnomination? The existence of jokes like those in the text answers that question.

4. Unless indigent defendants are defended by court-appointed attorneys, whose resources are even more meager.

5. To give an example: in Alameda County, California, the D.A.'s office (as an agency of law enforcement) has the legal right to access police files, while the public defender cannot. During jury selection, each side wants to dismiss as many unfavorable panelists as possible "for cause," i.e., as biased or otherwise unqualified to serve, rather than having to use a precious peremptory challenge. One thing that will trigger a cause challenge is evidence that the panelist has lied under oath. Panelists are often asked in the course of *voir dire* whether they have ever been arrested or convicted. Most often they answer in the negative: their prospective fellow jurors are sitting there, they are in the presence of Authority in the person of the judge—who wants to admit to bad behavior? But if the candidate is deemed unfavorable to the prosecution, the prosecutors may run a computer check on his/her record. If it comes up dirty, the prospective juror will be brought back to court, haled before the judge, and forced to explain the discrepancy under penalty of perjury. He/she will then be dismissed for cause. The defense has no equivalent privilege.

6. Recall the discussion in Chapter 4 of the differences between African-American Verbal Tradition (AVT) and Language of Wider Communication (LWC).

7. A disturbingly large number of cases have recently come to light in Illinois, in which persuasive evidence has been amassed that prosecutorial misconduct secured convictions on capital charges.

8. The first trial of Lyle and Erik Menendez in Los Angeles in 1994 ended in a hung jury. Since the brothers had confessed to the premeditated killing of their parents, the two juries' (one for each brother) failure to convict created widespread consternation and denunciations of the defense use of an "abuse excuse." Both were convicted in the retrial, and things settled down.

9. A classic case is presented in a PBS *Frontline* episode from 1984, "Inside the Jury." In it, a man named Leroy, who is a convicted felon and thus ineligible to possess a gun, stands accused of gun possession. He readily admits possession of the gun and also acknowledges both his awareness of the law that felons may not possess firearms and his status as a felon. Yet, after several hours of deliberation, a jury acquits him. As the jurors reasoned, Leroy (not a notably bright guy and a near-illiterate) bought the gun not in order to have a *gun,* for the reasons most of us would have one (to shoot people), but because he was jobless and saw an ad in a magazine offering instruction in how to be a detective. He sent for the brochure, and right there, high on the instructions list, was: Get a gun. So, wanting a job and being obedient, he did so. For him, one of the jurors (an English professor, of course) argued, the gun was not a *gun;* Leroy, in this context, did not possess a *gun,* but something closer to a "gun," a symbolic structure perhaps akin to the Lacanian phallus. Indeed, he was caught when he obediently brought the weapon into the courthouse, through the metal detector, in order to lawfully register it. If, the argument goes, he had meant his purchase to be a *gun,* rather than a "gun," he would not have done that.

10. In saying this I, like many analysts of the verdict, am second-guessing or interpreting the jury—reasserting my majoritarian right.

11. One oft-told example concerns a juror who, in response to a question concerning her feelings about science, replied that she had once gotten a false negative on a home pregnancy test, so she didn't believe in science at all.

12. Fiske points out that "some African Americans believe that scientific truth is not universal but white, if not in its essence, at least in its uses." They argue that "white" science seems always to "work against them and in favor of whites" (1996, 264). So there is a very real and dangerous parallelism between black attitudes toward justice and toward science, and one of the scarier aspects of the Simpson case is that it brought both together in a form that could not be ignored.

But as often, to allege a simple black/white dichotomy about the use of DNA evidence oversimplifies the case. *Everyone* prefers scientific results that prove a truth that we want to hear. So when, in 1998, a much more complex version of DNA testing argued that Thomas Jefferson had had a long sexual relationship with a black slave, Sally Hemings, and had fathered at least one of her children (see Smith 1998), there were no suggestions from the black community that the DNA was tainted.

13. And with its statistical samplings and bar graphs, the article (like a similar one in that day's *L.A. Times*) soothes its white readers' fears with the covert assurance that science is still trustworthy.

14. When I was in Sweden for a couple of weeks the next May, I found that the Swedes were as cognizant—even at that late date—of the minutiae of the case as were Americans.

15. To be intelligible to his readers, Gates had to make this point explicitly. The editorial writer, addressing approximately the same audience, sees no need to do so to make the case from the opposite perspective. See the discussion in Chapter 2 of the neutrality of the status quo. There *is* no real possibility for *mutatis mutandis*.

16. In Chapter 8, I discuss some of the consequences of this new media self-evaluation.

17. For discussion of this topic, with particular reference to the problem of pornography and women's discourse rights, see MacKinnon 1993.

CHAPTER 7

1. Disseminated by the OSB under the title "Resolution of the Board of Education Adopting the Report and Recommendations of the African-American Task Force: A Policy Statement and [sic] Directing the Superintendent of Schools To Improve the English Language Acquisition and Application Skills of African-American Students, No. $597-0063."

2. McWhorter (1998) claims that *all* speakers of nonstandard dialects can code-switch. But as a New Yorker growing up among people who were embarrassed about their "New York accents" yet were unable to change them, I don't think so. (Of course New Yorkers *understand* the standard language perfectly well.)

3. Part of the OSB's insistence on the former is probably due to the popular understanding of "dialect" as "inferior or uneducated form of the language." But for linguists, every form of a language is a dialect of that language—prestige, standard, or nonstandard depending on politics and power, but expressively and logically equivalent.

4. A favorite putative borrowing (suggested, for instance, by Robert MacNeil in the "Black on White" program of his series, *The Story of English*), is "OK"; it is claimed that a word similar in sound and sense is found in several West African languages. However, the word is first attested in New York in the 1830's and appears to be an abbreviation of "orl korrect," a fake-populist spelling of "all correct"; its popularity was enhanced by its association with Martin Van Buren, "Old Kinderhook," in the 1840 presidential campaign. This is exactly the kind of etymology that makes a linguist sniff, "dubious folk etymology," but in this case it seems to be right. In any case, if the word had come via speakers of African languages, it would not have shown up first so late or in that place.

5. From the Web site http://www.geocities.com/Hollywood/Lot/3340/ebonics.html#rule.

6. The amount of space given to the issue over a six-week period (from December 19, 1996, to the end of January 1997) is astonishing. Not surprisingly, the local papers outdid the national in reportage. Between December 19 and the end of January, a probably incomplete count of relevant coverage (news articles, Op-Ed pieces, columns, and editorials) in the four major Bay Area papers (*Oak-

land Tribune, San Francisco Chronicle, San Francisco Examiner, and *San Jose Mercury News*) stood at ninety, with the *Chron* contributing forty-five of that total. On the national level, using the NEWS database, there were twenty-two cites in the five papers sampled in December and twenty-eight in January.

7. For the record, "slang" occurs in all social groups in a society (see the delight of the middle-class Eynsford-Hill family, in *Pygmalion,* to discover that they know "the new slang"), though usually its forms originate among people without power or social clout: the young, the criminal, those in questionable occupations. Its forms tend to be ephemeral, and its meanings tend to cluster in the area of the unmentionable or the strongly emotional. Slang is purely lexical: we can speak of "slang words," but not "slang sounds" or a "slang rule of syntax."

Dialects like AAVE, on the other hand, are spoken by everyone, as we have seen, though some are more prestigious than others. Nonstandard dialects tend to persist as long as the groups that use them are isolated from mainstream speakers, and their forms are similarly long-lasting. Dialectal differences exist over the whole range of communicative competence. Sounds and words are usually where the most noticeable differences occur, but dialects also may differ in syntax and in pragmatics (e.g., politeness rules) as well as discourse properties (think of Johnnie Cochran's black discourse style vs. Christopher Darden's white one). AAVE thus spans the expressive range from very casual ("street talk" with a lot of "slang" in it) to serious and ceremonial, like any other dialect.

8. Our short-lived popularity is just one piece of evidence for the amount of interest the topic stirred up in the general populace. Among the others: according to *Newsweek* (John Leland and Nadine Joseph, "Hooked on Ebonics," January 13, 1997), "An America Online poll drew more responses than the one asking people whether O. J. Simpson was guilty." (This statistic requires a grain of salt: over a year had passed since the Simpson verdict, during which time many more people had joined AOL.)

9. I probably ought to attempt a definition of "linguist" here. A "linguist," as I use the term, is someone who has most if not all of the following characteristics: (1) has a Ph.D. in linguistics (not, e.g., communications or African-American studies) from the linguistics department of a major research university; (2) teaches linguistics courses at a university; (3) has published articles in scholarly journals edited by specialists in linguistics.

10. For instance, see William Labov, *Language in the Inner City* (University of Pennsylvania Press, 1972).

11. One of the most amazing moments I've ever seen on television occurred on a network evening news show on the Saturday after New Year's Day, 1997. They actually had a camera in the room where the discussion was going on—I recognized some colleagues seated there—and showed a few seconds of the discussion. That was the first and only time I know of that the popular media penetrated the LSA lair.

12 From the Web site of the Center for Applied Linguistics (http://www.cal. org/ebonics/wolfram.htm), January 30, 1997.

13. To be exact, linguists *were* quoted on occasion in all the media. But what we had to say had little influence on public opinion.

CHAPTER 8

1. The British favor "Naughtygate," which—in keeping with my argument—rhymes with "Watergate" in Standard British English.

2. According to perfumer, author, and psychotherapist Mandy Aftel (personal communication).

3. Yet some of the justifications for their own behavior advanced by the absolutists have a relativist tinge: "*Youthful* indiscretions"; "Not with anyone *in my office.*"

4. Some commentators have suggested that, because of the significant age and power difference between the parties, Lewinsky could not have given meaningful consent to the relationship. This point is not easily dismissed, but I think it is invalid.

As so often, the problem lies in deciding where along a continuum the presidential misalliance falls. We all agree that some forms of sexual relations can never be considered consensual, because one party is legally and otherwise incapable of giving meaningful consent: children or the mentally ill are good examples. Then there are situations in which the preexisting relationship, while theoretically between adults capable of consent, creates a childlike dependence of one upon the other (as in psychotherapy) or creates a more adult dependency, as between an employee and her immediate supervisor. In such cases it is probably true that meaningful consent cannot be given.

In other cases things are fuzzier. Some feminists take an absolute position. If power discrepancy makes consent questionable, and if men in this society virtually always have more power than women, then *any* sexual connection between men and women must be considered nonconsensual, so all heterosexual sex is rape. But most see this as an extreme position, interesting to argue but ultimately rendering meaningless essential legal concepts like "consent" and "rape." There are, however, ambiguous situations, and the Clinton-Lewinsky liaison is one. Yes, he was nominally her boss—but so distantly that he couldn't really have her fired or promoted. Yes, he was much older, and in a position of great influence: he was the president! Maybe we should treat Gategate as analogous to therapist-client liaisons.

The problem is that the more areas of nonconsensuality we establish, the more difficult we make it to see women as competent. The more relationships we categorize as actionable, the more childlike we see women as being, the more needy of protection. A Washington intern, living on her own, by her own account a woman with significant prior sexual experience, is not a child and should not be treated as such. This is not to deny the president's oafishness or sexual opportunism, but oafishness and opportunism are not prosecutable (or impeachable) offenses.

5. Sometimes the harassment charge is connected with Paula Jones's case against the president. But since that will never come to trial, we can never assess the plaintiff's story, and it is therefore inappropriate to *presuppose* its truthfulness in this way. The story of Juanita Broaddrick, who alleges that she was raped by then-governor Clinton in 1978, which surfaced post-impeachment, seems to me to have the same difficulties, and the same level of credibility, as Anita Hill's.

6. In the *New York Times* of October 15, Arthur Miller (1998) invokes the Salem analogy without making a literary genre comparison.

7. For some discussion of these difficulties, see Coleman and Kay 1981 and Sweetser 1990.

8. Reprinted from "Sad Movies (Make Me Cry)," © John D. Laudermilk, 1961.

9. The issue of whether all untruths under all circumstances are equally reprehensible is predictably thorny. Republicans argue that the perjurious nature of Clinton's lies renders them especially repugnant. As a linguist I tend to agree. Lying per se is dangerous enough, because it makes it harder for people to trust one another's utterances, as social animals must. Perjury is worse, because it erodes trust in the law to boot.

But distinctions get murkier as we explore. Is it worse to tell a flat-out lie or to encourage an addressee (as in the example here) to draw a false conclusion? I would argue for the latter, since that forces the innocent interlocutor into complicity in making the lie.

Another case: is it worse to lie under oath about something trivial (like sex) than to lie not under oath about something important, like collaborating in racism? *New York Times* columnist Frank Rich (1998) provides an interesting test case. Three of Clinton's harshest Congressional critics have been caught in bald-faced lies about their close relations with openly racist organizations. If we assume that racist behavior is more socially destructive than consensual sex, it follows that lying about the former is worse than lying about the latter. But how do we weigh the perjuriousness of the latter in this case, as against the non-perjury of the former? It's up to you.

10. For discussion of these three levels of language see Austin 1962.

11. For discussion of Quinn's covert classism, and incidentally a nice example of media representatives turning on each other, see Tomasky 1998.

12. The problem might be resolved if Americans were willing to overhaul their system of government. Many countries have two heads (e.g., president and premier; monarch and prime minister), one of whom performs the Daddy-like symbolic functions, the other the business-running role of the CEO. Then, if scandal hits Daddy or his family, the CEO can go on running the country; if scandal attaches to the CEO, it usually doesn't much matter, since no one pays that much attention to his private life.

References

Abramson, Jeffrey. 1996a. Editor's Introduction. In Abramson, ed., 1996b, pp. 1–29.

——, ed. 1996b. *Postmortem: The O. J. Simpson Case.* New York: Basic Books, Inc.

Adler, Jerry. 1990. Taking Offense. *Newsweek,* December 24.

Aftel, Mandy. 1996. *The Story of Your Life.* New York: Simon and Schuster.

Alter, Jonathan. 1998/1999. The Era of Bad Feeling. *Newsweek,* December 28/ January 4.

Alvarez, Lizette. 1998. Hillary Clinton: Popular and Hardly in Hiding. *New York Times,* August 12.

Amiel, Barbara, 1991. Feminist Harassment. *National Review,* November 4.

Austin, J. L. 1962. *How to Do Things with Words.* Cambridge, Mass.: Harvard University Press.

Babcock, Barbara. 1996. In Defense of the Criminal Jury. In Abramson, ed., 1996b, pp. 160–67.

Barkan, Joanne. 1997. Responses [to Bronstein 1997a]. *Dissent,* Summer.

Barringer, Felicity. 1991. The Thomas Nomination: Psychologists Try to Explain Why Thomas and Hill Offer Opposing Views. *New York Times,* October 13.

Barthes, Roland. 1972. *Mythologies.* Trans. Annette Lavers. New York: Hill and Wang.

Bazeley, Michael. 1996. Waging War of the Words. *Oakland Tribune,* December 20.

Beasley, Maurine. 1993. Covering Today's Woman: Mistreated by the Media? Or Not Treated at All? *American Journalism Review,* May.

Becklund, Laurie. 1991. Women's Old Angers Resurface: Many of Them Side With Clarence Thomas' Accuser, Not Because They Know Who Is Telling the Truth, But Because They Recall Sexual Harassment by Other Men. *Los Angeles Times,* October 11.

Bennet, James. 1996. The Ad Campaign: Liberal Use of "Extremist" Is the Winning Strategy. *New York Times,* November 7.

Bennetts, Leslie. 1994. Pinning Down Hillary. *Vanity Fair,* June.

Berman, Paul, ed. 1992. *Debating P.C.: The Controversy over Political Correctness on College Campuses.* New York: Laurel/Dell.

Bernstein, Richard. 1990. Ideas and Trends: The Rising Hegemony of the Politically Correct. *New York Times,* October 28.

Blauner, Bob. 1992. Talking Past Each Other: The Black and White Languages of Race. *San Francisco Chronicle,* August 2.

Blumenthal, Ellen. 1998. That Power-Mad Couple Seems Familiar. *New York Times,* March 1.

Boot, Max. 1990. McCarthyism on Campus. *Daily Californian,* November 27.

Brant, Martha, and Evan Thomas. 1996. Saint or Sinner? *Newsweek,* January 15.

Bray, Rosemary. 1991. Thomas-Hill Hearing Raised Deeply Buried Issues. *New York Times Magazine,* November 17.

———. 1992. Taking Sides against Ourselves. In Chrisman and Allen, eds., 1992, pp. 47–55.

Bronstein, Zelda. 1997a. Feminists, Pundits and Hillary Clinton. *Dissent,* Summer.

———. 1997b. Zelda Bronstein Replies. *Dissent,* Summer.

Brownstein, Ronald. 1991. The *Times* Poll: Public Tends to Believe Thomas by 48% to 35%. *Los Angeles Times,* October 14.

Bruck, Connie. 1994. Profile: Hillary the Pol. *New Yorker,* May 30.

Bugliosi, Vincent. 1996. *Outrage: The Five Reasons O. J. Simpson Got Away with Murder.* New York: Norton.

Burrell, Barbara. 1997. *Public Opinion, the First Ladyship, and Hillary Rodham Clinton.* New York and London: Garland.

Burros, Marian. 1995. Hillary Clinton Asks Help in Finding a Softer Image. *New York Times,* January 10.

Butler, Judith. 1997. *Excitable Speech: A Politics of the Performative.* New York: Routledge.

———. 1999. A "Bad Writer" Bites Back. *New York Times,* March 20.

Calling Grace Metalious. 1998. *Time,* October 19.

Carlson, Margaret. 1992. All Eyes on Hillary. *Time,* September 14.

Caroli, Betty Boyd. 1987. *First Ladies.* Oxford: Oxford University Press.

Carroll, Lewis. 1960. *Alice's Adventures in Wonderland* and *Through the Looking-Glass.* New York: Signet.

Cassius, Dio. 1906. *Dio's Annals of Rome.* Vol. 4, books 52–60. Trans. Herbert Baldwin Foster. Troy, N.Y.: Pafraet's Book Company.

Cheney, Lynne. 1995. *Telling the Truth: Why Our Culture and Our Country Have Stopped Making Sense.* New York: Simon and Schuster.

Chomsky, Noam A. 1965. *Aspects of the Theory of Syntax.* Cambridge, Mass.: M.I.T. Press.

Chrisman, Robert, and Robert L. Allen, eds. 1992. *Court of Appeal: The Black Community Speaks Out on the Racial and Sexual Politics of Clarence Thomas and Anita Hill.* New York: Ballantine.

Cicero, Q. Tullius. 1972. *Commentariolum petitionis*. Ed. Dantes Nardo. Milan: A. Mondadori.

Clift, Eleanor. 1992. Profile: Hillary Then and Now. *Newsweek*, July 22.

Clift, Eleanor, and Mark Miller. 1994. Saint or Sinner? *Newsweek*, April 11.

Clines, Francis X. 1998. From Political Debit to Force: Hillary Clinton. *New York Times*, November 22.

Clinton, Hillary Rodham. 1996. *It Takes a Village*. New York: Simon and Schuster.

Clymer, Adam. 1991. The Thomas Nomination: Parade of Witnesses Supports Hill's Story, Thomas' Integrity. *New York Times*, October 14.

Coleman, Linda, and Paul Kay. 1981. Prototype Semantics: The English Word *Lie*. *Language* 51 (1):26–44.

Cooper, Matthew. 1997. Lessons in How to Say I'm Sorry. *Newsweek*, November 7.

Corcoran, Katherine. 1993. Pilloried Clinton. *Washington Journalism Review*, January–February.

Cose, Ellis. 1997. Why Ebonics Is Irrelevant. *Newsweek*, January 13.

Crenshaw, Kimberlé. 1992. Whose Story Is It, Anyway? Feminist and Antiracist Appropriations of Anita Hill. In Morrison, ed., 1992b, pp. 402–40.

Crews, Frederick. 1995. *The Memory Wars: Freud's Legacy in Disrepute*. New York: New Yale Review Books.

Croce, Arlene. 1994/1995. A Critic at Bay: Discussing the Undiscussable. *New Yorker*, December 26/January 2.

Danforth, John C. 1994. *Resurrection: The Confirmation of Clarence Thomas*. New York: Viking.

Denby, David. 1983. The Decline of the *Village Voice*. *New Republic*, January 31.

Devine, Philip E. 1993. *Human Diversity and the Culture Wars: A Philosophical Perspective on Contemporary Cultural Conflict*. Westport, Conn.: Praeger.

Dowd, Maureen. 1991. The Thomas Nomination: With Each Round of Testimony, The Mood at the Hearing Sways. *New York Times*, October 14.

———. 1994. Amid Debate on Her Role, Hillary Clinton Pushes On. *New York Times*, September 29.

———. 1995. O.J. as Metaphor. *New York Times*, October 5.

———. 1996. Liberties: Pink Think. *New York Times*, September 15.

Duffy, Martha. 1995. Push Comes to Shove. *Time*, February 6.

Dworkin, Ronald. 1992. The Coming Battles over Free Speech. *New York Review of Books*, June 11.

Early, Gerald. 1998. The Wonder Boy. *New York Review of Books*, May 28.

Egan, Timothy. 1995. With Spotlight Shifted to Them, Some Simpson Jurors Speak Freely. *New York Times*, October 5.

Ehrenreich, Barbara. 1997. Responses [to Bronstein 1997a]. *Dissent*, Summer.

Ellerbee, Linda. 1990. Only When I Laugh. *San Francisco Chronicle*, July 1.

Elshtain, Jean Bethke. 1996. Suffer the Little Children. *New Republic*, March 4.

———. 1997. True Confessions. *New Republic*, November 10.

Emery, Noemi. 1993. The Androgyny Party. *Commentary*, June.

False Lessons of the Simpson Trial. 1995. Unsigned editorial, *New York Times*, October 5.

Farber, Daniel A., and Suzanna Sherry, 1993. Telling Stories out of School: An Essay on Legal Narratives. *Stanford Law Review* 45 (April): 807–55.

———. 1997. *Beyond All Reason: The Radical Assault on Truth in American Law.* Oxford: Oxford University Press.

Fineman, Howard. 1998. A Crisis at Home. *Newsweek*, December 21.

Fish, Stanley. 1980. *Is There a Text in This Class? The Authority of Interpretive Communities.* Cambridge, Mass.: Harvard University Press.

———. 1994. *There's No Such Thing as Free Speech . . . and It's a Good Thing, Too.* Oxford: Oxford University Press.

Fiske, John. 1996. *Media Matters: Race and Gender in U.S. Politics.* Minneapolis: University of Minnesota Press.

Fox-Genovese, Elizabeth. 1996. It Takes a Village and Other Lessons Children Teach Us. *National Review*, March 11.

Fraser, Nancy. 1992. Sex, Lies, and the Public Sphere: Some Reflections on the Confirmation of Clarence Thomas. *Critical Inquiry* 18 (Spring): 595–612.

Gates, Henry Louis, Jr. 1995. Thirteen Ways of Looking at a Black Man. *New Yorker*, October 23.

———. 1996. A Reporter at Large: Hating Hillary. *New Yorker*, February 26 and March 4.

Gates, Henry Louis, Jr., Anthony P. Griffin, Donald E. Lively, Robert C. Post, William B. Rubenstein, and Nadine Strossen. 1994. *Speaking of Race, Speaking of Sex: Hate Speech, Civil Rights, and Civil Liberties.* New York: New York University Press.

George, Lynell. 1995. Taking It Personally; Reflections on The Verdicts, the City, and Ourselves. *Los Angeles Times*, October 4.

Goffman, Erving. 1967. *Interaction Ritual.* New York: Doubleday.

Goodman, Ellen. 1996. A "Language" for Second-Class Life. *San Francisco Chronicle*, December 27.

Goodwin, Doris Kearns. 1993. Hillary and Eleanor. *Mother Jones*, January–February.

———. 1995. *No Ordinary Time.* New York: Simon and Schuster.

Goody, J., and I. Watt. 1972. The Consequences of Literacy. In P. Giglioli, ed., *Language and Social Context.* New York: Penguin.

Gopnik, Adam. 1998. American Studies. *New Yorker*, September 28.

Gottlieb, Martin. 1995. Deep Split in Reactions to Verdict. *New York Times*, October 4.

Greenblatt, Stephen. 1998. America's Raciest Read. *New York Times*, September 22.

Grier, Beverly. 1995. Making Sense of Our Differences: African American Women on Anita Hill. In Smitherman, ed., 1995a, pp. 150–58.

Gumperz, John J. 1982. *Discourse Strategies.* Cambridge, Eng.: Cambridge University Press.

Haberman, Clyde. 1998. NYC: Protesting Critics' Zeal on Clinton. *New York Times*, December 18.

Haiman, Franklyn. 1993. *"Speech Acts" and the First Amendment.* Carbondale and Edwardsville: Illinois State University Press.

Hall, Edward T. 1977. *Beyond Culture.* Garden City, N.J.: Anchor Books.

Hare, Nathan, and Julia Hare. 1992. The Clarence Thomas Hearings. In Chrisman and Allen, eds., 1992, pp. 78–83.

Heilbrunn, Jacob. 1997. Speech Therapy. *New Republic,* January 20.

Henderson, Stephen. 1998. Almond Pedicure: It's a Guy Thing. *New York Times,* August 10.

Herbert, Bob. 1995. Madness, Not Justice. *New York Times,* October 6.

Hertzberg, Hendrik. 1998. Talk of the Town: Wind From Washington: Old White House Type: Railsplitter; New White House Type: Hairsplitter. *New Yorker,* September 28.

Hill, Anita. 1997. *Speaking Truth to Power.* New York: Doubleday.

Honan, William H. 1997. To Masters of Language, a Long Overdue Toast. *New York Times,* December 31.

Howard, Lucy, with Arlyn Tobias Gajilan. 1998. Television: "Gay Every Single Week." *Newsweek,* May 11.

Hudson, R. A. 1980. *Sociolinguistics.* Cambridge, Eng.: Cambridge University Press.

Irving, Carl. 1991. UC Free Speech Concern Surfaces over Columbus. *San Francisco Examiner,* May 26.

Jackson, Jacquelyne Johnson. 1992. Them Against Us: Anita Hill vs. Clarence Thomas. In Chrisman and Allen, eds., 1992, pp. 99–105.

Jong, Erica. 1997. Responses [to Bronstein 1997a]. *Dissent,* Summer.

King, Florence. 1991. Never, Ever Come Out Swinging. *National Review,* December 2.

Kinsley, Michael. 1991. P.C.B.S. *New Republic,* May 20.

Kleinfeld, N. R. 1995. The Day (10 Minutes of It) the Nation Stood Still. *New York Times,* October 4.

Labaton, Stephen. 1995. Lessons of Simpson Case Are Reshaping the Law. *New York Times,* October 5.

Labov, William. 1972. The Social Motivation of a Sound Change. In *Sociolinguistic Patterns.* Philadelphia: University of Pennsylvania Press.

Lacayo, Richard. 1995. An Ugly End to It All. *Time,* October 9.

Lakoff, Robin T. 1984. The Pragmatics of Subordination. In *Papers from the Tenth Annual Meeting of the Berkeley Linguistic Society,* pp. 481–92.

———. 1990. *Talking Power.* New York: Basic Books.

———. 1996a. Many Stories, Multiple Meanings: Narrative in the O. J. Simpson Case. *Links & Letters* 3:49–60.

———. 1996b. The (Rise and Fall)[n] of Hillary Rodham Clinton. In Natasha Warner, Jocelyn Ahlers, Leela Bilmes, Monica Oliver, Suzanne Wertheim, and Melinda Chen, eds., *Gender and Belief Systems: Proceedings of the Fourth Berkeley Women and Language Conference, April 19–21, 1996.* Berkeley, Calif.: Berkeley Women and Language Group, pp. 387–402.

———. 1997a. The O. J. Simpson Case as an Exercise in Narrative Analysis. *Discourse Processes* 23 (3): 547–66.

————. 1997b. Radical Cheek. *Conscience*, Autumn, 21–22.

Leo, John. 1997. Ebonics? No Thonics! *U.S. News and World Report*, January 20.

Levinson, Stephen C. 1983. *Pragmatics*. Cambridge, Eng.: Cambridge University Press.

Lewis, Anthony. 1995. An American Dilemma. *New York Times*, October 6.

Lewis, Neil A. 1997. Black Scholars View Society with Prism of Race. *New York Times*, May 5.

Lind, Michael. 1995. Jury Dismissed: The Institution from the Dark Ages. *New Republic*, October 23.

Loftus, Elizabeth, 1979. *Eyewitness Testimony*. Cambridge, Mass.: Harvard University Press.

Lubman, Sarah. 1996. Roots of the Black English Push. *San Jose Mercury-News*, December 23.

MacKinnon, Catharine. 1993. *Only Words*. Cambridge, Mass.: Harvard University Press.

Malveaux, Julianne. 1992. No Peace in a Sisterly Space. In Chrisman and Allen, eds., 1992, pp. 143–47.

Mamet, David. 1992. *Oleanna*. New York: Vintage.

Maraniss, David. 1995. *First in His Class*. New York: Simon and Schuster.

Margolick, David. 1995. Jury Clears Simpson in Double Murder; Spellbound Nation Divides on Verdict. *New York Times*, October 4.

Martin, Steve. 1997. Shouts and Murmurs: A Public Apology. *New Yorker*, November 17.

Matsuda, Mari, Charles R. Lawrence III, Richard Delgado, and Kimberlé Williams Krenshaw. 1993. *Words That Wound: Critical Race Theory, Assaultive Speech, and the First Amendment*. Boulder, San Francisco, and Oxford: Westview Press.

Mayer, Jane, and Jill Abramson. 1994. *Strange Justice: The Selling of Clarence Thomas*. New York: Houghton Mifflin.

McWhorter, John. 1998. *The Word on the Street*. New York: Plenum.

Mead, Rebecca. 1998. Talk of the Town: Who Really Exploited Monica Lewinsky? *New Yorker*, September 28.

Menand, Louis. 1997. Comment: Johnny Be Good. *New Yorker*, January 13.

Mendoza-Denton, Norma. 1995. Pregnant Pauses: Silence and Authority in the Anita Hill–Clarence Thomas Hearings. In Kira Hall and Mary Bucholtz, eds., *Gender Articulated: Language and the Socially Constructed Self*. New York: Routledge, pp. 51–66.

Miller, Anita, ed. 1994. *The Complete Transcripts of the Clarence Thomas–Anita Hill Hearings, October 11, 12, 13, 1991*. Chicago: Academy Chicago Printers.

Miller, Arthur. 1998. Salem Revisited. *New York Times*, October 15.

Minton, Torri. 1998. Definition of Racial Slur Angers NAACP. *San Francisco Chronicle*, October 17.

Morrison, Toni. 1992a. Introduction: Friday on the Potomac. In Morrison, ed., 1992b, pp. vii–xxx.

————, ed. 1992b. *Race-ing Justice, En-Gendering Power*. New York: Pantheon.

———. 1998. Talk of the Town. *New Yorker,* October 5.

Mühlhäusler, Peter, and Rom Harré. 1990. *Pronouns and People: The Linguistic Construction of Social and Personal Identity.* Oxford: Oxford University Press.

Nabokov, Vladimir. 1955. *Lolita.* Greenwich, Conn.: Fawcett Publications.

Nagourney, Adam. 1997. Giuliani Gives an Apology on Criticism. *New York Times,* October 15.

Neilson, James. 1995. The Great P.C. Scare: Tyrannies of the Left. In J. Williams, ed., 1995, pp. 60–89.

Newton, Jim. 1995. Simpson Not Guilty: Drama Ends 474 Days after Arrests; Verdicts. *Los Angeles Times,* October 4.

Noonan, Peggy. 1991. A Bum Ride. *New York Times,* October 15.

Ofshe, Richard, and Ethan Watters. 1994. *Making Monsters: False Memories, Psychotherapy, and Sexual Hysteria.* Berkeley and Los Angeles: University of California Press.

Olson, Walter. 1992. The Hand That Rocks the Cradle. *National Review,* May 11.

Olszewski, Lori. 1996. Oakland Schools OK Black English. *San Francisco Chronicle,* December 19.

Ozick, Cynthia. 1998. Talk of the Town. *New Yorker,* October 12.

Paglia, Camille. 1996. A Psychological Portrait of Hillary: Ice Queen, Drag Queen. *New Republic,* March 4.

Patterson, Orlando. 1992. Race, Gender, and Liberal Fallacies. In Chrisman and Allen, eds., 1992, pp. 160–64.

———. 1998. Interview with Phil Ponce. *NewsHour with Jim Lehrer* (transcript), PBS, September 30.

Phelps, Timothy, and Helen Winternitz. 1992. *Capitol Games.* New York: Harper Perennial.

Pollitt, Katha. 1997a. Paula Jones, Class Act? *Nation,* March 17.

———. 1997b. Responses [to Bronstein 1997a]. *Dissent,* Summer.

Posner, Gerald. 1996. Throwing the Books at O.J. *Esquire,* November.

Quinn, Sally. 1998. Not in Their Backyard. *Washington Post,* November 2.

Reibstein, Larry. 1995. Judgment Day. *Newsweek,* October 9.

Reibstein, Larry, with Mark Miller, Donna Foote, and Tessa Namuth. 1995. What Went Wrong? *Newsweek,* October 16.

Remnick, David. 1998. The Sporting Scene: American Hunger. *New Yorker.* October 12.

Rich, Frank. 1995a. Journal: Dance of Death. *New York Times,* January 8.

———. 1995b. The L.A. Shock Treatment. *New York Times,* October 4.

———. 1998. Journal: Scandals sans Bimbos Need Not Apply. *New York Times,* December 26.

Rogan, Sandra L., Dianne G. Bystrom, Lynda Lee Kaid, and Christine S. Beck, eds. 1996. *The Lynching of Language: Gender, Politics, and Power in the Hill-Thomas Hearings.* Urbana: University of Illinois Press.

Rosen, Ruth. 1997. Responses [to Bronstein 1997a]. *Dissent,* Summer.

Rosenthal, A. M. 1995. Verdict on a Trial. *New York Times,* October 6.

Safire, William. 1998. On Language: Alone with "Alone," or What "Is" Is. *New York Times Magazine,* October 11.

Said, Edward. 1978. *Orientalism*. New York: Random House/Vintage.

Saint-Amand, Pierre. 1994. Terrorizing Marie Antoinette. Trans. Jennifer Curtiss Gage. *Critical Inquiry* 20 (Spring): 379–400.

Schafer, Roy. 1980. Narration in the Psychoanalytic Dialogue. *Critical Inquiry*, Autumn: 29–53.

Schoch, Russell. 1995. California Q & A: A Conversation with John Searle. *California Monthly*, February.

Seelye, Katharine Q. 1999. One Consolation for Clinton: Democratic Donations Surge. *New York Times*, March 20.

Seligman, Daniel. 1991. On Getting It. *Fortune*, November 18.

Shapiro, Walter. 1993. Whose Hillary Is She, Anyway? *Esquire*, August.

———. 1997. Mama Mia, That's a Mea Culpa. *Time*, June 30.

Shilts, Randy. 1989. AIDS: The Inside Story: Patiently Tiptoeing through The World of Word Twisters. *San Francisco Chronicle*, December 11.

Showalter, Elaine. 1997. *Hystories: Hysterical Epidemics and Modern Media*. New York: Columbia University Press.

Shuy, Roger. 1993. *Language Crimes: The Use and Abuse of Language Evidence in the Courtroom*. Oxford: Blackwell.

The Simpson Verdict. 1995. Unsigned editorial, *New York Times*, October 4.

Sleeper, Jim. 1996. Racial Theater. In Abramson, ed., 1996b, pp. 57–63.

Smith, Dinitia. 1998. The Enigma of Jefferson: Mind and Body in Conflict. *New York Times*, November 7.

———. 1999. Attacks on Scholars Include a Barbed Contest with "Prizes." *New York Times*, February 27.

Smitherman, Geneva, ed. 1995a. *African American Women Speak Out on Anita Hill–Clarence Thomas*. Detroit: Wayne State University Press.

———. 1995b. Testifyin, Sermonizin, and Signifyin: Anita Hill, Clarence Thomas, and the African American Verbal Tradition. In Smitherman, ed., 1995a, pp. 224–42.

Sowell, Thomas. 1996. Can Fans of Hillary Clinton Admit They Bought into a Lie? *Detroit News*, March 24.

Spence, Donald. 1982. *Narrative Truth and Historical Truth*. New York: Norton.

———. 1986. When Interpretation Masquerades as Explanation. *Journal of the American Psychoanalytic Association* 34 (1):3–21.

Staples, Brent. 1997. Editorial Notebook: The Trap of Ethnic Identity. *New York Times*, January 4.

Streisand, Betsy. 1995. And Justice for All. *U.S. News & World Report*, October 9.

Sweetser, Eve. 1990. *From Etymology to Pragmatics: Metaphorical and Cultural Aspects of Semantic Studies*. Cambridge, Eng: Cambridge University Press.

Tannen, Deborah. 1979. What's in a Frame? Surface Evidence for Underlying Expectations. In R. O. Freedle, ed., *New Directions in Discourse Processing*. Norwood, N.J.: Ablex, pp. 137–81.

———. 1984. *Conversational Style: Analyzing Talk Among Friends*. Norwood, N. J.: Ablex.

———. 1994. *Talking from Nine to Five*. New York: William Morrow.

———. 1998. *The Argument Culture*. New York: Random House.

Thernstrom, Abigail. 1991. Rough Justice: The Plot That Failed. *New Republic,* November 11.

Thernstrom, Abigail, and Henry D. Fetter. 1996. From Scottsboro to Simpson. *Public Interest,* Winter.

Thucydides. 1919–23. *History of the Peloponnesian War.* Trans. Charles Forster Smith. Cambridge, Mass.: Harvard University Press/Loeb Classical Library.

Tiersma, Peter. 1986. The Language of Offer and Acceptance: Speech Acts and the Question of Intent. 74 *California Law Review* 189.

———. 1987. The Language of Defamation. 66 *Texas Law Review* 303.

Tomasky, Michael. 1998. Off with Their Talking Heads. *New York,* November 22.

Toobin, Jeffrey. 1995. A Horrible Human Event. *New Yorker,* October 23.

———. 1996. *The Run of His Life: The People v. O. J. Simpson.* New York: Simon and Schuster.

Toufexis, Anastasia. 1991. When Can Memories Be Trusted? *Time,* October 28.

Trilling, Diana. 1996. Notes on the Trial of the Century. In Abramson, ed., 1996b, pp. 64–71.

Troutman-Robinson, Denise. 1995. The Tongue or the Sword: Which Is Master? In Smitherman, ed., 1995a, pp. 208–23.

Trudeau, Garry. 1996. The Framing of O. J. Simpson. *Time,* November 25.

Unreasonable Doubt. 1995. Unsigned editorial, *New Republic,* October 23.

Van Natta, Don, Jr. 1999a. Hillary Clinton's Campaign Spurs a Wave of GOP Fund Raising. *New York Times,* July 10.

———. 1999b. Fund-Raisers Find Bonanza in Impeachment. *New York Times,* July 20.

Verdict Is In: A City Divided; The Simpson Trial Has Raised Questions of Police Propriety and Racial Antipathy. 1995. Unsigned editorial, *Los Angeles Times,* October 4.

Verrillo, Erica. 1996. Who Is Anita Hill? A Discourse-Centered Inquiry into the Concept of Self in American Folk Psychology. In Rogan et al., 1996, pp. 61–83.

Wagner, Venise. 1996. "Ebonics" Uproar Overlooks L.A. Program. *San Francisco Examiner,* December 22.

Whitaker, Mark. 1995. Whites v. Blacks. *Newsweek,* October 16.

Whorf, Benjamin L. 1956. Languages and Logic. In J. B. Carroll, ed., *Language, Thought, and Culture: Selected Writings of Benjamin Lee Whorf.* Cambridge, Mass.: M.I.T. Press, pp. 233–45.

Wiegand, Shirley A. 1996. Analyzing the Testimony from a Legal Evidentiary Perspective: Using Judicial Language Judiciously. In Rogan et al., eds., 1996, pp. 3–23.

Will, George. 1998. Still Waiting for Lefty. *Newsweek,* May 25.

Williams, Jeffrey, ed. 1995. *P.C. Wars: Politics and Theory in the Academy.* New York: Routledge.

Williams, Patricia J. 1991. The Death of the Profane. In Patricia J. Williams, ed., *The Alchemy of Race and Rights.* Cambridge, Mass.: Harvard University Press, pp. 44–51.

———. 1998. In Living Black and White. *Washington Post Magazine,* March 29.

Williams, Robert. 1997. The Ebonics Controversy. *Journal of Black Psychology* 23.3 (August): 208–14.

Winn, Steven. 1998. High Court's Ruling Is Indecent. *San Francisco Chronicle,* June 26.

Wood, James. 1998. Madame Lewinsky; or Lord William's Lover. *New Republic,* October 5.

Woodward, Bob. 1994. *The Agenda.* New York: Pocket Books.

———. 1996. *The Choice.* New York: Simon and Schuster.

Index

Text: 10/13 Sabon
Display: Sabon
Composition: G&S Typesetters
Printing and binding: Thomson-Shore, Inc.